Income, Wealth, and the Maximum Principle

Income, Wealth, and the Maximum Principle

———— ✸ ————

MARTIN L. WEITZMAN

Harvard University Press

Cambridge, Massachusetts

London, England

2003

Library of Congress Cataloging-in-Publication Data

Weitzman, Martin L., 1942–
Income, wealth, and the maximum principle / Martin L. Weitzman.
p.   cm.
ISBN 0-674-01044-2 (alk. paper)
1. Economics—Mathematical models.   2. Mathematical optimization.
3. Maximum principles (Mathematics)   4. National income—Accounting.
5. Wealth—Mathematical models.   6. Economic development—Mathematical
models.   I. Title.
HB143.7.W45 2003
330′.01′5193—dc21   2002191337

Contents

Preface

It seems that I have been engaged in investigating the subject of income, wealth, and the maximum principle for some thirty-five years now. Very early on, in research begun in the late 1960s when I was just out of graduate school, it became apparent that the duality conditions of optimal control theory contained a gold mine of useful information. Pontryagin's maximum principle, which was then in vogue, could be translated into powerful, general, rigorous statements about the meaning of aggregate index numbers, including aggregate income, in a very general dynamic setting with heterogeneous capital and consumption. This line of research found early expression in a Cowles Foundation paper, written in 1970, which concerned the meaning of dynamic income and other aggregate indices in a multisector optimal growth setting. I have been with this subject, on and off, ever since.

In the course of such a long research program it becomes difficult to say precisely which ideas came from where. My first debt is therefore to the broad intellectual tradition of income and capital theory—especially as it has come down to us in its more modern form, associated with such great names in economics as Wicksell, Fisher, Lindahl, Hicks, Pigou, Ramsey, Hotelling, Samuelson, and Solow. More particularly, in the writing of this book I have benefited enormously from the insights, reactions, comments, criticisms, suggestions, and encouragement of a number of friends and colleagues, so many that I cannot list them all. Nevertheless, I want to single out for special thanks a few people who were especially generous in giving their time and help.

Jon Conrad, whom I did not know personally before this interaction, kindly read several chapters and gave many detailed useful comments. Geir Asheim, with whom I have been engaged in a long-standing and friendly debate over the meaning of "sustainability," provided me with a number of thoughtful criticisms on issues related to this thorny subject. Avinash Dixit and William Brock, two old friends, gave generously of their valuable time and helped me to sort out what was happening in the stochastic case. I am also especially indebted for their useful reactions to Thomas Aronsson, Gardner Brown, Linda Bui, Cynthia Lin, Karl-Gustaf Löfgren, Nick Oulton, Atle Seirstad, Knut Sydsaeter, Alexander Wagner, and Roberton Williams. None of these people, however, is responsible for the errors that may remain.

Finally, I would like to dedicate this book to Glenna. It's not easy to deal with me under ordinary circumstances, but preparing this book increased the intensity even more. She put up with a lot.

Income, Wealth, and the Maximum Principle

Introduction

This book grew out of the need to teach a version of natural resource economics and green accounting that would be understandable to advanced undergraduate and beginning graduate students. Such capital-theoretic topics involve at their very core the efficient dynamic allocation of resources (over an indefinitely protracted future, no less)—thereby exposing students to a much higher level of conceptual and mathematical challenges than they have encountered in any previous experience with static economic theory. And yet the economic theory of natural resources cannot be adequately covered without touching upon the basic structure of dynamic optimization (along with the dual interpretation of dynamic competitive equilibrium). To put the point another way, because the basic concepts are so central to dynamic resource allocation, there is no sense offering a second-rate dumbed-down version of optimal control theory and the maximum principle if the real thing can be repackaged in a form that is understandable to students, many of whom may need or want to know about it anyway. Optimal control theory is the most effective lens through which to see the fundamental unity of all capital theory, including, as special cases, the standard workhorse models of natural resource economics.

The key to an effective understanding of optimal control theory and the maximum principle for an audience of potential economists (or managers, or analytically inclined people interested in stock markets more generally) begins, I believe, with the realization that such "economist types" are usually interested only in special forms of the "optimal control problem." It really is useful for the "economist-type" student to start learning optimal control theory by focusing right away on the kind of problem that the "economist type" most typically wants to solve or understand in the first place. It turns out that such prototype-economic optimal control problems actually possess an unusually tractable recursive structure that can be used very advantageously to package and convey the basic theory. (In technical jargon, which only a person who is already knowledgeable about the subject would really understand at this stage, the prototype-economic optimal control problem involves maximizing the present discounted value of a time-autonomous objective, over an infinite time horizon, with an unconstrained end-state, subject to time-autonomous differential equations of motion, with the control set allowed to be state dependent, with non-negativity constraints on state variables, and where the reduced-form technology underlying the problem is essentially assumed to be convex.) Such prototype-economic forms constitute, I would guess roughly, maybe 90% or more of the optimal control problems that the practicing "economist type" actually wants to formulate and solve.

Viewed from this perspective, optimal control textbooks can be very confusing to an economics student trying to learn the basics of dynamic optimization theory. From the beginning, the student is forced to go through and sort out a large number of different issues involving, for example, fixed versus free end points, finite versus infinite horizons, finite versus infinite-horizon transversality conditions, state-free versus state-dependent control sets, constrained versus unconstrained state variables, convex versus nonconvex structures, time-dependent versus time-autonomous systems, necessary versus sufficient conditions, present-discounted-value costate variables versus current-value costate variables, present-discounted-value Hamiltonians versus current-value Hamiltonians, a costate variable of one for the objective function versus a costate variable of zero for the objective function, differentiable versus nondifferentiable state evaluation functions, and so on. Little wonder, then, that the student can become confused. Only limited advantage is taken, in deriving or explaining optimal control theory, of the fact that the vast majority of dynamic economic problems come already presorted into a particular characteristic form. This prototype-economic characteristic form lends itself much more readily than does the general case to applying, conceptualizing, and even rigorously proving basic results in optimal control theory.

In fact, the proofs are so much simpler for economic-type problems that—at least for the case of one control variable and one state variable—this book will be able to provide a fully rigorous proof of the maximum principle using methods that rely only on basic calculus. Moreover, the student who reads this book will learn how to unlock the secrets for solving all prototype-economic problems with one state variable—by simply applying consistently the key economic concept of the *stationary rate of return on capital*, which is introduced in Chapter 1 and used extensively throughout Part I. Just reducing an economic control problem to the canonical form where the control variable is net investment (and then mechanically calculating the stationary rate of return on capital) "solves" at least half of any given problem—and sometimes all of it. Even if a person should eventually desire to learn about how optimal control theory works in different settings, it is still a better learning strategy for the aspiring economist to first understand the prototype-economic case. (Besides, there may not be a need for such extensions, because the prototype-economic control problem covers the bulk of control problems that arise in economic settings.)

As an added bonus, the theory of the prototype-economic case is, I think, aesthetically very pleasing. For sheer mathematical beauty, the pure economic theory of the maximum principle and comprehensive income accounting can take pride of place as an economic counterpart to the elegant formulations of theoretical mechanics by W. R. Hamilton, C. G. J. Jacobi, and others. By itself this theoretical prettiness does not make the theory any more applicable, but it may facilitate the learning of it—on the principle that if you must learn something, it may help for it to be neat.

Thus far I have explained one motivating factor for the book. By taking advantage of the special structure of the prototype-economic form, I hope to lead the student as directly and as simply as possible to understanding—and to solving—the kinds of dynamic control problems that are most interesting to economists, yet without sacrificing rigor. There is also a second motivational strand, which for me was actually a more decisive factor in tipping the balance toward mustering the energy required to write a book.

The Hamiltonian of the prototype-economic optimal control problem takes a form that is immediately suggestive of an expression representing the "true income" or "net national product" (NNP) of the unit that is doing the maximizing. It turns out that there is a deep theoretical relationship between national income accounting and the current-value Hamiltonian of the corresponding optimal control problem. This relationship is known to specialist researchers in the field. A prime purpose of the book is to develop the pure economic theory of comprehensive national income accounting ("green accounting," for short) in a style and format that will be accessible to a wider professional audience.

This book, then, is intended for two types of readers. One type is the economics (or management science or finance) student trying to learn the basic theory of dynamic optimization in a much easier to understand prototype form specifically dedicated to economic applications. This "sub-book number one" might have been titled *Introduction to the Economics of Optimal Control Theory*.

The second intended audience is economists who may already know the basics of optimal control theory, but who may want to learn more about the modern theory of comprehensive national income accounting. (Although the phrase "national income accounting" is used throughout the book, it is really code for comprehensive income accounting by any unit—whether an individual, a firm, a sector, or an entire nation.) This contemporary economic theory of (national) income accounting already accompanies optimal control theory as a kind of "silent partner" in the background. With very little expenditure of extra effort, an economist who understands the rudiments of optimal control theory can enrich that understanding by picking up the connection with the theory of (national) income accounting almost "for free," as it were. This "sub-book number two" might have been titled *The Pure Theory of Comprehensive National Income Accounting*.

The theory of (national) income accounting, in and of itself, may be a topic of interest to many different kinds of economists—not just those specializing in natural resources. This "theory of accounting" identifies the welfare significance of NNP-type numbers. It explains how national income might be used in an ideal world to make welfare comparisons over time or across space. The theory can be useful in pointing out *which* items or activities ought to be included in comprehensive national income, as well as suggesting *how* they should be included. With a fully dynamic formulation, new light is shed on old topics in consumer surplus theory, cost-benefit analysis, and the theory of price deflators. The theory highlights an intriguing logical connection between "green" NNP and a particular measure of sustainability—the "sustainable-equivalent" utility level that the economy will be able to achieve over future time. More generally, the maximum principle, which was not available to classical pioneers such as Fisher, Lindahl, or Hicks, allows us to see in a new light some important answers to the vexing question "what is income?"—and to tie such answers directly to the equally vexing (and closely related) question "what is sustainability?"

In fact, I teach topics from both strands of the book, because both strands—the dynamic optimization strand and the green accounting strand—are critically important for understanding natural resource economics. In a well-defined sense, current competitive prices of natural resources (or capital stocks more generally) "foresee" the future effects of depletion (or accumulation)—and comprehensive NNP is a rigorous measure of "what the future portends" relative to the present. This same point pertains more generally to any kind of capital theory, of which the theory of natural resources is just a special case. The wealth and income-accounting side of a dynamic economy is an essential complement to the optimization and equilibrium side. This is the main intended message of the book.

Powerful and important as optimal control theory may be, there is no avoiding the fact that it involves subtle and sophisticated mathematics. A fully rigorous treatment of the general case—covering all of the mathematical details—is beyond the scope of any book aimed at educating the advanced undergraduate student or enlightening the average graduate economist. Even just stating an optimal control problem fully rigorously in the general case requires an understanding of real analysis, including measure theory, which is above the knowledge or aspiration level of the audience for whom this book is intended. And the topics of state-dependent control sets or non-negativity constraints on the state space (which so often are unavoidable aspects of modeling economic situations—and which this book covers) either are considered so advanced and complicated that they are not treated at all in many texts on optimal control theory, or else are not treated fully rigorously.

What, then, is the mathematical background needed for someone to profit from this book? A solid background knowledge of multivariable calculus is the only essential requirement. Other than that, it would help to know some elements of basic analysis (at a level that typically accompanies multivariable calculus), and some exposure to linear algebra and differential equations would also be helpful. Especially useful is a good working knowledge of standard static constrained optimization theory (Lagrangians and shadow prices), at a level that accompanies most of today's undergraduate microeconomics textbooks. (Incidentally, I also presume a decent knowledge of the economics contained in such textbooks.)

How is it possible to comprehend the economic content of a sophisticated mathematical technique such as the maximum principle of optimal control theory, and to be able to prove it rigorously, using just the basic methods of calculus? The key here is the special structure of the "prototype-economic" optimal control problem. The prototype-economic problem has enormous regularity not typical of the general class of optimal control problems. This particular class of problems allows what will be called the "wealth and income version" of the maximum principle to be proved first. Then the "standard version" of the maximum principle can be developed fully rigorously using only calculus methods. In a sense, this book reverses the traditional order of learning about dynamic economic optimization. Here we start with the wealth and income side, deriving the standard version of the maximum principle directly from the wealth and income version. This approach is easier, more intuitive, and more fully rigorous.

What ultimately lies behind the simpler proofs of the maximum principle for one-dimensional prototype-economic problems is the smooth differentiability of the state evaluation function. When the state evaluation function has a continuous derivative at every point along the optimal trajectory, all proofs become much easier. And then the rest of the prototype-economic structure kicks in by allowing a particularly intuitive form of the maximum principle to be derived as a theorem.

So the prototype-economic structure, which is already inherent in most economic applications, allows a recursive form of the maximum principle to be developed that is significantly easier to assimilate. By concentrating on the type of optimal control problem in which the typical economist is most interested anyway, I aspire to convey to that economist a better-motivated, more rigorous introduction to the maximum principle and a deeper understanding of the relationship between income and wealth. At least that is my hope.

The book is intended to serve what I view as an important gap in the literature, by combining together in one neat package capital theory and optimal control theory. Nevertheless, or perhaps because of this, the potential audience is likely to be varied. Since the people reading this book are likely to be coming from somewhat different places and looking for somewhat different things, the book is organized in a particular spatial order with an eye toward all readers being able to zero in on what they want.

Part I, which consists of the first four chapters, is essentially devoted to the *statement*, the *theory*, the *understanding*, and the *application* of the maximum principle to solve "economic-type" optimal control problems with *one* state variable or capital stock. Chapter 1 introduces the class of problems studied in Part I, makes the historical connection with the calculus of variations, begins a preliminary analysis of the meaning of convexity, and, most important, introduces the key solution concept of the *stationary rate of return on capital*. By using this economically intuitive concept almost mechanically, the careful reader of Part I will be able to solve and to analyze any one-dimensional prototype-economic optimal control problem.

Chapter 2 is devoted to stating carefully the prototype-economic optimal control problem with a single capital stock. The prototype-economic format keys on formulating the problem, through a change of variables if necessary, in terms of net investment as the critical "reduced-form" control variable. When net investment is chosen as the control instrument, it is easy to see what "economic" optimal control theory is all about through the crystal-clear lens of the stationary rate of return on capital. Chapter 2 also contains ten full examples of such economic optimal control problems. These examples include all of the classical one-dimensional dynamic optimization problems that have appeared in economics and have made such a lasting contribution to our understanding of capital theory. Few readers will want to plough through all ten problems *seriatum* at first read. But they are there—as references and as examples of how to see the unity of all dynamic economic problems and concepts.

Chapter 3 gives a fully rigorous statement and proof of the maximum principle for economic-type problems with one capital stock. The proof is "elementary" in the sense of being fully understandable to a reader with a good working knowledge of calculus and the willingness to follow a rather long mathematical argument. I know of no other rigorous "elementary" proof of the maximum principle. One section of Chapter 3 is devoted to explaining in detail the all-important economic interpretation and significance of the maximum principle. This economic interpretation of the maximum principle is alluded to in several books and articles, and is understood intuitively by knowledgeable economists, but I have never seen a complete and careful statement worked out in such a way that a novice learner could hope to follow fully the line of argument.

Chapter 4 is dedicated to solving, and analyzing in economically understandable terms, each of the ten prototype-economic optimal control problems introduced in Chapter 2. Again, the reader may not wish to plough through all of these solutions *seriatum*, but they are all there. A careful reader of Chapter 4 should be able to solve and analyze satisfactorily any one-capital economic problem that will materialize, right now or later in professional life. When a one-dimensional optimal control problem has been formulated in the prototype-economic format, which is always possible with a simple change of variables to make the reduced-form instrument be net investment—and when the stationary rate of return on capital has been routinely calculated—then the solution is relatively straightforward.

Part II of the book deals with extensions of the basic theory to cover multidimensional optimal control problems and uncertainty. The chapters in Part II emphasize the themes of *income, wealth,* and *sustainability.* This part of the book pushes further toward the frontier of active research and contains, inter alia, several new results.

Chapter 5, which inaugurates Part II, begins by stating and analyzing three economically important two-capital examples of optimal control theory. Then the duality between multidimensional optimal control theory and multi-dimensional dynamic competitive equilibrium is developed fully. Some sections of this chapter are needed primarily as background for the next chapter, and may be read lightly on first pass.

Chapter 6 is devoted to applying multidimensional optimal control theory in order to understand the answers to two basic questions about net national product. The first basic question is, What does NNP stand for? The second basic question is, How can NNP and other currently observable market data be used (at least in principle) to make rigorous welfare comparisons? The central aim of this chapter is to develop a unified theory of price deflators and welfare measures that will allow an observer to infer the relation between currently observable money NNP and present discounted utility or consumption, using only currently observable market information.

Chapter 7 extends into the realm of uncertainty the treatment of NNP and welfare begun in Chapter 6. This final chapter develops the key relationship between *stochastic income* and *stochastic wealth* (or welfare). Because stochastic diffusion processes, which form the backdrop for Chapter 7, are sufficiently demanding by themselves mathematically, only the simplest one-dimensional stochastic economic control problem is treated. Nevertheless, the interested reader should come away with a strong feel for the economics of the stochastic case and a good sense of how a multidimensional stochastic problem would be handled.

This book, then, tries to house within a unified framework all of the most important aspects of the economics of optimal control theory. Naturally there are many themes and subthemes. If, however, I were forced to select one single overarching theme of the book, I would repeat my earlier statement: the wealth and income-accounting side of a dynamic allocation resource process is an essential complement to the optimization and equilibrium side—because data based on currently observable competitive market processes can reveal useful and important information about future welfare.

The book is restricted to dynamic problems involving *continuous time*. Why some dynamic problems are formulated in continuous time while others are formulated in discrete time may seem mysterious, but each formulation has its advantages and disadvantages. The superiority of a continuous-time formulation for the class of dynamic optimization problems being considered here stems ultimately from the idea that situations describing the behavior of competitive stock markets are more naturally modeled in continuous time because such markets tend to equilibrate more or less instantaneously. Stock markets react immediately to news, not after a week, a day, or even an hour. To model such processes in discrete time is to introduce an artificial "lag" into stock market price adjustments. The book is organized around a basic economic idea called the "wealth and income version" of the maximum principle, which reflects the link between the instantaneous flow of income and the corresponding instantaneous evaluation of wealth. This wealth and income version holds only in continuous time—the corresponding statement in discrete time becomes a messy lagged approximation to what the continuous-time formulation is able to express so neatly and directly.

The book need not be read in exactly the order in which it is presented. Some readers may wish to understand just a few examples from Chapter 2, then take a quick view of the maximum principle in Chapter 3, finally see it applied to solve a few of the examples in Chapter 4, and only after this preliminary exploration turn toward learning the subject material in greater depth. Other readers may be more interested in learning techniques and solving problems than in understanding formal proofs of why the maximum principle works. Still others may already be acquainted with the techniques but want to see a relatively simple, yet mathematically rigorous, proof centered on economic concepts. A few readers may know the techniques and why they work, but want to understand better the economic significance or interpretation of the maximum principle. And some, of course, may wish to work through the material in the exact sequence being presented. The book is laid out in a logical sequence, but the reader can pick and choose, jumping forward and returning back in any order that feels comfortable. In principle, the various sections of each chapter are detachable from the others and may be learned in any convenient order. The sequence I have chosen is what I think, overall, represents the most logical unfolding of the subject, but my overriding objective is to place the learning material in logically ordered detachable subunits, so that different readers with different goals can roam freely at will, easily locating what they want. (Unless specially noted, references to a mathematical equation refer to the equation number in *that* chapter. Thus a reference in Chapter 4 to equation (11) refers to equation (11) of Chapter 4; by contrast a reference in Chapter 4 to equation (11) of Chapter 2 would be denoted (2.11).)

My ultimate hope is that this book will demystify dynamic economics—by helping to make the basic principles of capital theory accessible to a much wider audience, allowing more readers to understand this elegant and important subject.

PART I

Introduction to the Maximum Principle

1

---

*

The Calculus of Variations and
the Stationary Rate of Return on Capital

This introductory chapter provides background material and lays a conceptual foundation for what follows. One purpose is to provide a historical link between formulations of dynamic models as so-called calculus of variations problems and formulations in terms of so-called optimal control theory—which is the subject of the remaining chapters of this book. The calculus of variations is a greatly simplified special case of optimal control theory, and therefore it is a good setting in which to examine in their barest and most direct form certain core ideas that will play a key role throughout the rest of the book.

By far the most significant purpose of this chapter is to introduce in its simplest unadulterated form the very important concept of the *stationary rate of return on capital*. As we will see repeatedly throughout Part I, the stationary rate of return on capital is the key unifying concept for unlocking the secret of solving any one-capital prototype-economic problem.

This chapter also introduces the basic idea of convexity, whose role is perhaps easiest to appreciate in the simpler calculus of variations setting.

We begin with a simple example, a special instance of a class of continuous-time investment problems with quadratic adjustment costs. The example is intended to show how dynamic optimization problems may arise first in a discrete-time version in the mind's eye of the modeler, and how they are then "naturally" converted into a continuous-time formulation, which, it turns out, is much easier to solve because of the continuous-time feature.

Example: The Widget Entrepreneur's Problem

In a remote region of Transylvania, a widget entrepreneur is trying to decide how to start up a widget business and build it over time. If P is price, the demand for widgets in each period, D, is given by the linear demand function

$$D(P) = \frac{\overline{P} - P}{b}, \tag{1}$$

whose corresponding inverse demand function is

$$P(D) = \overline{P} - bD, \tag{2}$$

so that the revenue function can be written

$$\Phi(D) \equiv P(D)D = \overline{P}D - bD^2. \tag{3}$$

In the above formulation, b and $\overline{P}$ are positive constants and $P \leq \overline{P}$.

Widgets are made by robots. One trained robot can make one widget per period. There is a one-time cost of c to buy a robot. Robots last forever.

The widget entrepreneur has taken an elementary economics course and knows he is supposed to be producing where marginal revenue equals marginal cost. Suppose the competitive interest rate, representing the cost of capital for the widget manufacturer, is ρ per unit time. Then, setting marginal revenue $\overline{P} - 2bD$ equal to annuitized marginal cost ρc, he calculates the profit-maximizing number of widgets, and hence robots, to be

$$\hat{K} = \frac{\overline{P} - \rho c}{2b}. \tag{4}$$

If this were a truly static problem, then the above static analysis would suffice. But static problems are always approximations of dynamic situations, and the widget entrepreneur realizes that things are not so simple as the static elementary economics formulation. The complication is that each new robot must be "adjusted"—meaning each new robot must be individually installed and trained to produce widgets. And these individual adjustment sessions take time away from production, because each new robot must stand idle until the adjustments on it have been completed. The new robots are delivered at the beginning of each "period." The time it takes to adjust one new machine is τ. The new machines are all delivered together at the beginning of a production period, and the manager adjusts one at a time, right away, so they can start producing as soon as possible. If I new robots arrive at the beginning of a period, the manager must spend a total time of τI on new-robot adjustments. At adjustment time s, the manager will already have adjusted s/τ machines—meaning that the remaining $I - s/\tau$ new machines are waiting to be adjusted so they can begin producing widgets.

The total loss of widget production per period from the down time of I new machines is therefore

$$\int_0^{\tau I} (I - \frac{s}{\tau}) \, ds = aI^2, \tag{5}$$

where the parameter

$$a \equiv \tau/2 \tag{6}$$

might be called a *cost-of-adjustment coefficient*.

In the presence of adjustment costs, the widget entrepreneur faces a much more complicated *dynamic* problem than just finding the *static* stationary state where marginal revenue equals marginal cost, as with (4). Let $K(t)$ be the total number of robots on hand in period t (old and new) robots, while $I(t)$ represents the number of new robots that have just arrived at the beginning of period t. (The reason we use the symbols K and I here is that throughout the book they will stand for *capital* and *investment*, so we may as well get used to thinking in such terms right from the beginning.) Then the widget entrepreneur's problem is to

$$\text{maximize} \quad \sum_{t=1}^{\infty} \frac{1}{(1+\rho)^t} [\overline{P}K(t) - bK(t)^2 - cI(t) - aI(t)^2], \tag{7}$$

subject to the conditions

$$K(t) = K(t-1) + I(t), \tag{8}$$

and the initial condition

$$K(0) = 0. \tag{9}$$

The discrete-time formulation, with its periods of arbitrary length and its integer-valued variables $I(t)$, seems too "clunky" and too messy to analyze. So the widget entrepreneur, who knows calculus, formulates the problem more elegantly in continuous time to

$$\text{maximize} \quad \int_0^\infty [\overline{P}K(t) - bK(t)^2 - cI(t) - aI(t)^2]e^{-\rho t}\, dt \qquad (10)$$

subject to the differential equation

$$\dot{K}(t) = I(t), \qquad\qquad\qquad (11)$$

with the initial condition

$$K(0) = 0. \qquad\qquad\qquad (12)$$

Alas, the widget entrepreneur does not know how to solve such a problem and turns to us for help. Our first step is to recognize that (10)–(12) is a calculus of variations problem having a certain characteristic "prototype-economic" form. Let us abstract from the above example to examine this prototype-economic calculus of variations problem in a more general setting.

The Prototype-Economic Calculus of Variations Problem

Generalizing from the above example, let the function

$$G(K, I) \qquad\qquad\qquad (13)$$

represent the net current "take home" cash flow, which will here be called *immediate or direct gain,* as a function of the capital stock and investment flow. *For a given K,* the function $G(K, I)$ gives the relation between current net direct gain G and current net investment I. It is typically the case that

$$\frac{\partial G}{\partial I} = G_2(K, I) < 0, \qquad\qquad\qquad (14)$$

because investment usually comes at the expense of immediate gain. On the other hand, it is also typically the case that

$$\frac{\partial G}{\partial K} = G_1(K, I) \geq 0, \qquad\qquad\qquad (15)$$

because more capital usually generates more cash flow, other things being equal. Because $I = \dot{K}$, (14) and (15) taken together indicate that there is a tradeoff between present gain and future gain. Where to be ideally located along that tradeoff is the main issue.

A *prototype-economic calculus of variations problem* attempts to

$$\text{maximize} \quad \int_0^\infty G(K(t), I(t))e^{-\rho t} \, dt \tag{16}$$

subject to the differential equation

$$\dot{K}(t) = I(t), \tag{17}$$

with the initial condition

$$K(0) = K_0, \tag{18}$$

where K_0 is the inherited value of the capital stock at the beginning time zero.

It is readily confirmed that the widget entrepreneur's problem (10)–(12) is a prototype-economic calculus of variations problem with

$$G(K, I) \equiv \overline{P}K - bK^2 - cI - aI^2, \tag{19}$$

where we note that the direct-gain function (19) satisfies conditions (14) and (15).

We will not yet try to explain problem (16)–(18) fully, because it is better to discuss what it means and to give examples in the context of the more general optimal control version. Suffice it to say here that problems expressed in the form (16)–(18) crop up frequently in economics and in finance, management science, operations research, and several other economics-related fields.

Because neither the state variable $K(t)$ nor the control variable $I(t)$ is in any way constrained (in principle they are allowed to take on any values satisfying (17)), the prototype-economic problem (16)–(18) is considered to be a problem in the calculus of variations. Traditionally such a problem might be written in the form to

$$\text{maximize} \quad \int_a^b f(y(t), \dot{y}(t), t) \, dt \tag{20}$$

with the initial condition

$$y(a) = y_a. \tag{21}$$

In a typical application t represents time or position on a line. The variable $y(t)$ represents the *state* of the system at t. This "state" is required to be y_a at the beginning of the process and, in the above formulation, is left unconstrained at the end. The rate of change of $y(t)$—denoted $\dot{y}(t)$—can be interpreted as a *control instrument*. Taking the initial state y_a as given, the goal of the problem is to influence the trajectory of $y(t)$ by controlling the instrument $\dot{y}(t)$ over time in such a way that maximizes the objective function (20). To characterize a solution effectively, we need to put a little more structure on the problem. For now, we just assume that the function $f(y, \dot{y}, t)$ is "well behaved" in the sense of being smoothly differentiable everywhere of interest.

Note that the prototype-economic calculus of variations problem (20),(21) is a special case of (16),(17),(18) where $a = 0$, $b = \infty$, and which has the particular functional form

$$f(y, \dot{y}, t) = G(y, \dot{y})e^{-\rho t}. \tag{22}$$

The calculus of variations has a long and distinguished history. Centuries ago, Bernoulli, Euler, Lagrange, and other mathematicians of extremely high stature had already developed the basic theory and characterized the solution. Typical early applications were mostly to geometry (for example, the plane figure with maximum area that can be enclosed within a given perimeter length) and physics (for example, the curve along which a particle under the influence of gravity rolls in least time from one given point to another, which was solved by, among others, Isaac Newton). The applications to physics are legion, because, as Euler put it in the eighteenth century, "nothing at all takes place in the universe in which some rule of maximum or minimum does not appear" (as we will see, the same might be said of the "economics universe" too).

The solution of a calculus of variations problem is characterized by the famous Euler equation

$$\frac{\partial f}{\partial y} = \frac{d}{dt}\left(\frac{\partial f}{\partial \dot{y}}\right), \tag{23}$$

which must hold along an optimal trajectory. (To the reader who hasn't before seen and doesn't know the Euler equation (23): not to worry! The Euler equation is essentially a special "interior" case of the maximum principle, which we will cover fully in Chapter 3. Such a reader might want, however, to confirm that (23) is really a special case after reading Chapter 3.)

With the particular form (22), the Euler equation (23) then becomes

$$G_1 = \dot{G}_2 - \rho G_2. \tag{24}$$

We will not spend time now trying to prove directly that (24) constitutes a necessary optimality condition, because it will emerge as a special case of the maximum principle of optimal control theory. Instead, we concentrate here on important special aspects of a stationary solution, which will greatly strengthen our economic intuition and prove to be a useful connection with the maximum principle.

The Stationary Rate of Return on Capital

At this point we introduce a set of concepts as a way of looking at capital theory that will be of fundamental importance throughout the book. We begin with the idea of a "stationary state" and the fundamental concept of the stationary rate of return on capital. As a practical matter, the stationary state is a solution concept that finds its primary use in dynamic economics for the case of a single capital good. Generally speaking, the concept of a stationary state tends to be much less useful when there are multiple capital goods. Nevertheless, one-sector models are important, and it is difficult to overestimate the role that the "stationary state" has played in the way economists conceptualize (and solve) a great many (though not all) dynamic capital-theoretic problems.

A *stationary state* is simply a situation where capital is constant and, therefore, net investment is zero. In formal notation, a stationary state is a trajectory of capital and net investment of the particular form:

$$(K(t), I(t)) = (K, 0). \tag{25}$$

We begin our analysis of the stationary state by noting here that for any capital stock level K, we always have the option of remaining in the stationary state at that capital level merely by selecting $I(t) \equiv 0$. (The calculus of variations always allows this option because the control I is unrestricted.) The important question we now address is whether we *want* to remain in such a stationary state.

Suppose, therefore, that we have capital stock K and wish to analyze whether or not to break out of the corresponding stationary state by investing. If we invest nothing (net investment is zero), we can remain forever in state K, enjoying a constant income annuity flow equal to $G(K, 0)$, thereby yielding present discounted value of

$$\frac{G(K, 0)}{\rho}. \tag{26}$$

Our initial analysis is focused on answering the question, Do we want to remain in this stationary state, or can we do better? To begin, we perform a simple thought experiment about a possible transition from this stationary state to an adjacent or neighboring stationary state. Suppose we consider increasing our stock of capital by just ε units, having in mind thereafter to remain permanently in the new stationary state, whose capital stock is at the level $K + \varepsilon$. If we do this, our constant-income annuity flow would increase *in each period* by amount $G_1(K, 0)\varepsilon$, whose present discounted value is

$$\frac{G_1(K, 0)\varepsilon}{\rho}. \tag{27}$$

To achieve this long-run permanent stationary-state flow increase of $G_1(K, 0)\varepsilon$ per unit time, however, we must temporarily increase net investment in this period, from a level of zero to a level of ε. Such action results in a one-time immediate loss of gain

$$-G_2(K, 0)\varepsilon. \tag{28}$$

Thus we have shown that making a transition from stationary state K to stationary state $K + \varepsilon$ increases net present discounted value if and only if (27) is greater than (28). The same logic can be used to show that making a transition from stationary state K to stationary state $K - \varepsilon$ increases net present discounted value if and only if (28) is greater than (27).

Assuming $G_2(K, 0) < 0$, define:

$$R(K) \equiv \frac{G_1(K, 0)}{-G_2(K, 0)}. \tag{29}$$

We call $R(K)$ the *stationary rate of return on capital* (evaluated at capital stock level K). The function $R(K)$ represents one of the most important concepts in all of economics and will play a critical role throughout this book. It is natural to assume that

$$R'(K) \leq 0, \tag{30}$$

and in fact this condition will hold for every model we analyze.

The problem we are trying to solve is supposed to maximize the present discounted value of net gains. If the stationary rate of return on capital exceeds the interest rate, then (27) is bigger than (28) and we can attain a higher present discounted value of gains (than would be gotten by remaining in this stationary state) by investing some positive amount and moving to a more capital-intensive stationary state. If the stationary rate of return on capital is less than the discount rate, then (27) is smaller than (28) and we can attain a higher present discounted value of gains by disinvesting (investing some negative amount) and moving to a less capital-intensive stationary state. Therefore we do not want to remain "at rest" with any stock of capital whose stationary rate of return is not equal to the discount rate. This simple insight is surprisingly powerful and has important consequences for characterizing an optimal solution.

Equation (29) can equivalently be written as

$$\left. \frac{dI}{dK} \right|_{G=\overline{G}, I=0} = R(K). \tag{31}$$

Condition (31) indicates that $R(K)$ represents the rate at which present stocks of current dollars can be transformed into perpetual flows of annuity dollars (at the level of gain corresponding to zero investment). This means that $R(K)$ acts just like the yield on a infinitely long-term bond. Thus the answer to the question of whether to make positive or negative investments in executing a transition from one stationary state to another is essentially the answer to the following question: "If a person holds a portfolio of bonds whose annual yield in perpetuity is $R(K)$, while the going rate of interest is ρ, should that person be advised to buy or to sell such bonds?" The answer should be fairly obvious. If $R(K) > \rho$, you want to invest in more bonds. If $R(K) < \rho$, you want to disinvest your portfolio of such bonds. If $R(K) = \rho$, then on the margin you want neither to invest nor to disinvest in bonds.

A *stationary solution* of the Euler equation (24) is a stationary state (that is, a trajectory of the form $(K(t), \dot{K}(t)) \equiv (\hat{K}, 0)$), which also satisfies

$$R(\hat{K}) = \rho \tag{32}$$

for some $\hat{K}$. Using the definition (29), we readily confirm that equation (32) is a special case of (24) where $\dot{G}_2 \equiv 0$ (because the capital stock never changes), while the corresponding net investment level is constantly zero.

It can be verified that in the widget entrepreneur's problem the stationary solution (29) is precisely the static monopoly solution without adjustment costs, whose value of $\hat{K}$ is given by (4). This result presages a major theme of capital theory concerning the relationship between static and dynamic optimization. The static solution, which is almost always learned first in economics, typically represents a stationary case of the more general dynamic solution. Another theme, to be explored later, is that the dynamic solution often tries to attain, or at least to approach, its stationary solution (which is simultaneously the solution of the corresponding static problem).

The reader should be warned, however, that many interesting, important, and perfectly well-defined problems do not have a stationary solution. For example, if $b = 0$ in the widget entrepreneur's problem (10)–(12), which corresponds to a perfectly competitive widget market with infinite elasticity of demand, the problem is still meaningful—but the optimal solution is not stationary. In this case, where $b = 0$, it can be confirmed by direct substitution into (24) that the Euler condition implies the constant investment level

$$\bar{I} = \frac{\overline{P} - \rho c}{2a\rho}, \tag{33}$$

so that the corresponding capital stock trajectory is $K(t) = K_0 + \bar{I}t$, which is certainly not stationary (although it might legitimately be called "steady state," since capital is always expanding at the steady rate $\bar{I}$ per unit time).

Returning to the special case of a stationary solution to the Euler equation, let us temporarily wave aside the existence question. Even though existence need not occur generally, let us here suppose it so happens that there exists some value $\hat{K}$, which satisfies (32). (In the discussion that follows, it is easiest to make the harmless additional assumption that (30) holds with strict inequality at $K = \hat{K}$, implying $\hat{K}$ must be unique.)

It may seem like beating a dead horse, but the stationary rate of return is such a critically important concept that we explain it in yet one more way.

As another way to intuit the meaning of the basic condition (32), consider a heuristic hypothetical static version of the prototype-economic calculus of variations problem. The purpose of what follows is to demonstrate intuitively how economic "statics" is essentially a very special case of economic "dynamics"—with the statics concentrating exclusively on the stationary-state part of a dynamic solution. As we shall see throughout Part I, economic statics is usually economic dynamics restricted to an examination of stationary states only, where the corresponding static-equivalent flow price of a unit of capital is (on heuristic grounds) ρ.

Suppose we have the stationary capital stock $\hat{K}$. Suppose further we consider making a displacement change of ΔK, which requires a corresponding change of ΔI. We want to know whether or not we can receive higher static gain at the same "budget" as it cost us to attain the original stationary state. In a stationary equilibrium, it is natural to take the "price" of a unit of capital stock ΔK in terms of a unit of investment flow ΔI as the discount rate ρ—that is, displacement combinations that maintain the same budget should satisfy $\rho \Delta K = \Delta I$. This might be translated as a static flow interpretation of the idea that the "cost of capital" is the "imputed rental price" ρ, meaning a decision maker in this static world can "purchase" the gain that comes with an extra unit of capital by living with the adverse consequences (on direct gain) of investment's being perpetually higher in amount ρ per unit time. Thus in this heuristic thought experiment, our budget constraint for the proposed change is

$$\rho \Delta K - 1\Delta I = 0. \tag{34}$$

A *static heuristic version* of the prototype-economic calculus of variations problem is to select values of ΔK and ΔI to maximize the "utility" function $G(\hat{K} + \Delta K, \Delta I)$ subject to the budget constraint (34). The solution of such a problem must satisfy the well-known first-order condition

$$\frac{G_1(\hat{K} + \Delta K, \Delta I)}{\rho} = \frac{G_2(\hat{K} + \Delta K, \Delta I)}{-1}. \tag{35}$$

But the solution to (35) is just (32)! More formally, the solution of the problem of maximizing $G(\hat{K} + \Delta K, \Delta I)$ subject to the budget constraint (34) is $(\Delta K^*, \Delta I^*) = (0, 0)$. This result is general. The stationary solution (if it exists) solves the corresponding as-if-static flow version of the problem where the flow equivalent of the "cost of capital" is the "rental price" ρ.

Whichever story is employed, it is important to comprehend fully the economic significance of the optimal stationary state characterization (32). An economic interpretation of the optimal stationary state will prove invaluable for the one-dimensional case of a single capital good. Actually, the simple thought experiment of making an elementary investment or disinvestment perturbation to compare which of two adjacent stationary states is "better" will play a key role not just in enriching economic intuition, but also in proving rigorously a simple version of the maximum principle of optimal control theory.

As if this were not enough, a stationary state satisfying (32) has yet another important property, which was previously alluded to. Even though most economic problems do not start off with a stationary solution (that is, satisfying (32)) as their given initial state, many such problems often try to go to their stationary solution. This way of conceptualizing "what the optimal solution is trying to do" can be very useful for understanding the economics of the problem, especially for the case of a single capital good. An equation like (32) is woven throughout the fabric of so many economic applications of optimal control theory that it can truly be said to constitute a central solution concept. We will be analyzing stationary solutions in a wide variety of contexts, applying the same unifying capital-theoretic interpretations, only flavored somewhat differently to reflect the specific features of each particular economic context. And it all begins with the thought experiment of imagining being in a stationary state and asking the basic question, What would happen if we invested or disinvested a unit of capital and moved to a higher or lower stationary state?

Condition (32) is so important as a guide for investment that it might be called the "fundamental equation of capital theory." If at time t we find ourselves with capital stock $K(t)$, the most natural question in the world to ask is, Do we want to remain here? The answer is a tentative "yes" if $K(t)$ satisfies (32)—that is, if $K(t) = \hat{K}$. Suppose, though, that $K(t)$ does not satisfy (31).
If

$$R(K(t)) > \rho, \tag{36}$$

then we definitely do not want to "stay here." We want to make a positive investment in some capital—if we can.
If

$$R(K(t)) < \rho, \tag{37}$$

then we also do not want to "stay here." In this case we wish to disinvest, if it is possible—for example, by not replacing retired capital.

Capital theory (or optimal control theory, which for the economist is essentially the same thing) might be said to consist of a *qualitative* and a *quantitative* side. The qualitative part consists in making at any time one of the following three choices. Choice number one is to remain at the given level of capital stock, number two is to make some (positive) investment, and number three is to disinvest (make a negative investment). It turns out that this qualitative side of capital theory is covered amazingly completely by just checking which of the conditions, (37) or (36) or (32), pertains.

The quantitative side of capital theory is less simple. The qualitative side tells us in which direction net investment should move the capital stock. The quantitative side tells us how rapidly to move in the chosen direction. A full analysis of the quantitative side comes only with the maximum principle. But the first step here is to understand the economic intuition behind the basic qualitative principle of pushing investment in the direction of the sign of $[R(K) - \rho]$.

Introduction to the Role of Convexity (or Concavity) in Economic Problems

Next suppose, for the sake of argument, that not only does a unique stationary solution $\hat{K}$ exist, but it just so happens also that the economy starts off with the possibility of pursuing forever a stationary solution because the initial condition coincidentally satisfies (32), meaning

$$K_0 = \hat{K}. \tag{38}$$

If condition (38) is satisfied for the initial capital stock, does it imply that remaining in the stationary state is an optimal policy? Intuitively, the answer should be a resounding yes, due to the compelling economic logic describing qualitatively the direction of optimal investment behavior for situations characterized by (37), (36), or (32). As will emerge from example after example, in most economic situations the optimal policy is to try to go to the stationary solution (32), if one exists. Viewed this way, it then seems odd to find an economy lucky enough to start in a stationary optimal state (because the initial conditions happen to satisfy (38)), only to pull away and move in another direction.

So it seems economically plausible that when condition (38) holds we should want to remain in the stationary state. But to be able actually to infer such a conclusion in general, it turns out that we need to impose some additional conditions on the function $G(K, I)$. We will impose a structure that is natural to many economic scenarios—namely, *concavity of the objective function.*

The function $G(K, I)$ is concave if for any (K_1, I_1) and (K_2, I_2), and for all values of λ such that $0 \leq \lambda \leq 1$, then

$$
\begin{aligned}
& G(\lambda K_1 + (1 - \lambda)K_2, \lambda I_1 + (1 - \lambda)I_2) \\
& \geq \lambda G(K_1, I_1) + (1 - \lambda)G(K_2, I_2).
\end{aligned}
\tag{39}
$$

Inequality (39) represents a kind of two-dimensional *non-increasing-returns* condition. It turns out that non-increasing returns is naturally satisfied in a great many economic contexts, because it is just a generalization of the famous economic law of diminishing returns. This "law" is a natural assumption to make in many economic applications, because it follows from diminishing marginal utility, or diminishing marginal product, or diminishing marginal anything that is reflecting the limitations imposed by scarce resources, which lie in the background of any economic situation. Essentially, the concavity assumption corresponds to a non-positive-second-derivative curvature condition, which ensures that any local maximum is a global maximum. Of course there are exceptions where increasing returns are an important feature (and where they may even play a central role in modeling), but the point of departure for analyzing most economic situations is an assumption of nonincreasing returns like (39).

An equivalent way of stating the condition (39) for a smoothly differentiable function, in terms of three conditions on its second partial derivatives, is

$$
G_{11} \leq 0, \quad G_{22} \leq 0, \quad G_{11}G_{22} - (G_{12})^2 \geq 0,
\tag{40}
$$

which means that, *for all values of a and b,* the following quadratic-form condition holds

$$
G_{11}a^2 + G_{22}b^2 + 2G_{12}ab \leq 0.
\tag{41}
$$

Armed with these (equivalent) definitions, we now show that if the function $G(K, I)$ is concave, and if we start out in a stationary solution (that is, (38) holds), then an optimal policy is to remain forever in the stationary state, meaning for all t that

$$(K^*(t), I^*(t)) \equiv (\hat{K}, 0).$$

(42)

The proof of this important result is by contradiction and involves a typical variational argument. (The calculus of variations is the natural milieu for defining and investigating the stationary rate of return precisely because variations in net investment are unrestricted—and hence particularly easy to analyze.) Suppose the statement is not true. Suppose there is some continuously differentiable function $h(t)$ with $h(0) = \hat{K}$ having the property that

$$\int_0^\infty G(h(t), \dot{h}(t)) e^{-\rho t} \, dt > \int_0^\infty G(\hat{K}, 0) e^{-\rho t} \, dt.$$

(43)

Define the continuously differentiable function

$$f(t, \lambda) \equiv \lambda h(t) + (1 - \lambda) \hat{K}.$$

(44)

It is readily confirmed that when $\lambda = 0$, then $f(t, \lambda) = \hat{K}$, while when $\lambda = 1$, then $f(t, \lambda) = h(t)$. As λ is changed continuously from 0 to 1, we are moving smoothly along a straight line from $f(t, 0) = \hat{K}$ to $f(t, 1) = h(t)$. Furthermore, for all λ, we are starting from the same initial state because $f(0, \lambda) = \hat{K}$ for all λ.

Now define the function

$$\varphi(\lambda) \equiv \int_0^\infty G(f(t, \lambda), \dot{f}(t, \lambda)) e^{-\rho t} \, dt.$$

(45)

Taking the derivative of (45) with respect to λ, it is readily confirmed (using (44)) that

$$\varphi'(\lambda) = \int_0^\infty [G_1(f(t, \lambda), \dot{f}(t, \lambda))(h(t) - \hat{K})$$

(46)

$$+ G_2(f(t, \lambda), \dot{f}(t, \lambda)) \frac{d}{dt}(h(t) - \hat{K})] e^{-\rho t} \, dt.$$

Integrate the second term of the right-hand side of (46) by parts, and make use of the fact that $h(0) = \hat{K}$, which then yields

$$
\int_0^\infty [G_2 e^{-\rho t}] \frac{d}{dt}(h(t) - \hat{K}) \, dt
$$

$$
= \int_0^\infty -[(\dot{G}_2 - \rho G_2)e^{-\rho t}](h(t) - \hat{K}) \, dt.
$$

(47)

When $\lambda = 0$, then from (44) all variables in (46) and (47) are evaluated at the stationary solution $K(t) = \hat{K}$. In this case, $\dot{G}_2 = 0$ in (47), and substituting the resulting expression into (46), the latter becomes

$$
\varphi'(0) = \int_0^\infty [G_1(\hat{K}, 0) + \rho G_2(\hat{K}, 0)](h(t) - \hat{K})e^{-\rho t} \, dt.
$$

(48)

But now, by (29) and (32), the term within the square brackets of the right-hand side of (48) is zero, so we may conclude that

$$
\varphi'(0) = 0.
$$

(49)

Taking the second derivative of (45) with respect to λ by differentiating (46), and rearranging terms, we then obtain

$$
\varphi''(\lambda) = \int_0^\infty [G_{11}(h(t) - \hat{K})^2 + G_{22}(\dot{h}(t))^2
$$

$$
+ 2G_{12}(h(t) - \hat{K})(\dot{h}(t))]e^{-\rho t} \, dt.
$$

(50)

Applying (41) to (50), we have $\varphi''(\lambda) \leq 0$ for all possible continuously differentiable functions $h(t)$ and for all possible values of λ between 0 and 1. But now we have a contradiction! We have a smoothly differentiable function $\varphi(\lambda)$ with $\varphi'(0) = 0$, $\varphi''(\lambda) \leq 0$, and, from (43), $\varphi(1) > \varphi(0)$ (using the definitions (44) and (45)), which cannot all hold simultaneously. (How can the function $\varphi(\lambda)$ *increase* in going from $\lambda = 0$ to $\lambda = 1$, when its derivative at $\lambda = 0$ is zero and the second derivative is never positive?) The conclusion is that the premise (43) must be false.

Note carefully the logic that is involved here. From the economic interpretation of (32), which we have previously given, we have a strong economic sense that if we are lucky enough to start out in the stationary-state solution (42) (because (38) happens to hold), then it should be an optimal policy to remain at the stationary solution (42) forever. Yet to prove this, we need to have something like the local concavity condition (39). If (39) (or (40) or (41)) does not hold, then we can find some better solution—that is, some $\{h(t)\}$ satisfying (43)—which seems counterintuitive. The economic logic of this argument should strengthen our intuition that the non-increasing-returns concavity assumption (39) represents an economically reasonable condition to assume for many economic situations.

A classical calculus of variations problem is characterized by having no constraints whatsoever placed on possible values of $K(t)$ or $\dot{K}(t)$ (aside from regularity conditions, such as differentiability). It is precisely this aspect that makes the calculus of variations an ideal structure within which to define and analyze the stationary rate of return on capital. Yet this feature of no restrictions on variables is clearly unrealistic for most economic models, since, for example, negative capital stocks or unboundedly large (or small) investments make no economic sense. We need to have a "generalized" calculus of variations to deal with situations where feasible values of $K(t)$ or $\dot{K}(t)$ may have to be constrained in some way. Such a generalization is called *optimal control theory,* and to its development we now turn.

Bibliographic Note

As indicated, this chapter contains mainly background material from various strands of economics and mathematics. Economic applications of the calculus of variations are covered much more fully in Kamien and Schwartz (1991), part I. Another book that might be consulted here is Intriligator (1971). The important role of convexity in economics is exposited in the classic chapter 1 of Koopmans (1957). A history of the calculus of variations is in Goldstine (1980). A good overview of the historic and conceptual relationships between calculus of variations, the maximum principle, and dynamic programming is contained in Yong and Zhou (1999).

2

✳

The Prototype-Economic Control Problem

The Concept of an Economic Control Problem

It turns out that the calculus of variations is not the best way to formulate and solve "economic-like" dynamic optimization problems. The main issue is not so much that such problems cannot be forced into the mold of calculus of variations, because sometimes (though by no means always) they can. Rather, the main issue is that the calculus of variations framework is not the most natural or the easiest way to demonstrate the economic meaning and significance of a solution. Frank Ramsey and Harold Hotelling both expressed their seminal papers (Ramsey in 1928 on "optimal growth" and Hotelling in 1931 on "optimal extraction of an exhaustible resource") in terms of the calculus of variations because that was the only technique then available. But to best understand the contents of these two classic papers (as well as countless others in "economic-like" situations or contexts) nowadays, it is much better to formulate the problems in terms of so-called optimal control theory, which was not yet developed at the time when Ramsey and Hotelling were writing. If a beginning student has in mind economic applications but does not yet know any dynamic optimization theory, it is a far better use of time to bypass the calculus of variations altogether in favor of learning the material by applying the appropriate variant of so-called *optimal control theory*.

Modern control theory subsumes the calculus of variations as a special case. The additional generality of control theory can be crucial for many economic applications, because economic problems frequently have *inequality constraints,* including non-negativity conditions on variables, and constraints restricting some variables to lie within certain bounds. These situations simply cannot be handled by the calculus of variations, but, as we shall see, they are handled beautifully by optimal control theory. So the most immediate reason for an economist to study optimal control theory is to be able to solve important economic problems that cannot be handled by any other technique.

The second, and by far the most important, reason for an "economist type" to learn dynamic optimization in the framework of optimal control theory is that a solution is characterized by the famous *maximum principle*. The maximum principle is an extremely useful solution concept because it has a direct economic interpretation in terms of income and wealth that significantly complements our understanding of and economic intuition about capital theory. In this spirit the greater generality of optimal control theory is perhaps more like an additional bonus than a core reason for learning the dynamic-optimization material via the maximum principle. Even when an "economic-like" problem can be formulated and solved within the narrower confines of the calculus of variations, it is almost always better to phrase the problem in terms of optimal control theory and then to solve and interpret it by using the maximum principle.

Still on the subject of generality, there is yet a third reason why it behooves the aspiring economist fully to understand the optimal control approach to solving dynamic economic problems. The maximum principle shows vividly the fundamental unity of the solutions to all capital theory problems of an important and very broad class. It is not necessary to treat each case by special techniques to be able to highlight the essential economic themes. After covering the general theory, you will know beforehand what to look for to bring out the key economic features of a solution to any new problem in capital theory. One simply cannot conceptualize the scope of this impressive (and very useful) unity without the maximum principle of optimal control theory.

A fourth reason for economists to study the maximum principle falls under the rubric of things cultural, philosophical, aesthetic, historical, and/or connective—a kind of "art appreciation," if you will. There is a deep mathematical isomorphism between the basic unifying principles of capital theory exhibited by the maximum principle and the basic unifying principles of physics exhibited by Hamilton's famous canonical formulation. In physics, W. R. Hamilton's canonical equations of motion constitute one of the most fundamental of unifying laws, tying together such disparate fields as classical mechanics, thermodynamics, quantum mechanics, electricity and magnetism, and many other areas. Essentially, the methodology of a large part of modern physics has been to use the concepts of position and momentum that arise naturally in classical mechanics, and which are directly observable in that setting, to analyze the physical laws of thermodynamics, quantum mechanics, electricity and magnetism, and of other situations, where not only are position and momentum not observable, but it is often not even clear what they represent.

This and the next paragraph constitute a brief detour to explain the structural relation between Hamiltonian physics and Hamiltonian economics, which some readers may be interested to learn—but some others may not. For those who *are* interested in the isomorphism of the underlying mathematics, here is a quick translation key. What economists call "capital" corresponds to what the physicists call a "generalized coordinate," while economists' "price" of capital corresponds to their "generalized momentum." The current value Hamiltonian for economists is "income," while for the physicists it is "energy." Otherwise, the mathematical structure of the two systems is essentially isomorphic. Hamilton's famous canonical partial-differential equations of motion are essentially a version of the maximum principle. Jacobi's "transformation" or "substitution" or "potential" function is what an economist would call a "state evaluation function," which in economics is interpreted as representing "wealth" as a function of physical capital stocks. The so-called Hamilton-Jacobi equation, which is basically an elegantly compressed integral version of Hamilton's canonical partial-differential equations of motion, corresponds in an economic context to what in this book is called the "wealth and income version of the maximum principle."

There are some differences, of course, between Hamiltonian physics and Hamiltonian economics. The physicist almost always works with a system where energy is conserved, which corresponds in economics to a limiting case of zero discounting—and it is not clear what is the physical significance of positive discounting (does it represent a universe whose energy is "leaking out" at a constant rate ρ?). Economists are frequently interested in inequality constraints, for example the non-negativity of capital or the boundedness from below of net investment, and their prices are non-negative, whereas in physics it is as normal for position or momentum to be negative as positive. Nevertheless, what is most striking in the comparisons is the relative similarity of the underlying mathematical structure, rather than the differences. Thus when economists use the maximum principle to understand and unify capital theory, they are essentially following a centuries-old tradition of analyzing dynamical systems in a spirit inaugurated by Lagrange, Euler, Bernoulli, Hamilton, Jacobi, Weierstrauss, Cartheodory, and many of the other great pioneers of applied mathematics and theoretical physics. The maximum principle is the economist's version of dynamic elegance. This is one reason why, I think, the economic theory described in this book is likely to long endure. The truth or relevance of any theory is often elusive—even in physics, much less in economics. Therefore theories that possess an elegantly simple unified inner beauty and yet are "true enough" or "relevant enough" tend to have staying power, perhaps because they are so rare. I think that Hamiltonian economics is just such a rare candidate for long-term endurance.

We are now ready to state a slimmed-down one-dimensional core version of the optimal control problem that will be studied throughout the rest of the book.

The simplest prototype-economic control problem of general interest takes the form:

$$\text{maximize} \quad \int_0^\infty G(K(t), I(t))e^{-\rho t} \, dt \tag{1}$$

subject to

$$\dot{K}(t) = I(t), \tag{2}$$

and

$$m(K(t)) \le I(t) \le M(K(t)), \tag{3}$$

and

$$K(t) \ge 0, \tag{4}$$

and with the given initial condition

$$K(0) = K_0. \tag{5}$$

The reader should immediately take note that the optimal control problem (1)–(5) above appears to be a close relative of the calculus of variations problem (1.16)–(1.18) from the first chapter. Actually, the only differences are the constraint (3), which requires net investment to be chosen between some minimum value $m(K)$ and some maximum value $M(K)$, and the constraint (4), which requires the capital stock to be non-negative.

The flow variable $G(K(t), I(t))$, which appears in (1) above, represents the immediate or *direct gain* at time t of the economic system that is being modeled. Depending on the context, $G(K(t), I(t))$ might stand for the net flow of what could be called direct gain, dividend, cash flow, reward, payoff, profit, consumption, utility, or any other desideratum at time t.

The variable ρ appearing in the objective (1) represents the relevant *discount rate* to be applied to the direct gain. For a profit maximizer, ρ is the opportunity cost of capital or, more simply, the relevant rate of interest. For a utility maximizer, ρ represents the rate of pure time preference; there can even be an interpretation where ρ represents the per-period probability that the optimizer dies or the world perishes.

What about uncertain gains? There is a simple interpretation of the prototype-economic problem (1)–(5), which allows an important class of uncertainty to be routinely incorporated. For an expected-profit-maximizing firm making investments in an uncertain world, we interpret $G(K, I)$ as representing the *expected* direct-gain net cash flow from a project, while ρ is the competitive rate of return earned by alternative investments of this risk class. In the mathematical language of the standard capital-asset-pricing model, we might here write

$$\rho = r_f + \beta(r_m - r_f), \tag{6}$$

where r_f is the risk-free interest rate, r_m is the return on a market portfolio, and β is the "project beta," measuring the covariance of the project return with the market portfolio. Thus, with the appropriate interpretation of ρ, we are essentially able to handle by this prototype formulation any uncertain dynamic investment-optimization problem that can be framed in terms of the standard textbook capital-asset-pricing model.[1] As we will show throughout the book, this theme repeats itself. Many dynamic economics problems that (at first glance) appear not to possess a prototype architecture can, in fact, be transformed into (1)–(5) by a simple change of variables and/or a different interpretation of the discount rate ρ.

The maximand (1) is a stock of wealth-like magnitude representing the present discounted value of all instantaneous gains.

The *state variable* $K(t)$ represents (or is interpretable as) the level of a *capital stock* at time t. This interpretation is natural in most dynamic economic situations, although it should be clearly understood that the concept of a capital stock is intended to be very broad. Mineral deposits are capital stocks. Cows

1. On the capital-asset-pricing model (CAPM), see any introductory finance textbook, such as Brearley and Myers (2000).

on a dairy farm are capital stocks. Fish in a fishery are capital stocks. Clean air or water could be interpreted as a capital stock. There can even be "human capital" in the form of education and training skills. For some purposes, R&D activities may be conceptualized as involving the creation of "knowledge capital." Finally, of course, human-made means of production, like machinery, buildings, and roads, are perhaps the most conventional examples of capital stocks.

The word "capital" has a very elastic meaning in everyday usage. Throughout this book it will be essential to keep in mind that "capital" here means *physical capital,* as opposed to *wealth.* The latter concept will be fully developed starting with the next chapter. Both "capital" and "wealth" are extremely important concepts in economics, but (as understood by the economist) they are different.

What are the special properties of capital stocks that make this state variable different from state variables that appear in geometry or physics or engineering optimization problems? We will enumerate some other properties presently, but for now we note that the capital stocks appearing in economics-like situations are usually intended to be *non-negative*—as reflected in the *state constraint* $K(t) \geq 0$ in (4). Capital cannot be negative in many situations, because for petroleum reserves to be less than zero, for example, or for the stock of machinery to be negative essentially has no economic meaning. Most capital is quite naturally described as being inherently non-negative. Sometimes the condition $K(t) \geq 0$ must be imposed explicitly in some optimization problems to prevent the "solution" from instructing us to pump oil from empty wells or to turn machines back into the steel and coal from whence they came. Wherever the condition $K(t) \geq 0$ does not occur naturally, we can almost always make it happen by a natural redefinition—for example by redefining the measurement of air cleanliness to be zero in the worst possible state and positive in every other state.

The *instrument* $I(t)$ stands for the *net investment flow* at time t. Equation (2) simply says that the flow of net investment at any time always equals the rate of change of the corresponding capital stock. Thus investment here means *physical investment in physical capital.* In a sense, equation (2) represents more of a definition than an economic insight. Net investment is essentially defined as the instrument that controls the net accumulation of capital. If $G(K(t), I(t))$ stands for the flow of immediate present gain at time t, then in some abstract spirit $I(t)$ might be said to represent the flow of indirect future gain being accumulated into capital at time t, to be paid out later, indirectly, in the form of higher gains at some future time than would otherwise be available.

As we shall see, optimal control theory is general enough to allow almost any variable to serve as a control or instrument. We are forcing the instrument to be *net investment* here because when the control situation is posed in the "reduced form" of the prototype-economic problem, which can always be done by a change of variables, then the solution becomes very easy, to the point of being almost routine, and the economic intuition is always crystal clear. Once the problem is placed into the standard format (1)–(5), we can then mechanically calculate the stationary rate of return, which provides the critical solution concept for any situation involving one state variable. Thus, just to make a relatively simple change of variables that allows net investment to be "the" instrument is to take a giant forward step toward solving any control problem.

With human-made capital, like machinery and structures, we are accustomed to the idea that investment is positive, or at least it is usually positive. But there is no deep reason for this to be true. Investment in machinery is negative whenever gross investments are less than retirements, which sometimes happens. With mineral resources in the ground, investment is negative whenever we extract and use the mineral faster than new discoveries are replacing it in the ground, which occurs very often, even typically. Investment in clean air is negative whenever we are polluting more than we are cleaning up. Investment in forests is negative when the wood in trees is being cut down faster than it is being replanted. So while capital stock levels are usually represented by non-negative variables, investments may often be either negative or positive, depending on the situation and context. In one dimension, with just one capital good, the restrictions on net investment come in the form of an upper bound M (for *maximum*) and a lower bound m (for *minimum*), which might possibly depend on the state variable K, as shown in condition (3).

In economic situations we usually think of the possible combinations of goods and services as being determined by the level of the capital stocks, as well as other background fixed factors. The United States has more possibilities than China for both consumption and investment, primarily because the United States has a greater accumulation of capital—including human capital. Kuwait has more possibilities than Yemen because it has higher stocks of oil reserves. A manufacturing company with more physical plant and equipment has a greater range of production possibilities than the same company would have with less plant and equipment. At any time there is a tradeoff between present gains and future gains, determined by the capacity of the system. The capacity to trade off between consumption and investment is usually enhanced in absolute terms if more capital is present.

The *net gain function* $G(K, I)$ gives the maximum net cash flow of rewards as a function of the capital stock K that has been inherited from the past and the investment level I that is currently chosen. Usually it is presumed that

$$\frac{\partial G}{\partial I} = G_2(K, I) < 0, \tag{7}$$

because investment typically comes at the expense of current cash flow, while

$$\frac{\partial G}{\partial K} = G_1(K, I) > 0, \tag{8}$$

because more capital generates more cash flow, other things being equal.

It should be understood that the net gain function $G(K, I)$ describes the feasible combinations of G, I, and K that are available in principle at any instant of time. In our formulation, $G(K, I)$ represents a complete and timeless description of what is hypothetically possible at any instant, rather than a description of what is possible now, in the current situation. Right now, at time zero, we are stuck with the capital stock $K(0) = K_0$, which we inherited from the past. However, by choosing now a particular value of the net investment flow I, we will influence the amount of capital stock we will have at some future time T—that is, $K(T)$. The timeless net gain function $G(K, I)$ describes what combinations of G and I are achievable now, at time $t = 0$, with the currently inherited capital stock $K = K_0$, as well as what combinations of G and I will be achievable at any future time $t = T$, conditional on the capital stock then being $K = K(T)$, where we are allowed to think of $K(T)$ as assuming any (non-negative) value. The basic idea is that we currently are aware of all hypothetically possible combinations of G, I, and K, even though right now we are actually restricted to choosing from just a subset of those combinations of net gains $\tilde{G}$ and net investments $\tilde{I}$ satisfying the condition $\tilde{G} \leq G(K, \tilde{I})$ for quasi-fixed K.

Just to ensure that our terminology is consistent with the mathematical literature on dynamic optimization, let us take the opportunity here to review briefly some standard control-theory jargon in our own prototype-economic setup. In mathematical language, K is a *state variable* because its realization at any time is determined by past decisions and it describes completely the current state of the system. Our prototype problem has a *state constraint* of the form (4). By contrast with K, we call I a *control variable* because it represents an instrument that may be chosen at any time. What is the relevant *control set* that describes at any time the allowable values of I? In our prototype-economic formulation, the control set at any time is a *state-dependent* function of the capital stock at that time, which is defined as

$$S(K) \equiv \{I \mid m(K) \leq I \leq M(K)\}, \tag{9}$$

where $M(K)$ and $m(K)$ are functions giving, respectively, the *maximum* and the *minimum* allowable values of I. The notation $M(K) = +\infty$ means there is no upper limit on I, while the notation $m(K) = -\infty$ signifies the absence of a lower bound on I.

It should be apparent that the calculus of variations formulation (1.16)–(1.18) of the previous chapter is a special limiting case of the optimal control problem (1)–(5) of this chapter, where (4) is absent or irrelevant, and where (3) takes on the special values $M(K) = +\infty$ and $m(K) = -\infty$.

What is perhaps less apparent at this stage is the surprisingly large number of interesting economic problems that cannot be formulated in the calculus of variations form, but which can be formulated and solved as optimal control problems just by adding a simple constraint on I of the form (3) and/or a simple state-space constraint of the form (4). Also probably not apparent at this stage is how much more complicated the statement and rigorous proofs of the optimality conditions will become when the simple constraints (3) and (4) are added to what is otherwise a standard problem in the calculus of variations.

It is important to be clear about the relationship between the two sets

$$A \equiv \{(\tilde{G}, \tilde{I}, \tilde{K}) \mid \tilde{K} \geq 0, \ m(\tilde{K}) \leq \tilde{I} \leq M(\tilde{K}), \ \tilde{G} \leq G(\tilde{K}, \tilde{I})\}, \tag{10}$$

and

$$B(K) \equiv \{(\tilde{G}, \tilde{I}) \mid m(K) \leq \tilde{I} \leq M(K), \ \tilde{G} \leq G(K, \tilde{I})\}. \tag{11}$$

In a sense, A represents all *long-run hypothetically feasible combinations* of the triple (G, I, K), while $B(K)$ represents the *short-run actual combinations* of the pair (G, I) that would be currently available when the current capital stock is at level K. The point here is that the state variable K can be changed in the long run, but at any given instant of time it is quasi-fixed. Fortunately, we are dealing in this chapter with only three relevant variables (the state variable K and the two control variables $\tilde{G}$ and $\tilde{I}$, which appear in (11)), so it is possible to have in the mind's eye a vivid mental picture of the relationship between A and $B(K)$. The set A of attainable possibilities can be envisioned as a set in three dimensions, where the x-axis represents G, the y-axis represents I, and the z-axis represents K. For any given value of the state variable K, the corresponding two-dimensional control set $B(K)$, which describes feasible combinations of G and I given K, is a two-dimensional slice in the xy plane, that is, the intersection of the three-dimensional set A with the one-dimensional "slicing" plane $z = K$. The set $B(K)$ is essentially the same as the set A, except that K is being held constant for $B(K)$.

Because none of the relevant possibilities sets $(A, B(K), \text{ or } S(K))$ depends directly on calendar time t, the control problem (1)–(5) is sometimes called autonomous.[2] The only place where time enters explicitly into the problem is via the discounting term $e^{-\rho t}$, which appears in the objective (1). It seems to be a fact of life that most "economics-like" models posed as optimal control problems, both in the textbooks and in professional journal articles, are autonomous. This is certainly true of the Ramsey and Hotelling models previously cited, but it seems to hold more generally. Furthermore, if the time dependence of a nonautonomous situation involves exponential growth (of technological progress, the demand function, the probability of a regime switch, and so on) at a constant rate, it is often possible to reformulate the problem through a change of variables so that it becomes isomorphic to the form (1)–(5), with a possibly different interpretation of the discount rate ρ. Later in the book we will comment in a general way on what happens with time-dependent attainable-possibilities sets. However, it is left to explore in more advanced textbooks and articles what exactly transpires in situations when A depends explicitly on t. For now it is better to concentrate on learning well the simpler time-autonomous case, which constitutes the vast bulk of economic applications of optimal control theory anyway.

Note that the present-discounted-value objective (1) is to be maximized over an infinite time horizon starting now, at time zero. This infinite-horizon feature is very characteristic of dynamic economic formulations. The problem has no natural end, so to speak. The reason that a great many dynamic optimization models with economic overtones are formulated as infinite-horizon

---

2. Economists call such problems autonomous. Physicists or engineers use this term only when the problem has no direct dependence on time whatsoever—here meaning that $\rho = 0$ also, which for physicists typically means that energy is being conserved.

free-endpoint problems is essentially because any other way of stating the objective seems arbitrary. We could try to fix the final state at some arbitrary time T by specifying $K(T)$, but how would we know beforehand the correct amount of $K(T)$ to specify without first solving a further dynamic optimization problem describing the situation from time T on? Or we might leave the problem itself to determine the best value of $K(T)$ by specifying the value of capital at time T as the function $V(K(T))$ and then attempt to maximize a finite-horizon objective of the form

$$\int_0^T G(K(t), I(t)) \, e^{-\rho t} \, dt + e^{-\rho T} \, V(K(T)), \tag{12}$$

but once again the same basic kind of issue arises. How do we know beforehand the correct value function $V(K(T))$ to specify without first solving a further dynamic optimization problem that maximizes the objective from time T on as a parametric function of $K(T)$? The only way out of this infinite regress is to cut the Gordian knot by optimizing an infinite-horizon objective of the form (1) right from the very beginning. Hence most economic applications of optimal control are characterized by the unusual feature of being infinite-horizon free-endpoint dynamic optimization problems. By way of contrast, optimal control problems in physics or engineering less frequently take on this particular form.

Ten Classic Economic Problems

From this point on, the order followed by Part I of the book is as follows. We conclude this chapter by describing ten relatively simple one-dimensional dynamic optimization economic problems, which include several classical models. Then in Chapter 3 we develop rigorously the formal theory of the maximum principle, and explain its economic interpretation. Chapter 4 is devoted to solving formally and interpreting economically the ten problems introduced in this chapter. Readers are reminded that the book need not be read or the material learned in exactly this particular order. The spatial ordering of the book's contents has been constructed to allow readers to find readily what they want and to create their own best learning sequence.

The ten economic models are exhibited here in order to show in detail how each of them can be described as a specific example of the prototype-economic control problem (1)–(5). Each particular model can be conceptualized as differing from the others only in the specific way the attainable-possibilities set A is specified. We will exhibit the relevant direct gain function $G(K, I)$ and derive the all-important stationary rate of return on capital

$$R(K) \equiv \frac{G_1(K, 0)}{-G_2(K, 0)}, \tag{13}$$

which will play such a crucial role as a solution concept for the one-dimensional case. It will then be fairly evident why it makes sense to assume the condition

$$R'(K) \leq 0, \tag{14}$$

whenever the "usual" assumptions are made, and why it also makes sense to assume that if there exists a value of capital $\hat{K}$ satisfying

$$R(\hat{K}) = \rho, \tag{15}$$

then the condition

$$R'(\hat{K}) < 0, \tag{16}$$

is also likely to be satisfied. Condition (16) will make it easy to analyze how the stationary solution changes parametrically with the discount rate, since

$$\frac{d\hat{K}}{d\rho} = \frac{1}{R'(\hat{K})} < 0, \tag{17}$$

which is an intuitively plausible condition we would like to have the one-dimensional models possess anyway.

Later, in Chapter 4, we will apply the maximum principle to solve these ten models, which will serve to emphasize the enormous unifying power of modern capital theory as expressed by the maximum principle, since the same basic principles will recur in all of the situations.

PROBLEM 1: THE FAMILY FIRM
The form of this problem is perhaps the simplest and most basic of all optimal control economic models. To begin with, think of a family-owned business like a farm or a construction company. The family has maintained its capital equipment in the amount K_0 for some time and has not really thought carefully about whether to expand the business, to size it back, or to just remain

at the current level of capitalization K_0. Now the oldest child has just returned home from taking a business school course in dynamic decision making and is eager to try out a more analytical approach.

The family has two options for generating income. One is the difference between current revenues and current costs (including depreciation costs for worn-out capital) from the family business. The other is from placing deposits in a town bank that pays continuously compounded interest at the universally competitive rate ρ on all deposits. This town bank is also willing to lend money to the family firm at this same universally competitive rate ρ. The family firm can deposit or borrow as much money as it wants at any time, but all loans must be paid back in full.

To analyze what the family firm should do, the business school graduate first estimates the stationary net income possibilities from the family business as a function of its level of capitalization. This estimated relationship is illustrated as the curve in Figure 1. The horizontal axis represents the amount of capital stock owned by the firm, which is the variable K. The vertical axis represents the annual flow of net income generated by that capital, the variable Y. The stationary relationship between income and capital estimated by the business school graduate is the function $Y = F(K)$, depicted as the curve in Figure 1. This curve has $F'' < 0$, thereby exhibiting the law of diminishing returns.

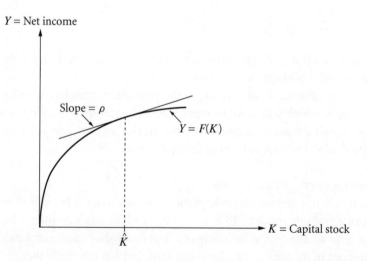

Figure 1 Long-run net income as a function of capital intensity.

It is important to stress that the function $Y = F(K)$ represents *net* income as a function of capital stock. If *gross* income possibilities from the family business as a function of its level of capitalization are given by the function $f(K)$, and if capital depreciates exponentially at decay rate μ, then the relation between the net and gross income functions is $F(K) = f(K) - \mu K$. The reason we are placing such emphasis on always expressing output and investment in net terms is that, once we have done so, we have transformed the one-capital-good problem into a standard form that is very easy to solve, analyze, and understand by using a powerful general approach based on the economically intuitive concept of the stationary rate of return on capital.

The business school graduate explains carefully and convincingly to the family that no matter what other consumption or investment plans they may have had before they thought of comparing their opportunities with what the bank is offering, they should now seek to maximize the present discounted value of their net earnings at the interest rate representing the opportunity cost of capital to them, here the rate ρ. The family accepts this logic, but even so it isn't clear whether the firm should be expanded or shrunk. And there are practical limits to the rate at which the family firm can change its capital. Because stripping down and selling off the very specific capital assets of the family firm at distress prices is costly, the only realistic way to shrink the capital stock is by failing to replace the worn-out capital that must be retired every year. To make this part simple, suppose that each year the fraction μ of capital wears out. At the other end of the investment scale, if the firm wishes to expand its capital base it can only absorb at most $\bar{I}$ of new capital each year. (Should anyone not like this constraint, $\bar{I}$ can be envisioned as being some very big number.)

Let $I(t)$ be a control variable representing the flow of net investment in the family business at time t. The gain flow generated by the family business at time t is the net income after investment $F(K(t)) - I(t)$. The problem faced by the family business, as interpreted by the business school graduate, is to control net investments $I(t)$ at time t in such a way as to

$$\text{maximize} \quad \int_0^\infty [F(K(t)) - I(t)] e^{-\rho t} \, dt \qquad (18)$$

subject to

$$\dot{K}(t) = I(t), \qquad (19)$$

and

$$-\mu K(t) \le I(t) \le \overline{I}, \tag{20}$$

and with the given initial condition

$$K(0) = K_0. \tag{21}$$

The family firm's problem is an optimal control problem of the form (1)–(5), where the relevant net gain function is

$$G(K, I) \equiv F(K) - I. \tag{22}$$

Applying formula (13) here, the stationary rate of return on capital for the family firm is

$$R(K) = F'(K). \tag{23}$$

PROBLEM 2: THE q-THEORY MODEL OF INVESTMENT

There is an important generalization of the family firm's problem that finds widespread application, among other places, as a core model in the macroeconomic literature on investment. As before, the long-run steady-state relationship between capital K and net income generated Y is given by the functional relationship $Y = F(K)$. And as before, net investment at time t, again denoted $I(t)$, must be subtracted from net income $Y(t)$ to determine net gain at time t.

But now there is an important additional investment cost to be considered when determining net gain. The new feature of this model, which is sometimes called the q-theory model of investment, is that the firm faces additional costs of adjustment to changes in capital stocks. In the family firm problem, the adjustment situation is a very simple special case where the adjustment costs are zero whenever net investment I satisfies the inequalities $-\mu K \le I \le \overline{I}$, and, in effect, are prohibitively expensive for any other values of I. In the q-theory model of investment, adjustment costs are given as some smoothly continuous function of I, say $\varphi(I)$, where the normalization convention usually takes the form

$$\varphi(0) = \varphi'(0) = 0, \tag{24}$$

with $\varphi'' > 0$. (The simplest example here is when $\varphi(I)$ is quadratic in I—an example of how this quadratic formulation might arise naturally was given in the widget entrepreneur's problem introduced at the beginning of Chapter 1.)

In the q-theory of investment, the flow of net gain at time t is given by the expression $F(K(t)) - I(t) - \varphi(I(t))$. The optimal control problem that forms the backbone of the q-theory of investment is of the form to

$$\text{maximize} \quad \int_0^\infty [F(K(t)) - I(t) - \varphi(I(t))]e^{-\rho t} \, dt \tag{25}$$

subject to

$$\dot{K}(t) = I(t), \tag{26}$$

and

$$-\mu K(t) \leq I(t), \tag{27}$$

and with the given initial condition

$$K(0) = K_0. \tag{28}$$

The q-theory model of investment is an optimal control problem of the type (1)–(5) with gain function

$$G(K, I) \equiv F(K) - I - \varphi(I). \tag{29}$$

Applying (13) to (29), the stationary rate of return on capital for the q-theory model of investment is

$$R(K) = F'(K). \tag{30}$$

PROBLEM 3: OPTIMAL MANAGEMENT OF THE FISHERY

The classical dynamic economic problem of optimal fishery management is typically presented as if seen through the eyes of a fictitious "sole owner," who may be conceptualized as being either a private firm or a government regulatory agency. The sole owner is assumed to be searching for a harvesting policy that maximizes net present discounted profits.

The problem here is of the form to choose the harvesting flow rate $\{h(t)\}$ to

$$\text{maximize} \quad \int_0^\infty \pi(x(t))h(t)e^{-\rho t}\, dt \tag{31}$$

subject to

$$\dot{x}(t) = F(x(t)) - h(t), \tag{32}$$

and

$$\underline{h} \le h(t) \le \bar{h}, \tag{33}$$

and with the given initial condition

$$x(0) = x_0. \tag{34}$$

For this model, $x(t)$ represents the stock of fish at time t, and $h(t)$ is the harvest flow taken at time t. In condition (33), $\bar{h}$ is some more or less arbitrary upper bound on harvesting; the lower bound $\underline{h}$ is perhaps somewhat less arbitrary because $\underline{h} \equiv 0$, at least, has a natural interpretation. (The upper and lower bounds are needed to make sense of the problem for technical reasons, as we shall see later.) The function $F(x)$ represents the net biological increase of the fish population, in the absence of any harvesting. The function $\pi(x)$ gives the net profits per fish caught when the stock of fish is x.

In the fisheries literature it is standard to take as unit profit the difference between price and catch cost, so that

$$\pi(x) = P - c(x), \tag{35}$$

where P represents the exogenously given world price of fish and $c(x)$ represents per unit "locating and harvesting cost" as a function of fish density x. A reader typically sees the form of the right-hand side of (35) rather than our more concise notation $\pi(x)$. From (35), the standard assumption $c'(x) < 0$ translates into the equivalent statement $\pi'(x) > 0$.

To reduce the problem of the sole owner of the fishery to the canonical form, it is necessary to reformulate it in terms of net investment. In this situation, net investment is the natural biological increment of the fish population minus the amount of fish being caught or harvested. (It is perhaps not yet entirely clear why we might want to take a problem out of the form in which it naturally suggests itself and recast it in the form of a prototype-economic problem—the reason is that the canonical form always permits the solution to be understood quickly, easily, and in the most economically intuitive way.)

With the change of variables $K \equiv x$ and $I \equiv F(x) - h$, and specifying $m(K) \equiv F(K) - \bar{h}$ and $M(K) \equiv F(K) - \underline{h}$, the optimal fishery harvesting problem is a prototype-economic problem with gain function

$$G(K, I) = \pi(K)[F(K) - I]. \tag{36}$$

From applying formula (13) to (36) (and remembering to evaluate at $I = 0$), the stationary rate of return on capital for this model of optimal fishery management is

$$R(K) = F'(K) + F(K)\frac{\pi'(K)}{\pi(K)}. \tag{37}$$

Equation (37) can be interpreted as saying that the stationary rate of return $R(K)$ consists of two terms representing the two economic effects that come from having a higher amount of fish capital here. The first effect, $F'(K)$, represents the increment of new fish population that comes with a higher parent fish stock. The second term on the right-hand side of (37) represents the additional profit from the lower unit harvesting cost that attends a larger fish population, since it is easier to locate and catch fish when there are more of them.

PROBLEM 4: NEOCLASSICAL OPTIMAL GROWTH

This famous problem (sometimes called the "Ramsey model" after its originator, Frank Ramsey) is described as being to

$$\text{maximize} \quad \int_0^\infty U(\Psi(t)/L(t))L(t)e^{-\theta t} \, dt \tag{38}$$

subject to

$$\dot{X}(t) = \Phi(X(t), L(t)) - \Psi(t), \tag{39}$$

$$-\mu X(t) \le \dot{X}(t) \le \Phi(X(t), L(t)), \tag{40}$$

$$L(t) = L_0 e^{nt}, \tag{41}$$

$$\Psi(t) \ge 0, \tag{42}$$

and with the given initial condition

$$X(0) = X_0. \tag{43}$$

In the above problem, Ψ is the flow of aggregate consumption (which may be considered the control variable), $U(\Psi/L)$ is the representative individual's utility function of per capita consumption, X is the aggregate capital stock, L is the population (which grows exponentially at rate n), $\Phi(X, L)$ is the aggregate production function net of depreciation (assumed to be homogeneous of degree one), and μ is the rate of capital depreciation. It is important to note that θ here represents the rate of pure time preference (the "rate of return on utility") as opposed to the "interest rate," which by a natural convention is the rate of return on the consumption good. (Later we will analyze the relation between "the rate of return on consumption"—the goods interest rate—and the rate of return on utility—the utility interest rate.)

The reader encountering this problem here for the first time should probably consider initially only the special case $n = 0$. What follows is essentially aimed at showing how to treat the case $n > 0$ by a change of variables, which reformulates the problem "as if" $n = 0$.

The most convenient way to transform the neoclassical optimal growth problem into a prototype-economic dynamic control model is to divide each variable by labor, so that the system is described entirely in per capita terms. Making use of the fact that the aggregate production function has constant returns to scale, dividing it by labor yields the equation

$$\dot{K} = F(K) - C, \tag{44}$$

where $C(= \Psi/L)$ here represents *consumption per capita*, while $K(= X/L)$ represents *capital per capita*, and

$$F(K) \equiv \Phi(K, 1) - nK \tag{45}$$

represents *net normalized output per capita*.

Transforming all variables into per capita terms, it may then be confirmed that the optimal neoclassical growth problem is a prototype-economic dynamic control model with $m(K) \equiv -(\mu + n)K$, $M(K) \equiv F(K) - nK$, $\rho \equiv \theta - n$, and having the gain function

$$G(K, I) \equiv U(F(K) - I). \tag{46}$$

From (13) applied to (46), the stationary rate of return on capital for the neoclassical model of optimal growth is

$$R(K) = F'(K). \tag{47}$$

PROBLEM 5: OPTIMAL EXTRACTION OF AN EXHAUSTIBLE RESOURCE
This is another classic problem, sometimes called the "Hotelling model" after its originator, Harold Hotelling. The problem here is to choose an extraction flow rate $\{E(t)\}$ to

$$\text{maximize} \quad \int_0^\infty [\Phi(E(t)) - C(S(t), E(t))]e^{-\rho t}\, dt \tag{48}$$

subject to

$$\dot{S}(t) = -E(t), \tag{49}$$

and

$$S(t) \geq 0, \tag{50}$$

and

$$E(t) \geq 0, \tag{51}$$

and with the given initial condition

$$S(0) = S_0. \tag{52}$$

In this problem, $S(t)$ is a state variable representing the stock of oil remaining in the reserve, while $E(t)$ is the extraction flow rate, both evaluated at time t. (Note that here we really need condition (50), whereas with previous problems this constraint was essentially superfluous.) Initially the stock of reserves is S_0. The function $\Phi(E)$ gives the flow of revenues from selling E barrels of oil per unit time. (In an alternative interpretation, $\Phi(E)$ is the area-under-the-demand-curve "total willingness to pay" utility of consuming E barrels of oil per unit time.) The cost function $C(S, E)$ represents the cost of extracting E barrels of oil per unit time when the remaining stock is S. (In the simplest case, traditionally analyzed first, $C(S, E)$ is assumed to be of the linear form $C(S, E) = cE$ for some constant c.) The parameter ρ stands here for the competitive interest rate. The function

$$G(S, -E) \equiv \Phi(E) - C(S, E) \tag{53}$$

represents *net profits* (revenues minus costs) as a function of remaining stocks and extraction flow rates.

The optimal extraction of an exhaustible resource is turned into an optimal control problem of the form (1)–(5) just by the change of variables $K \equiv S$ and $I \equiv -E$, and by specifying that $m(K) = -\infty$ and $M(K) = 0$.

From (13) applied to (53), the stationary rate of return on capital for this model of the optimal extraction of an exhaustible resource is

$$R(K) = \frac{-C_1(K, 0)}{\Phi'(0) - C_2(K, 0)}. \tag{54}$$

Referring to the above expression, it makes sense in this model to assume $C_1(K, 0) = 0$ because the cost of extracting "nothing" should not depend upon the stock of the reserves. With $C_1(K, 0) = 0$, condition (53) becomes

$$R(K) = 0, \tag{55}$$

which will be used later to provide a strong characterization of a solution to the Hotelling problem of optimally extracting an exhaustible resource.

The final five examples represent important economic problems posed at somewhat increased levels of abstraction.

PROBLEM 6: OPTIMAL EXTRACTION OF AN EXHAUSTIBLE RESOURCE FROM A RESERVE OF UNKNOWN SIZE

For a piece of equipment, like a truck, this problem might equally well have been called "Optimal Usage of Capital with an Uncertain Life."

Consider a piece of capital like a mine or a truck. Let the state variable Z stand for the total amount of ore that has thus far been extracted. (In the truck example, Z stands for the total mileage the truck has accumulated.) The ultimate size of the reserve is unknown and is given by the realization of a random variable having a known probability distribution. The probability that the capital "runs out" or "expires" between state Z and state $Z + dZ$ is given by $f(Z)dZ$, where the non-negative probability density function $f(Z)$ satisfies

$$\int_0^\infty f(Z)dZ = 1. \tag{56}$$

The cumulative probability distribution function corresponding to the density function $f(Z)$ is

$$F(Z) \equiv \int_0^Z f(Y)\,dY, \tag{57}$$

which expresses the probability that the capital gives out or expires before usage Z. Thus the probability that the mine or well contains reserves of at least Z (or the truck is good for mileage of at least Z) is $1 - F(Z)$, and the probability that the capital "runs out" or "expires" between state Z and state $Z + dZ$ conditional on capital having survived thus far is

$$\frac{f(Z)dZ}{1 - F(Z)}. \tag{58}$$

Suppose that usage intensity (extraction rate) of E at any time yields instantaneous profits given by the function $\Phi(E)$. Let ρ be the competitive interest rate. Let the aim (conditional on having survived thus far) be to control usage intensity as a function of time to maximize expected present discounted profits given the initial cumulative usage Z_0. Then the problem of "optimal extraction of an exhaustible resource from reserves of unknown size" (or, equivalently, the problem of "optimal consumption of capital with uncertain life") conditional on having already extracted amount Z_0 is to

$$\text{maximize} \quad \int_0^\infty \frac{1 - F(Z(t))}{1 - F(Z_0)} \Phi(E(t))e^{-\rho t}\,dt \tag{59}$$

subject to

$$\dot{Z}(t) = E(t), \tag{60}$$

and

$$E(t) \geq 0, \tag{61}$$

and with the given initial condition

$$Z(0) = Z_0. \tag{62}$$

The "optimal usage of capital with uncertain life" problem is a prototype-economic dynamic control model with $K(t) \equiv Z(t)$, $I(t) = E(t)$, $m(K) \equiv 0$, $K_0 \equiv Z_0$, and with gain function

$$G(K, I) \equiv \frac{[1 - F(K)]\Phi(I)}{1 - F(K_0)}. \tag{63}$$

This model should be compared with Problem 5. Here, to make things simple, costs are ignored (more precisely, they are restricted to being a function of the extraction rate E and are already included in the net profit function $\Phi(E)$), but the reserve size is uncertain. (Note: in this problem the capital stock is the cumulative oil already extracted, while in Problem 5 it is the oil reserves remaining below ground.)

Plugging (63) into our formula (13), the stationary rate of return on capital for this model of the optimal extraction of an exhaustible resource with unknown reserve size is

$$R(K) = \frac{f(K)\Phi(0)}{(1 - F(K))\Phi'(0)}. \tag{64}$$

From the above expression, it can be shown that if the limiting elasticity of demand is greater than one—which is needed for the problem to make sense in the first place, because otherwise the monopolist would make infinite profits by going to the limit of producing (almost) nothing and charging an (almost) infinite price—then

$$\lim_{E \to 0} \frac{\Phi'(E)}{\Phi(E)} = \infty, \tag{65}$$

so that condition (64) becomes

$$R(K) = 0, \tag{66}$$

which will provide a strong characterization of a solution to the problem of optimally extracting an exhaustible resource from a reserve of unknown size.

PROBLEM 7: OPTIMAL TREE HARVESTING

Suppose that, when it is cut down and brought to market, a tree of age T yields a net value given by the function

$$F(T). \tag{67}$$

Frequently in the literature, $F(T)$ is specified in the form

$$F(T) = Pf(T) - c + v, \tag{68}$$

where P is the exogenously given price of a unit of wood and $f(T)$ is the amount of wood yielded by a tree of age T, while c represents the total economic cost of cutting down the tree and bringing it to market. (In the forestry literature, the expression $Pf(T) - c$ is sometimes called the *net stumpage value* of the tree.) The parameter v stands for the *opportunity value* of the land being freed for its best subsequent economic use after the tree is felled (in forestry terminology, the *site value*)—which "best subsequent economic use" might well be the replanting of a sapling to start the tree-growing cycle anew. The relevant discount rate is ρ.

The famous *Wicksell problem* of capital theory is to choose the time of cutting T to

$$\underset{T}{\text{maximize}} \quad e^{-\rho T} F(T). \tag{69}$$

It might seem perverse to force such a direct statement as (69) into the seemingly far more arcane form of an optimal control problem. An optimal control formulation, however, will serve to reinforce economic intuition and to highlight quite dramatically the underlying unity of all time-and-capital problems.

An "as if continual harvesting" generalization of the Wicksell problem is to control the harvesting flow rate $\{h(t)\}$ to

$$\text{maximize} \quad \int_0^\infty h(t)\, \rho F(T(t)) e^{-\rho t}\, dt \tag{70}$$

subject to

$$\dot{T}(t) = 1 - h(t), \tag{71}$$

and

$$0 \leq h(t) \leq 1, \tag{72}$$

and with the given initial condition

$$T(0) = 0. \tag{73}$$

The original Wicksell formulation, in effect, limits the harvesting control variable $h(t)$ to be a step function, which has value zero until the cutting time and one thereafter. As we will see, the above generalization (70)–(73) yields the Wicksell solution anyway, as well as highlighting the underlying connection with all of the other capital-theoretic models that can be formulated as simple optimal control problems. For now, however, it suffices to note that the Wicksell problem is a special case of (70)–(73); therefore, if the optimal solution of (70)–(73) is a step function, then it must also represent the solution of the more restricted Wicksell problem (69). (The multiplicative constant ρ in the objective (70) makes no difference to the form of an optimal solution, but its presence equalizes stock and flow magnitudes so that the solutions of the two equivalent formulations yield identical values of the objective function.)

It is interesting to note that the "capital stock" in the optimal control problem (70)–(73) is $T(t)$, representing the *age* of the tree at time t. When you think about it, though, the tree at any particular age is the natural candidate for being a capital stock, because the corresponding "investment" here means allowing the tree to grow older by a year.

The optimal tree-harvesting-flow problem (70)–(73) is a prototype-economic dynamic control model with $K(t) \equiv T(t)$, $I(t) \equiv 1 - h(t)$, $m(K) \equiv 0$, $M(K) \equiv 1$, and with gain function

$$G(K, I) \equiv (1 - I)\rho F(K). \tag{74}$$

Using the definition (13) applied to (74), the stationary rate of return on capital for this model of optimal tree harvesting is calculated to be

$$R(K) = \frac{F'(K)}{F(K)}. \tag{75}$$

PROBLEM 8: POLLUTION-STOCK EXTERNALITY
On the planet Vulcan, the planetary economy can choose, within bounds, the level of consumption it wishes to produce, but, alas, each unit of consumption also produces jointly α units of bad air. The utility of consuming at level C is

$U(C)$, whereas the *disutility* of being forced to live with a stock B of bad air is $D(B)$. Furthermore, if the level of bad air exceeds an upper bound of $\overline{B}$, the planet melts and all life ceases. Over time, bad air on Vulcan recycles itself out of the atmosphere at rate μ. Finally, consumption cannot exceed some given fixed capacity $\overline{C}$.

The formal control problem is to choose values of $C(t)$ over time to

$$\text{maximize} \quad \int_0^\infty [U(C(t)) - D(B(t))]e^{-\rho t}\, dt \tag{76}$$

subject to

$$\dot{B}(t) = \alpha C(t) - \mu B(t), \tag{77}$$

and

$$0 \le C(t) \le \overline{C}, \tag{78}$$

and

$$0 \le B(t) \le \overline{B}, \tag{79}$$

and with the initial condition

$$B(0) = B_0. \tag{80}$$

To turn this problem into our standard form, we define the relevant capital stock to be the good of "clean air" rather than the bad of "dirty air," so that

$$K \equiv \overline{B} - B. \tag{81}$$

Then the relevant state-variable differential equation is transformed from (77) into

$$\dot{K}(t) = \mu \overline{B} - \mu K(t) - \alpha C(t). \tag{82}$$

By definition, net investment is $\dot{K}$, so that, from (82), $I = \mu \overline{B} - \mu K - \alpha C$. The simple pollution-stock externality problem (76)–(82) is a prototype-economic dynamic control model with $m(K) \equiv \mu(\overline{B} - K) - \alpha \overline{C}$, $M(K) \equiv \mu(\overline{B} - K)$, having the state constraint $K(t) \ge 0$ and initial condition $K_0 \equiv \overline{B} - B_0$, and with gain function

$$G(K, I) \equiv U([\mu(\overline{B} - K) - I]/\alpha) - D(\overline{B} - K). \tag{83}$$

From applying (13) to (83), the stationary rate of return on capital for this model of a pollution-stock externality is

$$R(K) = \alpha\left(\frac{D'}{U'}\right) - \mu, \tag{84}$$

where the standard notation D' and U' signifies the first derivative of the functions, here evaluated at $(K, 0)$.

PROBLEM 9: GROWTH WITH POLLUTION

In the previous problem, pollution was modeled as a pure *stock*. In this problem, pollution is modeled as a pure *flow*. Which assumption is more appropriate depends on the pollutant. For example, greenhouse gases act more like stocks; particulate matter in the air acts more like a reversible flow.

Suppose here that an economy has two different ways of producing output with one unit of capital. A "dirty" technology produces A of output, while emitting the flow amount γ of dirty air. A "clean" technology produces a of output, without any emission of pollutants. To make the problem economically sensible, we assume

$$A > a > \rho. \tag{85}$$

The problem is to find the right "mix" of clean and dirty technologies to maximize the present discounted value of the difference between utility of consumption $U(C)$ and disutility of bad air $D(B)$. Let θ be a *choice variable* representing the fractional *intensity of pollution* emitted per unit of capital. (Equivalently, θ is the fraction of capital dedicated to the clean technology, while $1 - \theta$ is the fraction embodied in the dirty technology.) The corresponding output, for given θ and K, is $[\theta A + (1 - \theta)a]K$. Then the formal control problem is to

$$\text{maximize} \quad \int_0^\infty [U(C(t)) - D(B(t))]e^{-\rho t}\,dt \tag{86}$$

subject to

$$\dot{K}(t) = [\theta(t)A + (1 - \theta(t))a]K(t) - C(t), \tag{87}$$

and

$$0 \leq \theta(t) \leq 1, \tag{88}$$

and

$$B(t) = \theta(t)\gamma K(t),\tag{89}$$

and with the given initial condition

$$K(0) = K_0.\tag{90}$$

This problem has *two* control variables, because there are two basic choices to be made—consumption versus investment and clean versus dirty technology. As we shall see, it is usually easier in practice to analyze problems in the form in which they are first formulated—simply because we typically have a better intuition about the underlying economics when the problem is expressed in familiar terms. Nevertheless, it is also important to understand the underlying unity of formulations and methodologies in capital theory in order to better separate the forest from the trees. To that end, we show formally how the growth with pollution problem can be reconfigured into our standard format, which expresses everything in capital stocks and net investment flows.

Define the gain function to be

$$G(K, I) \equiv \underset{0 \le \theta \le 1}{\text{maximum}} \ \{U([\theta A + (1 - \theta)a]K - I)\tag{91}$$
$$- D(\theta\gamma K)\}.$$

Because the constraint set

$$\{\theta | 0 \le \theta \le 1\}\tag{92}$$

does not depend on K or I, it can be shown that $G(K, I)$ is differentiable in K and I. If $\theta(K)$ is the value of θ that achieves the maximum in (91) when we set $I = 0$, then it can be shown from the definition (13) that the stationary rate of return on capital for this problem of growth with reversible pollution flows is

$$R(K) = \theta(K)A + (1 - \theta(K))a + \theta(K)\gamma\left(\frac{-D'}{U'}\right).\tag{93}$$

Although the growth with pollution problem (86)–(90) looks complicated, we will show in Chapter 4 that it is actually fairly easy to solve, and we will give an explicit solution for a particular class of commonly used utility functions. The point to be illustrated here is that even though $G(K, I)$ is defined indirectly as a solution of a maximization problem (here (91)), we are still able to apply the maximum principle "as if" we were applying it directly to the original problem (86)–(90). As long as the "reduced form" $G(K, I)$ is a concave function, it does not matter how many instruments or controls are lurking in the background. In a sense the instruments (here θ or C) are dummy variables—the important thing is that by maximizing over the instruments we are able to specify, at least theoretically (in a form like (91)), the reduced-form maximum value of G obtainable as a function of K and I.

As will be explained later, a very useful property is that the function $G(K, I)$ should be concave. This can be confirmed directly when the function $G(K, I)$ is given explicitly. But when the function $G(K, I)$ is defined implicitly, such a direct check is not possible. However, the function $G(K, I)$ defined here by (91) is concave, provided we make the usual assumption that $U(C)$ is concave ($U'' \leq 0$) and $D(B)$ is convex ($D'' \geq 0$). That $G(K, I)$ is a concave function is somewhat intuitive, but let us prove it here formally. (This kind of result recurs throughout economics, and it is useful to know how it is proved.)

The proof that $G(K, I)$ is concave is logically straightforward, but notationally very messy. Proofs that functions are concave (or that sets are convex) typically just show by brute force that the required definition is fulfilled. At first such proofs can seem overwhelming in their algebraic manipulations, but they all follow a similar pattern and with enough experience become routine. We put the proof in square parentheses here to indicate that, while it belongs in this place logically, it is somewhat of a digression from the main flow of the chapter; the interested reader can go through the argument now or may choose to come back to it later.

[*Proof that $G(K, I)$ is concave.* Recall the definition of a concave function. The function $G(K, I)$ is concave if for any (K_1, I_1) and (K_2, I_2), and for all values of λ such that $0 \leq \lambda \leq 1$, then

$$G(\lambda K_1 + (1 - \lambda)K_2, \ \lambda I_1 + (1 - \lambda)I_2) \geq \lambda G(K_1, I_1) + (1 - \lambda)G(K_2, I_2). \tag{94}$$

Let the solution of problem (91) be θ_1 for (K_1, I_1) and be θ_2 for (K_2, I_2). Consider the following proposed "convex combination" value

$$\theta(\lambda) \equiv \lambda\theta_1 + (1 - \lambda)\theta_2. \tag{95}$$

The first thing to note is that because $\theta(\lambda)$ is a weighted average of two numbers between zero and one, it must also be between zero and one. Thus, because it satisfies the constraint $0 \leq \theta(\lambda) \leq 1$, we have that $\theta(\lambda)$ is a *feasible* solution of (91), although it need not be an optimal solution. For $(K, I) \equiv (\lambda K_1 + (1 - \lambda)K_2, \; \lambda I_1 + (1 - \lambda)I_2)$ the value of the objective function on the right-hand side of (91) is

$$U([\theta(\lambda)A + (1 - \theta(\lambda))a][\lambda K_1 + (1 - \lambda)K_2] \\ - (\lambda I_1 + (1 - \lambda)I_2)) - D(\theta(\lambda)\gamma(\lambda K_1 + (1 - \lambda)K_2). \tag{96}$$

Now substitute from (95) into (96) and rewrite the latter expression as

$$U(\lambda[\theta_1 A + (1 - \theta_1)K_1 - I_1] + (1 - \lambda)[\theta_2 A + (1 - \theta_2)K_2 - I_2]) \\ - D(\lambda[\theta_1 \gamma K_1] + (1 - \lambda)[\theta_2 \gamma K_2]). \tag{97}$$

From the definition of concavity of $U(C)$, we have that the expression

$$U(\lambda[\theta_1 A + (1 - \theta_1)K_1 - I_1] \\ + (1 - \lambda)[\theta_2 A + (1 - \theta_2)K_2 - I_2]) \tag{98}$$

is greater than or equal to

$$\lambda U(\theta_1 A + (1 - \theta_1)K_1 - I_1) \\ + (1 - \lambda)U(\theta_2 A + (1 - \theta_2)K_2 - I_2). \tag{99}$$

Since $D(B)$ is assumed to be a convex function, it follows that $-D(B)$ is a concave function. From the definition of concavity of $-D(B)$ we have

$$- D(\lambda[\theta_1 \gamma K_1] + (1 - \lambda)[\theta_2 \gamma K_2]) \\ \geq -\lambda D(\theta_1 \gamma K_1) - (1 - \lambda)D(\theta_2 \gamma K_2). \tag{100}$$

Substituting from (98), (99), and (100) into (97), concavity of the functions shows that for $\theta = \theta(\lambda)$ and $(K, I) \equiv (\lambda K_1 + (1 - \lambda)K_2, \; \lambda I_1 + (1 - \lambda)I_2)$ the value of expression (97) (or, equivalently, (96)) is greater than or equal to

$$\lambda[U(\theta_1 A + (1 - \theta_1)K_1 - I_1) - D(\theta_1 \gamma K_1)] \\ + (1 - \lambda)[U(\theta_2 A + (1 - \theta_2)K_2 - I_2) - D(\theta_2 \gamma K_2)], \tag{101}$$

which by the definition of θ_1 and θ_2 is just equal to

$$\lambda G(K_1, I_1) + (1 - \lambda)G(K_2, I_2). \tag{102}$$

Now it remains only to put the pieces together. Note that expression (96) represents just an achievable value of the objective function. An optimal value, which is denoted $G(\lambda K_1 + (1 - \lambda)K_2, \; \lambda I_1 + (1 - \lambda)I_2)$, is at least as big as (96). Thus we have proved that

$$
\begin{aligned}
G(\lambda K_1 &+ (1 - \lambda)K_2, \lambda I_1 + (1 - \lambda)I_2) \\
&\geq \lambda G(K_1, I_1) + (1 - \lambda)G(K_2, I_2),
\end{aligned}
\tag{103}
$$

which means that $G(K, I)$ is a concave function.   ∎]

PROBLEM 10: IRREVERSIBLE INVESTMENT

A standing forest of F_0 hectares exists at the current time zero. The recreational and aesthetic flow value per hectare of standing forest is γ per unit time. If the forest is cut and developed, the social value is β per hectare per unit time. A one-time cost of c must be paid to clear a hectare of forest and convert it into developed land. Additionally, there is some upper bound $\overline{C}$ on the maximum number of hectares of forest that can be developed per unit time, representing some limitation on conversion capacity. (In practice, we will simplify the problem by taking $\overline{C}$ to be arbitrarily large, but formally we need to specify $\overline{C}$ as finite to make the problem well defined, mathematically.) Once the forest is cut and developed, the process is considered irreversible for all practical purposes. Thus in the abstraction of this model, forests can be cleared and converted into developed land, but it is not practical to convert developed land back into standing forest.

If global warming occurs, then the value of a standing forest, including carbon sequestration value, is α per hectare per unit time. To make things interesting to analyze, we assume that there is a genuine economic conflict whose resolution is unclear beforehand, meaning here that

$$
\alpha > \beta - rc > \gamma,
\tag{104}
$$

where r is the relevant discount rate.

It is uncertain whether global warming will be serious or not. More important in this problem, it is even uncertain when we will learn whether it is serious or not. We model this uncertainty as follows.

Suppose that decisive news about the significance of global warming arrives as a Poisson event, with exponential waiting time, meaning that the probability that decisive news will arrive between time t and time $t + dt$ is

$$
\theta e^{-\theta t} dt,
\tag{105}
$$

where the parameter θ measures the intensity of the Poisson process. Thus the *average* wait until decisive news arrives is

$$w \equiv \int_0^\infty t\theta e^{-\theta t}\,dt = \frac{1}{\theta}. \tag{106}$$

The decisive news can be bad (global warming is serious) with probability b, or good (global warming is not serious) with probability $1-b$. (Note that "bad" news about global warming here is "good" news for the forest and vice versa.)

Once the news about the seriousness of global warming arrives, we do not need optimal control theory to tell us what is an optimal policy, because it is so easy to comprehend and to express. If the news about global warming is bad, then development should cease immediately and all existing forest should be preserved—because each hectare delivers a flow value α of environmental services, which by (104) is greater than the annuitized net development value $\beta - rc$. With benefit of hindsight in this case, when the bad news arrives we will wish that we had left all of the forest intact. If decisive bad news about global warming arrives at a time when the level of standing forest is F, then the present discounted value *at that time* of following an optimal policy *from that time on* is

$$\Phi_b(F) \equiv \frac{\alpha F + \beta(F_0 - F)}{r}. \tag{107}$$

If the decisive news about global warming is good, then all of the remaining forest should be cut down and developed as rapidly as possible, because the net development value $\beta - rc$ exceeds the non-global-warming aesthetic and recreational value γ of a hectare of standing forest. If we could, we would cut down and convert immediately into developed land all of the remaining forest, thereafter earning the total flow value βF_0 per unit time on the fully developed land. But there is a capacity constraint of $\overline{C}$ on the maximum rate at which this conversion can occur. If we cut down and develop a forest stock of size F at the maximum feasible rate, it will take time

$$T(F) \equiv F/\overline{C} \tag{108}$$

to accomplish the conversion.

If decisive good news about global warming arrives at a time when the size of the remaining forest is F, then the present discounted value *at that time* of following an optimal policy *from that time on* is

$$\Phi_g(F) \equiv \int_0^T [\gamma(F - \overline{C}s) + \beta(F_0 - F + \overline{C}s) - c\overline{C}]e^{-rs} \, ds$$

$$+ e^{-rT} \frac{\beta F_0}{r},$$
(109)

where T is the linear function (108) of F. We are most interested in the limiting case when $\overline{C}$ is indefinitely large, which turns (109) into the much simpler expression

$$\lim_{\overline{C} \to \infty} \Phi_g(F) = \frac{\beta F_0}{r} - cF.$$
(110)

The best development plan (contingent on not yet receiving news of the status of global warming) solves an optimal control problem whose control variable at time t is the cutting rate $C(t)$, and whose maximand is the expected present discounted net value expression

$$\int_0^\infty \{ \int_0^t [\gamma F(s) + \beta(F_0 - F(s)) - cC(s)]e^{-rs} \, ds$$

$$+ be^{-rt}\Phi_b(F(t)) + (1 - b)e^{-rt}\Phi_g(F(t)) \} \theta e^{-\theta t} \, dt.$$
(111)

Integrating the first expression of (111) by parts yields

$$\int_0^\infty \{ \int_0^t [\gamma F(s) + \beta(F_0 - F(s)) - cC(s)]e^{-rs} ds \} \theta e^{-\theta t} \, dt$$

$$= \int_0^\infty [\gamma F(t) + \beta(F_0 - F(t)) - cC(t)]e^{-(r+\theta)t} \, dt.$$
(112)

Now substitute from (112) into (111) and rearrange terms. Letting $C(t)$ be the planned cutting at time t contingent upon no news yet arriving, the optimal control problem becomes that of *maximizing*

$$\int_0^\infty \{[\gamma F(t) + \beta(F_0 - F(t)) - cC(t)] + b\theta \Phi_b(F(t))$$

$$+ (1 - b)\theta \Phi_g(F(t))\} e^{-(r+\theta)t} \, dt \tag{113}$$

subject to

$$\dot{F}(t) = -C(t), \tag{114}$$

and

$$0 \le C(t) \le \overline{C}, \tag{115}$$

and with the given initial condition

$$F(0) = F_0. \tag{116}$$

The above optimal control problem looks extremely complicated. Actually, as will be shown in Chapter 4, it is exceedingly easy to solve. For now we just note that the irreversible investment problem is a prototype-economic dynamic control model with $\rho \equiv r + \theta$, $K(t) \equiv F(t)$, $I(t) \equiv -C(t)$, $m(K) \equiv -\overline{C}$, $M(K) \equiv 0$, and whose gain function is

$$G(K, I) \equiv \gamma K + \beta(F_0 - K) + cI$$
$$+ b\theta \Phi_b(K) + (1 - b)\theta \Phi_g(K). \tag{117}$$

Applying the definition (13) to expression (117), the stationary rate of return on capital for this irreversible investment problem, in the limiting case (which we will later analyze) when $\overline{C}$ is made indefinitely large, is

$$R(K) \equiv \frac{\gamma - \beta + \frac{b\theta}{r}(\alpha - \beta) - (1 - b)\theta c}{-c}, \tag{118}$$

which, we note here, is a constant, independent of K.

This concludes the chapter's brief survey of applications. The ten examples of the prototype-economic problem of optimal control theory represent models that have all appeared in the economic literature, some of them very prominently featured. They are examples of a branch of economics called *capital theory*. We now seek a unified solution concept to characterize the solutions of all such capital theory problems. This unified solution concept, called the maximum principle of optimal control theory, shows that the same basic connecting principles arise again and again in seemingly very different capital-theoretic situations. Because the maximum principle is such a natural way of expressing the fundamental unity of all capital theory, with very little exaggeration it is almost possible to say that the maximum principle *is* capital theory—at least for the important broad class of introductory models treated in this chapter.

Bibliographic Note

The idea of making formal the concept of a "prototype-economic control problem"—by identifying the three essential characteristic features of such a problem as convexity, time-autonomy, and infinite horizon—is new here, but examples of such problems have been treated for a long time now. (See, for example, Arrow and Kurz 1970, Seierstad and Sydsaeter 1987, or Kamien and Schwartz 1991.) Some overviews of the conceptual and historical relationship between calculus of variations, optimal control theory, and dynamic programming are contained in Intriligator (1971), in Kamien and Schwartz (1991), and especially in Yong and Zhou (1999). Optimal control theory in its modern form first appeared in the extremely influential book of Pontryagin et al. (1962), which introduced the maximum principle, and by now it has been applied extensively throughout economics.

The q-theory of investment is covered at an elementary level, with many further references, in Romer (1996). Another introductory treatment, with references, appears in Dixit and Pindyck (1994).

The problem of the sole owner of the fishery is covered extensively and treated elegantly in Clark (1990). It is also motivated nicely and its management implications are discussed especially well in Conrad (1999).

The Hotelling problem of the optimal extraction of a nonrenewable resource is motivated and explained (without equations) especially nicely in Solow (1974). For comprehensive introductory treatments (with equations) see Conrad (1999) or Dasgupta and Heal (1979). Hotelling's original formulation in terms of the calculus of variations (Hotelling 1931) still reads well today. The case of an uncertain reserve was treated by Loury (1979).

The famous Ramsey-Cass-Koopmans model of optimal economic growth appears in many places throughout economics. A good introductory treatment is in Romer (1996). The formulation of Cass (1965), which is expressed in terms of the maximum principle of optimal control theory, remains readable today, as does the original seminal article of Ramsey (1928), which is expressed in terms of the calculus of variations.

The unusual formulation of a continuous-harvesting version of the tree-cutting problem is new here; this device is being employed primarily to emphasize the connection with other forms of capital theory. However, the tree-cutting (or wine-aging) problem itself has been in the mainstream of economics for a long time now. A very accessible introductory treatment of basic models in the economics of forestry is contained in Conrad (1999). Samuelson (1976) is a classic unifying account of the various theoretical constructions used historically in forest economics.

Dynamic pollution externality problems of various forms are covered in a number of books and articles. See, for example, Keeler, Spence, and Zeckhauser (1972), Conrad and Clark (1987), Stokey (1998), or Conrad (1999).

The treatment of irreversible investment as an optimal control problem is new here. However, conceptually related formulations appear in Arrow and Fisher (1974), Hanemann (1989), Dixit and Pindyck (1994), and Conrad (1999).

3

---------------- ✴ ----------------

The Maximum Principle in One Dimension

Technical Aspects of the Economic Control Problem

The goals of this chapter are to state carefully, then to prove rigorously, and finally to interpret intuitively the maximum principle of optimal control theory for the prototype-economic one-dimensional problem described in the previous chapter. The material of this chapter is presented in a logical sequence—but there is no reason it must be read in this order. For example, some readers may want to go straight to the economic interpretation, which is in the last section. As usual, it depends on the reader's background and interests.

In this chapter we will also specify a complete characterization of the solution to an important quadratic control problem, which will be very useful in its applications. Although the one-dimensional case is more special than many economists realize, it nevertheless forms the basis for much of our intuition about capital theory. We begin by expressing precisely what we mean by an "optimal" control.

It seems natural in an economics problem to require any admissible control to be a *piecewise-continuous* function of time. This requirement means that, within any given finite time interval, the control must be everywhere continuous in time with the possible exception of at most a finite number of points of time—at which the control function is allowed to "jump" discontinuously. It would be very difficult to give economic meaning to a control that is *not* piecewise continuous. We would then have to imagine a form of investment that is "continuously discontinuous," so to speak, which is not worth thinking about because it is too strange to implement, if it even exists.

The trajectory $\{K(t), I(t)\}$ is said to be *feasible* if the control $\{I(t)\}$ is piecewise continuous and if for all times $t \geq 0$

$$m(K(t)) \leq I(t) \leq M(K(t)), \tag{1}$$

and

$$\dot{K}(t) = I(t), \tag{2}$$

and

$$K(t) \geq 0, \tag{3}$$

and if

$$K(0) = K_0. \tag{4}$$

The trajectory $\{K^*(t), I^*(t)\}$ is said to be *optimal* if it is feasible and if for any other feasible trajectory $\{K(t), I(t)\}$,

$$\int_0^\infty G(K^*(t), I^*(t))e^{-\rho t}\, dt \geq \int_0^\infty G(K(t), I(t))e^{-\rho t}\, dt. \tag{5}$$

(Note that we are implicitly assuming that the infinite horizon integrals of (5) are well defined for any comparisons of interest—that is, they converge.)

Before proceeding with our statement of the maximum principle, it is necessary to impose some further conditions on the three functions $G(K, I)$, $M(K)$, and $m(K)$ that appear in the problem. There is some leeway in exactly how to express the required conditions. In essence, there is a loose tradeoff between simplicity and generality. From a strictly mathematical viewpoint it is possible to impose somewhat less restrictive assumptions, but I have chosen to characterize the functions $G(K, I)$, $M(K)$, and $m(K)$ in the simplest and economically most plausible way. Thus at a cost of some relatively minor and uninteresting loss of generality, I have opted for clarity of exposition (as might be seen, for example, through the eyes of an aspiring economist trying to learn the maximum principle). This accords with the general philosophy behind this book: to choose unity of approach, simplicity, and elegance ahead of mathematical generality.

To make things easier, assume without significant loss of generality that, for all $K > 0$, $M(K)$ and $m(K)$ satisfy the conditions

$$M'(K) \geq 0, \qquad M''(K) \leq 0, \tag{6}$$

and

$$m'(K) \leq 0, \qquad m''(K) \geq 0. \tag{7}$$

If we remember the symbolism that $m = -\infty$ means I is unbounded from below, while $M = +\infty$ means I is unbounded from above, casual inspection leaves at least the impression that conditions (6) and (7) are more or less naturally satisfied and do not seem unduly restrictive for the ten examples of Chapter 2. (We employ the notational convention $m'' \geq 0$ whenever $m = -\infty$ and $M'' \leq 0$ whenever $M = +\infty$, so these cases are formally covered too.)

For convenience, we also assume for all $K \geq 0$ that

$$m(K) \leq 0 \leq M(K), \tag{8}$$

a condition that seems not unduly restrictive and was satisfied in each of the ten examples of Chapter 2.

Recourse to a simple diagram should convince the reader that when (6), (7), (8) hold, then it implies that *if $m(K) = 0$ for any $K > 0$, then $m(K) \equiv 0$ for all $K > 0$, and if $M(K) = 0$ for any $K > 0$, then $M(K) \equiv 0$ for all $K > 0$.* (Just try drawing the curves as if you were trying to make a counterexample to show that this is *not* true, and you will see that you can't make such a drawing.)

We do not deal directly with the state space constraint (3) because the relevant theory is messy and largely incidental to the aims of this book. The easier route, which we take here, is to enforce (3) indirectly by requiring as an assumption that

$$m(0) = 0, \tag{9}$$

which prohibits negative investments when capital is zero.

It is convenient to assume that $G(K, I)$ is defined and is smoothly differentiable for all $K \geq 0$ and for all I satisfying

$$m(K) \leq I \leq M(K). \tag{10}$$

As a convenient but harmless normalization convention, we assume that $G(K, I)$ has been scaled so that

$$G(0, 0) = 0, \tag{11}$$

and that an optimal trajectory exists starting from $K(0) = 0$.

For the sake of simplicity it will also prove convenient to assume the conditions

$$G_1 \geq 0 \tag{12}$$

and

$$G_2 < 0. \tag{13}$$

Most economic optimization models come naturally in the form of what is called a *convex optimization problem*. This characterizes most economic models, because most economic situations arise naturally in what is called a *convex environment*, and therefore possess a *convex structure*. All of these terms ("convex optimization problem," "convex environment," "convex structure") signify exactly the same thing. Formally, they all signify that the set of *hypothetically feasible combinations of G, I, and K,*

$$A \equiv \{(G, I, K) \mid K \geq 0, m(K) \leq I \leq M(K), G \leq G(K, I)\}, \tag{14}$$

is *convex*, which means that if (G, I, K) is feasible and (G', I', K') is feasible, then for all values of the "weight" λ satisfying $0 \leq \lambda \leq 1$, the "weighted average" is also feasible—that is,

$$(\lambda G + (1 - \lambda)G', \lambda I + (1 - \lambda)I', \lambda K + (1 - \lambda)K') \, \varepsilon \, A. \tag{15}$$

By assuming that $M'' \leq 0$ and $m'' \geq 0$, we have already ensured that the bounds on investment have a convex architecture. To impose a convex structure overall it remains only to postulate that $G(K, I)$ is a concave function. Recalling the definition, $G(K, I)$ is a concave function if for any (K_1, I_1) and (K_2, I_2), and for all values of λ such that $0 \leq \lambda \leq 1$, then

$$\begin{aligned} G(\lambda K_1 + (1 - \lambda)K_2, \, \lambda I_1 + (1 - \lambda)I_2) \\ \geq \lambda G(K_1, I_1) + (1 - \lambda)G(K_2, I_2). \end{aligned} \tag{16}$$

In the present smoothly differentiable context, concavity of $G(K, I)$ also means that

$$G_{11} \leq 0, \quad G_{22} \leq 0, \quad G_{11}G_{22} - (G_{12})^2 \geq 0. \tag{17}$$

Depending on the situation, it is sometimes easier to confirm concavity by mechanically checking that formula (17) is satisfied, rather than trying to evaluate (16), but the two approaches are ultimately equivalent.

In Chapter 1 we have already given a general reason why it is plausible to assume in many economic problems that $G(K, I)$ is a concave function. (See the discussion in Chapter 1 concerning the inequalities (1.39)–(1.41).)[1]

---

1. A quick reminder about the notation used for referencing equations in the book. Equation (16) refers to equation (16) of the *current* chapter (here Chapter 3), while equation (1.39) refers to equation (39) of Chapter 1.

Here, however, let us check directly that (16) or (17) holds in each of the ten examples of prototype-economic problems described in Chapter 2.

In Problem 1 (the family firm problem) of Chapter 2 it is routine to assume $F'' \leq 0$, which means that G defined by (2.22) satisfies (17) everywhere.

In Problem 2 (the q-theory of investment problem), the conditions $F'' \leq 0$ and $\varphi'' \geq 0$ are always imposed, thereby ensuring that G defined by (2.29) satisfies (17) everywhere.

In Problem 3 (optimal management of the fishery), it is usually assumed that $\pi' \geq 0$ and $\pi'' \leq 0$. (In (2.35), this assumption takes the form that $c' \leq 0$ and $c'' \geq 0$.) It is additionally assumed usually that $F'' \leq 0$, at least in the range that is relevant for the problem. These assumptions ensure that for G defined by (2.36), it must be true that (17) is always satisfied, at least in the relevant part of the range of x where $F(x) \geq 0$.

In Problem 4 (neoclassical optimal growth), the standard routine assumptions are $F' \geq 0$, $U' \geq 0$, $U'' \leq 0$, $F'' \leq 0$, which imply that G defined by (2.46) causes (16) to hold everywhere.

In Problem 5 (optimal extraction of an exhaustible resource), the standard assumption in (2.53) is that $\Phi'' \leq 0$, $C_{11} \leq 0$, $C_{22} \geq 0$, and $C_{12} = 0$. Such assumptions make (16) hold everywhere.

In Problem 6 (optimal extraction of an exhaustible resource from a reserve of unknown size), it is always assumed that $\Phi'' \leq 0$. An additional condition on the probability distribution is needed to guarantee concavity of G in (2.63). One such condition is the assumption that the probability of expiring, conditional on having survived, increases at a nondecreasing rate over survival life. (This assumption is satisfied for most commonly used probability functions, such as the exponential or gamma distributions.)

In Problem 7 (optimal tree harvesting), it is usual to assume of $F(T)$ that $F'' \leq 0$ in the relevant part of its range, which is sufficient to ensure concavity here of $G(K, I)$ defined by (2.74).

In Problem 8 (pollution-stock externality), the usual assumption is $U'' \leq 0$ and $V'' \geq 0$, which is sufficient for (17) to hold.

In Problem 9 (growth with pollution), we cannot apply formula (17) straightaway. However, in Chapter 2 we proved directly, using definition (16), that $G(K, I)$ is a concave function.

In Problem 10 (irreversible investment), it is tediously confirmed by brute force differentiation that (17) holds when $G(K, I)$ is defined by (2.117).

What do the underlying curvature assumptions in the ten problems, which all imply (16) or (17), have in common? They are all describing some slightly less restrictive version of the law of diminishing returns, which might be called the *law of nonincreasing returns*. Notice throughout the examples that the second derivatives of "bad things" like costs or the disutility of pollution are always assumed to be non-negative, while the second derivatives of "good things" like output, revenue, profit, and utility functions are always assumed to be nonpositive. Loosely speaking, if the law of nonincreasing returns is built into every nook and cranny of the underlying substructure of a model, then the overall model has a "convex structure" (meaning the feasible alternatives set A is convex, that is, satisfies condition (15)). Convexity begets convexity. If a model is nonconvex, some subcomponent of the underlying architecture must be nonconvex. If every subcomponent of a model is convex, then the overall architecture of the model must be convex. Not every economic model has a convex architecture, but most do. The solutions of all convex optimization problems share a generically similar structure, since global and local optima coincide, while the solutions of nonconvex problems are idiosyncratic and difficult to characterize in general terms.

Here, in the simple prototype-economic control problem, the most complicated part of having a convex structure means that $G(K, I)$ is a concave function. While we showed the concavity of $G(K, I)$ directly here by brute force verification of (16) or (17), with some experience it is possible almost to "feel" the presence of a convex structure. The general rule is that when each individual building block of the model exhibits the law of nonincreasing returns, then the overall model must exhibit a convex structure—meaning the set A describing feasible combinations of (G, K, I) will be convex.

Because this kind of issue represents an important point that arises frequently throughout economics, let us prove formally here that concavity of the function $G(K, I)$ and concavity of the function $M(K)$ and convexity of the function $m(K)$ imply that the *set A* of hypothetically feasible combinations of G, I, and K described by (14) is convex. Suppose, then, that

$$(G', K', I') \ \varepsilon \ A \tag{18}$$

and

$$(G'', K'', I'') \ \varepsilon \ A, \tag{19}$$

where the operator notation "ε" means "is a member of" or "belongs to."

By definition (14), statements (18) and (19) imply the following four inequalities:

$$m(K') \leq I' \leq M(K'), \tag{20}$$

$$m(K'') \leq I'' \leq M(K''), \tag{21}$$

$$G' \leq G(K', I'), \tag{22}$$

$$G'' \leq G(K'', I''). \tag{23}$$

Now consider for any value of λ satisfying $0 \leq \lambda \leq 1$ the "convex combination"

$$(G, K, I) \equiv (\lambda G' + (1 - \lambda)G'', \ \lambda K' + (1 - \lambda)K'', \\ \lambda I' + (1 - \lambda)I''). \tag{24}$$

The question we are addressing is whether the convex combination point (24) belongs to A, given from (18) and (19) that both of its component parts belong to A.

From concavity of the function $M(K)$ we know that

$$M(\lambda K' + (1 - \lambda)K'') \geq \lambda M(K') + (1 - \lambda)M(K''), \tag{25}$$

while from convexity of the function $m(K)$ we know that

$$m(\lambda K' + (1 - \lambda)K'') \leq \lambda m(K') + (1 - \lambda)m(K''). \tag{26}$$

Combining (20),(21) with (25),(26), we then have

$$m(\lambda K' + (1 - \lambda)K'') \leq \lambda I' + (1 - \lambda)I'' \\ \leq M(\lambda K' + (1 - \lambda)K''), \tag{27}$$

while from concavity of the function $G(K, I)$, we have

$$G(\lambda K' + (1 - \lambda)K'', \lambda I' + (1 - \lambda)I'') \\ \geq \lambda G(K', I') + (1 - \lambda)G(K'', I''). \tag{28}$$

Substituting from inequalities (22) and (23) into the right-hand side of (28), we then derive

$$G(\lambda K' + (1 - \lambda)K'', \lambda I' + (1 - \lambda)I'') \geq \lambda G' + (1 - \lambda)G''. \tag{29}$$

All that remains is to confirm from (27), (29), and the definition (14) that

$$(\lambda G' + (1 - \lambda)G'',\ \lambda K' + (1 - \lambda)K'',\ \lambda I' + (1 - \lambda)I'')\ \varepsilon\ A, \quad (30)$$

which is the condition to be proved. ∎

Statement of the One-Dimensional Maximum Principle

We previously defined the *stationary rate of return on capital* (evaluated at capital stock K) as the function

$$R(K) \equiv \frac{G_1(K, 0)}{-G_2(K, 0)}. \quad (31)$$

Differentiating (31), we obtain

$$R'(K) = \frac{-G_{11}(K, 0)}{G_2(K, 0)} + \frac{G_1(K, 0)\, G_{12}(K, 0)}{(G_2(K, 0))^2}. \quad (32)$$

This is negative under the relatively harmless assumption $G_1 G_{12} < G_2 G_{11}$, which indicates that the marginal rate of substitution (31) between K and I declines as K increases for fixed $I = 0$.

As was previously indicated in the context of the calculus of variations, there is no general reason why an optimal control problem should possess a stationary solution. But *if* there exists a stationary solution, then it is useful to postulate its uniqueness and accessibility, which will make it much easier to analyze the full solution of the optimal control problem—consisting of both nonstationary and stationary parts. "Uniqueness" basically means there is just one such solution; "accessibility" essentially means the problem can "get to" such a solution.

Assumption (Uniqueness and Accessibility of a Stationary State). If there exists a value $\hat{K} > 0$ satisfying

$$R(\hat{K}) = \rho, \quad (33)$$

then

$$R'(\hat{K}) < 0, \quad (34)$$

which means $\hat{K}$ is unique, and

$$m(\hat{K}) < 0 < M(\hat{K}),\tag{35}$$

which means $\hat{K}$ is locally accessible from above and below.

The maximum principle holds even without the uniqueness and accessibility assumptions. But it is somewhat more difficult to prove, and the slightly greater generality does not seem worth the effort. Besides, in most of the applications when a stationary solution exists, we will want to describe the important connection between an optimal solution and a stationary solution, for which uniqueness and accessibility conditions are very convenient. So, while it is not really necessary to assume the accessibility condition or the uniqueness of a stationary state, it does make everything easier and captures the economic situations in which we are most interested anyway.

It seems to be a fact that for optimal control problems in the economics literature having a stationary solution, accessibility and uniqueness are assumed, at least implicitly. Although we do not spend the time here to confirm the fact directly, we merely remark that in each of the ten problems discussed in the last chapter, the uniqueness and accessibility of a stationary solution—when it exists—seems like a harmless assumption. This will come out clearly enough in the next chapter when we discuss the solutions to some of the problems from Chapter 2.

We now introduce the variable p. Although it is too early yet to explain why, the dual variable $p(t)$ will stand for the *shadow price of capital at time t*, expressed in terms of the current value of gain at time t (as opposed to being discounted back to time zero). As in static optimization theory, p represents the extra value of the objective function that could be obtained upon re-optimization after relaxing the corresponding constraint equation by one (small) unit. The corresponding constraint equation here is (2). In this dynamic setting, $p(t)$ is what is sometimes called the (current value) "co-state variable" associated (at time t) with the state-variable differential equation (2).

Next, without yet thinking deeply about why we are doing it, we mechanically write the so-called Hamiltonian expression:

$$H \equiv G(K, I) + pI.\tag{36}$$

A function of K and p that will play a critical role in the maximum principle is the maximized Hamiltonian function

$$\tilde{H}(K, p) \equiv \underset{m(K)\leq I \leq M(K)}{\text{maximum}} [G(K, I) + pI].\tag{37}$$

To anyone not acquainted with optimal control theory, (36) and (37) will at first appear to be little more than some kind of a definition. Our definition of a "Hamiltonian," which we will be using throughout this book, corresponds to what in the optimal control literature is sometimes called more technically the "current value Hamiltonian"—because the numeraire in which it is expressed at any time is the current value of gain at that time (as opposed to the present discounted value, discounted back to time zero). As we will presently see, our (current value) Hamiltonian has an important economic interpretation, because it corresponds closely to the economist's notion of (current) income. However, the concept of the Hamiltonian as income will take on a life of its own only when the full theory is understood and has been applied to a number of problems. Just as Lagrangian constructs at first seem like very strange artifices in static constrained optimization theory, so do Hamiltonian-income constructs in optimal control theory appear strange and artificial upon first acquaintance. And just as Lagrangians eventually become familiar and natural friends after repeated usage to solve constrained (static) optimization problems, the same thing will happen with Hamiltonians in (dynamic) optimal control theory. So, at first acquaintance there is nothing yet to "understand" about (36) or (37)—they are just definitions of flowlike entities, which resemble income, and this will turn out to be very useful for analyzing problems in capital theory.

The first substantive thing to note about the maximized Hamiltonian function $\tilde{H}(K, p)$ is that it is well defined for all $K \geq 0$ and for all p whenever $m(K) > -\infty$ and $M(K) < \infty$ (that is, $m(K)$ and $M(K)$ are both finite, which can always be imposed without affecting the spirit of the problem by artificially selecting suitably large M or suitably small m). The function $\tilde{H}(K, p)$ is then well defined because the operation defining it consists of maximizing a continuous function over a closed and bounded set, which always has a solution.

For a *given* K, the function $G(K, I)$ is a concave function of I, implying here (with the underlying assumptions about smooth differentiability) that $G_{22} \leq 0$. There are then essentially only two kinds of solutions $\tilde{I}(K)$ to the maximization problem (37). (For notational convenience, we are suppressing the dependence of $\tilde{I}$ on p.) One kind is an interior solution, where

$$m(K) < \tilde{I}(K) < M(K) \tag{38}$$

and

$$p = -G_2(K, \tilde{I}(K)). \tag{39}$$

In this case, by the envelope theorem (since (39) holds),

$$\frac{\partial \tilde{H}}{\partial K} = G_1(K, \tilde{I}(K)). \tag{40}$$

The other kind is a corner solution, where either

$$\tilde{I}(K) = M(K) \tag{41}$$

and

$$p > -G_2(K, \tilde{I}(K)), \tag{42}$$

or

$$\tilde{I}(K) = m(K) \tag{43}$$

and

$$p < -G_2(K, \tilde{I}(K)). \tag{44}$$

If (41),(42) holds, then

$$\frac{\partial \tilde{H}}{\partial K} = G_1(K, \tilde{I}(K)) + [G_2(K, \tilde{I}(K)) + p]M'(K), \tag{45}$$

while if (43),(44) holds, then

$$\frac{\partial \tilde{H}}{\partial K} = G_1(K, \tilde{I}(K)) + [G_2(K, \tilde{I}(K)) + p]m'(K). \tag{46}$$

Thus, except possibly for the singular situation where (39) happens to hold at a corner (that is, where (41) or (43) holds), which corresponds to a point of possible discontinuity for the optimal control, the function $\tilde{H}(K, p)$ is differentiable with respect to K. Furthermore, it is a standard result from the theory of cost or profit functions that whenever $\tilde{I}(K)$ is unique, then

$$\frac{\partial \tilde{H}}{\partial p} = \tilde{I}(K). \tag{47}$$

We are now in a position to state the main result of this chapter.

Theorem (One-Dimensional Maximum Principle).   *Under the assumptions of the prototype-economic model enumerated in this chapter, for the feasible* *trajectory* $\{K^*(t), I^*(t)\}$ *to be optimal it is necessary and sufficient that there exists a continuous non-negative price trajectory* $\{p(t)\}$ *satisfying for all* $t \geq 0$ *the condition*

[#1]: $$G(K^*(t), I^*(t)) + p(t)I^*(t) = \tilde{H}(K^*(t), p(t)), \qquad (48)$$

and satisfying for all $t \geq 0$ *along the trajectory* $\{K^*(t), I^*(t)\}$ *(except possibly at points of discontinuity of* $I^*(t)$*) the differential equation*

[#2]: $$\dot{p}(t) = -\frac{\partial \tilde{H}}{\partial K} + \rho p(t), \qquad (49)$$

and satisfying the transversality condition

[#3]: $$\lim_{t \to \infty} p(t)K^*(t)e^{-\rho t} = 0. \qquad (50)$$

Proof of the One-Dimensional Maximum Principle

At this point of the book there is an argument for attempting to interpret and apply the maximum principle right away, before proving it, so as immediately to build understanding and intuition for someone trying to learn how to use it. (The important economic interpretation of the maximum principle is given in the last section of this chapter, while the entire next chapter is devoted to applications. A reader who wants to see these aspects now may go straightaway to the pertinent sections.) However, there is also an argument for placing the proof of the maximum principle at this point. One reason is the traditional logic of having a proof immediately follow the statement of a theorem. Another reason is the fact that the proof is economically intuitive and will itself provide strong economic motivation for the conditions [#1], [#2], and [#3]. In any event, we are speaking here only of the spatial arrangement of the material—readers are encouraged to follow the temporal sequence that feels most comfortable and which best fits their individual needs or wants.

Although the proof of the one-dimensional maximum principle given here is, so far as I know, completely rigorous, it relies only on a good working knowledge of basic calculus and analysis. Even if each separate link is understandable, however, a long chain of reasoning is still involved. The proof shows the intimate connection between dynamic programming and the maximum principle. Most important, the proof indicates precisely where the dual prices come from and what they represent. Furthermore, this proof deals quite explicitly with possible stationary states, and contains much detail that will later become useful, even indispensable, for solving particular problems. Because many of the basic points in the proof need to be understood anyway for a person to become a good optimal control problem solver, and because the proof tries as much as possible to be based on economically intuitive reasoning, it is recommended that anyone seeking to learn thoroughly the applications of optimal control theory to dynamic economic problems should read through and absorb the proof of optimality for this one-dimensional case.

We will prove first the necessity of the maximum principle, and then its sufficiency.

Proof of Necessity. Define the *state evaluation function* as

$$V(X) \equiv \text{maximum} \int_0^\infty G(K(t), I(t))e^{-\rho t}\, dt \qquad (51)$$

subject to the differential equation

$$\dot{K}(t) = I(t), \qquad (52)$$

and the constraints

$$m(K(t)) \le I(t) \le M(K(t)), \qquad (53)$$

and with the initial condition

$$K(0) = X. \qquad (54)$$

The above problem (51)–(54) represents exactly the problem we are trying to solve for the special case $X = K_0$. Therefore, since we are assuming the original problem is meaningful, we know that the state evaluation function $V(X)$ is well defined and exists at the point $X = K_0$. Furthermore, by the very definition of optimality it must hold for all $t \ge 0$ along an optimal trajectory that

$$V(K_0) = \int_0^t G(K^*(s), I^*(s))e^{-\rho s}\, ds + e^{-\rho t}V(K^*(t)). \qquad (55)$$

Equation (55) is sometimes called the "principle of optimality" of dynamic programming. The basic idea behind it is that all subtrajectories of an optimal trajectory must also be optimal. Although the equation is intuitively apparent, a rigorous proof can readily be supplied based on the idea that if (55) does *not* hold, then there is a fundamental contradiction with the definition of optimality—either for the original trajectory defined on the time interval $[0, \infty)$ or for the subtrajectory defined on the interval $[0, t)$.

We can rewrite (55) as

$$V(K^*(t)) = e^{\rho t}[V(K_0) - \int_0^t G(K^*(s), I^*(s))e^{-\rho s}\, ds]. \tag{56}$$

Equation (56) implies that the state evaluation function $V(X)$ is well defined and exists everywhere along an optimal trajectory, which is all that we need for this proof.

We pause now to prove a useful lemma about $V(X)$.

Lemma. *Wherever it is defined, $V(X)$ is a concave, nondecreasing, nonnegative function.*

[*Proof of Lemma.* That the function $V(X)$ must be monotone nondecreasing in X follows more or less directly from (12) and the free disposal of gain inherent in (14). The essential idea here is that with free disposal, more initial capital is always better than less initial capital because the trajectory of the less-initial-capital economy can always be duplicated by the more-initial-capital economy. Let $\{X^*(t), I^*(t)\}$ represent an optimal trajectory starting from X. Suppose $X' > X$. Then by (6),(7), the trajectory $\{X^*(t) + X' - X, I^*(t)\}$ is a *feasible* trajectory, which begins from X'. But using (12) and the definition (51) we must have

$$
\begin{aligned}
V(X') &\geq \int_0^\infty G(X^*(t) + X' - X, I^*(t))e^{-\rho t}\, dt \\
&\geq \int_0^\infty G(X^*(t), I^*(t))e^{-\rho t}\, dt \equiv V(X),
\end{aligned} \tag{57}
$$

which is the desired monotonicity condition.

From (11) it follows that $V(0) \geq 0$, which, combined with monotonicity, implies that $V(X) \geq 0$ for all $X \geq 0$.

Finally, concavity of $V(X)$ follows more or less directly from the convexity of the set A of hypothetically feasible combinations defined by (14). Consider two optimal trajectories, $\{X_1^*(t),\ I_1^*(t)\}$ and $\{X_2^*(t),\ I_2^*(t)\}$, starting, respectively, from initial conditions X_1 and X_2. Then we have

$$V(X_1) = \int_0^\infty G(X_1^*(t),\ I_1^*(t))e^{-\rho t}\ dt \tag{58}$$

with

$$m(X_1^*(t)) \leq I_1^*(t) \leq M(X_1^*(t)), \tag{59}$$

and

$$V(X_2) = \int_0^\infty G(X_2^*(t),\ I_2^*(t))e^{-\rho t}\ dt \tag{60}$$

with

$$m(X_2^*(t)) \leq I_2^*(t) \leq M(X_2^*(t)). \tag{61}$$

We now ask the following question. Is it *feasible* to produce, for any $0 \leq \lambda \leq 1$, the "convex combination trajectory" $\{\lambda X_1^*(t) + (1-\lambda)X_2^*(t),\ \lambda I_1^*(t) + (1-\lambda)I_2^*(t)\}$ starting from the initial state $\lambda X_1 + (1-\lambda)X_2$? The answer is *yes*, as we now show.

Multiply (59) by $\lambda \geq 0$ and (61) by $(1-\lambda) \geq 0$ and then add them together, yielding

$$\lambda m(X_1^*(t)) + (1-\lambda)m(X_2^*(t)) \leq \lambda I_1^*(t) + (1-\lambda)I_2^*(t)$$
$$\leq \lambda M(X_1^*(t)) + (1-\lambda)M(X_2^*(t)). \tag{62}$$

From concavity of $M(X)$ we have

$$\lambda M(X_1^*(t)) + (1-\lambda)M(X_2^*(t)) \leq M(\lambda X_1^*(t)$$
$$+ (1-\lambda)X_2^*(t)), \tag{63}$$

while convexity of $m(X)$ yields

$$\lambda m(X_1^*(t)) + (1 - \lambda)m(X_2^*(t)) \geq m(\lambda X_1^*(t) + (1 - \lambda)X_2^*(t)). \quad (64)$$

Making use of (63) and (64), we can transform inequality (62) into

$$m(\lambda X_1^*(t)) + (1 - \lambda)X_2^*(t)) \leq \lambda I_1^*(t) + (1 - \lambda)I_2^*(t)$$
$$\leq M(\lambda X_1^*(t) + (1 - \lambda)X_2^*(t)). \quad (65)$$

The inequality (65) proves that it is *feasible* to produce, for any $0 \leq \lambda \leq 1$, the convex combination trajectory $\{\lambda X_1^*(t) + (1 - \lambda)X_2^*(t), \lambda I_1^*(t) + (1 - \lambda)I_2^*(t)\}$ starting from the initial state $\lambda X_1 + (1 - \lambda)X_2$. The next natural question to ask is this. What present discounted gain does the convex combination trajectory give? The answer is

$$\int_0^\infty G(\lambda X_1^*(t) + (1 - \lambda)X_2^*(t), \lambda I_1^*(t) + (1 - \lambda)I_2^*(t))e^{-\rho t}\, dt. \quad (66)$$

So the *optimal* trajectory starting from an initial state $\lambda X_1 + (1 - \lambda)X_2$ must yield at least as high a value of present discounted gain as the *feasible* trajectory (66), that is,

$$V(\lambda X_1 + (1 - \lambda)X_2) \geq \int_0^\infty G(\lambda X_1^*(t) + (1 - \lambda)X_2^*(t),$$
$$\lambda I_1^*(t) + (1 - \lambda)I_2^*(t))e^{-\rho t}\, dt. \quad (67)$$

Concavity of $G(K, I)$ implies that

$$G(\lambda X_1^*(t) + (1 - \lambda)X_2^*(t), \lambda I_1^*(t) + (1 - \lambda)I_2^*(t))$$
$$\geq \lambda G(X_1^*(t), I_1^*(t)) + (1 - \lambda)G(X_2^*(t), I_2^*(t)). \quad (68)$$

Combining (67) with (68) and making use of (58) and (60) yields the conclusion

$$V(\lambda X_1 + (1 - \lambda)X_2) \geq \lambda V(X_1) + (1 - \lambda)V(X_2). \quad (69)$$

Inequality (69) means exactly that $V(X)$ is concave, which concludes the lemma. ∎]

Back now to the main body of the proof, where we define next the *wealth function at time t*

$$W(t) \equiv V(K^*(t)). \tag{70}$$

Substituting from (56) into (70), we have

$$W(t) = e^{\rho t}[W(0) - \int_0^t G(K^*(s), I^*(s))e^{-\rho s}\, ds]. \tag{71}$$

It follows immediately from (71) that $W(t)$ is differentiable and satisfies the differential equation

$$\dot{W}(t) = \rho W(t) - G(K^*(t), I^*(t)). \tag{72}$$

Because $W(t)$ is differentiable, it follows from the definition (70) and the fact that a concave function must have right- and left-hand-side derivatives that, if $I^*(t) \neq 0$, then

$$V'(K^*(t)) = \frac{\dot{W}(t)}{I^*(t)}. \tag{73}$$

We now treat the case $I^*(t) \neq 0$. (After we have proved the maximum principle for this case, we will prove it next for the case $I^*(t) = 0$.)

Substituting from (73) and (70) into (72) yields, after rearrangement, the equation

$$\rho V(K^*(t)) = G(K^*(t), I^*(t)) + V'(K^*(t))I^*(t). \tag{74}$$

For the time interval between time t and time $t + \tau$, consider any feasible trajectory $\{K(t), I(t)\}$ that begins at time t with the initial condition $K(t) = K^*(t)$, and after time $t + \tau$ follows an optimal trajectory starting from the then-initial state $K(t + \tau)$ (but is not necessarily optimal between times t and $t + \tau$). The difference between the value of such a policy and the optimal policy starting from time t, discounted back to time t, is

$$\varphi(\tau) \equiv \int_t^{t+\tau} G(K(s), I(s))e^{-\rho(s-t)}\, ds$$
$$+ e^{-\rho\tau}V(K(t + \tau)) - V(K^*(t)). \tag{75}$$

By the fact that any feasible trajectory yields a value of the objective function no greater than the optimum, and the definition of the function (75), we have that

$$\varphi(\tau) \le 0, \tag{76}$$

while

$$\varphi(0) = 0. \tag{77}$$

Now note from (75) that $\varphi(\tau)$ is differentiable from the right at $\tau = 0$, which from (76) and (77) must imply that

$$\varphi'(0) \le 0. \tag{78}$$

Differentiating (75) from the right at $\tau = 0$, while remembering that the "initial condition at time $t + \tau$" for $\tau = 0$ is $K(t) = K^*(t)$, and then applying (78) yields

$$G(K^*(t), I(t)) + V'(K^*(t))I(t) - \rho V(K^*(t)) \le 0. \tag{79}$$

Combining (79) with (74), we then have

$$\begin{aligned} &G(K^*(t), I(t)) + V'(K^*(t))I(t) \\ &\le G(K^*(t), I^*(t)) + V'(K^*(t))I^*(t). \end{aligned} \tag{80}$$

Next, define the relevant investment good *price* at time t to be equal to the *derivative of the state evaluation function* along an optimal trajectory at that time:

$$p(t) \equiv V'(K^*(t)). \tag{81}$$

Equation (81) represents an extremely important statement, whose significance should be fully appreciated. *The price that appears in the maximum principle equals the derivative of the state evaluation function.* The result that prices are derivatives of the state evaluation function provides a rigorous justification for dynamic benefit-cost analysis, which essentially uses net present discounted values appraised at such prices to evaluate projects involving time.

From the fact that $V(K)$ is monotone nondecreasing in K, it follows at once from the definition (81) that

$$p(t) \ge 0. \tag{82}$$

Using definitions (37) and (81), the inequality (80) is equivalent to the statement

$$\tilde{H}(K^*(t), p(t)) = G(K^*(t), I^*(t)) + p(t)I^*(t), \tag{83}$$

which is exactly condition [#1] of the maximum principle.

Note that in the course of proving equation (83), we have simultaneously proved (by equation (74)) the condition

$$\tilde{H}(K^*(t), p(t)) = \rho V(K^*(t)). \tag{84}$$

Although we do not yet examine the significance of (84) here, we note for later reference that it is what we will eventually identify as a basic accounting equation, because it characterizes "income" $\tilde{H}$ as the return on "wealth" V. It should be appreciated that equation (84) has been proved *before proving* the maximum principle, and indeed it is being used to prove the maximum principle. In this spirit, the "basic equation of green accounting" (84) may legitimately be called "basic" in the sense of being prior to, or more primitive than, the standard form of the maximum principle.

Since (84) holds identically for *all* $t \geq 0$ (whenever $I^*(t) \neq 0$), and since the right-hand side of (84) is differentiable, differentiating both sides of the equation with respect to time and evaluating along an optimal trajectory yields

$$\frac{\partial \tilde{H}}{\partial K} \dot{K}^* + \frac{\partial \tilde{H}}{\partial p} \dot{p} = \rho V'(K^*) \dot{K}^*. \tag{85}$$

Using equations (2), (47), and (81) to substitute for terms in (85), it becomes transformed into the equivalent equation

$$\frac{\partial \tilde{H}}{\partial K} I^*(t) + I^*(t)\dot{p}(t) = \rho p(t)I^*(t), \tag{86}$$

which proves condition [#2] of the maximum principle for all times t when $I^*(t) \neq 0$.

Let us now deal with the case $I^*(t) = 0$.

Let T be the *first time* when $I^*(t)$ becomes zero. In other words,

$$I^*(T) = 0, \tag{87}$$

while

$$0 \leq t < T \implies I^*(t) \neq 0. \tag{88}$$

Notice that if the optimal trajectory spends any finite time in the state where $I^*(T) = 0$, then it is optimal to spend all of the remaining time $t > T$ in the state where $I^*(t) = 0$, simply because, when the capital stock is unchanged, the future looks the same from time point T as it does from time point $T + dt$.

There are essentially three possible reasons why the optimal program first has zero net investment at time T. It may be that

$$R(K^*(T)) > \rho, \tag{89}$$

but the program is blocked from positive investments because

$$M(K^*(T)) = 0, \tag{90}$$

or it may be that

$$R(K^*(T)) < \rho, \tag{91}$$

but the program is blocked from negative investments because

$$m(K^*(T)) = 0. \tag{92}$$

The third and economically most interesting possibility is that the optimal program is not blocked at all, but first *chooses* zero investment at time T because it has just then entered the stationary-solution state

$$K^*(T) = \hat{K}. \tag{93}$$

Let us examine this third and economically most interesting possibility now. Assuming (93), define the stationary-state price to be

$$\overline{p} \equiv \frac{G_1(\hat{K}, 0)}{\rho} = -G_2(\hat{K}, 0). \tag{94}$$

Using (35), (38), (39), and (94), we readily confirm, from the (necessary and sufficient) first-order conditions on an interior solution, that

$$\tilde{H}(\hat{K}, \overline{p}) = G(\hat{K}, 0), \tag{95}$$

which proves condition [#1] of the maximum principle in this stationary state, while condition [#2] of the maximum principle follows directly from (40) and (94), since here, in the stationary solution, we have $\dot{p} = 0$. It remains to show that $p(t)$ is continuous across the boundary $t = T$. (Actually, this seemingly simple continuity of $p(t)$ across the boundary $t = T$ is the most intricate part of the entire proof.)

We note first from (95) and the definition of a stationary state that

$$\tilde{H}(\hat{K}, \overline{p}) = \rho V(\hat{K}), \tag{96}$$

so the basic equation of green accounting (84) continues to hold here in the stationary solution.

For any function $f(t)$ continuous on the interval $[0, T)$, we employ the standard notation

$$f(T^-) \equiv \lim_{\substack{t \to T \\ t < T}} f(t). \tag{97}$$

Because of the fact that

$$K^*(T^-) = K^*(T) = \hat{K}, \tag{98}$$

it follows that $V(K^*(T^-)) = V(K^*(T)) = V(\hat{K})$, and hence, from (96) and (74),

$$\lim_{t \to T^-} G(K^*(t), I^*(t)) + p(t)I^*(t)$$
$$[= \lim_{t \to T^-} G(\hat{K}, I^*(t)) + p(t)I^*(t)] = G(\hat{K}, 0). \tag{99}$$

Divide (99) by $I^*(t) \neq 0$ and rearrange terms, yielding

$$p(T^-) = \lim_{t \to T^-} -\frac{G(\hat{K}, I^*(t)) - G(\hat{K}, 0)}{I^*(t)}. \tag{100}$$

If $I^*(T^-) = 0$, then (100) immediately implies the desired conclusion, that is,

$$I^*(T^-) = 0 \implies p(T^-) = -G_2(\hat{K}, 0) \,(= \overline{p}). \tag{101}$$

If $I^*(T^-) \neq 0$, then we need a different strategy to prove (101). Making use of (98), replace (99) by the notationally more convenient equation

$$G(K^*(T^-), I^*(T^-)) + p(T^-)I^*(T^-) = G(\hat{K}, 0). \tag{102}$$

From maximizing the Hamiltonian in the stationary state at time T, we have

$$G(\hat{K}, 0) \geq G(\hat{K}, I^*(T^-)) + \overline{p}I^*(T^-). \tag{103}$$

Making use of (98) to compare (102) with (103), it follows directly that

$$I^*(T^-) > 0 \Rightarrow p(T^-) \geq \overline{p}, \tag{104}$$

and

$$I^*(T^-) < 0 \Rightarrow p(T^-) \leq \overline{p}. \tag{105}$$

Next, for all τ satisfying

$$0 < \tau \leq T, \tag{106}$$

consider the function

$$\varphi(\tau) \equiv \int_0^\tau G(K^*(t), I^*(t))e^{-\rho t}\, dt + e^{-\rho \tau} G(K^*(\tau), 0)/\rho. \tag{107}$$

The function defined by (107) represents the value of following the previously optimal policy until time τ, and thereafter a stationary policy of zero net investment, which new policy is allowed by condition (8).

Because T is an optimal time for investment to first become zero, for all $\tau \leq T$ we have

$$\varphi(\tau) \leq \varphi(T), \tag{108}$$

which implies

$$\varphi'(T^-) \geq 0. \tag{109}$$

Applying (109) to (107), we then derive

$$G(K^*(T^-), I^*(T^-)) + G_1(K^*(T^-), 0)I^*(T^-)/\rho \\ - G(K^*(T^-), 0) \geq 0. \tag{110}$$

If we make use of (94) and (98) to compare (110) with (102), it follows directly that

$$I^*(T^-) > 0 \Rightarrow p(T^-) \leq \overline{p}, \tag{111}$$

and

$$I^*(T^-) < 0 \Rightarrow p(T^-) \geq \overline{p}. \tag{112}$$

Comparing (111),(112) with (104),(105), (and since (101) also holds), we have now proved the desired continuity result

$$p(T^-) = \overline{p}. \tag{113}$$

This result implies more than the continuity of $p(t)$. When there exists a unique accessible stationary state $\hat{K}$, result (113) essentially means that the state evaluation function is differentiable at $\hat{K}$. The underlying reason is the symmetry of approaching $\hat{K}$ from above and below. Condition (113) shows that if $\hat{K}$ is approached from below, then $p(t)$ defined by (81) approaches the left-hand side directional derivative of the concave function $V(K)$ evaluated at $K = \hat{K}$, which in its turn equals $\overline{p}$ defined by (94). But this argument is essentially symmetrical for the case $K > \hat{K}$. If $\hat{K}$ is approached from above, the same style of reasoning shows that the right-hand side directional derivative of the concave function $V(K)$ exists at $\hat{K}$ and also equals $\overline{p}$ defined by (94).

Because right- and left-hand side derivatives of $V(K)$ exist at $\hat{K}$, and are equal to each other, we have demonstrated that $V'(\hat{K})$ is a proper derivative, and that it equals $\overline{p}$. Since we have already shown that the state evaluation function is continuously differentiable all along the optimal approach to $\hat{K}$, we have now proved the following important proposition. When there exists a unique accessible stationary solution, and the optimal policy is to enter it at some point, then the state evaluation function is continuously differentiable all along the optimal trajectory (in the stationary state and on the approach to it).

Previously, any "simple" proof of the maximum principle has depended critically on the ad hoc assumption that the state evaluation function is continuously differentiable. As has been widely recognized, the strategy of this so-called dynamic programming proof of the maximum principle represents a very unsatisfactory methodology, because the state evaluation function is not a given primitive, whose properties we know from first principles, but rather is a derived construct, whose properties need to be proved from more basic characteristics of the problem. By limiting ourselves to a prototype-economic control problem, we essentially are able to *derive* the continuous differentiability of the state evaluation function, instead of arbitrarily assuming this critical property.

The proof for the case of "blocked" investments is similar. Here we define the stationary price

$$\overline{p} \equiv \frac{G_1(K^*(T), 0)}{\rho}. \tag{114}$$

When (89),(90) hold, then

$$\overline{p} > -G_2(K^*(T), 0), \tag{115}$$

and the maximized Hamiltonian (37) is achieved at the upper-corner solution

$$\tilde{I} = M(K^*(T)) = 0, \tag{116}$$

while if (91),(92) hold, then

$$\overline{p} < -G_2(K^*(T), 0), \tag{117}$$

and the maximized Hamiltonian (37) is achieved at the lower-corner solution

$$\tilde{I} = m(K^*(T)) = 0. \tag{118}$$

The differential equation condition [#2] of the maximum principle then follows directly from the definition (114), since here, in a stationary condition, $\dot{p} = 0$. (Note that investment is actually frozen at zero because if $m(K) = 0$ for any $K > 0$, then $m(K) \equiv 0$ and $m'(K) \equiv 0$ for all $K > 0$, and if $M(K) = 0$ for any $K > 0$, then $M(K) \equiv 0$ and $M'(K) \equiv 0$ for all $K > 0$.) It remains then just to show that $p(t)$ is continuous across the boundary $t = T$, which is omitted here since the proof is very similar to the case of a stationary solution.

Back to the more interesting case of unblocked investment. We note from the definition of a stationary state that, for all $t \geq T$ (during which time $K^*(t) \equiv \hat{K}$),

$$\tilde{H}(K^*(t), \overline{p}) = G(K^*(t), 0) = \rho V(K^*(t)), \tag{119}$$

so that the basic equation of green accounting (84) continues to hold in this case.

It remains only to prove the transversality condition. If the trajectory enters a stationary state at time T, the transversality condition obviously holds because, when $K^*(t) \equiv \hat{K}$,

$$\lim_{t \to \infty} \overline{p} K^*(t) e^{-\rho t} = 0. \tag{120}$$

If the optimal trajectory never enters a stationary state because $I^*(t) \neq 0$ for all t, then the state evaluation function is differentiable at all times along an optimal trajectory. Since $V(K)$ is a concave function, it must be true that

$$V(0) - V(K^*(t)) \leq V'(K^*(t))[0 - K^*(t)], \tag{121}$$

because a concave function everywhere lies below its tangent. Using definition (81), rewrite (121) in the equivalent form

$$p(t)K^*(t) \leq V(K^*(t)) - V(0). \tag{122}$$

Because the state evaluation function is nondecreasing in K, the right-hand side of (122) is non-negative. Furthermore, it must be the case that

$$\lim_{t \to \infty} e^{-\rho t} V(K^*(t)) = \lim_{t \to \infty} \int_t^\infty G(K^*(s), I^*(s))e^{-\rho s} \, ds = 0, \tag{123}$$

or else the objective function integral would not converge and the optimal control problem would not be well defined, contrary to what has been assumed.

Condition (123) implies that

$$\lim_{t \to \infty} e^{-\rho t}[V(K^*(t) - V(0)] = 0. \tag{124}$$

Since both $p(t)$ and $K^*(t)$ are non-negative, the expression

$$p(t)K^*(t)e^{-\rho t} \tag{125}$$

is bounded below by zero and, from (122), is bounded above by a non-negative sequence that, from (124), converges to zero. We have thus proved that in this case

$$\lim_{t \to \infty} p(t)K^*(t)e^{-\rho t} = 0. \tag{126}$$

This completes the proof of necessity for the one-dimensional maximum principle. Note the critical roles played in the proof by the state evaluation function $V(K)$ and the stationary rate of return function $R(K)$. ∎

Proof of Sufficiency. The first thing to show is that the maximized Hamiltonian

$$\tilde{H}(K, p) \equiv \underset{m(K) \leq I \leq M(K)}{\text{maximum}} \quad [G(K, I) + pI] \tag{127}$$

is a *concave function of K* for any given p. This time we show the required condition by using the fact, which we already proved under the assumed curvature restrictions on the relevant functions, that the set A of hypothetically feasible combinations of G, I, and K defined by (14) is *convex*. Suppose, then, that I' is a solution of (127) corresponding to K', while I'' is a solution corresponding to K''. Thus,

$$G(K', I') + pI' = \tilde{H}(K', p), \tag{128}$$

and

$$G(K'', I'') + pI'' = \tilde{H}(K'', p). \tag{129}$$

For any λ satisfying $0 \leq \lambda \leq 1$, define

$$K_\lambda \equiv \lambda K' + (1 - \lambda) K'' \tag{130}$$

and

$$I_\lambda \equiv \lambda I' + (1 - \lambda) I''. \tag{131}$$

Define

$$G_\lambda \equiv \lambda G(K', I') + (1 - \lambda) G(K'', I''). \tag{132}$$

From convexity of A,

$$(G_\lambda, K_\lambda, I_\lambda) \ \varepsilon \ A, \tag{133}$$

which implies from the definition (14) that

$$m(K_\lambda) \leq I_\lambda \leq M(K_\lambda) \tag{134}$$

and

$$G_\lambda \leq G(K_\lambda, I_\lambda). \tag{135}$$

Since (133) holds, by the definition (127) of $\tilde{H}$ as representing a *maximum*, it must be true that

$$G(K_\lambda, I_\lambda) + pI_\lambda \leq \tilde{H}(K_\lambda, p). \tag{136}$$

Now substitute from (135) into (136), yielding

$$G_\lambda + pI_\lambda \leq \tilde{H}(K_\lambda, p). \tag{137}$$

It remains only to use equations (128)–(132) to change (137) into a form that renders the desired conclusion

$$\lambda \tilde{H}(K', p) + (1 - \lambda)\tilde{H}(K'', p) \leq \tilde{H}(\lambda K' + (1 - \lambda)K'', p), \quad (138)$$

thereby showing that the maximized Hamiltonian is a concave function of K for any given p.

On to the main body of the sufficiency proof. Let $\{K(t), I(t)\}$ represent any feasible trajectory starting from

$$K(0) = K_0. \tag{139}$$

Because a concave function lies everywhere below or on its tangent,

$$\tilde{H}(K(t), p(t)) - \tilde{H}(K^*(t), p(t))$$
$$\leq \tilde{H}_1(K^*(t), p(t))(K(t) - K^*(t)), \tag{140}$$

for all t. Furthermore, from the definition (127), it also holds for all t that

$$G(K(t), I(t)) + p(t)I(t) \leq \tilde{H}(K(t), p(t)), \tag{141}$$

while from the maximum principle

$$\tilde{H}(K^*(t), p(t)) = G(K^*(t), I^*(t)) + p(t)I^*(t), \tag{142}$$

and

$$\tilde{H}_1(K^*(t), p(t)) = \rho p(t) - \dot{p}(t), \tag{143}$$

for all t.

Next, substitute from (141), (142), and (143) into (140), multiply by $e^{-\rho t}$ and integrate over time, yielding the conclusion that the expression

$$\int_0^\infty [G(K(t), I(t)) + p(t)I(t)$$
$$- G(K^*(t), I^*(t)) - p(t)I^*(t)]e^{-\rho t} \, dt \tag{144}$$

is less than or equal to the expression

$$\int_0^\infty [\rho p(t) - \dot{p}(t)][K(t) - K^*(t)]e^{-\rho t} \, dt. \tag{145}$$

Integrating the above expression by parts and substituting I for $\dot{K}$, (145) is equal to

$$[p(t)e^{-\rho t}(K^*(t) - K(t))]\,|_0^\infty + \int_0^\infty p(t)[I(t) - I^*(t)]e^{-\rho t}\,dt. \tag{146}$$

Canceling terms in $p(t)I(t)$ and $p(t)I^*(t)$ from both sides of (146) and (144), we obtain the inequality

$$\int_0^\infty [G(K(t), I(t)) - G(K^*(t), I^*(t)]e^{-\rho t}\,dt \tag{147}$$

$$\leq [p(t)e^{-\rho t}(K^*(t) - K(t))]\,|_0^\infty.$$

Applying the transversality and initial conditions to the right-hand side of (147), we have

$$[p(t)e^{-\rho t}(K^*(t) - K(t))]\,|_0^\infty = \lim_{t\to\infty} p(t)e^{-\rho t}(-K(t)). \tag{148}$$

The right-hand limit in (148) is clearly nonpositive, so that combining (148) with (147) and transposing terms turns (147) into the desired conclusion

$$\int_0^\infty G(K(t), I(t))e^{-\rho t}\,dt \leq \int_0^\infty G(K^*(t), I^*(t))e^{-\rho t}\,dt. \tag{149}$$

Inequality (149) proves sufficiency. Thus at this point we have proved rigorously that in a convex setting the one-dimensional maximum principle is both necessary and sufficient for a feasible trajectory to be optimal. ∎

A Quadratic Application of the Maximum Principle

Now let us immediately show how to use the maximum principle to solve a special but very important case. We seek to obtain a complete solution for a quadratic gain function. This complete solution to the quadratic case will prove extremely useful for characterizing and analyzing the optimal behavior of a number of problems in the next chapter.

Suppose there exists a unique stationary solution $\hat{K}$. Suppose further that there are no effective upper or lower bounds on investment, which implies that everywhere along an optimal trajectory the Hamiltonian is maximized at an interior solution. (Such a case is as if we have a calculus of variations problem.) In this situation, we know that an optimal trajectory must converge to the unblocked stationary solution. Consider the *quadratic gain function*

$$G(K, I) = G(\hat{K}, 0) + G_1(K - \hat{K}) + G_2 I + G_{11}\frac{(K - \hat{K})^2}{2}$$
$$+ G_{22}\frac{I^2}{2} + G_{12}(K - \hat{K})I, \tag{150}$$

where all of the coefficients G_1, G_2, G_{11}, G_{22}, and G_{12} are treated as being constant. The functional form (150) is an exact local representation in the neighborhood of the stationary solution $(\hat{K}, 0)$, and it is a good enough global approximation to be useful in analyzing many of the examples we will be discussing.

We assume that (150) is concave in K and strictly concave in I, the latter condition meaning here that $G_{22} < 0$. Because $\hat{K}$ is a stationary equilibrium,

$$-\rho G_2 = G_1. \tag{151}$$

For convenience we make the change of variable

$$X \equiv K - \hat{K}, \tag{152}$$

and apply the maximum principle to the state variable X.

Omitting the constant first term in the right-hand side of (150) as being irrelevant, we find that the Hamiltonian is

$$H = G_1 X + G_2 I + G_{11}\frac{X^2}{2} + G_{22}\frac{I^2}{2} + G_{12}XI + pI, \tag{153}$$

and it is maximized with respect to I at the interior solution $\tilde{I}(X, p)$, where the accompanying first-order condition is

$$\tilde{I}(X, p) = \frac{p + G_2 + G_{12}X}{-G_{22}}. \tag{154}$$

Using the expression for $\tilde{I}(X, p)$ from (154), the maximized Hamiltonian is

$$\tilde{H}(X, p) = G_1 X + G_2 \tilde{I}(X, p) + G_{11} \frac{X^2}{2} + G_{22} \frac{\tilde{I}(X, p)^2}{2} \tag{155}$$
$$+ G_{12} X \tilde{I}(X, p) + p \tilde{I}(X, p),$$

and, differentiating (155) while again making use of the first-order condition (154), after canceling terms we obtain

$$\frac{\partial \tilde{H}}{\partial X} = G_1 + G_{11} X + G_{12} \tilde{I}(X, p). \tag{156}$$

Inverting equation (154) to solve for p in terms of $I = \tilde{I}$, we have along an optimal trajectory that

$$p(t) = -[G_2 + G_{12} X(t) + G_{22} I(t)], \tag{157}$$

and therefore

$$\dot{p}(t) = -G_{12} \dot{X}(t) - G_{22} \dot{I}(t). \tag{158}$$

Making use of (156), (157), (158), and (151), condition [#2] of the maximum principle becomes, after canceling terms,

$$-G_{22} \dot{I} + \rho G_{22} I + [G_{11} + \rho G_{12}] X = 0, \tag{159}$$

which can be rewritten as the second-order linear differential equation

$$\frac{d^2 X}{dt^2} - \rho \frac{dX}{dt} + \frac{G_{11} + \rho G_{12}}{-G_{22}} X. \tag{160}$$

The only solution of (160) that converges to zero is of the form

$$X(t) = X(0) e^{-at}, \tag{161}$$

for some positive a, which must satisfy, from plugging (161) into (160), the characteristic quadratic equation

$$a^2 + \rho a + \frac{G_{11} + \rho G_{12}}{-G_{22}} = 0. \tag{162}$$

The positive root of (162) is

$$a = \sqrt{\left(\frac{\rho}{2}\right)^2 + \frac{G_{11} + \rho G_{12}}{G_{22}}} - \frac{\rho}{2}. \tag{163}$$

We now have a complete solution to the quadratic optimal control economic problem in the two equivalent and useful forms

$$I^*(t) = a[\hat{K} - K(t)], \tag{164}$$

and

$$K^*(t) = \hat{K} + [K_0 - \hat{K}]e^{-at}. \tag{165}$$

The complete solution of the quadratic case (164),(165) will prove very helpful in analyzing several applied problems in the next chapter.

The Wealth and Income Version of the Maximum Principle

There is yet one very important technical item to cover before we are finished with formal statements and proofs of the maximum principle. We have stated and proved what might be called a "standard version" of the maximum principle. There is another version of the principle that, for economics problems, is at least as useful as the standard version. We will call this form the *wealth and income* version of the maximum principle. (It corresponds to what in physics is sometimes called Jacobi's integral form of Hamilton's equations of motion, or, more briefly, the Hamilton-Jacobi formulation.)

As before, define the *state evaluation function* as

$$V(X) \equiv \text{maximum} \int_0^\infty G(K(t), I(t))e^{-\rho t} \, dt \tag{166}$$

subject to the differential equation

$$\dot{K}(t) = I(t), \tag{167}$$

and the constraints

$$m(K(t)) \leq I(t) \leq M(K(t)), \tag{168}$$

and with the initial condition

$$K(0) = X. \tag{169}$$

Theorem (Wealth and Income Version of the One-Dimensional Maximum Principle). *Under the assumptions of the prototype-economic model enumerated in this chapter, for the feasible trajectory* $\{K^*(t), I^*(t)\}$ *to be optimal it is necessary and sufficient that there exists a continuous non-negative price trajectory* $\{p(t)\}$ *satisfying for all* $t \geq 0$ *the "wealth and income" condition*

$$[\#4]: \quad \rho V(K^*(t)) = G(K^*(t), I^*(t)) + p(t)I^*(t)$$
$$= \tilde{H}(K^*(t), p(t)). \tag{170}$$

The first question that leaps to mind concerns the relationship between the "standard" version of the maximum principle (conditions [#1], [#2], and [#3]) and the "wealth and income" version [#4]. The short answer is that, for economics problems of the type considered in this book, the two versions are equivalent. In the proof of the standard version of the maximum principle, remember, we derived condition [#4] first, and only after [#4] was proved did we then derive conditions [#1], [#2], [#3] by making use of [#4]. Although the proof earlier in this chapter contains the details, we simply note here that one can almost "see" that conditions [#1], [#2], [#3] are contained within [#4]. Condition [#1] is exactly the second equality of [#4]. Condition [#2] comes directly from differentiating both sides of the first equality of [#4] with respect to time, and setting the two time derivatives equal to each other. Therefore, we might say that [#2] is a *differential equation form* of [#4] or, what is the same thing, [#4] is an *integral equation form* of [#2]. The important point is that the first equality of [#4] is simply a different way of writing [#2]. Finally, condition [#3] is essentially a straightforward consequence of the fact that the integral defining the state evaluation function must converge for the problem to be meaningful in the first place.

Having already derived conditions [#1], [#2], [#3] by making use of [#4], let us now go the other way by showing that [#4] follows directly from conditions [#1], [#2], and [#3].

As was already noted, condition [#1] is exactly the second equality of [#4]. It therefore remains only to prove the first equality of [#4].

Differentiating the maximized Hamiltonian $\tilde{H}(K(t), p(t))$ and evaluating it along the optimal trajectory, we have

$$\frac{d\tilde{H}}{dt} = \frac{\partial \tilde{H}}{\partial K} \dot{K}^*(t) + \frac{\partial \tilde{H}}{\partial p} \dot{p}(t). \tag{171}$$

Along an optimal trajectory, from the definition of $\tilde{H}(K^*(t), p(t))$, from applying [#1], and from the theory of cost or profit functions, we must have

$$\frac{\partial \tilde{H}}{\partial p} = I^*(t). \tag{172}$$

Now combine (172) and [#2] to transform (171) into

$$\frac{d\tilde{H}}{dt} = \rho p(t) I^*(t). \tag{173}$$

Use [#1] to change (173) into the equivalent linear differential equation

$$\frac{d\tilde{H}}{dt} = \rho \tilde{H} - \rho G(K^*(t), I^*(t)), \tag{174}$$

which has the solution

$$\tilde{H}(K^*(t), p(t)) = \rho \int_t^\infty G(K^*(s), I^*(s)) e^{-\rho(s-t)} \, ds \tag{175}$$

$$+ \lim_{\tau \to \infty} \tilde{H}(K^*(\tau), p(\tau)) e^{-\rho(\tau-t)}.$$

Now if a solution of the original problem exists, so that the optimized objective integral converges, it must be true that

$$\lim_{\tau \to \infty} G(K^*(\tau), I^*(\tau)) e^{-\rho \tau} = 0. \tag{176}$$

From [#3], we must have

$$\lim_{\tau \to \infty} p(\tau) \left[K_0 + \int_0^\tau I^*(s) \, ds \right] e^{-\rho \tau} = 0, \tag{177}$$

which cannot hold unless

$$\lim_{\tau \to \infty} p(\tau) I^*(\tau) e^{-\rho \tau} = 0. \tag{178}$$

Combining (176), (178), and [#1], we see that the second term of the right-hand side of equation (175) vanishes, and (175) then becomes

$$\tilde{H}(K^*(t), p(t)) = \rho \int_t^\infty G(K^*(s), I^*(s))e^{-\rho(s-t)} \, ds, \qquad (179)$$

which signifies we have the desired result

$$\tilde{H}(K^*(t), p(t)) = \rho V(K^*(t)). \qquad (180)$$

Thus, after proving that each implies the other, we can assert rigorously that conditions [#1], [#2], [#3] *are equivalent to* condition [#4].

The Economic Interpretation of the Maximum Principle

Having finished with the technical mathematics, we now come to the extremely important issue of interpreting the maximum principle in economic terms. But before doing so, we pause to reflect methodologically on what it signifies more generally to give an "economic interpretation" to the first-order conditions that characterize the solution of a constrained optimization problem.

Probably the single most important idea in all of economics is Adam Smith's famous insight that ferocious competition in the marketplace, far from being the formula for chaos and decay that it seems at first glance to be, actually induces an allocation so orderly that the result is as if guided by an "invisible hand." The rigorous mathematical essence of the modern version of the invisible hand principle is that there exists a fundamental isomorphism between "resource allocation as a constrained optimization problem" and "resource allocation as a competitive equilibrium." Loosely speaking, with convexity, every allocation of resources that can be described as a solution of a constrained optimization problem can also be described or interpreted as being the outcome of a competitive equilibrium—and vice versa. To understand the one is to understand the other.

It is difficult to overestimate the importance of this "invisible hand" duality principle. If we can envision the basic properties of a competitive equilibrium for some resource allocation scenario, then we can envision the basic properties of a solution to the corresponding constrained optimization problem—and vice versa. Therefore, it follows, if we have a good intuition for how competitive markets work, then we can apply this intuition to help us to characterize the solutions of constrained optimization problems. The maximum principle of optimal control theory fits this paradigm exactly—with one important new feature that comes from augmenting the *flows* of static economics with the *stocks* of dynamic economics. The extra time dimension added by a dynamic resource allocation setting introduces a new economic process on the dual side that has no genuine counterpart in static flow economics—namely, the operation of a competitive market for stocks.

Now we are ready to ask a crucial question. What is the economic interpretation of the maximum principle? There are really two equivalent economic interpretations of the maximum principle, corresponding to the two equivalent versions of the maximum principle. One interpretation (the wealth and income version) makes more intuitive sense when the maximizing unit is viewed as a *firm*. The other interpretation (the standard version) is more intuitive when the fundamental unit is a *nation*. They are, however, two sides of the same coin. The two forms of the maximum principle are mathematically identical, but which interpretation is more useful in a particular application depends on what is considered observable and what is the desired direction of inference.

The economic interpretation of the maximum principle is that it is essentially describing the *dynamic competitive equilibrium of a stock market*. But a stock market in what? The wealth and income version of the maximum principle is describing a dynamic competitive equilibrium in *shares of the firm*; these shares are assets entitling the owner to claims on future dividends. By contrast, the standard version of the maximum principle is describing a dynamic competitive equilibrium in *real stocks of physical capital*.

The distinction between whether a "firm" or a "nation" is the more appropriate unit of conceptualization hinges mainly on which variables are considered directly observable and which others need to be inferred indirectly. If the gain of the firm is interpretable as dividends, and if shares in the firm are traded on a competitive stock market, then it is natural to assume that share prices are measured in the same monetary units as dividends and that both are directly observable. By way of contrast, for this "firm" interpretation, the shadow price of capital (or investment) serves as more of an inside accounting device for the firm and a guide for the internal allocation of resources. This internal accounting price of investment goods, in most instances, is specific to the firm and perhaps not directly observable outside the firm. Also, with this interpretation, ρ stands for the relevant interest rate, which in principle is observable (or at least it can be calculated). So, with the "firm" interpretation, immediate gains (here dividends) are measured in ordinary monetary units, the stock market price on shares is observable, and the relevant interest rate is also observed (or calculated as the firm's competitive cost of capital).

By contrast, if the unit is the "nation" it seems natural to assume that the competitive market prices of real investment goods are observable as transaction prices in the markets where the real investment goods are bought and sold. But the present discounted value of the future welfare that the nation is "producing" is not directly observable—because there is no economywide stock market in "national utiles," and even if there were, neither utility functions nor pure rates of time preference ρ are directly observable. With the fundamental unit being the nation, we will be interested in using the theory to infer the present discounted value of the nation's future welfare from its current comprehensive net national income or product.

Because both interpretations are ultimately equivalent, we are free to use both, or to alternate back and forth between them. The wealth and income version of the maximum principle will typically be more directly useful for understanding the behavior of firms maximizing present discounted profits, whereas the standard version of the maximum principle will be more directly useful for analyzing a nation maximizing present discounted utility. As we shall see, however, combining the wealth and income version with the standard version will give us insights into many facets of capital theory—including, in particular, the theory of comprehensive (national) income accounting—which neither version alone could reveal.

Let us begin with the firm as the maximizing unit. The wealth and income version of the maximum principle is the condition

$$[\#4]: \quad \rho V(K^*(t)) = G(K^*(t), I^*(t)) + p(t)I^*(t)$$
$$= \tilde{H}(K^*(t), p(t)). \tag{181}$$

In the setting of a firm embedded within an economy that has a perfectly competitive stock market, $V(K^*(t))$ in [#4] represents the competitive stock market value at time t of all shares in the company. (A "share" of the firm's stock entitles the owner to the same "share" of the firm's future dividends.) The price $p(t)$ appearing in [#4] is an internal accounting or transfer price representing the value of an extra unit of physical capital to the firm. The expression $G(K^*(t), I^*(t))$ represents the cash flow of dividends paid out at time t, while $I^*(t)$ represents the firm's net investment. The Hamiltonian expression

$G(K^*(t), I^*(t)) + p(t)I^*(t)$ represents the firm's properly accounted net income at time t. We assume that the setting is a perfect capital market where money can be borrowed or lent at the relevant competitive interest rate for the firm, which is ρ. The wealth and income version of the maximum principle essentially requires a basic consistency between the firm's investment behavior, its properly accounted income, and the stock market value of its shares. The firm's investment policy is optimal if and only if its stock market share price is consistent with its current earnings—dividends plus net investment—where the accounting price of investment is the true value of an extra unit of capital to the firm, which accounting price simultaneously is "as if" being used internally to guide optimal investment decisions.

Turning to a more detailed analysis, we begin by noting that condition [#4] is really more like two conditions compressed into one. The first part of condition [#4] (the second equality) means that at any time the firm is acting to maximize its true income, that is, the value of its dividends plus net investment, where net investment is evaluated at the internal shadow price of capital $p(t)$. If the optimal control solution is like a movie unfolding over time, then the second equality of [#4] is like a "still frame" at instant t. It is a static description, indicating that the firm is on its production possibilities frontier at a point where the marginal rate of transformation between current gains and investment in future gains exactly equals the current efficiency price of investment relative to current gains, which is $p(t)$. Furthermore, this investment goods price $p(t)$ is not just any price, but, as we know from the proof, is exactly *the* marginal value to the firm's optimal program of an extra unit of capital—that is, $p(t) = V'(K^*(t))$.

Behind the scenes, the firm might be manipulating several dozen control variables to attain the maximized value of its net income, which is represented in compressed form by the second equality of [#4]. The reduced form of the firm's decision here is completely described by the second equality of condition [#4], because it signifies that all underlying control variables have been chosen to place the firm on its production possibilities frontier at just the precise point where the marginal rate of transformation between dividends and net investment is equal to the efficiency price of an extra unit of investment. This is why we problem solvers can leave the Hamiltonian expressed in the original control variables in which the problem was originally stated—if that is more convenient for solving the problem or for conceptualizing the solution. As long as the firm maximizes its true income (the Hamiltonian) over all relevant control variables taking the investment price as if given, it does not matter whether I is directly controlled, as in this formulation, or whether it is indirectly controlled by an arbitrary collection of control variables. In the most abstract formulation, any number of control variables, subject to any number of constraints, may simultaneously be determining direct gain G and net investment I. The controls are like dummy variables—we are not interested in them per se, but only in the netted-out aggregate possibilities frontier between G and I. None of the background detail about control variables or control sets really matters. The only thing that matters is that net income (with net investment evaluated at its correct efficiency price) is being maximized at each instant of time.

The second part of condition [#4] (the first equality) requires that what the firm believes is its true net income—dividends plus net investments evaluated at the true efficiency price of investment—should actually reflect the market rate of return (times the share price) for this firm. The expression $G(K^*(t), I^*(t)) + p(t)I^*(t)$ represents the true income that the firm would be reporting to its shareholders at time t as dividends plus the value of net investment, if the accounting were complete and accurate at prices representing true investment opportunity costs. The first equality of [#4] signifies that the true income the firm is generating per share should be equal to what its shareholders could obtain if they sold a share and deposited the proceeds in a bank paying interest at rate ρ. So, what the firm is accounting as its income at true efficiency prices must, in equilibrium, be the same fraction of its stock market value as what could be earned elsewhere throughout the economy. Note that it is not dividends per share price that equals the interest rate, but true income per share price. A startup company with a valuable idea or patent may pay no dividends now, yet its "true income" in the form of highly internally valued investment may be substantial, anticipating the dividends to come at some future time.

It is important to understand that the wealth and income version contains within itself an implicit "theory" of income accounting. This theory tells us what is supposed to be the exact meaning and significance of the bottom line of a firm's accounting statement—that is, its net income or earnings—in an ideal accounting system. Of course, real world accounting systems are not ideal. For example, they are not always able to price investments at true opportunity cost or to calculate economic depreciation accurately. Nor do they account well for inflation. But the theory is still very valuable, because it both indicates what income accounting is intended to accomplish for a firm and gives a precise rationale explaining why investors might be interested in looking at the firm's earnings divided by its share value (and why they might want to compare this ratio with the firm's cost of capital). In short, the theory tells us what is good accounting, and it also tells us why good accounting matters—because it provides the previously missing theoretical link between true net income and financial value.

What about the standard version of the maximum principle? Briefly, the standard version (conditions [#1], [#2], [#3]) is describing an economywide dynamic competitive equilibrium with a perfect capital market. The standard version of the maximum principle reveals a deep connection between optimization over time and market equilibrium over time. Essentially, the basic invisible-hand theorem here says that an economic situation is being optimally controlled over time if and only if the situation can simultaneously be interpreted as describing a dynamic competitive equilibrium with a perfect capital market in the "real" capital stocks. If quantities are being optimized in a dynamic economic model, they must be accompanied by prices in such a way that any observers would swear they are witnessing an economy with a perfect capital market in dynamic competitive equilibrium. Conversely, if price and quantity trajectories in a model of an economy behave as if the model were describing a dynamic competitive equilibrium with a perfect capital market, then the quantities must be at their optimal values.

To best understand the economic content of the standard version of the maximum principle, it is convenient to create a fictitious nation, called, say, the "competitive confederation." Instead of a single unit solving its own optimal control problem, we think in terms of a "nation" consisting of a very large number of "representative agents," each having the same optimal control problem with respect to international economic conditions outside the nation, but competing vigorously with each other for capital within the nation. So each representative agent in the competitive confederation is optimizing the same optimal control problem against the external world, but internally all must compete for capital on perfectly competitive capital markets.

A convenient way to think of the nation's having a perfect capital market at real interest rate ρ is to postulate an imaginary national bank where any amount of capital may be borrowed or deposited at interest rate ρ under the condition that all loans must eventually be paid off. (Without this provision, every self-interested agent would borrow indefinitely large amounts and never pay back.) The unit of account in this nation is naturally the unit in which immediate gains are measured in the optimal control problem, which might represent units of some kind of reward, payoff, dividend, consumption, utility, or any other desideratum in which the objective of the problem is expressed. In effect, the national bank is a place where gains can be deposited or borrowed at interest rate ρ.

We now show that the standard version of the maximum principle is describing the dynamic economy wide competitive equilibrium that would occur in such an idealized nation or competitive confederation.

Suppose the perfectly competitive price of the single capital good at time t is $p(t)$. This means that at time t any representative agent can buy or sell any amount of capital at the given price $p(t)$.

The first condition of the maximum principle is

$$[\#1]: \qquad G(K^*(t), I^*(t)) + p(t)I^*(t) = \tilde{H}(K^*(t), p(t)). \qquad (182)$$

This condition signifies that at all times the representative agents are acting to maximize net "national" product, taking prices as given. Envisioning an optimal control problem as a movie unfolding over time, condition [#1] represents a "still frame" photographed at instant t. It is a static description, indicating that at time t the economy is on its production possibilities frontier at a point where the marginal rate of transformation between current gains and investment (in future gains) is exactly the current competitive price of investment relative to current gains, which is $p(t)$. Furthermore, this investment-goods price $p(t)$ is not just any price, but, as we know from the proof earlier in this chapter, is exactly *the* marginal value to the optimal program at time t of an extra unit of capital—that is, $p(t) = V'(K^*(t))$, at least when $I^*(t) \neq 0$.

Behind the scenes, the representative agents of the economy might be manipulating thousands, or even millions of intermediate control variables to attain by the "invisible hand" the maximized reduced-form value of net national product expression [#1]. The reduced form of even the most complicated competitive equilibrium is that all intermediate control variables have been set (by internal competition in intermediate goods) so that the economy is placed on its production possibilities frontier at the precise point where marginal rates of transformation between final outputs are equal to their price ratios, which is exactly the reduced-form condition [#1].

Condition [#1] means that no matter how complicated are the internal workings of the competitive confederation economy, any observers of these microeconomic inner workings will come away thinking they are witnessing a static competitive equilibrium. This is why we can leave the Hamiltonian expressed in the original control variables in which the problem was originally stated, if that is a more convenient form for solving the problem or interpreting the solution. As long as we maximize the Hamiltonian over all control variables, it does not matter whether I is directly controlled, as in this formulation, or whether it is indirectly controlled by an arbitrarily large collection of intermediate control variables. In the most abstract formulation any number of control variables, subject to any number of intermediate-materials-balancing constraints in the background, may be simultaneously determining direct gain G and net investment I. The control variables are like dummy variables here—we are no more interested in them per se than we are in intermediate goods like metallic ores or chemical feedstocks. We are interested only in the netted-out aggregate possibilities frontier between G and I. None of the background detail about control variables or control sets really matters. The only thing that matters is that net national product is being maximized (as if at fixed prices) for each instant of time.

The second condition of the maximum principle is the differential equation

$$[\#2]: \qquad \dot{p}(t) = -\frac{\partial \tilde{H}}{\partial K} + \rho p(t), \qquad (183)$$

which holds everywhere along an optimal trajectory.

Unlike [#1], which is a description of a perfectly competitive static economy, condition [#2] is a uniquely dynamic description of a capital-stock market in competitive equilibrium. This kind of dynamic competitive equilibrium is sometimes called an "equilibrium in price expectations" or a "rational expectations equilibrium." To understand this dynamic competitive equilibrium interpretation, we need to begin with the concept of "arbitrage." *Arbitrage* is the simultaneous purchase and sale of equivalent securities in order to make pure positive profits from discrepancies in their expected future prices. Condition [#2] is essentially saying that in a perfectly competitive capital market no pure profits can be made from arbitrage. Condition [#2] is a dynamic version of the basic static principle that prices in competitive equilibrium are determined where supply equals demand—because otherwise someone could make pure profits from arbitrage.

Let ε represent a very small period of time. Suppose that a representative agent buys a dollar's worth of capital at time t (at unit price $p(t)$), uses it to produce extra income at the flow rate $[\partial \tilde{H}/\partial K]/p(t)$ during the interval between time t and time $t + \varepsilon$, and then sells the capital at time $t + \varepsilon$ for a price of $p(t + \varepsilon)$ dollars. At time $t + \varepsilon$ the representative agent will then have made a *net* gain in dollars of

$$\frac{\varepsilon \dfrac{\partial \tilde{H}}{\partial K} + p(t + \varepsilon) - p(t)}{p(t)}. \tag{184}$$

If the representative agent instead placed the dollar as a deposit in the national bank at time t, then the net amount gained from this investment at time $t + \varepsilon$ would be

$$\rho \varepsilon. \tag{185}$$

In a perfectly competitive capital market where no pure profits can be made from arbitrage, (184) must equal (185), which can be rewritten as the condition

$$\frac{p(t + \varepsilon) - p(t)}{\varepsilon} = -\frac{\partial \tilde{H}}{\partial K} + \rho p(t). \tag{186}$$

Taking the limit as $\varepsilon \to 0$, equation (186) becomes exactly condition [#2] of the maximum principle. If [#2] did *not* hold, then the economy would be in disequilibrium and pure profits could be made from arbitrage by moving money from private investment to the national bank (if (185) exceeds (184)), or from the national bank to private investment (if (184) exceeds (185)). By transferring funds from one investment vehicle to the other, this arbitrage activity would put pressure on capital-stock prices to move in a direction closer to satisfying [#2], and such price movements would not cease until no more pure profits could be made from arbitrage, meaning condition [#2] holds fully in equilibrium. (This same style of argument interprets economically why prices must be continuous even across boundary points of discontinuity of the control $I^*(t)$—because otherwise pure profits could be made from arbitrage just before and after the boundary time.)

The third condition of the maximum principle is

$$[\#3]: \qquad \lim_{t \to \infty} p(t) K^*(t) e^{-\rho t} = 0. \tag{187}$$

To begin to understand the role of this "transversality condition" [#3], we need to ask the following question. If a competitive economy is on a price-quantity trajectory satisfying conditions [#1] and [#2], is it possible that it is *not* on an optimal trajectory? The general answer, which came out indirectly in the proof of necessity, is yes. In the general case, we need the transversality condition [#3] to obtain optimality. Conditions [#1] and [#2] guarantee only intertemporal optimality. If $K(t)$ is the capital stock at time t on a price-quantity trajectory satisfying conditions [#1] and [#2], then it can be shown that there is no better way to go from $K(0)$ at time 0 to $K(t)$ at time t—that is, the trajectory maximizes present discounted gains in going from $K(0)$ at time 0 to $K(t)$ at time t. But maybe $K(t)$ is the "wrong" amount of capital to have at time t. Without the transversality condition [#3], the economy could be "efficiently" piling up uselessly large amounts of capital into the indefinite future. Without [#3], we may be myopically stuck in a situation where we are efficiently accumulating capital in every finite subperiod, but we are inefficiently overaccumulating capital for the infinite-horizon period in which we are really interested.

It seems clear from the proof of necessity that we generally need condition [#3] to hold for optimality. But how would the representative agents in the competitive confederation know how to act to make [#3] happen? What is their "signal" that [#3] should hold? The answer, which is analogous to the explanation of [#2], is driven by the ability to make pure profits from arbitrage in a disequilibrium state of a perfectly competitive capital market where [#3] fails to hold.

For, suppose the contrary of [#3]. Suppose instead that

$$\lim_{t \to \infty} p(t) K(t) e^{-\rho t} = A, \tag{188}$$

where $A > 0$. (This is a mathematical description of an economic "bubble," in this stock of K, over time.) Then by following a competitive trajectory until time T, and then selling off all of the capital stock at time T, a representative agent could attain present discounted value

$$\int_0^T G(K(t), I(t))e^{-\rho t} \, dt + p(T)K(T)e^{-\rho T}. \tag{189}$$

As T is made arbitrarily larger, expression (189) comes arbitrarily close to

$$\int_0^\infty G(K(t), I(t))e^{-\rho t} \, dt + A. \tag{190}$$

Which would you rather have—an infinitely long income stream whose present discounted value is

$$\int_0^\infty G(K(t), I(t))e^{-\rho t} \, dt, \tag{191}$$

or a very long, but finite, opportunity whose present discounted value (189) comes arbitrarily close to (190), and is therefore arbitrarily close to being bigger than (191) by amount $A > 0$? Your answer should be the present discounted value (189), which is arbitrarily close in value to (190), and therefore strictly greater than (191). With a perfect capital market, if you cashed in a lump sum arbitrarily close to (190) at some time T and deposited it in the national bank, you could enjoy a stream of gains that would be higher at each instant of time than $G(K(t), I(t))$ by an amount arbitrarily close to the annuity stream ρA.

But in so analyzing the situation, you would not be alone in your reasoning. Every representative agent can reason in the same way. The overhang of capital stocks waiting to be liquidated would put downward pressure now on the entire price trajectory of capital until the value of A in (188) would be driven down to zero, at which time desire for pure arbitrage profits from cashing in future investments would cease. The essential idea here is that if bubbles are commonly perceived to exist in some stocks, then the idea of desiring to liquidate such stocks at some distant future time for pure profit will ultimately translate into pushing down their price now. If A in (188) is positive, the price of capital now, $p(0)$, cannot represent a dynamic competitive equilibrium because $p(0)$ is "too high" relative to the present discounted gain (191).

To sum up, any group of economists observing a nation over time on a trajectory simultaneously satisfying [#1], [#2], and [#3] would swear under oath that they were witnessing a dynamic competitive equilibrium with a perfect capital market at interest rate ρ. So if we can imagine for some economic model or situation what a dynamic competitive equilibrium with a perfect capital market at interest rate ρ would look like, then we can simultaneously imagine the solution to the optimal control problem. The ability to envision these two dual sides of an optimal control problem is frequently invaluable in suggesting the form of a solution. Furthermore, this way of looking at things gives economists a leg up on solving optimal control problems, because we usually have a comparative advantage in imagining what the corresponding dynamic competitive equilibrium should look like.

Rather than trying here to explain further the theoretical significance of conditions [#1], [#2], [#3], and [#4], it is probably better to demonstrate their specific roles in the solution of actual problems. The next chapter does this. Then, in later chapters, motivated by the applications, we develop the general multidimensional theory of heterogeneous capital more fully.

Bibliographic Note

The maximum principle is "proved," for a situation where the state evaluation function is continuously differentiable, in several basic textbooks, including Kamien and Schwartz (1991), Intriligator (1971), and Clark (1990). A rigorous statement and applications, without proofs, is contained in Seiderstad and Sydsaeter (1987). The treatment of Arrow and Kurz (1970), while not rigorous, is useful for its economic insights.

I do not know of any "elementary" book that proves rigorously the maximum principle when the state evaluation function is not assumed to be differentiable, even for the case of one state variable. Moreover, the proof of this chapter covers fully the economically important situation where the control set depends upon the state variable, which is typically considered an advanced and very difficult topic. The proof of this chapter (for the continuous-time case) parallels closely the proof in Weitzman (1973) (for the discrete-time case). The classic original statement of the maximum principle is Pontryagin et al. (1962).

Much of the material on the economic interpretation of the maximum principle is new. A previous earlier treatment is Dorfman (1969). The "wealth and income version" essentially stems from work first reported in Weitzman (1970).

4

✳

Applications of the Maximum Principle
in One Dimension

This chapter shows how to use the maximum principle to solve the ten one-dimensional problems introduced in Chapter 2.

SOLUTION OF PROBLEM 1: THE FAMILY FIRM

We start by solving and then analyzing the family firm problem. This model is a particularly good one to begin with, because the solution is so intuitive and yet the problem leads naturally to the examination of a number of important themes in optimal control theory that will be repeated and amplified in much more general models. So the family firm problem is simple and intuitive, yet rich and suggestive.

The problem faced by the family firm is to control net investments $I(t)$ at time t in such a way as to

$$\text{maximize} \quad \int_0^\infty [F(K(t)) - I(t)]e^{-\rho t} \, dt \tag{1}$$

subject to

$$\dot{K}(t) = I(t), \tag{2}$$

and

$$-\mu K(t) \leq I(t) \leq \overline{I}, \tag{3}$$

and with the given initial condition

$$K(0) = K_0. \tag{4}$$

For the family firm's problem, the net gain function is

$$G(K, I) \equiv F(K) - I. \tag{5}$$

We have already defined the very important concept of a stationary rate of return on capital (evaluated at capital stock K) as being expressed by the function

$$R(K) \equiv \frac{G_1(K, 0)}{-G_2(K, 0)}. \tag{6}$$

In the family firm model, it is readily calculated that

$$R(K) = F'(K), \tag{7}$$

and it is natural for us to assume a unique stationary capital stock $\hat{K}$ satisfying

$$R(\hat{K}) = F'(\hat{K}) = \rho, \tag{8}$$

because

$$R'(\hat{K}) = F''(\hat{K}) < 0. \tag{9}$$

What is the optimal investment policy for the family firm's control problem? The solution's basic idea should be fairly intuitive, at least in broad outline. At capital stock level K, the rate of return to capital in the family firm is $F'(K)$, whereas the rate of return available on the alternative investment (the bank) is ρ. The family firm would never want to remain stationary in a situation where $F'(K) \neq \rho$. Capital should be increased if $F'(K) > \rho$, decreased if $F'(K) < \rho$, and unchanged if $F'(K) = \rho$. Next question: if changes are to be made, how fast should capital be changed? In this model, the answer is as fast as possible, because every day spent in a state where $F'(K) \neq \rho$ is a day with lower present-discounted cash flow than might otherwise be obtained.

Let us analyze this problem formally. The Hamiltonian here is

$$H \equiv F(K) - I + pI, \tag{10}$$

where p stands for the internal value or opportunity price of an extra unit of capital to the firm.

The next step is to calculate the maximum value of the Hamiltonian over all feasible values of I. In this case it is relatively easy to do, because we are maximizing a linear function. With $\tilde{I}(p)$ denoting the Hamiltonian-maximizing value of net investment as a function of its price (and, for notational convenience, suppressing dependence of $\tilde{I}$ on K), there are three possibilities:

$$p > 1 \Rightarrow \tilde{I}(p) = \overline{I} \Rightarrow \tilde{H}(K, p) = F(K) + (p - 1)\overline{I}, \tag{11}$$

or

$$p < 1 \Rightarrow \tilde{I}(p) = -\mu K \Rightarrow \tilde{H}(K, p) = F(K) + (1 - p)\mu K, \tag{12}$$

or, in the case of an indeterminate solution, $\tilde{I}(p)$ can be any feasible value, that is,

$$p = 1 \Rightarrow -\mu K \leq \tilde{I}(p) \leq \overline{I} \Rightarrow \tilde{H}(K, p) = F(K). \tag{13}$$

Since the variable p represents the value of an extra unit of capital to an optimal program, it seems natural to guess that when $K < \hat{K}$, then the value of an extra dollar's worth of capital is more than a dollar ($p > 1$ because $F'(K) > p$), as there is no other way in which the price can "signal" that net investment must be positive. Similarly, it also seems natural to guess that when $K > \hat{K}$, then the value of an extra dollar's worth of capital is less than a dollar ($p < 1$ because $F'(K) < p$), since there is no other way in which the price can "signal" that net investment must be negative.

So, an educated guess here is that $K < \hat{K} \Rightarrow p = V'(K) > 1$, while $K > \hat{K} \Rightarrow p = V'(K) < 1$. It also seems like a good guess that $V'(\hat{K}) = 1$, because the value of an extra unit of capital in the stationary state, which the optimal policy wants to get to and stay in, should be exactly one.

Thus far, we have used the necessity of condition [#1] of the maximum principle (here (11), (12), (13)) to suggest strongly the form of an optimal solution. Let us therefore propose this form of solution and then prove it is optimal by sufficiency of the maximum principle in the convex environment of Problem 1.

What we are proposing as a solution here is the *most rapid approach* to the stationary state and, after reaching it, remaining there forever. (In optimal control terminology, this is also called a "bang-bang" solution.) Using mathematical notation, we are therefore proposing the following solution. If $K_0 < \hat{K}$, then $I^*(t) = \overline{I}$ for $0 \leq t < T$, where $T \equiv (\hat{K} - K_0)/\overline{I}$, and thereafter $I^*(t) = 0$ for $t \geq T$. If $K_0 > \hat{K}$, then $I^*(t) = -\mu K(t)$ for $0 \leq t < T$, where here $T \equiv (\log \hat{K} - \log K_0)/\mu$, and thereafter $I^*(t) = 0$ for $t \geq T$. If $K_0 = \hat{K}$, then $I^*(t) = 0$ for all $t \geq 0$.

To prove that this most rapid approach or bang-bang policy is optimal, we must show that it satisfies the three basic conditions of the maximum principle. We want to construct a price trajectory that supports our proposed quantity policy. We work backward in time, starting with the proposed stationary solution $K = \hat{K}$, $p = 1$. The transversality condition [#3] of Chapter 3 is obviously fulfilled in a stationary state where $K^*(t) = \hat{K}$ and $p(t) = 1$ are both constant for $t \geq T$. Similarly, it is readily confirmed that conditions [#1] and [#2] of Chapter 3 are both satisfied in the stationary state. From (11), (12), and (13) we want to show in our proposed solution that when $K_0 < \hat{K}$, then $p(t) > 1$ for $0 \leq t < T$, and that when $K_0 > \hat{K}$, then $p(t) < 1$ for $0 \leq t < T$. And we also must show that the continuity condition $p(T^-) = 1$ is satisfied.

We begin with the case $K_0 < \hat{K}$. From (11), in this case we are proposing for $0 \leq t < T$ that

$$-\frac{\partial \tilde{H}}{\partial K} = -F'(K(t)), \tag{14}$$

and therefore condition [#2] here becomes

$$\dot{p}(t) = -F'(K(t)) + \rho p(t), \tag{15}$$

with the terminal condition $p(T) = 1$.

Defining here

$$q(t) \equiv p(t) - 1, \tag{16}$$

we can rewrite (15) as

$$\dot{q}(t) = [\rho - F'(K(t))] + \rho q(t). \tag{17}$$

Along with the differential equation $\dot{K} = \bar{I}$ and the boundary conditions $q(T) = 0$ and $K(T) = \hat{K}$, the differential equation (17) is well defined. We need to show consistency by proving $q(t) > 0$ for $0 \leq t < T$.

Now the term in the square brackets of (17) is zero at $t = T$ and *strictly negative* for $0 \leq t < T$ (because then $F'(K(t)) > \rho$, since $K(t) < \hat{K}$). It follows from (17) that if $q(\tau) \leq 0$ for *any* $\tau < T$, then $\dot{q}(t) < 0$ for *all* t satisfying $\tau \leq t < T$, and thus $q(T) < 0$. Therefore, if we are to have $q(T) = 0$, then any $q(t)$ satisfying the differential equation (17) must be *strictly positive* for $0 \leq t < T$. Thus we have shown that $p(t) > 1$ for $0 \leq t < T$.

This proves the optimality of the most rapid approach policy for $K_0 < \hat{K}$, because we have exhibited a proposed trajectory of $\{I^*(t)\}$ and $\{p(t)\}$ that simultaneously satisfies all three conditions of the maximum principle.

The proof of optimality of the most rapid approach policy for the case $K_0 > \hat{K}$ is a mirror image of the proof that was just given for the case $K_0 < \hat{K}$. To make sure the understanding is complete, though, let us give it here in detail.

Suppose, now, that $K_0 > \hat{K}$. From (12), in this case we are proposing for $0 \le t < T$ that

$$-\frac{\partial \tilde{H}}{\partial K} = -F'(K) + (p-1)\mu, \tag{18}$$

and therefore condition [#2] here becomes

$$\dot{p}(t) = -F'(K(t)) + (p(t)-1)\mu + \rho p(t), \tag{19}$$

with the terminal condition $p(T) = 1$.

Again defining

$$q(t) \equiv p(t) - 1, \tag{20}$$

we can rewrite (19) as

$$\dot{q}(t) = [\rho - F'(K(t))] + (\rho + \mu)q(t). \tag{21}$$

Along with the differential equation $\dot{K} = -\mu K$ and the boundary conditions $q(T) = 0$ and $K(T) = \hat{K}$, the differential equation (21) is well defined. Consistency here requires we show that $q(t) < 0$ for $0 \le t < T$.

Now the term in square brackets of (17) is zero at $t = T$ and *strictly positive* for $0 \le t < T$ (because then $F'(K(t)) < \rho$, since $K(t) > \hat{K}$). It follows from (21) that if $q(\tau) \ge 0$ for *any* $\tau < T$, then $\dot{q}(t) > 0$ for *all* t satisfying $\tau \le t < T$, and thus $q(T) > 0$. Therefore, if $q(T) = 0$, then any $q(t)$ satisfying the differential equation (21) must be *strictly negative* for $0 \le t < T$. Thus, $p(t) < 1$ for $0 \le t < T$.

This proves the optimality of the most rapid approach policy for $K_0 > \hat{K}$, because we have exhibited a proposed trajectory of $\{I^*(t)\}$ and $\{p(t)\}$ that simultaneously satisfies all three conditions of the maximum principle.

Pulling all of the pieces together, we have proved rigorously that the optimal investment policy for the family firm problem is a most rapid approach to $K = \hat{K}$.

The interested reader should be able to show what happens if $F'(K) < \rho$ for all $K \geq 0$. In this case the firm should liquidate its capital as rapidly as possible, because the rate of return inside the firm is less than what is available on alternative outside investments.

Most Rapid Approach Problems

The conceptual simplicity of a MRA (most rapid approach) policy is a starting point for understanding the solutions of many optimal control problems, which at first glance may appear to be much more complicated than the family firm problem. Inspired by this simple example, we now ask an important question. What feature of the family firm problem gave rise to the optimality of a most rapid approach to the stationary state? What is the general class of problems for which the optimal control is MRA?

The general feature that gives rise to a MRA solution is linearity in investment of the gain function. This means that the gain function can be expressed in the form

$$G(K, I) = A(K) + B(K)I, \tag{22}$$

where $A(K)$ and $B(K)$ are concave functions with $B(K) < 0$. As we will soon be investigating, models of the form (22) include, among others, the optimal fisheries management problem, the optimal tree harvesting problem, and the problem of irreversible investment—as well as the family firm problem.

Applying our by now standard formula $R = -G_1/G_2$ to (22), we find that the very important rate of return to capital in a stationary state here is

$$R(K) = \frac{A'(K)}{-B(K)}. \tag{23}$$

Armed with the maximum principle and guided by our treatment of the simple prototype family firm problem, we now can readily state and prove that when a problem has the special (linear in I) structure (22) the optimal policy is MRA. We state this as follows.

With (22) and the underlying assumptions of Chapter 3, an optimal policy is completely characterized as follows

$$R(K(t)) > \rho \;\Rightarrow\; I^*(t) = M(K(t)), \tag{24}$$

$$R(K(t)) < \rho \;\Rightarrow\; I^*(t) = m(K(t)), \tag{25}$$

and the policy (24),(25) continues until such time T when either further invest-ment is "blocked" by zero or a stationary state $K(T) = \hat{K}$ has been reached, after which net investment is zero.

We prove this assertion here for the case of a unique accessible stationary state. The proof for the case of blocked investments is very similar. From the definition of uniqueness and accessibility, and making use of the discussion in Chapter 3 sandwiched between equations (3.8) and (3.9), we have

$$K < \hat{K} \;\Rightarrow\; R(K) > \rho, \, M(K) > 0, \tag{26}$$

and

$$K > \hat{K} \;\Rightarrow\; R(K) < \rho, \, m(K) < 0. \tag{27}$$

Let us analyze this problem formally. The Hamiltonian here is

$$H \equiv A(K) + B(K)I + pI, \tag{28}$$

where p stands for the marginal value or opportunity price of an extra unit of capital.

The next step is to calculate the maximized Hamiltonian over all feasible values of I. In this case it is relatively easy to do because we are maximizing a linear function. With $\tilde{I}(p)$ denoting the Hamiltonian-maximizing value of investment as a function of its price, there are three possibilities. Either

$$p > -B(K) \;\Rightarrow\; \tilde{I}(p) = M(K) \;\Rightarrow\; \tilde{H}(K, p)$$
$$= A(K) + [p + B(K)]M(K), \tag{29}$$

or

$$-B(K) > p \;\Rightarrow\; \tilde{I}(p) = m(K) \;\Rightarrow\; \tilde{H}(K, p)$$
$$= A(K) + [p + B(K)]m(K), \tag{30}$$

or, in the case of an indeterminate solution where $\tilde{I}(p)$ can be *any* feasible value,

$$p = -B(K) \;\Rightarrow\; m(K) \leq \tilde{I}(p) \leq M(K)$$
$$\Rightarrow \tilde{H}(K, p) = A(K). \tag{31}$$

Since the variable p represents the value of an extra unit of capital, it seems natural to suppose that when $K = \hat{K}$, then the value of an extra unit of capital is the direct marginal gain $-B(\hat{K})$ of being freed from buying a unit of investment (because in a stationary state we don't want to keep an extra unit of capital), so that $p = -B(\hat{K})$. It also seems natural to suppose that $K < \hat{K} \Rightarrow p > -B(K)$ (because there is no other way to send a decentralized price signal that net investment should be positive when $R(K) > \rho$) and that $K > \hat{K} \Rightarrow -B(K) > p$ (because there is no other way to send a decentralized price signal that net investment should be negative when $R(K) < \rho$). We are thus here using the necessity of condition [#1] of the maximum principle (as (29), (30), and (31)) to suggest strongly the general form of a solution. Let us therefore propose this form of solution and then prove it is optimal by sufficiency of the maximum principle in the convex environment of the problem.

What we are proposing as a solution is a most rapid approach to the stationary state and, after reaching it, remaining there forever. In mathematical notation, we are therefore proposing the following solution. If $K_0 < \hat{K}$, then $I^*(t) = M(K(t))$ for $0 \leq t < T$, where T is the first time when $K(t) = \hat{K}$, and thereafter $I^*(t) = 0$ for $t \geq T$. If $K_0 > \hat{K}$, then we are proposing as an optimal solution that $I^*(t) = m(K(t))$ for $0 \leq t < T$, where again T is the first time when $K(t) = \hat{K}$, and thereafter $I^*(t) = 0$ for $t \geq T$. If $K_0 = \hat{K}$, then we propose $I^*(t) = 0$ for all $t \geq 0$.

To prove that this MRA policy is optimal, we must show that it satisfies the three basic conditions of the maximum principle. The transversality condition [#3] is obviously fulfilled in a stationary state where $K^*(t) = \hat{K}$ and $p(t) = -B(\hat{K})$ are both constant for $t \geq T$ (as was shown in the proof of necessity from Chapter 3). Likewise, it is readily confirmed that conditions [#1] and [#2] are satisfied in a stationary solution. From (23), (24), and (25) we want to show in our proposed solution that when $K_0 < \hat{K}$ then $p(t) > -B(K(t))$ for $0 \leq t < T$, and that when $K_0 > \hat{K}$ then $-B(K(t)) > p(t)$ for $0 \leq t < T$. Moreover, to satisfy continuity, we must also have $p(T^-) = -B(\hat{K})$.

We begin with the case $K_0 < \hat{K}$. From (29), in this case we are proposing for $0 \leq t < T$ that

$$-\frac{\partial \tilde{H}}{\partial K} = -[A'(K) + (p + B(K))M'(K) + B'(K)M(K)], \qquad (32)$$

and therefore condition [#2] here becomes

$$\dot{p}(t) = -[A'(K(t)) + (p(t) + B(K(t)))M'(K(t)) \\ + B'(K(t))M(K(t))] + \rho p(t), \qquad (33)$$

with the terminal condition $p(T) = -B(\hat{K})$.

Defining here

$$q(t) \equiv p(t) + B(K(t)), \qquad (34)$$

and making use of (23), we can rewrite (33) as

$$\dot{q}(t) = [B(K(t))(R(K(t)) - \rho)] + q(t)(\rho - M'(K(t))), \qquad (35)$$

where $K(t)$ is the solution of the differential equation $\dot{K} = M(K(t))$ with the boundary condition $K(T) = \hat{K}$.

Now the term in the square brackets of (35) is zero at time $t = T$ and *strictly negative* for $0 \leq t < T$ (because then $R(K(t)) > \rho$, while $B < 0$). Although we could handle the more general case by an extended argument, it is easiest and most convenient to make here the harmless assumption that $M'(K(t)) \leq \rho$. It then follows from (35) that if $q(\tau) \leq 0$ for *any* $\tau < T$, then $\dot{q}(t) < 0$ for *all* t satisfying $\tau \leq t < T$, and thus $q(T) < 0$. Therefore, if we are to have $q(T) = 0$, then $q(t)$ satisfying the differential equation (35) must be *strictly positive* for $0 \leq t < T$. Thus from the definition (34) we have shown that $p(t) > -B(K(t))$ for $0 \leq t < T$.

This proves the optimality of the MRA policy for $K_0 < \hat{K}$, because we have exhibited a proposed trajectory of $\{I^*(t)\}$ and $\{p(t)\}$ that simultaneously satisfies all three conditions of the maximum principle.

The proof of optimality of the MRA policy for the case $K_0 > \hat{K}$ is a mirror image of the proof that was just given for the case $K_0 < \hat{K}$.

Suppose that $K_0 > \hat{K}$. From (25), in this case we are proposing for $0 \leq t < T$ that

$$-\frac{\partial \tilde{H}}{\partial K} = -[A'(K) + (p + B(K))m'(K) + B'(K)m(K)], \qquad (36)$$

and therefore condition [#2] here becomes

$$\dot{p}(t) = -[A'(K(t)) + (p(t) + B(K(t)))m'(K(t))$$
$$+ B'(K(t))m(K(t))] + \rho p(t), \tag{37}$$

with the terminal condition $p(T) = -B(\hat{K})$.

Defining here

$$q(t) \equiv p(t) + B(K(t)), \tag{38}$$

and making use of (23), we can rewrite (37) as

$$\dot{q}(t) = [B(K(t))(R(K(t)) - \rho)] + q(t)(\rho - m'(K(t))). \tag{39}$$

Now the term in the square brackets of (39) is zero at $t = T$ and *strictly positive* for $0 \leq t < T$ (because then $R(K(t)) < \rho$, while $B < 0$). It follows from (39) that if $q(\tau) \geq 0$ for *any* $\tau < T$, then $\dot{q}(t) > 0$ for *all* t satisfying $\tau \leq t < T$, and thus $q(T) > 0$. Therefore, if $q(T) = 0$, then $q(t)$ satisfying the differential equation (39) must be *strictly negative* for $0 \leq t < T$. Thus $-B(K(t)) > p(t)$ for $0 \leq t < T$, and there are no inconsistencies in applying the maximum principle to the proposed solution.

This proves the optimality of the MRA policy for $K_0 > \hat{K}$, because we have exhibited a proposed trajectory of $\{I^*(t)\}$ and $\{p(t)\}$ that simultaneously satisfies all three (sufficient) conditions of the maximum principle.

Putting all of the pieces together, we have proved rigorously that the optimal investment policy for a gain function that is linear in investment is a most rapid approach to the stationary state $K = \hat{K}$. This is a powerful result that will be very useful, and the relative ease with which it was proved is therefore testimony to the power and usefulness of the maximum principle itself.

The proof of the case where investment is blocked at time T, because either

$$R(K(T)) > \rho, \qquad M(K(T)) = 0 \tag{40}$$

or

$$R(K(T)) < \rho, \qquad m(K(T)) = 0 \tag{41}$$

is very similar in structure. First, the necessity of the maximum principle suggests very strongly that the optimal investment policy is the most rapid approach to the blocked state. Then this policy is proposed and shown to satisfy consistently all three parts of the maximum principle, which means it is satisfying the sufficient conditions for optimality. The exact details are left as an exercise.

Having completely characterized the solution for a gain function that is linear in investment, the next natural question to ask is what happens when the gain function is *not* linear in investment. It turns out that the most rapid approach to the stationary state is still a very useful point of departure for analyzing nonlinear problems, even though it is not optimal for the nonlinear case. As an example of what is meant by this, take the family firm problem. If we add the single feature of a nonlinear utility of consumption function $U(C)$, then the family firm problem becomes transformed into the neoclassical optimal growth problem with gain function

$$G(K, I) = U(F(K) - I), \tag{42}$$

while, if instead of a curved utility function we add the single feature of an adjustment cost $\varphi(I)$ for investment (with $\varphi'' > 0$ and the normalization $\varphi(0) = \varphi'(0) = 0$), the family firm problem is transformed into the q-theory of investment model with gain function

$$G(K, I) = F(K) - I - \varphi(I). \tag{43}$$

In both of these cases (42) and (43), it is readily confirmed that the stationary rate of return on capital is exactly the same as for the original family firm problem, namely

$$R(K) = F'(K). \tag{44}$$

We can now intuit what is the qualitative effect of adding a curved utility function or a curved adjustment cost. The solution will still attempt to "get to" the stationary state $\hat{K}$ where $R(\hat{K}) = \rho$. Only now, with nonlinear utility or cost-of-adjustment functions, it is no longer optimal to make a most rapid approach. The optimal policy calls for moderating the speed of approach to the steady state, with the degree of moderation related positively to the curvature of the utility or adjustment functions. If there is very small curvature, so that the functions are almost linear, the approach to the stationary state will be very rapid, while still not the "most rapid." At the opposite extreme, with a very highly curved utility or adjustment function, the optimal policy cannot afford to be so extreme as MRA because of the large potential losses from strongly diminishing marginal utility or sharply increasing costs of adjustment. So models nonlinear in investment or utility act here like models linear in investment or utility in wanting to approach a stationary state—but with the sole difference being moderation in the speed of approach, depending on the degree of nonlinearity.

Before getting into a full-blown discussion of what happens when the gain function is nonlinear in investment, however, we first want to analyze concretely some other linear models.

SOLUTION OF PROBLEM 3: OPTIMAL MANAGEMENT OF THE FISHERY

Perhaps the most famous of all models whose gain function is linear in investment is the standard model of the optimal management of the fishery by a "sole owner." In the standard fishery management model, the capital K stands for the physical stock of fish. The fishery problem is of the form (22), with

$$A(K) = F(K)\pi(K) \tag{45}$$

and

$$B(K) = -\pi(K). \tag{46}$$

The rate of return on capital in a stationary state here is

$$R(K) = F'(K) + \frac{F(K)\pi'(K)}{\pi(K)}. \tag{47}$$

In the simple fishery model, $F(K)$ represents the net (flow) biological increment in the fish population (per unit time) as a function of the existing population stock level. The standard assumptions made about $F(K)$ are the usual production function conditions

$$F(0) = 0, \qquad F'(0) > 0, \qquad F''(K) < 0. \tag{48}$$

(Certainly these assumptions are met for the commonly used logistic growth function.)

The function $\pi(K)$ represents the unit harvesting profitability (per fish caught) when the fish population is K. In the fisheries literature, $\pi(K)$ usually appears in the form

$$\pi(K) = P - c(K), \tag{49}$$

where P is the given fixed price per unit of fish and $c(K)$ is the unit harvesting cost.

The standard assumptions here are

$$\pi'(K) \geq 0, \qquad \pi''(K) \leq 0, \tag{50}$$

which correspond to $c'(K) \leq 0$, $c''(K) \geq 0$. The reason that unit harvesting profitability is assumed to be nondecreasing in fish population is that the cost of catching a ton of fish increases (or at least does not decrease) when there are less fish to be caught.

Recall that the equation corresponding to (47) for the family firm (and many other models in capital theory) is simply

$$R(K) = F'(K). \tag{51}$$

Formula (47) is the same formula as (51)—the stationary rate of return on capital is just the marginal product of capital—except for adding the second term on the right-hand side of the equation (47). Why is the term $F(K)\pi'(K)/\pi(K)$, which is non-negative in sign, added to $F'(K)$ to obtain the stationary rate of return for the fishery, while such a term is altogether absent for the family firm (or many other situations in capital theory)? The answer is connected with the measurement of capital. In the family firm problem, which is typical of a wide class of capital-theoretic environments, capital can naturally be measured in dollars, so the cash value of the capital and the physical amount of the capital (tons of trucks, number of trucks, total horsepower of truck fleet, and so on) are essentially the same thing—each way of measuring capital is just some linear multiple of the other. In the fishery problem, the cash value of the capital stock is not just the physical stock of fish. The formula giving the stationary rate of return on capital (47) for the fishery is the same as the more familiar marginal productivity of capital formula (51) when capital is measured in units of cash value. The following argument is heuristic, but should convey the intended idea.

Suppose we are in a stationary state (not necessarily the optimum) at fish stock level K. What is the marginal value of an extra fish in the sea? If we were given as a gift an extra fish in the sea, we could remain in the same stationary state just after harvesting the extra fish, yielding extra immediate profit $\pi(K)$. Thus, if $\Psi(K)$ represents the *stock cash value* of the fish stock K in a stationary state, we may figuratively write

$$\Psi'(K) = \pi(K). \tag{52}$$

If $\Phi(K)$ represents the *flow cash value* of the flow of annual profits from a fish stock maintained in stationary state K, then

$$\Phi(K) = \pi(K)F(K). \tag{53}$$

The marginal product of fish capital measured in cash values is heuristically $d\Phi/d\Psi$, which can be written as

$$\frac{d\Phi}{d\Psi} = \frac{\Phi'(K)}{\Psi'(K)}. \tag{54}$$

Using (52) and (53) to evaluate (54), and comparing with (47), we then have the result

$$R(K) = \frac{d\Phi}{d\Psi}. \tag{55}$$

Equation (55) conveys the important general principle that the stationary rate of return on capital is the marginal product of capital when everything is measured in equivalent cash values. In the family firm problem, the basic principle (55) reduces to the simple familiar marginal productivity formula (51); for the fishery, (55) takes the less familiar form (47), reflecting the fact that the cash value of a stock of fish increases nonlinearly because it is cheaper to find and catch fish when there are more of them. But both formulas are expressing exactly the same idea—the stationary rate of return on capital must equal the marginal product of capital when all flow and stock variables are properly calibrated in units of equivalent cash value.

We know from the general theory we just developed that when the gain function is linear in investment, as for the fishery problem, that the optimal investment (or harvesting) policy is a most rapid approach to the stationary solution $\hat{K}$ satisfying $R(\hat{K}) = \rho$. Using (55), the economic interpretation of such a policy is that the stock of fish should be pushed as rapidly to, and maintained at, the level where the marginal product of fish capital, measured in cash values, equals the discount rate. Expressed in terms of the conventionally measured stock of fish K (as opposed to being measured in cash values), the condition $R(\hat{K}) = \rho$, which characterizes a stationary solution, turns expression (47) into the form

$$F'(\hat{K}) = \rho - \frac{F(\hat{K})\pi'(\hat{K})}{\pi(\hat{K})}. \tag{56}$$

The second term being subtracted in the right-hand side of (56) is

$$\frac{F(\hat{K})\pi'(\hat{K})}{\pi(\hat{K})}, \tag{57}$$

which is positive if $\pi'(\hat{K}) > 0$. (It is zero if $\pi'(\hat{K}) = 0$, which essentially brings us back to a version of the family firm model.) The term (57) represents what might be called a *stock effect*. When the cost of fishing decreases as the fish population is increased, then it is natural for us to expect a modification of the simple family firm formula, which is biased in favor of increased fish-capital population levels. Note that when (57) is positive, then the fish stock value $\hat{K}$ satisfying (56) is larger than the fish stock value satisfying the family-firm rule (51), because the situation is "as if" the family firm were facing a lower discount rate. From formula (57) the strength of this stock effect depends in a natural way on the sensitivity of harvesting costs to the level of the stock. If harvesting costs increase dramatically as fish stocks are depleted, the stock effect will bias optimal management toward maintaining much higher stocks of fish.

Is it possible that (57) could be bigger than ρ, so that, from (56), the marginal physical product of capital measured in fish terms is actually *negative*? The answer, at least in principle, is *yes*. To understand why, imagine a fanciful scenario where fish populations above a certain critical level cause the fish to jump into the nets, so fishing costs are negligable, while below that same critical population level the fish are prohibitively expensive to locate and catch. In this purposely extreme example, the optimal fish stock level $\hat{K}$ satisfying (56) would be determined primarily on the cost side, almost irrespective of the shape of the reproduction function $F(K)$, at the population where the fish are costlessly jumping into the nets (while they are nearly impossible to find at any lower density).

Is it ever possible that it is economically "optimal" to drive a fish population to extinction? The answer, unfortunately, is yes. If $R(0^+) < \rho$, then a stationary solution does not exist and equation (56) is replaced by the limiting inequality $F'(\varepsilon) < \rho - F(\varepsilon)\pi'(\varepsilon)/\pi(\varepsilon)$ holding for all "very small" ε. In this case, the economically optimal policy is a "corner solution" of harvesting all of the fish as rapidly as possible, until the entire fish population is wiped out. The underlying rationale behind choosing extinction is not very complicated. After all, the sole owner is considering the fish stock to be just another form of capital. If the asset does not provide a suitably high rate of return relative to the alternatives, then it is optimal to liquidate the stock. (This situation can be viewed as an example of a problem with access to the stationary solution blocked, since the owner would like to make negative investments in fish stocks, because the stationary rate of return is less than the discount rate, but is prevented from so doing by the blocking corner condition $m(0) = 0$.) Note that extinction would only be economically "optimal" if a number of criteria were met. First of all, it must be relatively inexpensive to find and harvest the fish, even at extremely low population densities—so that $\pi(x) = P - c(x) > 0$, even for very small x. (Otherwise it is simply not optimal to harvest any fish when $\pi < 0$.) Additionally, the particular fish species must be unable to reproduce at a sufficiently rapid rate. (If the intrinsic potential growth rate of the fish population exceeds the discount rate—so that $F(\varepsilon)/\varepsilon > \rho$ for arbitrarily small ε—then extinction would never be chosen by the sole owner; this is analogous to the family firm not wanting to liquidate all capital if $F'(0) > \rho$.) Needless to say, actual decisions about the extinction of species involve many more considerations than the simple economic criteria of this simplest of all dynamic fishery models.

We know that the optimal fishery policy is a most rapid approach to the stationary solution $\hat{K}$ satisfying (56) (assuming its existence). Which part of the maximum principle signals this? It is essentially the condition characterizing the investment level at time t as being the value which maximizes the Hamiltonian at that time. The Hamiltonian here is

$$H = \pi(K(t))[F(K(t)) - I] + p(t)I. \tag{58}$$

If

$$p(t) > \pi(K(t)), \tag{59}$$

then it means that the indirect value of leaving an extra fish in the sea $p(t)$ exceeds the net direct value of the harvested fish $\pi(K(t))$, and the Hamiltonian (58) will be maximized when investment is set at its highest possible value— that is, harvesting is set at its lowest possible value. Thus, $p(t) > \pi(K(t))$ is the signal to harvest fish at the lowest possible rate.

If

$$p(t) < \pi(K(t)), \tag{60}$$

then it means that the direct value of one more harvested fish $\pi(K(t))$ exceeds the indirect value of leaving the fish in the sea $p(t)$, and the Hamiltonian (58) will be maximized when investment is set at its lowest possible value. Thus $p(t) < \pi(K(t))$ is the signal to harvest fish at the highest possible rate. The signal to harvest fish at the stationary-state level $h = F(\hat{K})$ is that the shadow price on the value of leaving a fish unharvested is $\hat{p} = \pi(\hat{K})$. If the fishery managers established a landing fee of $\hat{p} = \pi(\hat{K})$, but otherwise left the fishermen alone, such a policy would automatically induce the same optimal path as if the fishery were directed by a profit-maximizing sole owner.

We have presented our economist's approach to optimal fishery management as the solution to an optimal control problem. Let us now briefly consider what corresponds to the most rapidly approached stationary solution for some other models of fishery management.

The simplest model of fishery management is laissez-faire. If the fishery were managed as unregulated common property, then free access would induce fishermen to enter whenever unit harvesting profitability was positive and to exit whenever unit harvesting profitability was negative. At the equilibrium free-access number of fishermen, when no one chooses to enter or exit, profitability can be neither positive nor negative. The free-access equilibrium population $\underline{K}$ therefore satisfies

$$\pi(\underline{K}) = 0. \tag{61}$$

(If $\pi(0) > 0$, then the fish population is driven to extinction under common-property free access and $\underline{K} = 0$.)

Of course, historically several other principles have been proposed as guidance for fisheries management. Maximum sustainable biological yield, which is sometimes recommended, is attained at a population K_s that maximizes $F(K)$, thereby satisfying the condition

$$F(K_s) = \max_{K} F(K). \tag{62}$$

This concept of maximum sustainable yield may (or may not) have some biological motivation, but it is inadequate as an economic criterion because it takes no account whatsoever of harvesting costs, fish values, or interest rates. The maximum sustainable economic rent is an economic generalization of the purely biological principle (62), which attempts to maximize the total sustained economic profits, thereby resulting in fish population $\overline{K}$ satisfying

$$\pi(\overline{K})F(\overline{K}) = \max_{K} \pi(K)F(K). \tag{63}$$

Criterion (63) at least pays some attention to the economic flow of profitability, but is still unsatisfactory to the economist because it seems to disregard altogether any role for the rate at which these flow profits are discounted.

Let us calculate and compare with (61), (62), and (63) the stationary state that comes out of our approach of modeling the fishery as if it were controlled by a sole owner whose goal is to maximize present discounted profits. The best way to make such a comparison, it turns out, is by posing the question: How does the optimal stationary fish population depend on the discount rate?

It is relatively easy to show that an increase in the discount rate ρ causes a decrease in the optimal stationary fish stock $\hat{K}$. If the optimal stationary stock as a function of the discount rate ρ is denoted $\hat{K}(\rho)$, then it follows straightaway from performing comparative statics on (47) and (56) and making use of the underlying convexity-curvature assumptions of the model, that

$$\hat{K}'(\rho) = \frac{1}{R'(\hat{K}(\rho))} < 0. \tag{64}$$

Thus the economically optimal fish population is inversely related to the discount rate, as might have been expected. It is then instructive to examine the form of an optimal stationary state $\hat{K}(\rho)$ for extreme values of ρ. We consider the two limiting cases, $\rho \to 0$ and $\rho \to \infty$.

As $\rho \to 0$, condition (56) becomes

$$\pi(\hat{K}(0))F'(\hat{K}(0)) + \pi'(\hat{K}(0))F(\hat{K}(0)) = 0. \tag{65}$$

We note that (65) is the first-order condition characterizing a solution of the maximization problem (63). We therefore conclude that

$$\hat{K}(0) = \overline{K}. \tag{66}$$

We have derived the important result that a fishery management policy of maximizing sustainable economic yield is equivalent to applying a zero discount rate.

As $\rho \to \infty$, condition (56) can hold with $F'(\hat{K})$ being finite only if $\pi(\hat{K}) \to 0$. Thus

$$\pi(\hat{K}(\infty)) = 0. \tag{67}$$

Comparing (67) with (61), we then conclude that

$$\hat{K}(\infty) = \underline{K}. \tag{68}$$

We have derived the important result that a fishery management policy of uncontrolled free access is equivalent to applying an infinite discount rate.

As we shall see, these two basic principles characterize essentially all situations in natural resource economics. A zero discount rate is equivalent to a policy of maximizing sustainable economic yield (fishermen act as if they are conservationists), while an infinite discount rate is equivalent to a policy indistinguishable from what would happen if the natural resource were managed by treating it as common property with free access (fishermen act as if there were "no tomorrow").

Our solution of the optimal fish harvesting problem therefore contains as two polar cases the most conservative management policy (maximizing sustainable economic rent) and the least conservative management policy (free access to common property). The optimal management policy for positive discount rates is thus in between these two extremes—another general theme we will see repeated throughout natural resource economics.

The generality of this set of repeating themes in natural resource economics stems from a commonly shared structure. Consider the structure of *any* problem of the most rapid approach type, whose gain function is linear in investment (that is, $G(K, I) = A(K) + B(K)I$). Then setting the stationary rate of return equal to ρ defines the stationary-optimal capital stock as the implicit solution of the equation

$$\rho = \frac{A'(\hat{K}(\rho))}{-B(\hat{K}(\rho))}. \tag{69}$$

Thus, when $\rho \to 0$, condition (69) becomes

$$A'(\hat{K}(0)) = 0, \tag{70}$$

which always has the interpretation of being a management policy of maximizing sustainable economic yield.

When $\rho \to \infty$, condition (69) becomes

$$B(\hat{K}(\infty)) = 0, \tag{71}$$

which always has the interpretation of being a management policy of uncontrolled free access.

As a brief aside, and without yet getting involved in the details, we can intuit what would happen in the fishery model if we were to introduce a utility or revenue function that is nonlinear in the fish harvest—or if there are nonlinear adjustment costs to changing harvest levels. The stationary-state analysis will remain entirely relevant, because we will never voluntarily want to rest in a stationary position where $R(K) \neq \rho$. The only difference is that the approach to the relevant stationary state will be slower—in proportion to the degree of curvature of the utility or adjustment functions.

Suppose that, besides yielding economic value through harvesting, the stock of a natural resource also gives direct utility in the form of an amenity value. (For example, people may like to view the natural resource, or they may just feel more satisfied knowing that more of it exists, or the natural resource stock may provide some vital ecosystem services.) Given an "amenity value function" $\varphi(K)$, the reader should be able to show that the optimal policy for managing a fishery with amenity value is still the most rapid approach to a stationary state, with the only difference here being that the equation characterizing the stationary stock $\hat{K}$ now includes a term to account for the amenity value. A good exercise is to derive the condition characterizing the stationary stock when there is economic *and* amenity value, and to analyze exactly how this optimal stock level $\hat{K}$ is influenced by the amenity value function $\varphi(K)$.

SOLUTION OF PROBLEM 7: OPTIMAL TREE HARVESTING
Another model whose gain function is linear in investment is the optimal tree harvesting model (problem 7). This model can be posed and solved directly, without invoking optimal control theory—so a formulation in terms of optimal control theory serves more to enrich an intuitive understanding of the maximum principle (as capital theory) than to serve as a mechanism for actually solving a problem that could not otherwise be solved.

Suppose that, when it is cut down and brought to market, a tree of age T yields a net value given by the function

$$F(T). \tag{72}$$

Frequently in the forestry literature, $F(T)$ is specified in the form

$$F(T) = Pf(T) - c + v, \tag{73}$$

where P is the given market price of wood and the function $f(T)$ is (in forestry terminology) the "merchantable volume" of wood yielded by a tree of age T. The parameter c represents the total economic cost of cutting down the tree, processing it for sale, and bringing the wood to market. (In the forestry literature, the expression $Pf(T) - c$ is called the *net stumpage value* of the tree.) The parameter v stands for the *opportunity value* (in lumbering terminology the *land expectation* or *site value*) of the land being freed for its best subsequent economic use after the tree is felled—which "best subsequent economic use" might well be the replanting of a seedling to start the tree-growing cycle anew.

The famous Wicksell problem of capital theory is to choose the time of cutting T to

$$\text{maximize} \quad e^{-\rho T} F(T). \tag{74}$$

It might seem perverse to force such a direct statement as (74) into the seemingly more arcane form of an optimal control problem. However an optimal control formulation will serve to reinforce economic intuition and to highlight quite dramatically the underlying unity of all time-and-capital problems.

In the optimal control version of the Wicksell problem, the "capital stock" is the age of the tree (more precisely, it is the tree of that age). The corresponding act of "investment" here means allowing the tree to grow older by a year.

Suppose we fancifully imagined that "the forest" could be continuously harvested in the spirit of "the fishery." For this artificial fishery-like forest, the harvest-flow generalization of the Wicksell problem in capital theory is to control the investment rate $\{I(t)\}$ to

$$\text{maximize} \quad \int_0^\infty \rho F(K(t))[1 - I(t)]e^{-\rho t} \, dt \tag{75}$$

subject to

$$\dot{K}(t) = I(t), \tag{76}$$

and

$$0 \le I(t) \le 1, \tag{77}$$

and with the given initial condition

$$K(0) = 0. \tag{78}$$

The original Wicksell formulation in effect limits the investment $I(t)$ to be a step function, which takes on value one when the tree is growing (or until it is cut), and takes on value zero thereafter. As we shall see, the above harvest-flow generalization yields the Wicksell solution anyway. For now it suffices to note that the Wicksell problem is a special case of (75)–(78); therefore, if the optimal solution of (75)–(78) is a step function, as will turn out to be the case, then it must also represent the solution of the more restricted Wicksell problem (74).

It is useful to pose the Wicksell model formally as an optimal control model of capital accumulation, because it highlights the underlying connection between growth and aging processes where capital is time (aging of wine is another well-known example) and the bulk of all other capital-theoretic models that can be formulated as simple optimal control problems where capital is not time. Posing the problem this way allows us to see rigorously what we otherwise can only intuit in models of tree cutting, wine aging, animal raising, and many other problems of growth and aging—the important idea that in many situations age is capital, but that otherwise the same general principles of capital theory apply.

So, for this Wicksell problem, let us identify "capital" with "age." Applying the definition (6), the stationary rate of return on capital in the optimal tree harvesting problem is

$$R(K) = \frac{F'(K)}{F(K)}. \tag{79}$$

From the general consideration that the gain function of the Wicksell problem is linear in investment, we know that the optimal solution involves a most rapid approach to the stationary state $\hat{K}$ where $R(\hat{K}) = \rho$, which by (79) is equivalent to the condition

$$\frac{F'(\hat{K})}{F(\hat{K})} = \rho. \tag{80}$$

Let us see what is happening specifically in this particular optimal control problem. The Hamiltonian here is

$$H = \rho F(K)[1 - I] + pI, \tag{81}$$

where p stands for the marginal value of letting a tree of age K grow for one more year.

The next step is to calculate the maximum value of the Hamiltonian over all feasible values of I. This part is easy because we are maximizing a linear function over the unit interval. With $\tilde{I}(p)$ denoting the Hamiltonian-maximizing value of investment as a function of its price, from (81) there are three possibilities:

$$p > \rho F(K) \Rightarrow \tilde{I}(p) = 1 \Rightarrow \tilde{H}(K, p) = p, \tag{82}$$

or

$$p < \rho F(K) \Rightarrow \tilde{I}(p) = 0 \Rightarrow \tilde{H}(K, p) = \rho F(K), \tag{83}$$

or, the case of an indeterminate solution where $\tilde{I}(p)$ can be any feasible value,

$$p = \rho F(K) \Rightarrow 0 \le \tilde{I}(p) \le 1 \Rightarrow \tilde{H}(K, p) = \rho F(K). \tag{84}$$

A most rapid approach to $\hat{K}$ from below must mean maximal possible investment. It is now not difficult to guess at the form of an optimal policy. Combining (79) and (80) with (82), an intuitive chain of reasoning is that

$$K < \hat{K} \Leftrightarrow \frac{F'(K)}{F(K)} > \rho \Rightarrow p > \rho F(K) \Rightarrow \tilde{I}(p)$$
$$= 1 \Rightarrow \tilde{H}(K, p) = p, \tag{85}$$

in which case we have

$$-\frac{\partial \tilde{H}}{\partial K} = 0, \tag{86}$$

and therefore condition [#2] here becomes

$$\dot{p}(t) = \rho p(t), \tag{87}$$

with the "terminal condition"

$$p(\hat{K}) = \rho F(\hat{K}) = F'(\hat{K}). \tag{88}$$

Combining (87) with (88) yields

$$p(t) = \rho F(\hat{K})e^{\rho(t-\hat{K})}. \tag{89}$$

By the optimality of $\hat{K}$ for the problem (74), we must then have for $K(t) < \hat{K}$ that

$$F(K(t))e^{-\rho t} < F(\hat{K})e^{-\rho \hat{K}}. \tag{90}$$

Combining (90) with (89), we obtain the basic result that for $K(t) < \hat{K}$

$$p(t) > \rho F(K(t)). \tag{91}$$

From (91) we can say that the signal *not* to cut down the tree is that the shadow indirect value of allowing the tree to grow exceeds the direct value of harvesting it. (It is never optimal to allow a tree to grow to an age T where $F'(T)/F(T) < \rho$, but if we acquired such an "economically overripe tree" that had $T > \hat{K}$ from a non–profit-maximizing owner, the signal to cut it down immediately would be that the shadow indirect value of allowing the tree to grow was less than the direct value of harvesting it.)

We now make some important observations about the role of the hitherto obscure parameter v, which stands for the *opportunity value* of the land being freed for its best subsequent economic use after the tree is felled. Suppose that, instead of being concerned about the fate of an individual tree, which is the Wicksell problem, we are interested in the infinite-horizon optimal rotation of a one-tree lot (or, more realistically, of a woodlot consisting of a stand of cohort trees). In this case, the opportunity value v of the land being freed for its best subsequent economic use after the tree is felled is the present discounted value of a infinite-horizon rotation policy that begins with the replanting of a seedling to start the tree-growing cycle anew.

Suppose the parameter c now includes all costs of replanting (as well as logging, processing, and transportation costs). In the optimal rotation problem, we are analyzing the most profitable sequence of harvesting and replanting times over an infinite horizon. We assume that, in the underlying specification (73), the parameters P, c, and ρ, and the function $f(T)$ are unchanging over all future time. (The parameter v in (73) will be endogenously determined, as we are about to show.) In this kind of stationary environment, the future always looks the same at every instant just after a woodlot has been cut and replanted, irrespective of the calendar time when this operation is done. Suppose we are now at such a time instant, just after the woodlot has been cut and replanted. If we decide now that it is optimal to plan on the seedling growing to age T^*, at which time we harvest it and replant, then we will henceforth always decide in like instants just after cutting and replanting that it is optimal to allow a seedling to grow to age T^*—because the future looks the same from all such instants, and hence the optimal planned lifetime of the tree is the same.

Let T be some rotation period. Suppose the competitive market value of the land (in forestry terminology the land expectation or the site value), right after it has been cut and replanted, is v. The famous *Faustmann model* of optimal forest rotation states that the site value is the solution to the problem of maximizing present discounted profits:

$$v = \underset{T}{\text{maximum}} \quad [Pf(T) - c][e^{-\rho T} + e^{-\rho 2T} \\ + e^{-\rho 3T} + e^{-\rho 4T} + \ldots]. \tag{92}$$

Substituting the appropriate expression for the sum of the infinite geometric series within the square brackets, we can rewrite (92) in the equivalent form

$$v = \underset{T}{\text{maximum}} \quad \frac{[Pf(T) - c]e^{-\rho T}}{1 - e^{-\rho T}}. \tag{93}$$

Let the optimal Faustmann rotation period be K^*. From setting the derivative of the maximand of (93) equal to zero, we derive the first-order condition

$$Pf'(K^*) = \frac{\rho[Pf(K^*) - c]}{1 - e^{-\rho K^*}}. \tag{94}$$

Equation (94) is the famous *Faustmann formula* for the optimal rotation period K^*.

After some algebraic manipulation, (94) can be combined with (93) to yield the following expression for the maximized site value:

$$v = \frac{Pf'(K^*)}{\rho} - Pf(K^*) + c. \tag{95}$$

We are now interested to compare the solution of the Faustmann problem with the solution of the Wicksell problem. Plugging formula (73) into the Wicksell condition (80), we derive that the Wicksell harvesting time $\hat{K}$ satisfies the condition

$$\frac{Pf'(\hat{K})}{\rho} - Pf(\hat{K}) + c = v. \tag{96}$$

Furthermore, $\hat{K}$ is the unique solution of (96) because of the concavity-curvature condition $f'' < 0$.

Let us now make the very natural assumption that the site value v in the Wicksell solution (96) is competitively determined by formula (95). Comparing (95) with (96), we have at once that $\hat{K} = K^*$, because both $\hat{K}$ and K^* are unique solutions of the same equation.

In the forestry literature, the Faustmann model and the Faustmann formula are typically contrasted with the Wicksell model and the Wicksell formula. In a serious sense, this is a false dichotomy. The Wicksell model ostensibly takes the site value as exogenously given, often as zero, although there is evidence that Wicksell himself understood that it would be fallacious to perform comparative statics when treating v as if it were constant.[1] The Faustmann and Wicksell models are identical when proper account is taken of the market site value of forest land. The two models represent two equivalent ways of looking at optimal forestry management. The Wicksell approach emphasizes how to think about harvesting an individual tree. The Faustmann approach emphasizes how to think about the harvesting cycle of an ongoing stand of trees. As long as the opportunity value of the woodlot is properly assessed and included, both models yield identical conclusions. It is essentially a case of looking at two sides of a single problem that more properly should be called the *Faustmann-Wicksell model* of forestry management.

In what follows, we use the symbols $\hat{K}$ and K^* interchangeably—and symbolize both by $\hat{K}$—since they are the same when both are embedded within a properly specified model where v is endogenously determined by (94),(95). Doing comparative statics on the Faustmann-Wicksell formula (95), it is relatively easy to show that an increase in the discount rate ρ (or in the price-cost ratio P/c) causes a decrease in the optimal rotation age. Thus if the optimal age as a function of the discount rate ρ is denoted $\hat{K}(\rho)$, then it follows straightaway from performing comparative statics on (95), with $\hat{K}(\rho) \equiv K^*(\rho)$, and making use of the underlying convexity-curvature assumptions of the model, that

$$\hat{K}'(\rho) < 0, \tag{97}$$

whose meaning should be economically intuitive.

---

1. See the interesting historical discussion in Löfgren (1999).

It is instructive to examine the form of an optimal forestry policy for extreme values of ρ. We consider the two limiting cases, $\rho \to 0$ and $\rho \to \infty$. In the limit as $\rho \to 0$, the Faustmann-Wicksell condition (94) becomes

$$\frac{Pf'(\hat{K}(0))}{Pf(\hat{K}(0)) - c} = \lim_{\rho \to 0} \frac{\rho}{1 - e^{-\rho \hat{K}(0)}}. \tag{98}$$

Using l'Hôpital's rule to evaluate the right-hand limit yields

$$\lim_{\rho \to 0} \frac{\rho}{1 - e^{-\rho \hat{K}(0)}} = \frac{1}{\hat{K}(0)}, \tag{99}$$

so that (98) implies

$$Pf'(\hat{K}(0)) = \frac{Pf(\hat{K}(0)) - c}{\hat{K}(0)}. \tag{100}$$

Now, it is readily confirmed that equation (100) is precisely the first-order condition for the problem of maximizing over all K the average profit per unit of time

$$\frac{Pf(K) - c}{K}. \tag{101}$$

We have therefore derived the important result that a forestry management policy of maximizing average sustainable economic yield is equivalent to applying a zero discount rate.

As $\rho \to \infty$, the Faustmann-Wicksell condition (94) can hold only if $Pf(\hat{K}) \to c$. Thus $\hat{K}(\infty)$ must satisfy the condition

$$Pf(\hat{K}(\infty)) = c. \tag{102}$$

But equation (102) is describing the outcome of competitive free access to a tree lot that no one owns. As soon as the net stumpage value of harvesting the tree rises to just above zero, every itinerant forester is eager to cut down the tree and take the profits. (Note from (93) that with $\rho \to \infty$ the site value v becomes worthless.) We have thus derived the basic result that a forestry policy of uncontrolled free access is equivalent to applying an infinite discount rate.

These results in forestry management parallel the analogous results in fishery management. Actually, the above two basic principles apply to virtually all situations in natural resource economics. A zero discount rate is equivalent to a policy of maximizing average sustainable economic yield, while an infinite discount rate is equivalent to a policy indistinguishable from what would happen if the natural resource were managed by treating it as common property with free access.

Our solution of the optimal forestry management problem therefore contains as two polar cases the most conservative management policy (maximizing average sustainable economic return, which means foresters act like conservationists) and the least conservative management policy (free access to common property, which means foresters act as if there were "no tomorrow"). The optimal management policy for positive discount rates is in between these two extremes—again a general theme we are seeing repeated throughout natural resource economics.

Finally, let us analyze for the Faustmann-Wicksell model the meaning of the "wealth and income" form of the maximum principle. Applying (82) and (89) to condition [#4], we obtain the equation

$$\rho V(T) = \rho F(\hat{K})e^{\rho(T-\hat{K})}, \tag{103}$$

which must hold for all ages T of the tree satisfying $0 < T < \hat{K}$. Plugging (73) and (93) into (103), we obtain the equation

$$V(T) = ve^{\rho T}, \tag{104}$$

holding for all ages T of the tree satisfying $0 < T < \hat{K}$.

Equation (104) informs us of the competitive *stock market price* (per tree) of a site with a tree of age T, where $0 < T < \hat{K}$. Note the inherent sawtooth pattern over time of (104) as the stock market value rises continuously from v for just-planted seedlings to $ve^{\rho \hat{K}}$ for trees just about to be harvested, and then crashes discontinuously down to v again just after the cutting and replanting. Note too that the stock market price of a one-tree woodlot just before harvesting, $ve^{\rho \hat{K}}$, equals the price just after harvesting, v, plus the dividend (per marketed tree) of net stumpage value $Pf(\hat{K}) - c$ because, from (93),

$$[e^{\rho \hat{K}} - 1]v = Pf(\hat{K}) - c. \tag{105}$$

The wealth and income version of the maximum principle here is telling us that the optimal Faustmann-Wicksell forestry policy is equivalent to the sawtooth competitive stock market trajectory (104), with the interpretation (105) that the price of the forest just before cutting must equal the ex dividend price of the share, plus the amount of the cut-tree dividend. Thus the general theme is again manifested—to solve the Faustmann-Wicksell model is to comprehend how the model would behave in a competitive stock market. If a forester understands well the competitive-equilibrium relationship between site value and net stumpage value, that forester understands well the solution of the Faustmann-Wicksell model.

By way of making a transition here to the next model to be analyzed, the Faustmann-Wicksell formulation neglects or shunts aside at least one important real-world consideration. Underexploitation of forests can easily be rectified, but overexploitation may not be reversible for decades or even centuries. This feature would not matter if we lived in a world of perfect certainty, where we never made mistakes or came to regret our actions—but of course we do not live in such a world. The next problem to be analyzed addresses this type of one-sided irreversibility, which seems to characterize many resource-management situations.

SOLUTION OF PROBLEM 10: IRREVERSIBLE INVESTMENT

In Chapter 2, the final model formulated was called the "irreversible investment problem." Without going over all of the notation again here, the relevant gain function for this problem is

$$
\begin{aligned}
G(K, I) \equiv \gamma K + \beta(F_0 - K) + cI \\
+ b\theta \Phi_b(K) + (1 - b)\theta \Phi_g(K),
\end{aligned}
\tag{106}
$$

where

$$
\Phi_b(K) \equiv \frac{\alpha K + \beta(F_0 - K)}{r},
\tag{107}
$$

and

$$
\Phi_g(K) \equiv \int_0^{K/\overline{C}} [\gamma(K - \overline{C}s) + \beta(F_0 - K + \overline{C}s) - c\overline{C}]e^{-rs}ds
\tag{108}
$$

$$
+ e^{-rK/\overline{C}}\frac{\beta F_0}{r}.
$$

Recall that $\overline{C}$ stands for the maximal rate at which the forest can be cut down and developed. It does not at all destroy the spirit of the problem to make $\overline{C}$ be very big—quite the opposite, since we are concentrating on the irreversibility aspect, which becomes, if anything, sharper for large $\overline{C}$. In the limiting case as $\overline{C}$ is made indefinitely large, expression (108) becomes

$$
\lim_{\overline{C} \to \infty} [\int_0^{K/\overline{C}} [\gamma(K - \overline{C}s) + \beta(F_0 - K + \overline{C}s) - c\overline{C}]e^{-rs}\, ds
$$
$$
+ e^{-rK/\overline{C}}\frac{\beta F_0}{r}] = \frac{\beta F_0}{r} - cK,
$$

(109)

and the gain function (106) becomes, after rearranging terms,

$$
G(K, I) = [\gamma - \beta + \frac{b\theta}{r}(\alpha - \beta) - (1 - b)\theta c]K
$$
$$
+ cI + \beta F_0(1 + \frac{\theta}{r}).
$$

(110)

Problem 10 started off looking incredibly complicated, but has now become incredibly simple. Not only is the gain function linear in I, with a constant coefficient, but it is also linear in K as well. The stationary rate of return on capital with the gain function (110) is

$$
R(K) \equiv \frac{\gamma - \beta + \dfrac{b\theta}{r}(\alpha - \beta) - (1 - b)\theta c}{-c},
$$

(111)

which, being a constant, is independent of K.

As we now know from the general theory of a gain function that is linear in investment, the optimal policy is a most rapid approach. In this problem there is not a stationary solution, since (111) is either greater or less than ρ for all K (except with probability-measure zero). The MRA goes here to a blocked investment state—either the smallest possible value of K, that is, the corner solution $K = 0$ (cut down the forest as soon as possible), or the largest possible value of K, that is, the corner solution $K = F_0$ (leave the forest intact, at least until news of global warming is received). Using the by now standard criterion about the relation of $R(K)$ to ρ, from (111) it is optimal to remain at the blocked initial position $K = F_0$ by retaining intact the entire forest (until good news is obtained) if

$$\rho < \frac{\gamma - \beta + \frac{b\theta}{r}(\alpha - \beta) - (1 - b)\theta c}{-c}, \qquad (112)$$

while it is optimal to cut down and develop the forest as rapidly as possible (MRA to $K = 0$) if

$$\rho > \frac{\gamma - \beta + \frac{b\theta}{r}(\alpha - \beta) - (1 - b)\theta c}{-c}. \qquad (113)$$

Remembering that in this problem $\rho \equiv r + \theta$ and $w \equiv 1/\theta$, from rearranging (113) we derive that the optimality criterion for cutting down and developing the forest immediately is

$$\frac{b[\alpha - (\beta - rc)]}{(1 - b)[(\beta - rc) - \gamma]} < \frac{wr}{1 - b}. \qquad (114)$$

Otherwise (if (114) does not hold) it is optimal to preserve the forest until such time as good news about global warming might arrive.

Let us call (114) the "irreversible investment criterion" (for this problem). The theory of irreversible investments has significant implications for economics generally and for environmental and natural resource economics particularly. In this context it is important to understand how and why the irreversible investment criterion differs from more standard investment criteria.

If the act of cutting down the forest were completely reversible, then the optimal policy would be to cut it down immediately (because $(\beta - rc) > \gamma$), and later, if and when bad news about global warming arrived, to restore it immediately (because $\alpha > (\beta - rc)$).

The more interesting comparison is between the irreversible investment criterion (114) (which takes account of the option value of waiting) and the standard benefit-cost investment criterion (which ignores the option value of waiting).

If the forest is cut down and developed immediately, the present discounted gain (per hectare) is

$$\frac{\beta - rc}{r}. \qquad (115)$$

If the forest is left intact forever, the expected present discounted gain (per hectare) is

$$
\int_0^\infty [[\int_0^t \gamma e^{-rs} ds + b \int_t^\infty \alpha e^{-rs} ds
$$

$$
\tag{116}
$$

$$
+ (1-b) \int_t^\infty \gamma e^{-rs} ds] \theta e^{-\theta t} \, dt,
$$

which by straightforward evaluation of the integrals reduces to

$$
\frac{\theta}{r} [\frac{\gamma}{\theta} + \frac{b(\alpha - \gamma)}{r + \theta}].
\tag{117}
$$

Thus it is better to cut and develop the forest immediately rather than leave it standing forever if (115) exceeds (117), that is, if

$$
\frac{\beta - rc}{r} > \frac{\theta}{r} [\frac{\gamma}{\theta} + \frac{b(\alpha - \gamma)}{r + \theta}].
\tag{118}
$$

Some algebraic manipulation confirms that condition (118) can be rewritten in the equivalent form

$$
\frac{b[\alpha - (\beta - rc)]}{(1-b)[(\beta - rc) - \gamma]} < 1 + \frac{wr}{1-b}.
\tag{119}
$$

Thus the standard benefit-cost investment criterion tells us it is optimal to cut down now and develop immediately the forest if condition (119) holds. Our task here is to compare the two investment criteria (114) and (119).

The left-hand side of both expressions (114) and (119) is the same ratio of the probability-weighted comparative advantage of having a forest with no development if there *is* global warming divided by the probability-weighted comparative advantage of having development with no forest if there is *not* global warming. Other things being equal, a high value of this ratio of expected comparative advantages favors preserving the forest in *both* situations. The identical role being played by this same ratio of expected net benefits in the left-hand side of both inequalities (114) and (119) should be intuitively clear.

On the other side of the inequality, the first thing to notice is that the right-hand side of (119) is always larger than the right-hand side of (114). Thus the irreversible investment criterion for cutting down immediately is

stricter than the standard benefit-cost investment criterion. The positive difference between the right-hand side of (119) and the right-hand side of
(114) is expressing a "real option value" of being able to wait before making an irreversible decision. Note that the mere fact that investment is irreversible does not necessarily mean that not investing is optimal. A project
may well pass the irreversible investment criterion (114)—it just represents
a higher threshold or hurdle than the standard benefit-cost investment criterion (119).

The most dramatic way to get a sense of the difference between the two
investment criteria is to consider the extreme case where the average waiting
time until news about global warming arrives, the parameter w, is very small.
Setting $w = 0$ in (114), the irreversible investment criterion tells us *always*
to wait until news arrives before doing any cutting. Setting $w = 0$ in (119),
the standard benefit-cost investment criterion tells us to cut down the forest
immediately if

$$b[\alpha - (\beta - rc)] < (1 - b)[(\beta - rc) - \gamma], \tag{120}$$

that is, if the expected net benefits of preserving the forest are less than the
expected net benefits of cutting down the forest. Suppose, as is not unreasonable for some situations, that condition (120) holds very strongly, meaning the
right-hand side of the inequality is much bigger than the left-hand side. Then
we have a seemingly paradoxical situation where the standard benefit-cost criterion is telling us very strongly to cut down the forest immediately, while the
irreversible investment criterion (114) is telling us equally strongly to let the
forest stand.

The resolution of the seeming paradox lies in the opportunity cost of information gathering. The decisive factor in inducing us to delay cutting is that
the opportunity cost of obtaining the relevant information is very low, since
we do not expect to have to wait long for the decisive news to arrive. The expected net benefits of preserving the forest may be much less than the expected
net benefits of cutting down the forest, and it may be highly likely that we will
end up cutting down the forest anyway (because b is small)—and yet, if the
expected waiting time is sufficiently small, it still will always pay to wait a little
bit of time to make sure we are doing the right thing.

Another way to see vividly the role of information gathering is to consider
the extreme case $b = 1$, which means that it is not a question of whether or
not we will be having global warming, but that it is only a question of when

it will arrive. In this limiting case $b = 1$, the irreversible investment criterion (114) is identical to the standard benefit-cost investment criterion (119). (The way to see this is first to cancel out the term $(1 - b)$ from the denominators of both sides before going to the limit.) The reason that both criteria coincide here is that waiting does not help us to resolve which state of the world will be relevant, since we already know that information. In this case nothing is lost by treating the situation as if we must decide today whether or not to cut the forest, and both criteria tell us to cut the forest today if and only if

$$[\alpha - (\beta - rc)] < wr[(\beta - rc) - \gamma], \tag{121}$$

which can be interpreted as saying that the expected net benefits of preserving the forest in this case ($b = 1$) are less than the expected net benefits of cutting down the forest. Any difference between the irreversible investment criterion (114) and the standard benefit-cost criterion (119) can arise only if there is some informational gain from waiting—that is, only if $b < 1$.

Turning to yet another extreme case, we ask, What happens in the limit if the expected waiting time for the news—the parameter w—is very large? Inspecting formulas (114) and (119), we see that the irreversible investment criterion and the standard benefit-cost investment criterion are identical in the case where w is indefinitely large, and both are telling us to cut down the forest now. This should be intuitively obvious—if global warming is indefinitely remote, in the limit (with positive discounting) we should proceed as if it is not going to occur, which always favors immediate development because of the postulated higher net benefits. An analogous extreme case with identical consequences, for similar reasons, is when the probability of global warming—the parameter b—is infinitesimally small.

A final interesting pair of extreme cases concerns what happens when the discount rate is forced to assume each of its two extreme values. To simplify the analysis, we henceforth suppose $c = 0$ (thereby eliminating the complication of keeping stock and flow costs comparable). Then in the limit as $r \to \infty$, the investment criteria (114) and (119) both tell us to cut the forest down and develop the site immediately (because we care only about the immediate benefits). In the limit as $r \to 0$, the irreversible investment criterion (114) tells us always to wait (because we care here mostly about the limiting benefits, which we can only ascertain by waiting to find out whether or not global warming will occur). By contrast, note that as $r \to 0$ the standard benefit-cost criterion (120) would (incorrectly) have us decide now solely on the basis of whether expected long-run benefits under preservation $(1 - b)\gamma + b\alpha$ are greater or less than long-run benefits under development β.

The analysis of Problem 10 has involved many algebraic manipulations, which is typical of irreversible investment problems. The algebra of irreversible investments is not always easy, but the subject is important for environmental economics and other applications of "real options theory." This concludes our discussion of irreversible investment, and with it our application of most rapid approach policies.

Nonlinear Problems

The remainder of the examples involve situations where the gain functions are not linear in investment, and hence a most rapid approach policy is not optimal. As we will see clearly, however, a previous knowledge of the MRA case will serve us very well as a point of departure for understanding what is optimal policy in the more general nonlinear case.

SOLUTION OF PROBLEM 2: THE q-THEORY MODEL OF INVESTMENT
The first nonlinear (in investment) model to be analyzed here is the q-theory of investment model. In its simplest form, the optimal control problem that forms the backbone of the q-theory of investment is to

$$\text{maximize} \quad \int_0^\infty [F(K(t)) - I(t) - \varphi(I(t))]e^{-\rho t} \, dt \qquad (122)$$

subject to

$$\dot{K}(t) = I(t), \qquad (123)$$

and with the given initial condition

$$K(0) = K_0. \qquad (124)$$

If we go back to our simplest optimal control model, the family firm problem, then the q-theory of investment model essentially differs just by having a nonlinear cost of adjustment $\varphi(I)$, where $\varphi(0) = \varphi'(0) = 0$ and $\varphi'' > 0$. The stationary rate of return for the q-theory of investment model is

$$R(K) = F'(K), \tag{125}$$

which is the same as for the family firm, so we know that the direction of investment depends here too on the sign of $[F'(K) - \rho]$. In a sense, the q-theory of investment model would also like to get to the stationary state quickly, but if the capital stock changes too quickly a significant adjustment cost must be paid—and therefore some balanced moderation is required.

With p representing the marginal value of a unit of capital to the firm, the Hamiltonian here is

$$H = F(K) - I - \varphi(I) + pI. \tag{126}$$

Maximizing the Hamiltonian over the control variable I obtains the interior solution

$$\varphi'(I^*(t)) = p(t) - 1, \tag{127}$$

while the differential equation of motion of the co-state variable here is

$$\dot{p}(t) = \rho p(t) - F'(K^*(t)). \tag{128}$$

In the investment literature, equation (128) is often rewritten in the directly interpretable integrated solution form

$$p(t) = \int_t^\infty e^{-\rho(s-t)} F'(K^*(s))\, ds, \tag{129}$$

which represents the worth to the firm now of an extra unit of capital as the present discounted value of the increase in future output that the extra unit provides.

From (127), in order to make the correct investment decision at time t the firm does not need to know anything more about the future other than the information that is summarized in $p(t)$. In this model, $p(t)$, which represents the internal accounting value to the firm of an extra unit of capital or investment, is a "sufficient statistic" for the firm's investment decision.

The external purchase price of capital here is unity, with the difference between internal value of capital and external purchase price, by (127), being the marginal adjustment cost. The marginal value of an extra unit of capital differs from one because, with a gift of capital, no adjustment costs need be paid.

The ratio of the value to the firm of an extra unit of capital divided by its replacement cost—denoted p in this model—is known as *Tobin's q*. The q-theory model is used extensively throughout economics, especially in the macroeconomic investment literature. It provides an important link between a firm's investment behavior and its stock market value, because if shares in the firm are competitively traded then it is intuitive, at least qualitatively, that there must be some positive relation between the internal value of capital to the firm and the stock market price of its shares. But what is the exact quantitative relationship?

The empirical literature on Tobin's q is bedeviled by the fact that what is relevant to the firm's investment at any time t is *marginal q*—because $p(t) = V'(K^*(t))$—while what is observable at time t is the firm's stock market valuation $V(K^*(t))$. The empirical problem is that an observer is typically quite unsure about the relationship of $V'(K^*(t))$ to $V(K^*(t))$. We now show, however, that we can quantify this relationship in an operationally meaningful way by using the wealth and income version of the maximum principle.

Condition [#4] applied to this problem is

$$\rho V(K^*(t)) = F(K^*(t)) - I^*(t) - \varphi(I^*(t)) + p(t)I^*(t), \qquad (130)$$

which can be used to measure Tobin's q empirically as follows.

Define the *yield discrepancy* between the firm's net cash flow at time t and what a risk-equivalent bond would pay as

$$\Delta(t) \equiv \rho V(K^*(t)) - [F(K^*(t)) - I^*(t) - \varphi(I^*(t))]. \qquad (131)$$

Using definition (131), equation (130) can be rewritten as

$$p(t) = \frac{\Delta(t)}{I^*(t)}. \qquad (132)$$

Tobin's *marginal q* (that is, our p), which is the price-like signal relevant for investment theory, is not directly observable. But formula (132) allows us to infer that it should be equal to the firm's "yield discrepancy," divided by the amount of investment, all of which are, in principle, observable. Thus the wealth and income version informs us that, at least in theory, the firm's internal accounting price of capital is exactly its yield discrepancy per dollar of investment.

Our primary interest here in the q-theory model is not to exposit a new measurement tool for empirical work, but rather to indicate what the introduction of adjustment costs does to the investment behavior of what would otherwise be a MRA model, like the family firm or the fishery. With adjustment costs, the model still wants to get to its stationary state, only now an optimal policy typically approaches the stationary state gradually and asymptotically rather than crashing into it by a "bang-bang" most rapid approach. That is to say, the presence of adjustment costs acts to smooth investment behavior over time, but does not otherwise alter the fact that the model goes to its stationary state.

To see clearly what is happening here, let us take a particular functional form. The second-order Taylor-series approximation of the production function around the stationary state $F'(\hat{K}) = \rho$ is

$$F(K) = F(\hat{K}) + \rho(K - \hat{K}) + \frac{F''}{2}(K - \hat{K})^2, \tag{133}$$

where F'' is here treated as a negative constant.

Instead of viewing (133) as a valid local approximation, we will take this quadratic form as a globally accurate description of the production function, which is not a terrible assumption for many practical purposes. We then have the marginal product of capital being the linear function

$$F'(K) = \rho + (K - \hat{K})F''. \tag{134}$$

Suppose the adjustment cost function is also quadratic

$$\varphi(I) = \frac{\alpha}{2}I^2, \tag{135}$$

where α is a parameter measuring the slope of the marginal adjustment cost function. If we combine together into one differential equation (123), (127), (128), (134), and (135), we obtain

$$\alpha\frac{d^2K}{dt^2} = \rho\alpha\frac{dK}{dt} - (K - \hat{K})F''. \tag{136}$$

The only solution of the second-order differential equation (136) that converges to $\hat{K}$ (as an optimal solution must) is of the form

$$K(t) - \hat{K} = (K(0) - \hat{K})e^{-at}, \tag{137}$$

for some positive a, which implies the very simple linear capital stock adjustment equation

$$I^*(t) = a(\hat{K} - K(t)). \tag{138}$$

From plugging (137) into (136), the *adjustment speed coefficient a* satisfies the characteristic quadratic equation

$$\alpha a^2 + \rho\alpha a + F'' = 0. \tag{139}$$

The only positive solution of (139) is

$$a = \sqrt{\left(\frac{\rho}{2}\right)^2 - \frac{F''}{\alpha}} - \frac{\rho}{2}. \tag{140}$$

We could also have derived (140) by applying the general theory of quadratic gain functions developed in the last chapter. The reader should confirm that (140) is a special case of equation (3.163) where $G_{11} = F''$, $G_{22} = -\alpha$, $G_{12} = 0$.

Notice in (140) that, since $F'' < 0$, the speed of adjustment is inversely related to the cost of adjustment. If you think about it, this makes perfectly good sense. The extreme case $\alpha \to 0$ brings us back into the world of most rapid approach, while the other extreme case $\alpha \to \infty$ causes adjustments to be infinitesimally slow. In-between values of α warrant adjustment speeds in between the two extremes.

From (140) it is also apparent that the speed of adjustment is directly related to the curvature of the long-run production function. Again, this is as it should be, since, other things being equal, stronger curvature implies bigger losses from *not* being at the stationary solution. Because we cannot afford to sustain the enormous losses of being out of a stationary state, the extreme case $F'' \to -\infty$ causes us in the limit to go to a most rapid approach policy. The other extreme of approaching a linear production function as $F'' \to 0$ causes adjustments to be infinitesimally slow, because then the comparative role of adjustment costs becomes paramount.

Finally, (140) is telling us that speed of adjustment is inversely related to the discount rate. With the future being highly discounted relative to the present, other things being equal, there is not much sense in sacrificing current output to move more rapidly to a stationary solution, which helps only in the long run. By contrast, other things being equal, with a very low discount rate it is a good idea to give up some current income in favor of raising the flow of income coming in over an indefinite future.

The q-theory of investment model constitutes one class of problems non-linear in investment, because $\varphi'' > 0$ implies

$$G_{22} < 0. \tag{141}$$

The other main source of nonlinearity causing condition (141) to hold is curvature of the revenue or utility functions—as in the neoclassical optimal growth Problem 5. Mathematically, all problems with (141) holding are of the same generic form, and all display generically similar properties. Models featuring (141) approach their stationary states gradually, with the speed of approach dependent on relative curvatures. Thus if the sole owner of the fishery were a monopolist, whose revenue function is the analogue in the fishery setting of a utility function in the optimal growth setting, the optimal policy would be to go to the relevant stationary state, but gradually and asymptotically rather than by crashing into it with a "bang-bang" most rapid approach. In all such models, condition (141) causes optimal behavior to smooth investments over time, but does not otherwise alter the fact that the model goes to its stationary state—that is, where the stationary rate of return on capital equals the discount rate.

SOLUTION OF PROBLEM 4: NEOCLASSICAL OPTIMAL GROWTH

We next analyze the neoclassical optimal growth problem. This famous optimal control problem has an enormous literature, in which it has been examined from many different angles. We will stress here the similarity of the behavior of the optimal neoclassical growth trajectory with the behavior, just analyzed, of the q-theory model of investment. In a sense, both models display less than most rapid approaches to their stationary states because of "costs of adjustment," broadly construed—with the slowness of the approach directly related to the magnitude of these costs of adjustment.

We will not here examine in much detail other aspects of the neoclassical optimal growth model, because in the next chapter we will treat a much more general multisector optimal growth model with any number of heterogeneous investment and consumption goods. As we shall see, the one-sector neoclassical optimal growth model is useful as a prototype forerunner of some basic themes that will emerge in the multisector generalization. As we shall also see, the neoclassical optimal growth model is somewhat misleading, because this extremely special case of a one-good one-sector world with a strictly linear production-possibilities tradeoff between homogeneous consumption and investment obscures a number of very important economic aspects that can only be framed and understood in a context where production possibilities involve *multiple* consumption and investment goods. (In a sense the neoclassical optimal growth model is too simple, because the price of consumption equals the price of investment equals the price of output equals the price of capital, and we do not have to sort out or make sense of a number of important, realistic, and interesting issues involving the meaning and significance of commonly encountered price-quantity aggregates like real investment, real consumption, consumer surplus, or, what is a major focus of attention in this book, national income.)

In the neoclassical optimal growth problem, the direct gain function is of the form

$$G(K, I) = U(F(K) - I),\tag{142}$$

and it is conveniently assumed that the utility function has enough curvature that the upper and lower bounds on investment are not operative and an interior solution always prevails. (The case of corner solutions is readily handled by the maximum principle, but it needlessly obscures the underlying economics.) The stationary rate of return on capital here is

$$R(K) = F'(K).\tag{143}$$

By this point we should have an immediate intuition about the form of an optimal solution. The neoclassical optimal growth solution is drawn toward the stationary state $\hat{K}$, which in the optimal growth literature is called the "modified golden rule," where

$$R(\hat{K}) = F'(\hat{K}) = \rho,\tag{144}$$

but it also wants to go slowly, because of the curvature $U'' < 0$. Without a curved utility function, if $U'' = 0$, then by (142) the gain function becomes linear in investment and the optimal trajectory wants to go to its stationary state as rapidly as possible. On the other hand, if the utility function shows unboundedly strong diminishing returns to consumption, in the presence of any positive discounting at all we will not want to give away even the tiniest bit of consumption this period in favor of having more consumption next period (because it is as if people would starve to death below the current consumption level), which signifies an unboundedly slow approach to the stationary state. Thus we know intuitively beforehand that the speed of approach will depend inversely on the curvature of the utility function.

The Hamiltonian for this problem is

$$H = U(F(K) - I) + pI, \tag{145}$$

and the maximized Hamiltonian is achieved at the investment level $\tilde{I}(K, p)$ satisfying the interior first-order condition

$$U'(F(K) - \tilde{I}(K, p)) = p, \tag{146}$$

which identifies the price p as representing here the marginal utility of consumption. It is then readily confirmed by using the envelope theorem (that is, differentiating (145) and using the first-order condition (146) to cancel terms) that

$$\frac{\partial \tilde{H}}{\partial K} = pF'(K). \tag{147}$$

Condition [#2] of the maximum principle can then be expressed for this model as the equation

$$\dot{p}(t) = -p(t)F'(K^*(t)) + \rho p(t), \tag{148}$$

which may be rewritten as

$$F'(K^*(t)) = -\frac{\dot{p}(t)}{p(t)} + \rho. \tag{149}$$

Define now the *elasticity of marginal utility* with respect to consumption as

$$\eta \equiv -\frac{dU'}{dC}\frac{C}{U'} = -\frac{CU''}{U'}. \tag{150}$$

Viewed as a parameter, η equals the percentage decrease in marginal utility per percentage increase in consumption. It is a measure of the curvature of the utility function, which quantifies how rapidly diminishing returns to consumption set in as consumption levels are increased.

Combining (146) with (150), expression (149) then becomes

$$F' = \eta g + \rho, \tag{151}$$

where

$$g \equiv \frac{\dot{C}}{C} \tag{152}$$

is the growth of consumption along an optimal trajectory.

Equation (151) is a famous relationship of optimal growth theory, because it connects the *real interest rate*, which is just the marginal product of capital, to underlying parameters of tastes and technology. It is critically important to understand that a high real interest rate could be generated by a high rate of pure time preference, or the ability of the economy to grow rapidly, or a high elasticity of marginal utility—or by a combination of all three. The *goods interest rate* F', which corresponds to the real rate of return we see reflected in bond and stock markets (and what is relevant for benefit-cost analysis), is not the same thing as the *utility interest rate* ρ, which, ignoring the growth of population or technological progress, is the not directly observable rate of pure time preference for utility. It is perfectly consistent to have a zero rate of pure time preference ($\rho = 0$) and a positive real interest rate, provided that a dollar of consumption withheld today can be turned into more than a dollar's worth of consumption tomorrow. (This is the case Ramsey focused on in his seminal 1927 optimal growth paper.) As long as capital is productive, the real interest rate will be positive no matter what the rate of pure time preference.

Equation (151) is essentially a compressed way of writing the maximum principle for the highly aggregated economy of the neoclassical one-sector world. What is (151) trying to tell us? Suppose our neoclassical one-sector economy is riding along its optimal trajectory. Now let us perform a natural thought experiment by perturbing consumption in two arbitrarily short adjacent periods separated by time length dt. To begin, we withhold from consumption one unit of the good for this period t and invest it instead. We then ask the following question. How much extra consumption can we enjoy next period, at time $t + dt$, while still maintaining intact the rest of the optimal trajectory? The answer is $F'dt$ units of extra consumption, because if a unit of capital is "on loan" for one period of length dt, then it can produce $F'dt$ units of extra output during that period and still leave as a bequest the same amount of capital for future production. Thus, F' represents the economy's competitive real interest rate expressed in terms of goods.

Because ρ represents the exogenously imposed *rate of pure time preference on utility*, an optimal trajectory must have the property that if one unit of utility was sacrificed this period we should be able to receive back an extra amount of $\rho\,dt$ units of utility next period without altering future utility possibilities. (If this were not true, we could automatically increase the present discounted value of utility by shifting utiles from one period to the other, meaning the original path could not have been optimal.) In the utility thought experiment, when we withhold one unit of consumption this period, we lose U' units of utility this period. So next period we should receive back as compensation the utility amount $U'[1 + \rho dt]$ along an optimal trajectory. In fact, how much utility do we receive back by the goods thought experiment described in the previous paragraph? At time $t + dt$, the marginal utility of consumption will be $[U' + U''\dot{C}dt]$, so we receive back in utiles the amount $[U' + U''\dot{C}dt][1 + F'dt]$. These two equivalent approaches must yield the same extra utility, and so must be equal to each other for very small dt, which means

$$U'[1 + \rho dt] = [U' + U''\dot{C}dt][1 + F'dt]. \tag{153}$$

Condition (153) can hold for all arbitrarily small but positive dt if and only if the equality (151) holds. Thus condition (151) essentially describes as a requirement of optimality that the goods rate of return F' equals the utility rate of return ρ plus the appropriate correction factor for translating from units of utility to units of goods, which is captured by the term ηg.

We know from (143) that the stationary rate of return on capital (K here) is just $F'(K)$. We also know that optimal net investment is positive, negative, or zero, according to the sign of $[F'(K) - \rho]$. Suppose for the sake of argument that $[F'(K) - \rho]$ is positive. Then net investment should be positive, but how large is it? How fast should we be approaching the stationary state $\hat{K}$, where $F'(\hat{K}) - \rho = 0$?

It is difficult to give a mathematically concise answer to this question under the most general circumstances. But we can see what the speed of convergence depends upon locally, in the neighborhood of the optimal stationary state $\hat{K}$, which is good enough to give a solid intuition about what must be happening globally.

From (151),(152) we have

$$\dot{C} = -\frac{U'}{U''}[F' - \rho], \tag{154}$$

where all variables are evaluated along an optimal trajectory. We also know that

$$\dot{K} = F - C, \tag{155}$$

which, when we differentiate both sides with respect to time, becomes

$$\frac{d^2K}{dt^2} = F'(K)\dot{K} - \dot{C}. \tag{156}$$

If we substitute from (154) into (156), we obtain the second-order differential equation

$$\frac{d^2K}{dt^2} = F'(K)\frac{dK}{dt} + \frac{U'}{U''}[F'(K) - \rho], \tag{157}$$

which must hold all along an optimal trajectory.

Now, a famous theorem in nonlinear differential equations (due originally to Poincaré), when applied here, states that as $K^*(t)$ approaches its limit point $\hat{K}$, the solution of the nonlinear differential equation (157) approaches the solution of the "linearized" version

$$\frac{d^2K}{dt^2} = F'(\hat{K})\frac{dK}{dt} + \frac{U'(F(\hat{K}))}{U''(F(\hat{K}))}F''(\hat{K})[K - \hat{K}], \tag{158}$$

where the linearized coefficients are evaluated at the limit point $\hat{K}$.

The only solution of the differential equation (158) that converges to $\hat{K}$ is of the form

$$K(t) - \hat{K} = [K(0) - \hat{K}]e^{-at}, \tag{159}$$

for some positive a, which implies the very simple linear capital stock adjustment equation

$$I^*(t) = a(\hat{K} - K(t)). \tag{160}$$

Plugging (160) into (159), the "speed of adjustment" coefficient a is the positive root of the characteristic quadratic equation

$$a^2 + F'a - \frac{U'}{U''}F'' = 0, \tag{161}$$

which is

$$a = \left[-F' + \sqrt{(F')^2 + 4U'F''/U''} \right] \Big/ 2. \tag{162}$$

Substituting $F' = \rho$ and $\eta = -FU''/U'$ evaluated at the stationary solution $\hat{K}$, (162) can be rewritten in the economically more meaningful form

$$a = \sqrt{\left(\frac{\rho}{2}\right)^2 - \frac{F''F}{\eta}} - \frac{\rho}{2}. \tag{163}$$

We could alternatively have derived (163) by applying the general theory of quadratic gain functions developed in the last chapter. The reader should confirm that (163) above is a special case of equation (3.163), where $G_{11} = U'F'' + U''(F')^2$, $G_{22} = U''$, $G_{12} = -U''F'$.

Comparing (163) with the "adjustment cost" result (140), the local behavior of the two models is identical, with the analogue of the "adjustment cost coefficient" in the neoclassical optimal growth model being

$$\alpha = \frac{\eta}{F}. \tag{164}$$

Notice in (163) that, since $F'' < 0$, the speed of adjustment is inversely related to the elasticity of marginal utility. We anticipated such a relationship in the discussion that accompanied the definition of the elasticity of marginal utility. The extreme case $\eta \to 0$ brings us back into the world of MRA, because the utility function then becomes linear in investment. The opposite extreme $\eta \to \infty$ causes adjustments to be infinitesimally slow, because of the super-high losses to utility from unboundedly strong diminishing returns to consumption. In-between values of η warrant adjustment speeds in between the two extremes.

From (163) it is also apparent that the speed of adjustment is directly related to the curvature of the production function. Again, this is as it should be, because, other things being equal, stronger curvature implies bigger losses from *not* being in the stationary solution. Because we cannot afford to sustain the enormous losses of being out of a stationary state, other things being equal the extreme case $F'' \to -\infty$ causes us in the limit to go to a MRA policy, while the other extreme of approaching a linear production function, as $F'' \to 0$, causes adjustments to be infinitesimally slow because the comparative role of a curved utility function becomes paramount.

Finally, (163) is telling us that speed of adjustment is inversely related to the rate of pure time preference. With a very high utility discount rate, other things being equal there is not much sense in sacrificing current consumption to move more rapidly to a stationary solution. By contrast, other things being equal, with a very low utility discount rate it is a good idea to give up some consumption now, in favor of raising the level of relatively heavily weighted future consumption flows.

The effects of steady technological progress can be incorporated into the neoclassical optimal growth model by making the following three additional assumptions: (1) output is a constant returns to scale production function of capital and augmented labor; (2) technological progress is labor augmenting at a constant growth rate; (3) the utility function is isoelastic, meaning η in (150) is constant. When all quantities are then expressed in units of effective or augmented labor, the resulting model is isomorphic to the form we have been analyzing here.

Even though we have not analyzed such a situation formally, we should now have a good intuitive sense of what is optimal behavior if the sole owner of the fishery *both* is a monopolist (alternatively, a utility-maximizing social planner) *and also* has costs of adjustment. The monopolist owner with adjustment costs will still want to go the stationary state, but will now approach that stationary state gradually. The speed of approach will be slower as the demand curve has higher *elasticity* (in this situation, the elasticity of demand with respect to price acts just like the parameter η in the utility function of the neoclassical optimal growth model). The approach will also be more gradual as the cost of adjustment (the parameter α in the q-theory of investment model) is higher. It is left as an exercise to show formally that the monopoly fishery with adjustment costs does indeed exhibit just this pattern of optimal behavior.

SOLUTION OF PROBLEM 5: OPTIMAL EXTRACTION OF AN EXHAUSTIBLE RESOURCE

We next examine the solution to the famous Hotelling model of the optimal extraction of an exhaustible resource. In this problem, $S(t)$ is a state variable representing the stock of oil reserves remaining in the ground, while $E(t)$ is the extraction flow rate, with both non-negative variables evaluated at time t. Initially, the stock of reserves is S_0. The function $\Phi(E)$ gives the flow of revenues from selling E barrels of oil per unit time if the oil well is privately owned by a monopolist. (In this case, if $D^{-1}(E)$ is the inverse demand function giving price as a function of amount demanded, then $\Phi(E) = E D^{-1}(E)$.)

An alternative interpretation is that $\Phi(E)$ gives the social *utility* of consuming E barrels of oil per unit time if the well is publicly owned. (With social utility equal to the "area under the demand curve," which represents the consumer's "total willingness to pay," this interpretation, as we will show, gives the same outcome as if the oil wells were owned by a large number of perfect competitors.)

The cost function $C(S, E)$ represents the cost of extracting oil at a flow rate E when the remaining stock is S. (In the base case, traditionally analyzed first, $C(S, E)$ is taken to be some constant unit extraction cost γ times E— or even zero, which makes things simpler yet.) The parameter ρ stands for the competitive interest rate. The gain function $G(S, E)$ represents *net profits* (revenues minus costs) or *net utility* as a function of remaining reserves and extraction flow rates. The control problem is to

$$\text{maximize} \quad \int_0^\infty [\Phi(E(t)) - C(S(t), E(t))]e^{-\rho t} \, dt \tag{165}$$

subject to

$$\dot{S}(t) = -E(t), \tag{166}$$

and

$$S(t) \geq 0, \tag{167}$$

and

$$E(t) \geq 0, \tag{168}$$

and with the given initial condition

$$S(0) = S_0. \tag{169}$$

To fortify our intuition about this problem, we begin our analysis with the simplest possible case of costless extraction. When $C(S, E) = 0$, it is readily confirmed that the stationary rate of return on capital for this model of the optimal extraction of an exhaustible resource is

$$R(K) = 0, \tag{170}$$

which, by the theory we have developed, means we *always want to disinvest* (that is, $E^*(t) > 0$) whenever we are *not blocked* (that is, $S^*(t) > 0$). If the gain function were linear, we would want to empty out the oil wells as rapidly as possible (under positive discounting), but with a curved gain function we will wish to approach zero reserves more gradually, depending on the degree of curvature of the revenue or utility function.

Let $p(t)$ be the co-state variable to the differential equation (166), representing the efficiency or shadow price of the resource at time t. By applying our usual interpretation to the particular context of this model, $p(t)$ is the value of receiving a "gift" of one more unit of the exhaustible resource in the ground at time t. Another way of saying the same thing is that $p(t)$ is the "scarcity price" at time t, representing the value of leaving one more unit of the exhaustible resource in situ—to be balanced against the alternative value of extracting and selling it. Yet some other names for $p(t)$ are "marginal user cost" or "royalty" or "dynamic rent" or "Hotelling rent" (per unit extracted, at time t).

The relevant Hamiltonian for this problem is

$$H = \Phi(E) - pE, \tag{171}$$

where the minus sign appears on the right-hand side of (171) because extraction E represents negative investment in capital—that is, $I = -E$, where I is true net investment. Thus in this extraction situation, Hamiltonian income is less than current gain $\Phi(E)$, because capital is being depleted, and the competitive stock market share value is less than the capitalized value of current gains because, for this "wasting asset" as it is sometimes called, the current gains cannot be maintained indefinitely. Applying condition [#1] of the maximum principle, the Hamiltonian is maximized at that extraction rate $E^*(t)$, which satisfies the first-order condition

$$\Phi'(E^*(t)) = p(t), \tag{172}$$

meaning that in an optimal policy, with the monopoly interpretation, the marginal revenue of extracting and selling one more unit of the resource for the monopolist should exactly equal the marginal shadow value of leaving the unit in the ground. This is the dynamic analogue of the static condition "marginal revenue equals marginal cost," except that here "marginal cost" is the "scarcity price" or "Hotelling rent" on the extra barrel. Note that for the monopolist $p(t)$ is not the price paid by the consumer, but instead, by (172), it equals *marginal* revenue. The price paid by the consumer is the *average* revenue, or $\Phi(E^*(t))/E^*(t)$, which for the monopolist is higher than marginal revenue.

In the situation where $\Phi(E)$ represents the utility of consumption, (172) has an interesting interpretation as the perfectly competitive solution. Suppose the inverse demand function (the market-clearing price that people are willing to pay for E) is

$$P = D^{-1}(E). \tag{173}$$

Then the corresponding consumer-surplus utility function is the "total willingness to pay" expression

$$\Phi(E) = \int_0^E D^{-1}(X)\,dX, \tag{174}$$

which is represented graphically by the familiar "area under the demand curve," and (172) becomes

$$P(t) = D^{-1}(E^*(t)) = p(t). \tag{175}$$

Condition (175) means that the price consumers pay for the resource $P(t) = D^{-1}(E^*(t))$ equals the efficiency or scarcity or competitive price of the resource $p(t)$, which is the same situation *as if* there is perfect competition in the extraction industry because the "law of one price" is holding. (Consumers are acting as if $\{P(t)\}$ represents a competitive equilibrium price trajectory for buyers, and producers are acting as if $\{p(t)\}$ is a competitive equilibrium price trajectory for sellers. The only remaining condition needed to be an economywide competitive equilibrium is the law of one price: $P(t) = p(t)$ for all t.) This insight is important, because it means that we can model the behavior of a perfectly competitive extractive industry by just postulating maximization of the present discounted value of an "area under the demand curve" utility function of the form (174). (Just such a "trick" was originally proposed by Harold Hotelling himself to handle the competitive case.) In this way, a dynamic competitive equilibrium can be modeled "as if" it is the solution of a control problem maximizing present discounted utility, where utility is measured by the consumer-surplus "area under the demand curve" representing "total willingness to pay." Thus the formulation here covers both the monopoly case and the perfectly competitive case—depending upon the interpretation of the gain function.

Examining (171) and (172), we note immediately in this problem that, because S does not appear in the Hamiltonian,

$$\frac{\partial \tilde{H}}{\partial S} = 0, \tag{176}$$

which means that condition [#2] of the maximum principle here takes the special form

$$\dot{p}(t) = \rho p(t). \tag{177}$$

The solution of (177) is

$$p(t) = p(0)e^{\rho t} \tag{178}$$

for some initial value $p(0)$.

Condition (178) is the famous *Hotelling rule:* The in situ shadow or efficiency or scarcity or opportunity or royalty price of an exhaustible resource must grow at the rate of interest. With zero extraction costs, (178) means for the zero-cost monopolist that marginal revenue must grow at the rate of interest, while for the zero-cost competitive industry, price must grow at the rate of interest. If condition (178) did not hold, an arbitrageur in a nation of competitive oil extractors could make pure profits either by buying oil in the ground on money borrowed from the bank (if the in situ price is appreciating faster than the interest rate) or by selling oil in the ground and depositing the sales money in the bank (if the in situ price is appreciating slower than the interest rate). The underlying principle is that in dynamic competitive equilibrium, a storable nonproducing asset must appreciate at the going rate of interest. This holds for any asset that pays no dividends, is traded in a competitive market, and costs nothing to store or extract. Hotelling's great insight was to note that an exhaustible resource is just a special form of capital, and hence, with a perfect capital market, it must earn the same rate of return as any other form of capital. (As we have seen, it is the same with fisheries or forests—they are all forms of natural capital that will be optimally managed only when they are earning competitive rates of return.)

How is the initial scarcity price $p(0)$ determined? For each parametrically chosen value of $p(0)$ there is a corresponding trajectory of total "amount demanded" (equals "amount extracted" in equilibrium), which satisfies condition (172), given the chosen value of $p(0)$. The easiest way to see this is in the competitive industry, where (from (175) and (178))

$$E^*(t) = D(p(0)e^{\rho t}). \tag{179}$$

(A completely analogous argument holds for the monopoly case, where (172) represents marginal revenue.) Because $p(t)$ is increasing over time (exponentially, at rate ρ), the corresponding trajectory of "amount demanded" from the competitive industry $D(p(t))$ must decline over time, eventually reaching zero. For only one chosen value of $p(0)$ in (179) will exactly all of the exhaustible resource be extracted, that is, only one value of $p(0)$ will make total demand equal total supply:

$$\int_0^\infty D(p(0)e^{\rho t})\, dt = S_0. \tag{180}$$

If $p(0)$ is initially chosen too low, then the integral on the left-hand side of (180), representing the total amount extracted and sold, will be more than the existing reserves. If $p(0)$ is chosen too high, then the integral on the left-hand side of (180), representing the total amount extracted and sold, will be less than the existing reserves. By trial and error, raising the initial price $p(0)$ when total extraction exceeds total reserves, and lowering the initial price $p(0)$ when total reserves exceed total extraction, we could find, in the limit as the successive approximations are made finer and finer, the exact initial scarcity price $p(0)$ that just equates total extraction and sales with total reserves. (Note that it also follows immediately from the above argument that higher S_0 translates into lower $p(0)$, because a lower price trajectory is required to clear the market of the higher reserves.)

What is there about the maximum principle that communicates the important message that in an optimal solution total extraction of the stock of oil must equal total reserves? It cannot be the first two conditions, which have already been used, and which do not send any such signal. It must be the transversality condition [#3], here being

$$
\begin{aligned}
0 &= \lim_{t \to \infty} p(t) S^*(t) e^{-\rho t} = \lim_{t \to \infty} p(0) e^{\rho t} S^*(t) e^{-\rho t} \\
&= \lim_{t \to \infty} p(0) S^*(t) = \lim_{t \to \infty} S^*(t),
\end{aligned} \tag{181}
$$

which means

$$
\int_0^\infty E^*(t)\, dt = S_0, \tag{182}
$$

that is, $p(0)$ must be selected to make (180) hold.

Whenever a stationary solution fails to exist, the transversality condition can be critically important in allocating resources optimally—and this is the perfect example. Conditions [#1] and [#2] of the maximum principle are describing intertemporal optimality only. If a trajectory satisfies condition [#1] (172) and condition [#2] (178), it will be going "optimally" from an oil reserve of size S_0 at time zero to an oil reserve of size $S(t)$ at time t (that is, maximizing present discounted gains), but there is no assurance without the transversality condition [#3] that it is optimal to actually be at reserve $S(t)$ at time t. We might be keeping so much oil in the ground that we end up never using it all in the limit. The market "signal" ensuring that (182) holds is that *otherwise* the transversality condition [#3] fails and then, by the general argument at the end of Chapter 3, pure profits can be made from arbitrage. If the left-hand side of (182) exceeds the right-hand side, then pure profits can be made effortlessly by the arbitrage operations of buying such oil in the ground on money borrowed at interest rate ρ and "cashing in" the well when oil prices inevitably appreciate at a rate greater than ρ as supplies run out. If the right-hand side of (182) exceeds the left-hand side, then selling such oil in the ground and depositing the proceeds in a bank paying interest ρ is a better investment, because the overhang of unsold oil will eventually cause oil prices to appreciate at a slower rate than ρ.

Let us solve explicitly a particular example of the problem of optimal extraction of exhaustible resources. Consider a revenue function or utility function of the isoelastic form

$$
\Phi(E) = A E^{(1-1/\theta)}, \tag{183}
$$

where $\theta > 1$ is the *elasticity of demand*, while A is a positive constant. Extraction costs are zero.

Condition [#1] of the maximum principle (here (172)) becomes

$$A \left(1 - \frac{1}{\theta}\right) (E^*(t))^{-1/\theta} = p(t), \tag{184}$$

so that, from condition [#2] (here (177)) if $p(t)$ grows exponentially at rate ρ, then $E^*(t)$ must grow exponentially at rate $-\rho\theta$. Thus

$$E^*(t) = E(0)e^{-\rho\theta t}, \tag{185}$$

where from the transversality condition [#3] (here (181), which is equivalent to (182)),

$$E(0) = S_0 \rho\theta. \tag{186}$$

With equations (185) and (186), we have used the maximum principle to *characterize completely* for this problem (with isoelastic demand and zero extraction costs) the optimal extraction pattern of a nonrenewable resource. We leave it as an exercise to specify exactly the corresponding optimal price trajectory and to analyze how the optimal solution depends upon the underlying parameters S_0, ρ, and θ.

The simple Hotelling model demonstrates clearly that a nonrenewable resource can command a positive price, which could be made arbitrarily large depending on the parameters of the problem, even though it costs nothing to extract the resource. Such a conclusion holds both for the monopolist and for the perfect competitor. This is the dynamic analogue of agricultural land commanding a positive pure rent even under perfect competition.

Now let us put extraction costs into the model. Suppose, to keep things simple to begin with, that extraction costs are simply a constant γ per unit extracted. Then the entire model goes through exactly as before provided we now interpret the relevant price here as being the net price—meaning the gross marginal value of an extra unit of the resource minus the extraction cost γ. Condition (172) is then replaced by the condition

$$\Phi'(E^*(t)) - \gamma = p(t). \tag{187}$$

In this model, then, from (187) the difference between marginal value $\Phi'(E^*(t))$ and marginal cost γ equals the "opportunity cost," "user cost," "royalty," "Hotelling rent," or whatever other name is used for $p(t)$ at time t. For the monopolist here, Hotelling's rule $\dot{p}/p = \rho$ takes the form

$$\frac{d}{dt}(MR - \gamma) = \rho[MR - \gamma], \tag{188}$$

which means that marginal revenue (MR) minus marginal cost (γ) grows at the rate of interest. For the competitive industry, Hotelling's rule $\dot{p}/p = \rho$ then takes the form

$$\frac{d}{dt}(P - \gamma) = \rho[P - \gamma], \tag{189}$$

which can be rewritten as

$$P(t) = \gamma + (P(0) - \gamma)e^{\rho t}. \tag{190}$$

It should be confirmed mathematically from (190) and understood intuitively that as the unit extraction cost γ increases, the price trajectory the consumer faces in the competitive case becomes less steeply sloped over time and simultaneously shifts up. The corresponding competitive extraction trajectory declines more gradually over time (because the price trajectory is less steep) and simultaneously shifts down (because the total area under the extraction schedule still equals the total amount of the reserve).

Notice what happens to the optimal price and quantity trajectories as the discount rate varies. As ρ is made larger, the price trajectory is tilted more sharply upward over time and simultaneously shifted down, because with a higher rate of price appreciation, the initial price must be lower to induce consumers to buy all of that rapidly appreciating oil. Since the price is growing faster in this case, the corresponding extraction trajectory is tilted more downward over time and simultaneously shifted up because demand toward the end is choked off more rapidly by the more rapidly rising price, and therefore must be balanced by greater demand at the beginning. The total area under the extraction trajectory is always equal to S_0, but when the discount rate is made higher, more of this area is concentrated at the beginning of the extraction process. As usual, it is interesting to examine what happens for extreme values of ρ. We consider the two limiting cases, $\rho \to 0$ and $\rho \to \infty$.

For the extreme case $\rho \to 0$, the price and quantity trajectories approach being completely flat across time with the quantity per unit time approaching zero in the limit. Such a quantity trajectory has the usual property of maximizing (in the limit) the average gain per unit time. For the other extreme case $\rho \to \infty$, the price at the beginning of the trajectory goes to the extraction cost γ (otherwise the price trajectory from (190) would become so high so soon that it would choke off all demand while leaving some oil reserves remaining in the ground)—with the familiar interpretation that the optimizer is treating the natural resource as if there were free access, so it is as if every potential producer queues up and draws at the well when the price is only just barely the slightest bit above extraction cost. In this case the nonrenewable resource is drawn down rapidly because the price just covers the extraction cost.

Equation (187) generalizes readily to the case where extraction costs depend only on the speed of extraction, so that

$$C(S, E) = C(E), \tag{191}$$

in which case it emerges directly from the maximum principle that the Hotelling rule holds in the form

$$\Phi'(E^*(t)) - C'(E^*(t)) = [\Phi'(E^*(0)) - C'(E^*(0))]e^{\rho t}. \tag{192}$$

The logic behind (192) remains the same basic principle of no pure profits from arbitrage. If condition (192) did not hold in a dynamic competitive equilibrium, then an arbitrageur could make pure profits by either buying the oil in the ground on money borrowed from the bank (if the in-situ competitive price minus marginal extraction cost is appreciating faster than the interest rate) or selling the oil in the ground and depositing the sales money in the bank (if the in-situ competitive price minus marginal extraction cost is appreciating slower than the interest rate).

The expression on the left-hand side of equation (192) represents unit Hotelling net rent $p(t)$ at time t. For the competitive industry as a whole, total Hotelling rent at time t is $[P(t) - C'(E^*(t))][E^*(t)]$, which represents the appropriate "economic depletion" term to be subtracted from gross income to give the true measure of net income, whose capitalized value would be reflected exactly in the competitive stock market price of all shares outstanding. The basic expression "[price minus marginal cost] times [stock depletion]" is a standard formula for economic depreciation when stocks are declining. As we shall see in Part II, it represents in a precise sense the loss of sustainable-equivalent future welfare due to current consumption of a depletable resource stock.

The *simple* Hotelling rule does not hold if extraction costs depend in any way on the stock of the resource remaining. In this case (192) is replaced by a somewhat more complicated rule, which takes account of the fact that when we extract an extra unit in the present, we are adversely affecting the future costs of extraction. In this case a "corrected version" of Hotelling's rule continues to hold, where instead of just current marginal cost C', the relevant inclusive marginal cost expression now includes an additional term representing the present discounted value of the amount by which future extraction costs are increased from extracting an extra barrel now. Otherwise, the analysis is similar to previous cases.

As a last example here of the Hotelling version of "maximum-principle reasoning" we describe the competitive equilibrium for a given demand curve $D(P)$ when extraction costs are constant at γ and there exists a constant-returns-to-scale "backstop technology" that can supply any amount of the exhaustible resource at fixed price $\bar{c}$, representing the unit cost of production of the backstop technology. While we interpret the model here in the setting of the perfectly competitive industry, the results are qualitatively similar for the case of a monopoly extractor, where $\Phi(E)$ stands for revenue rather than "area under the demand curve" utility.

To make the problem interesting, we assume that

$$\bar{c} > \gamma \tag{193}$$

and

$$D(\bar{c}) > 0. \tag{194}$$

We leave as an exercise the formal statement of the optimal control problem, which we are "solving" here by exhibiting the corresponding dynamic competitive equilibrium.

The solution consists of two phases. In phase 1, oil is extracted and the backstop technology is not used. In phase 2, no oil remains and the backstop technology is the exclusive source of all energy.

Let T be the time of the "switch point" when the backstop technology first comes on line. Since the price must be continuous across any switch point, this means

$$P(T) = \bar{c}. \tag{195}$$

Plugging (195) into the price trajectory (190) and rearranging terms, we derive the initial price

$$P(0) = \gamma + (\bar{c} - \gamma)e^{-\rho T}. \tag{196}$$

From (196) and (190), we then have a complete description of the equilibrium price trajectory

$$P(t) = \gamma + (\bar{c} - \gamma)e^{\rho(t-T)} \tag{197}$$

for $t < T$ and $P(t) = \bar{c}$ for $t \geq T$.

The "switch time" T is determined by the condition

$$\int_0^T D(\gamma + (\bar{c} - \gamma)e^{\rho(t-T)})\, dt = S_0, \tag{198}$$

which just equates total sales with total purchases.

For example, if the demand curve is of the linear form

$$D(P) = a - bP, \tag{199}$$

then it is readily confirmed from (198) that T is the implicit solution of the equation

$$(a - b\gamma)T - b(\bar{c} - \gamma)(1 - e^{-\rho T})/\rho = S_0. \tag{200}$$

In summary, the Hotelling analysis supports the main thesis of this chapter. To solve the Hotelling problem in any one of its many variants is to envision how a competitive stock market would allocate the exhaustible resource for that particular variant.

SOLUTION OF PROBLEM 6: OPTIMAL EXTRACTION OF AN EXHAUSTIBLE RESOURCE FROM A RESERVE OF UNKNOWN SIZE

We now analyze problem 6, which is an interesting twist on the Hotelling problem, where extraction costs are zero but the size of the mineral reserve is uncertain. We do not repeat the formal statement of the problem here, and leave as an exercise the application of the standard version of the maximum principle to characterize a solution. Instead, we focus here on the wealth and income version of the maximum principle, which for this problem extends into the realm of uncertainty the interpretation of the Hamiltonian as sustainable-equivalent gain.

The relevant Hamiltonian here is

$$\frac{1 - F(Z)}{1 - F(Z_0)} \Phi(E) - pE, \tag{201}$$

which has an interior maximum where

$$p(t) = \frac{1 - F(Z^*(t))}{1 - F(Z_0)} \Phi'(E^*(t)). \tag{202}$$

Since (202) holds all along an optimal trajectory, it must hold at time $t = 0$ when $Z^*(0) = Z(0) = Z_0$, which yields

$$p(0) = \Phi'(E^*(0)). \tag{203}$$

Next, consider $Z_0 = Z(0)$ to be a parameter characterizing the state we now find ourselves in. Applying the wealth and income version of the maximum principle, and making use of (203) we obtain at the current time that

$$\rho V(Z(0)) = \Phi(E^*(0)) - \Phi'(E^*(0))E^*(0), \tag{204}$$

which has a very interesting economic interpretation.

In a deterministic setting, the state evaluation function represents the present discounted value of an optimal policy. With uncertainty, the present discounted value of an optimal policy is a random variable, and the state evaluation function represents its expectation. More specifically here, $V(Z(0))$ in (204) is the expected present discounted value of following an optimal policy for a mine or well with uncertain reserves, out of which $Z(0)$ units have already been extracted. Because competitive share values must capitalize expected future dividends, $V(Z(0))$ is also the competitive stock market price of shares of the mine or well with uncertain reserves, out of which $Z(0)$ units have already been extracted. The "accounting price" $\Phi'(E^*(0))$ represents the opportunity cost of leaving in the ground an extra unit of the resource. The term $\Phi'(E^*(0))E^*(0)$ then represents depletion (for an oil well) or depreciation (for a truck), evaluated at the correctly accounted opportunity cost. (Generally speaking, a term like $\Phi'(E^*(0))E^*(0)$ measures what might be called "true economic depreciation.") The right-hand side of (204) represents net income, taking proper account of depletion or depreciation. Equation (204) then says that the return on the stock market evaluation at any time of

shares of the well or truck equals net income (taking proper account of depletion or depreciation at that time), independent of the probability distribution
of reserves or life expectancy.

Why is this result holding independent of the probability distribution? The
reason is that, for an optimal policy, the opportunity cost of the in-situ resource already accounts for the uncertainty.

In a later chapter we will treat more comprehensively the wealth and income
version of the maximum principle in the presence of uncertainty. We note
here only that the spirit of this particular example will be replicated in more
general settings. If the uncertainty manifests itself through the capital stocks,
as with this example, then there is still an interpretation like (204) of the
Hamiltonian as representing the stationary certainty equivalent of the *expected*
present discounted value of an optimal policy.

SOLUTION OF PROBLEM 8: POLLUTION-STOCK EXTERNALITY

The form of the pollution-stock externality problem should be vaguely recog-
nizable as having a gain function that is nonlinear in investment. We have seen
several such problems already. Our plan of attack for analyzing Problem 8 now
follows a predictable course.

Question number one: Does a stationary solution exist?

Answer: Yes. Formula (2.83) says that for this problem the stationary rate
of return is $R(K) = \alpha D'/U' - \mu$. The existence of a unique solution to the
equation $R(\hat{K}) = \rho$ then follows from the underlying second-derivative curvature assumptions on the functions U and D. When the stationary solution
$R(\hat{K}) = \rho$ is expressed in terms of the original variables of this problem, it
becomes (in obvious notation)

$$\alpha \frac{D'(\hat{B})}{U'(\hat{C})} - \mu = \rho, \tag{205}$$

where $\alpha\hat{C} = \mu\hat{B}$ corresponds to the stationarity condition $\hat{I} = 0$.

Question number two: Is the stationary solution attainable?

Answer: Yes. The only possible blocking constraints are $C \leq \overline{C}$ or $B \leq \overline{B}$,
and these cannot block access to (205) when $\overline{C}$ and $\overline{B}$ are larger than the
stationary-solution values $\hat{C}$ and $\hat{B}$.

Question number three: What is the economic interpretation of the stationary solution?

Answer: Let us analyze the stationary solution in terms of the variables and
concepts in which the problem was originally posed. On Vulcan, the basic

tradeoff is between the greater current pleasure of consuming more now and the greater future displeasure from built-up stocks of bad air, which will hurt more later. Producing one unit more of consumption simultaneously releases α units of bad air, which decays exponentially over time at rate μ.

Suppose we are in a stationary solution $\alpha \hat{C} = \mu \hat{B}$ where (205) holds. Consider a "thought-experimental" perturbation of consuming ε more units right now. This would give us a one-time immediate utility boost of

$$U'\varepsilon, \tag{206}$$

but on the down side, production of ε extra units of consumption will release $\alpha\varepsilon$ units of bad air. At time t from now, the remaining extra bad air from the thought experiment is $\alpha\varepsilon e^{-\mu t}$, which causes disutility at that time of

$$D'\alpha\varepsilon e^{-\mu t}, \tag{207}$$

and therefore the present-discounted disutility caused by the thought-experimental release of $\alpha\varepsilon$ units of bad air is

$$\int_0^\infty [D'\alpha\varepsilon e^{-\mu t}]e^{-\rho t}\, dt. \tag{208}$$

In a stationary solution, the marginal gain (206) should be exactly offset by the marginal loss (208), which is precisely what the stationary-solution condition (205) is saying. Thus, as usual, the stationary solution is the optimal solution for a "correctly translated" static version of the problem, where stocks and flows trade off against each other at rate ρ. This simple example, however, indicates clearly that, without detailed knowledge of the underlying dynamic model, it may be very difficult, or even impossible, to find a "correctly translated" static version of the problem. The standard textbook formula for finding the optimal level of pollution in a simplistic static-flow world is to equate the "marginal benefit" of clean air with its "marginal cost" of cleanup. Here the reader should seriously attempt to identify what in condition (205) might correspond to "marginal benefit" and what might correspond to "marginal cost." It is left as an exercise to summarize the outcome of such an attempt and to infer what it means. (The overarching message is that you really need to understand "dynamics" in order to do "statics" properly.) It is also left to the reader to perform a comparative-statics parametric analysis on the stationary solution (205) and to confirm that the results make economic sense.

Question number four: What is the approach speed to the stationary solution?

Answer: If both utility functions $U(C)$ and $D(B)$ are taken to be quadratic, we can obtain an exact solution. (For our purposes this is a good enough global approximation, and it is always an exact approximation within a neighborhood of the stationary solution.) Following previous procedures, we obtain a second-order linear differential equation in the capital stock (here B), which results in a quadratic equation for the speed of adjustment. We apply to this particular case equation (3.163) of the general theory of quadratic gain functions developed in the last chapter, where here $G_{11} = U''\mu^2/\alpha^2 - D''$, $G_{22} = U''/\alpha^2$, $G_{12} = -U''\mu/\alpha^2$. The appropriate (positive) root for the speed of adjustment a is given by the equation

$$a = \sqrt{\left(\frac{\rho}{2}\right)^2 - \frac{D''\alpha^2}{U''} + \mu^2 - \mu\rho} - \frac{\rho}{2}, \tag{209}$$

and we can completely characterize the solution to the pollution-stock externality problem (in the case of quadratic utilities) by the simple linear differential equation

$$\dot{B}(t) = a[\hat{B} - B(t)], \tag{210}$$

whose solution is

$$B(t) = \hat{B} - [\hat{B} - B_0]e^{-at}. \tag{211}$$

The details, which should be familiar from the previous examples, are left to the reader.

Question number five: What is the economic interpretation of the approach speed to the stationary solution?

Answer: We leave details to the reader after a few general remarks. From (209), the speed of approach is directly related to the curvature of the disutility of pollution function and inversely related to the curvature of the utility of consumption function. The reader should confirm that such a conclusion makes good economic sense. Also, from (209), the speed of approach varies directly with the rate of decay of the stock pollutant and inversely with the discount rate. Again, the reader should confirm that such a conclusion makes good economic sense. Note that as $\mu \to \infty$, the optimal policy becomes in the limit a most rapid approach to the steady state. Here too, a good economic understanding of why such a result obtains is important.

To summarize our approach to the problem: we began with the stationary solution that represents what "would be" the solution of a corresponding static version of the problem (although, as we have seen, it is not quite that simple). Then we gave an economic interpretation of the stationary solution, and analyzed what it depends upon. Next we confirmed that nothing in the model blocks us from attaining this stationary state over time. Using the maximum principle, we then calculated (for a quadratic approximation) the speed of convergence to the stationary state and analyzed what it depends upon. There is really not much more to analyze or to understand in such models.

The above concise description summarizes the standard operating procedure for solving and analyzing one-dimensional problems with unblocked stationary states. We have also seen examples of what happens when there is no stationary state (for example, extraction of nonrenewable resources) or when the stationary state is blocked (for example, the irreversible investment problem). The final problem we analyze in this chapter also fails to have a stationary state, but for a different reason than anything we have so far encountered.

SOLUTION OF PROBLEM 9: GROWTH WITH POLLUTION

The last problem analyzed in this chapter is the "growth with pollution" model of Chapter 2. So that this problem will have a closed-form solution that is relatively easy to analyze, we assume particularly simple functional specifications of the utility functions. The utility of consumption is presumed to be logarithmic

$$U(C) = \log(C), \tag{212}$$

while the disutility of bad air is linear

$$D(B) = \alpha B, \tag{213}$$

where α here parameterizes the unpleasantness of bad air relative to the pleasure of consumption. More general specifications yield qualitatively similar results, but the solutions are harder to explain briefly and concisely. The main message intended to be conveyed is independent of the utility functions.

With the above utility functions (212) and (213), and with $\{C(t), \theta(t)\}$ being the controls, the "growth with pollution" problem (2.86)–(2.90) takes the form to

$$\text{maximize} \quad \int_0^\infty [\log(C(t)) - \beta\theta(t)K(t)]e^{-\rho t} \, dt \tag{214}$$

subject to

$$\dot{K}(t) = [\theta(t)A + (1 - \theta(t))a]K(t) - C(t), \tag{215}$$

with the control constraints

$$0 \leq \theta(t) \leq 1, \tag{216}$$

and with the given initial condition

$$K(0) = K_0, \tag{217}$$

where $\beta \equiv \alpha\gamma$ is a reduced-form parameter of the problem.

The "dirty" technology produces more output per unit expenditure of capital (A, as compared with a for the "clean" technology), but it also emits γ units of bad air per unit of capital, thereby creating additional disutility of $\beta = \alpha\gamma$ relative to the clean technology. Problem (214)–(217) has two control instruments: C, standing for consumption, and θ, standing for the fraction of capital stock that is of the dirty type. By this point, we should be unafraid to work directly with the original control variables (here C and θ), rather than having to transform the problem into an equivalent form where the only control variable is net investment I.

As we will soon see, the solution to the above problem (214)–(217) consists of two stages: a first stage where only the dirty technology (which is cheaper per unit output) is used, and a second stage where only the clean technology (which is costlier per unit output) is employed. To understand the nature of the growth with pollution problem, it will be useful to analyze the second stage as an optimal growth problem—in its own right, with its own interesting features. Suppose, then, it has been decreed that only the clean technology, whose output to capital ratio is a, may be used.

The subproblem we then wish to solve is to

$$\text{maximize} \quad \int_0^\infty \log(C(t))e^{-\rho t}\, dt \tag{218}$$

subject to

$$\dot{K}(t) = aK(t) - C(t), \tag{219}$$

and with the given initial condition

$$K(0) = K_0. \tag{220}$$

The relevant Hamiltonian here is

$$H = \log(C) + pI, \tag{221}$$

which is maximized over $C + I = aK$, yielding the interior solution

$$\frac{1}{C(t)} = p(t). \tag{222}$$

Condition [#2] of the maximum principle here becomes

$$\rho - \frac{\dot{p}(t)}{p(t)} = a, \tag{223}$$

which is a special case of the fundamental equation of optimal growth theory (149).

Combining (222) and (223), it follows that

$$\frac{\dot{C}(t)}{C(t)} = g_a, \tag{224}$$

where

$$g_a \equiv a - \rho. \tag{225}$$

The capital accumulation equation going along with (224) is

$$\dot{K}(t) = aK(t) - C(0)e^{g_a t}, \tag{226}$$

and it is readily shown that the only value of $C(0)$ consistent with capital being non-negative and with the transversality condition being satisfied is

$$C(0) = \rho K(0), \tag{227}$$

which means, since $\dot{K}/K = a - \rho$, that the entire system (consumption, capital, output, investment) grows at the constant rate g_a. The net savings rate corresponding to (227) is

$$s = \frac{a - \rho}{a}. \tag{228}$$

Thus we have a complete characterization of the solution to the optimal growth problem (218)–(220). In this problem, a represents the economywide competitive interest rate, because it denotes how much extra consumption is available next period from postponing a unit of consumption in this period.

When the rate of return to capital is a, then the economy saves at the rate s given by (228) and grows at the rate g_a given by equation (225).

It should be easy to see now what happens in the extreme case where pollution is not a concern at all—that is, there is no disutility of pollution ($\beta = 0$). This is just like the situation previously analyzed, except for A replacing a. In this case, the only difference is that using the dirty technology would give a higher rate of return to capital (A instead of a), a higher savings rate, and a higher corresponding growth rate

$$g_A \equiv A - \rho. \tag{229}$$

We can now intuit the outlines of a full solution to the growth with pollution problem. At the very beginning, in the limiting primitive state of humanity with very low capital and output, where the marginal utility of consumption $U'(C) = 1/C$ greatly exceeds the marginal disutility of pollution β, the economy will act as if the rate of return on capital is A and the growth rate is $g_A = A - \rho$. Throughout this first stage pollution builds over time. By the second stage, when the economy has built up high capacity and is relatively rich with consumer goods, the comparative disutility of pollution will weigh greater than the marginal utility of consumption, and the economy will choose the clean technology, whose rate of return on capital is a and whose optimal growth rate is $g_a = a - \rho$. In between *starting* at the capital-poor, high rate of return, high growth rate beginning, and *finishing* at the capital-rich, low rate of return, low growth rate end, the economy must somehow make a transition, presumably by having a declining rate of return and slowing growth rate throughout some intermediate transition time of phase 1. We now turn to working out the details of exactly how growth rates and rates of return on capital change over time in the presence of a pollution externality. These algebraic details are somewhat intricate, but they will yield a closed-form solution whose economic message should be clear.

The Hamiltonian for the problem of growth with pollution is

$$H = \log(C) - \beta\theta K + p\{[\theta A + (1 - \theta)a]K - C\}. \tag{230}$$

We can now directly maximize the Hamiltonian with respect to the two control variables C and θ, thereby cutting through the artifice of forcing the gain function into the standard form $G(K, I)$ and then maximizing over I. (Remember, what counts is that the Hamiltonian is maximized with respect to all control variables, not that we waste time and effort forcing the problem into a mold where we have an explicit expression for $G(K, I)$, which plays no direct role in deriving a solution anyway.)

Maximizing with respect to C gives the usual condition $U'(C) = p$, which here becomes

$$\frac{1}{C^*(t)} = p(t), \tag{231}$$

where $C^*(t)$ is the optimal consumption flow at time t.

Maximizing with respect to θ over the control set $0 \leq \theta \leq 1$ yields the following characterization:

Case 1 (upper-corner solution):

$$p(A - a) > \beta \Rightarrow \theta = 1; \tag{232}$$

Case 2 (lower-corner solution):

$$p(A - a) < \beta \Rightarrow \theta = 0; \tag{233}$$

Case 3 (indeterminate interior solution):

$$p(A - a) = \beta \Rightarrow 0 \leq \theta \leq 1. \tag{234}$$

Let $\theta(t)$ represent the optimized value of θ at time t (which therefore satisfies (232),(233),(234)). For all three cases, condition [#2] of the maximum principle applied here yields

$$\dot{p}(t) = \rho p(t) + \beta \theta(t) - p(t)[\theta(t)A + (1 - \theta(t))a]. \tag{235}$$

As already noted, the maximum principle suggests the following form of an optimal solution. There are two stages of growth. Stage 1 is characterized by $\theta = 1$ and lasts from time $t = 0$ until some time $t = T$. Stage 2 is characterized by $\theta = 0$ and lasts from time $t = T$ to time $t = \infty$.

To characterize a complete optimal solution, we now work *backward* in time. We have already characterized the constant growth phase 2. It begins with the switch-point condition

$$\beta = p(T)(A - a), \tag{236}$$

which corresponds to (234) and holds at the exact instant of time $t = T$ (but not thereafter and not before). It is left to the reader to confirm (from (235) and (236)) that (233) holds for $t > T$, and hence $\theta = 0$ holding all through this second phase is mutually consistent with (233) and (235). Throughout phase 2, the rate of return on capital is a and the growth rate of the entire economy is $g_a = a - \rho$.

Combining (236) with (231), it follows that the optimal consumption level at the switch-point time $t = T$ is

$$C^*(T) = \frac{A - a}{\beta}. \tag{237}$$

Next, combining (237) with the savings rate condition (228) (which implies $C^*(T) = \rho K^*(T)$), it must be true at time T that

$$K^*(T) = \frac{A - a}{\beta \rho}. \tag{238}$$

Thus the time when stage 2 growth begins, at time T, is exactly signaled by the capital stock first attaining the level (238). It is left to the reader to analyze how (238) varies with the underlying parameters of the problem and to confirm that the results make economic sense.

In stage 1, condition [#2] of the maximum principle (equation (235) with $\theta = 1$) informs us that the social rate of return on capital at time $t (< T)$ is

$$\rho - \frac{\dot{p}(t)}{p(t)} = A - \frac{\beta}{p(t)}. \tag{239}$$

(That the expression on the left side of equality (239) represents the efficiency or social rate of return follows from equation (149) of optimal growth theory, which indicates that this expression acts as if it is the marginal product of capital, answering the question: how much extra consumption can society obtain next period per unit delayed from being consumed this period?)

It is readily confirmed, by direct checking, that the solution of the differential equation (239) with the boundary condition (236) is

$$p(t) = \frac{\beta}{A - \rho}[1 + \frac{a - \rho}{A - a}e^{-(A-\rho)(t-T)}], \tag{240}$$

and, by (231), $C^*(t) = 1/p(t)$ is completely determined.

Plugging the above formula (240) back into (239), the rate of return on capital in stage 1 at time $t (< T)$ is

$$\rho - \frac{\dot{p}(t)}{p(t)} = A - \frac{A - \rho}{1 + \dfrac{a - \rho}{A - a} e^{-(A-\rho)(t-T)}}, \tag{241}$$

while the corresponding growth of consumption is

$$\frac{\dot{C}^*(t)}{C^*(t)} = A - \rho - \frac{A - \rho}{1 + \dfrac{a - \rho}{A - a} e^{-(A-\rho)(t-T)}}. \tag{242}$$

We have now completely characterized the behavior of the system in stage 1. Time $t = 0$ corresponds to the initial condition $K(0) = K_0$. Time $t = T$ corresponds to the boundary condition (238). The smaller (larger) is $K(0)$ relative to $K^*(T)$, the larger (smaller) is T. Suppose we are at the initial time $t = 0$ in the formulas (241) and (242). Then other things being equal, as T is larger, stage 2 is farther off in the future, and from (241) the rate of return on capital approaches A in the limit as T approaches infinity, while from (242) the limiting growth rate of C approaches $g_A = A - \rho$. On the other hand, as T is smaller and stage 2 is nearer, from (241) the rate of return on capital approaches a, while from (242) the growth rate of C approaches $g_a = a - \rho$ in the limit as T approaches zero when t is already zero.

The algebra required to confirm the optimality of the proposed closed-form solution is involved, even for this relatively simple specification. What is perhaps more important here is to understand the economic rationale. Equation (241) indicates that throughout stage 1 the rate of return on capital declines continuously from a value approaching back in time to A if the initial capital stock approaches zero in an "early industrialization" state, to a value approaching a at time $t = T$, and it remains at a thereafter throughout stage 2. Similarly for consumption, throughout stage 1 the growth of consumption is declining continuously from a value approaching back in time eventually to $g_A = A - \rho$, if the initial capital stock approaches zero in the early industrial state, to a value approaching $g_a = a - \rho$ at time $t = T$, and it remains at g_a thereafter throughout stage 2.

These "continuous slowing" results may have important implications. Dynamic pollution externalities cause a lowering of rates of return and a slowing of growth rates over time. But this lowering of rates of return and slowing of growth rates should *precede* the switch to a cleaner technology. In stage 1, when an entirely dirty technology is being used, the optimally controlled economy foresees the coming switch to a clean technology, and reacts by slowing growth rates and lowering rates of return appropriately in just such a way that there is a perfectly smooth transition to stage 2.

In terms of a pollution externality like global warming, which is essentially a pollution-stock externality with very complicated lags and feedbacks, the qualitative story being told by this ultra-simple flow model holds up remarkably well and can serve as a kind of "first approximation" for organizing the broad outlines of how we conceptualize this complicated problem. The business-as-usual fossil fuel–based technology corresponds to what is here being called the "dirty" technology. The "clean" technology corresponds to generating energy from nuclear power, or solar cells, or windmills, or hydroelectric tidal dams, or whatever is the cheapest alternative energy source that does not emit carbon dioxide. In the early part of stage 1 (the pre-1950 period?), the rate of return on capital should be just below the aggregate rate of return (for the entire global economy) based on a dirty energy sector, and should decline gradually over time to approach the aggregate rate of return based on a clean energy sector. Ballpark estimates of A and a are not difficult to make. Suppose that the aggregate economywide real rate of return on capital for the economy based on carbon dioxide is, say, 5%. Then an energy-generating sector that is nuclear based should yield an aggregate economywide rate of return on capital that is slightly lower, say, around 4.7% or 4.8%, because aggregate output per unit of aggregate capital is now slightly lower (by some 4% to 6%), from being forced to generate energy more expensively without fossil fuels.

Throughout stage 1, the rate of return should be decreasing and the growth rate should be declining to what is appropriate for the all-clean technology. In stage 2, starting at time T, the world economy is based on a non–carbon dioxide energy sector, and the rate of return to capital is correspondingly lower by the difference in aggregate output per unit of aggregate capital between the dirty and clean technologies. Although the switch from dirty to clean technologies may seem dramatically sudden in this model, behind the scenes rates of return and rates of growth are seamlessly meshing across the boundary between stages 1 and 2. This important insight (seamless meshing of real discount and growth rates) is robust, surviving much more general specifications. The core message of this ultra-simple "model" is that an insightful first-approximation way to view the aggregate welfare impacts of global warming is to ask yourself, What would happen if I were forced to change from a bank account paying 5% interest per year to a bank account paying 4.7% or 4.8%?

This concludes our treatment of the one-dimensional maximum principle, and therefore signals the end not only of this chapter but of Part I as well. Henceforth, throughout Part II, we will be concerned with situations involving multiple heterogeneous capital goods and/or situations with uncertainty in capital accumulation.

PART II

Comprehensive Accounting and
the Maximum Principle

5

---　✳　---

Optimal Multisector Growth and Dynamic Competitive Equilibrium

Introduction via Three Examples

This book is composed of two interconnected modules. Part I is essentially an introduction to the economic theory of the maximum principle. In Part I we never went beyond models with a single capital stock. On the other hand, in Part I we used the maximum principle to characterize in sharp detail the exact form of an optimal solution for a wide variety of economically important one-dimensional dynamic problems.

Part II is both more general in its scope and more narrowly targeted in its aims. This chapter and the next will deal with an arbitrarily large number of different kinds of capital, but will focus more sharply on the meaning and significance of comprehensive or inclusive income accounting in such a general multisector setting.

We begin with three specific examples that both illustrate the multidimensional maximum principle and indicate our goals for this second module of the book. Although at this point we have not yet developed formally optimal control theory for two or more state variables (that comes later in the chapter), the three two-capital examples we are about to analyze are simple enough that the particular two-dimensional application of the maximum principle we will use should appear as an intuitive (if not yet fully rigorous) generalization of the one-dimensional case. Most multidimensional optimal control problems are difficult—sometimes very difficult—to solve and analyze. These three heterogeneous-capital examples have been chosen not only because their solutions are relatively easy to characterize but because they introduce some basic themes of national income accounting, which will be developed formally later in this and throughout the next chapter.

MODEL A: TWO GRADES OF HOTELLING DEPOSITS

Consider the following natural extension of the Hotelling problem treated in the last chapter. There are two deposits or fields of a nonrenewable resource. The first deposit or field, of amount S_1^0, is relatively "easy" to extract at "low" unit extraction costs c_1. The second deposit or field, of amount S_2^0, is relatively "difficult" to extract at "high" unit extraction costs c_2. Without loss of generality, we are therefore assuming

$$c_1 < c_2. \tag{1}$$

We imagine that deposits of both types are owned by large numbers of competitive extractors. "Total willingness to pay" utility is specified by the money-metric "area under the demand curve" expression

$$U(E) = \int_0^E D^{-1}(C)dC, \tag{2}$$

where $D^{-1}(C)$ is the inverse demand function giving price P as a function of quantity demanded C. In keeping with the discussion of Chapter 4, the dynamic competitive equilibrium is here the solution of the problem to

$$\text{maximize} \quad \int_0^\infty [U(E_1(t) + E_2(t)) \tag{3}$$

$$- c_1 E_1(t) - c_2 E_2(t)]e^{-\rho t} \, dt$$

subject to

$$\dot{S}_1(t) = -E_1(t), \tag{4}$$

$$\dot{S}_2(t) = -E_2(t), \tag{5}$$

and

$$E_1(t) \geq 0, \qquad E_2(t) \geq 0, \qquad S_1(t) \geq 0, \qquad S_2(t) \geq 0, \tag{6}$$

and with the given initial conditions

$$S_1(0) = S_1^0, \qquad S_2(0) = S_2^0. \tag{7}$$

Let p_1 and p_2 be the respective competitive prices of the two mines (or wells), per unit of the two ore-deposit types. The relevant Hamiltonian here is of the form

$$H = U(E_1 + E_2) - (p_1 + c_1)E_1 - (p_2 + c_2)E_2. \tag{8}$$

The Hamiltonian expression (8) combines three basic components of current income: *total willingness to pay* $U(E_1 + E_2)$ for resource services $E_1 + E_2$ (in the sense of the "area under the demand curve" expression (2)) minus *extraction costs* $c_1E_1 + c_2E_2$ minus *economic depletion* $p_1E_1 + p_2E_2$. It is the accounting for depletion—the subtraction of the total Hotelling rent term $p_1E_1 + p_2E_2$—that "greens" expression (8) by indicating the amount by which current well-being comes at the expense of future well-being. As will soon become apparent, an operational way of measuring the total Hotelling rent $p_1E_1 + p_2E_2$ is by the equivalent depletion formula $(E_1 + E_2)P - (c_1E_1 + c_2E_2)$, where P represents the competitive market price of a unit of the extracted resource.

Maximizing the Hamiltonian (8) over the control variables E_1 and E_2 yields the three alternative solution forms

$$p_1 + c_1 < p_2 + c_2 \Rightarrow U'(E_1) = p_1 + c_1, \quad E_2 = 0, \tag{9}$$

or

$$p_1 + c_1 > p_2 + c_2 \Rightarrow E_1 = 0, \quad U'(E_2) = p_2 + c_2, \tag{10}$$

or

$$p_1 + c_1 = p_2 + c_2 \Rightarrow U'(E_1 + E_2) = p_1 + c_1 = p_2 + c_2. \tag{11}$$

Because the maximized Hamiltonian is independent of S_1 and S_2, the corresponding capital-pricing differential equations are

$$\dot{p}_1(t) = \rho p_1(t) \tag{12}$$

and

$$\dot{p}_2(t) = \rho p_2(t). \tag{13}$$

Having studied carefully the solution of the one-capital version for a single deposit or field in the last chapter, the reader will not find it difficult to guess the corresponding two-capital solution for the two-grades problem being examined here. There will be two phases. In phase 1, lasting from time $t = 0$ to time $t = T$, only ore of type 1 will be extracted. Throughout phase 2, which begins at time T and continues thereafter indefinitely, only ore of type 2 is extracted.

Throughout stage 1, from equation (9),

$$P(t) = p_1(t) + c_1, \tag{14}$$

where $P(t)(= U'(E(t)))$ is the competitive postextraction market price of the resource, while throughout stage 2, from equation (10),

$$P(t) = p_2(t) + c_2. \tag{15}$$

At the switch-over time T, from equation (11),

$$P(T) = p_1(T) + c_1 = p_2(T) + c_2. \tag{16}$$

Combining (16) with (12) and (13) yields

$$p_1(t) + c_1 = P(T)e^{\rho(t-T)} + c_1(1 - e^{\rho(t-T)}) \tag{17}$$

and

$$p_2(t) + c_2 = P(T)e^{\rho(t-T)} + c_2(1 - e^{\rho(t-T)}). \tag{18}$$

The immediate implication of (17), (18), and (1) is that

$$t < T \implies p_1(t) + c_1 < p_2(t) + c_2 \tag{19}$$

and

$$t > T \implies p_1(t) + c_1 > p_2(t) + c_2. \tag{20}$$

Combining (14), (15), (19), and (20), we then have

$$P(t) = \min\{p_1(t) + c_1, p_2(t) + c_2\}. \tag{21}$$

Figure 2 depicts the relationship between $p_1(t) + c_1$, $p_2(t) + c_2$, and $P(t)$.

Using (17), (18), (19), (20), and (21), the proposed solution is completely characterized by specifying the unique values of T and $P(T)$ satisfying the two conditions

$$\int_0^T D(P(T)e^{\rho(t-T)} + c_1(1 - e^{\rho(t-T)}))\, dt = S_1^0 \tag{22}$$

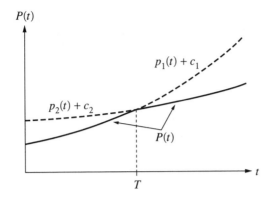

Figure 2 Equilibrium Hotelling price trajectory.

and

$$\int_{T}^{\infty} D(P(T)e^{\rho(t-T)} + c_2(1 - e^{\rho(t-T)})) \, dt = S_2^0. \tag{23}$$

What is the signal to owners of type 2 reserves that they should not be producing during phase 1? It is that

$$t < T \implies p_2(t) > P(t) - c_2, \tag{24}$$

meaning the value of leaving the mineral in the ground $p_2(t)$ exceeds the net profitability of extracting and selling it $P(t) - c_2$. Equivalently here,

$$t < T \implies \frac{\frac{d}{dt}(P(t) - c_2)}{P(t) - c_2} = \frac{\dot{p}_1}{p_1 + c_1 - c_2} > \frac{\dot{p}_1}{p_1} = \rho, \tag{25}$$

which sends essentially the same signal as (24)—that is, it is more profitable to leave the mineral in the ground because its net value is appreciating faster than the rate of interest.

Analogously, the signal to owners of type 1 reserves that their wells should be empty of oil during phase 2 is that

$$t > T \implies p_1(t) > P(t) - c_1, \tag{26}$$

that is, the value of leaving the mineral in the ground $p_1(t)$ is greater than the net profitability of extracting and selling it $P(t) - c_1$, which, along with the transversality condition, implies that no type-1 oil should remain unexploited at any time throughout phase 2. A more intuitive rendition is the dynamic version:

$$t > T \implies \frac{\frac{d}{dt}(P(t) - c_1)}{P(t) - c_1} = \frac{\dot{p}_2}{p_2 + c_2 - c_1} < \frac{\dot{p}_2}{p_2} = \rho, \tag{27}$$

that is, the net value of leaving grade 1 mineral in the ground during phase 2 is appreciating more slowly than the rate of interest, implying it should be drawn down and sold immediately.

This concludes the analysis of a dynamic competitive equilibrium for two grades of nonrenewable resource deposits. In the last chapter we analyzed the dynamic competitive equilibrium for a single grade of nonrenewable resource deposit with a backstop technology. We leave as an exercise the analysis of a dynamic competitive equilibrium for *two* grades of nonrenewable deposits *and* a backstop technology.

MODEL B: SHIFTABLE VERSUS NONSHIFTABLE CAPITAL

In the course of analyzing Problem 9 in the previous chapter, we solved a one-sector growth model (4.218)–(4.220) for a situation where homogeneous aggregate output is linearly proportional to aggregate capital (with output/capital coefficient a) and utility is a logarithmic function of consumption. We now seek to pose and solve a natural two-sector generalization of the same problem. (This model is a variant of what is sometimes called the Fel'dman-Mahalanobis model of economic growth; for more background, see Weitzman (1971).)

For convenience, we rewrite the one-sector version here as being the optimal control problem to

$$\text{maximize} \quad \int_0^\infty U(C(t))e^{-\rho t}\, dt \tag{28}$$

subject to

$$C(t) + I(t) = aK(t) \tag{29}$$

and

$$\dot{K}(t) = I(t), \tag{30}$$

and with the given initial condition

$$K(0) = K_0, \tag{31}$$

where the utility function is of the logarithmic form

$$U(C) = \log(C). \tag{32}$$

The "net savings rate" at time t for the above model is defined as

$$s(t) \equiv \frac{I(t)}{C(t) + I(t)}. \tag{33}$$

In effect, we characterized completely the solution to (28)–(32) as being to follow a policy of saving at the constant rate

$$s^* = \frac{a - \rho}{a}, \tag{34}$$

which corresponds to having every part of the economy grow exponentially at the constant rate $g^* = a - \rho$.

The nonshiftable-capital model we will analyze here consists of two sectors: the consumption-goods sector ("department 2") and the investment-goods sector ("department 1"). We make the plausible assumption that at any given instant of time the productive capacity of each sector is quasi-fixed and nonshiftable, but that over time the proportions can be continuously altered by directing new investments to one or the other of the two sectors. Such a description accords well with the familiar putty-clay nature of real-world investment. The cement and steel of the investment-goods sector are pliable general-purpose construction materials that can be used to increase the capacity of either sector until they are hardened into concrete shells and bolted-down specific machinery, dedicated to producing either more consumption (bakeries, urban housing, and so forth) or more investment (steel mills, cement factories, and so forth), at which point the two types of capital are considered to be *as if* frozen in place and are no longer shiftable.

To make the one- and two-sector versions comparable here, we assume that the utility of consumption for both models is the same logarithmic function (32), and that the output/capital coefficient is the same value a in both sectors of the two-sector model (as well as for the single aggregated sector of the one-sector model).

The simplest two-sector putty-clay analogue of the problem (28)–(31) is to

$$\text{maximize} \quad \int_0^\infty U(C(t))e^{-\rho t}\, dt \tag{35}$$

subject to

$$C(t) = aK_2(t), \tag{36}$$

$$I(t) = aK_1(t), \tag{37}$$

and

$$\dot{K}_1(t) = I_1(t), \tag{38}$$

$$\dot{K}_2(t) = I_2(t), \tag{39}$$

and

$$I_1(t) + I_2(t) = I(t), \tag{40}$$

and

$$0 \le I_1(t) \le I(t), \tag{41}$$

$$0 \le I_2(t) \le I(t), \tag{42}$$

and with the given initial conditions

$$K_1(0) = K_0^1, \tag{43}$$

$$K_2(0) = K_0^2, \tag{44}$$

where $U(C)$ in (35) is the logarithm function (32).

What is the relationship between the one-sector optimal growth model (28)–(31) and its two-sector putty-clay generalization (35)–(44)? To make both models tightly conformable, let us assume

$$K(0) = K_1(0) + K_2(0). \tag{45}$$

Figure 3 depicts the relationship between the two models when (45) holds. At time zero (now), the one-sector version has a straight-line production

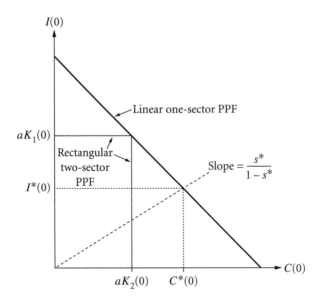

Figure 3 Shiftable versus nonshiftable capital. PPF = production possibilities frontier.

possibilities frontier with a slope of -1, and the decision maker is free to choose *any* non-negative values of $C(0)$ and $I(0)$ satisfying

$$C(0) + I(0) = aK(0). \qquad (46)$$

By contrast, the two-sector putty-clay version is "stuck" at time zero with its historically inherited "as if fixed coefficients" values of $C(0)$ and $I(0)$, which satisfy

$$C(0) = aK_2(0), \qquad (47)$$

and

$$I(0) = aK_1(0). \qquad (48)$$

Thus the two-sector model here has a *rectangular*-shaped production possibilities frontier in Figure 3 (described by (47),(48)), while the one-sector aggregated version has a *linear* production possibilities frontier in Figure 3 (described by (46)). We know that the currently producible historically given two-sector combination $(C(0), I(0)) = (aK_1(0), aK_2(0))$ is a point lying on the linear production possibilities frontier of the one-sector version. This particular point, however, need not represent an optimal combination of consumption and investment for the aggregate one-sector model. Imagine, though, that it does. Suppose, by pure coincidence, that the initial capital stocks of the two-sector model just so happen to satisfy the one-sector optimal savings condition—that is,

$$\frac{K_1(0)}{K_1(0) + K_2(0)} = s^*, \tag{49}$$

where s^* is given by equation (34).

Generally, the one-sector aggregate version has more production-possibility options than the two-sector putty-clay version, because the rectangular production possibilities set represented by (47),(48) is contained within the corresponding linear production possibilities set represented by (45). This implies that the maximized value of the objective function (28) of the less restricted one-sector problem (28)–(31) is greater than or equal to the maximized value of the same objective function (35) of the more restricted two-sector problem (35)–(44). However, when (49) holds initially, the two-sector putty-clay model can choose to "imitate" exactly the optimal one-sector constant-saving policy by selecting $I_1(t)$ at all times $t \geq 0$ so that

$$\frac{I_1(t)}{I(t)} = s^*. \tag{50}$$

Therefore it follows, if (49) holds, that both the one- and the two-sector models have the identical optimal consumption trajectory (both economies save at the same savings rate (34)) and the same optimal value of the objective function.

The relevant Hamiltonian for the two-sector optimal control problem is

$$H = U(aK_2) + p_1 I_1 + p_2 I_2. \tag{51}$$

Even without getting deeply involved in the details of the maximum principle here, we now find it possible to make an educated guess about the form of an optimal policy. If condition (49) holds initially, then the optimal two-sector policy is to maintain these same ideal capital stock proportions forever thereafter by always obeying (50). If condition (49) does not hold initially, then an educated guess might be that the optimal two-sector investment policy is a *most rapid approach* to the ideal savings ratio of capital stocks, which satisfies

$$\frac{K_1(t)}{K_1(t) + K_2(t)} = s^*, \tag{52}$$

and then, once condition (52) has been attained, the optimal policy remains forever in a state where (52) holds by following thereafter investment policy (50). A formal proof of the optimality of such a most rapid approach to the "ideal proportions" (52) hinges on showing that the conditions

$$\frac{K_1(t)}{K_1(t) + K_2(t)} < s^*, \qquad p_1(t) > p_2(t), \tag{53}$$

$$I_1^*(t) = a K_1(t), \qquad I_2^*(t) = 0$$

and

$$\frac{K_1(t)}{K_1(t) + K_2(t)} > s^*, \qquad p_1(t) < p_2(t), \tag{54}$$

$$I_1^*(t) = 0, \qquad I_2^*(t) = a K_1(t)$$

are mutually consistent with the corresponding price differential equations of motion

$$\dot{p}_1(t) = \rho p_1(t) - a \ \max\{p_1(t), p_2(t)\}, \tag{55}$$
$$\dot{p}_2(t) = \rho p_2(t) - a U'(a K_2(t)).$$

and also with the appropriate transversality conditions

$$\lim_{t \to \infty} p_1(t) K_1(t) e^{-\rho t} = \lim_{t \to \infty} p_2(t) K_2(t) e^{-\rho t} = 0. \tag{56}$$

(We leave the formal proof as an exercise, with the additional hint that if $t = T$ is the *first time* when condition (52) holds, then $p_1(t) = p_2(t)$ for all $t \geq T$.)

EXPLORING THE CONCEPT OF INCOME

Notice what is happening here. Figuratively speaking, the two-sector model is trying to act like the one-sector model. In the first (adjustment) stage, the two-sector model is modifying its structure (as rapidly as possible) to conform with the ideal proportions that the corresponding one-sector model would choose. After attaining these ideal proportions, the two-sector model subsequently looks exactly like the one-sector model it is trying to imitate. This kind of behavior is characteristic of a wide class of problems in optimal growth theory. By dealing with the one-sector optimal growth model, we are often implicitly covering (for free, as it were) the second-stage behavior of a more general multisector model.

Having employed the relatively simple device of the two-sector nonshiftable-capital dynamic problem (35)–(44) to indicate how the maximum principle may be used to clarify the relationship between one- and two-sector versions of an optimal growth problem, we now utilize this same apparatus to explore in a very tentative way some aspects of the concept of "national income." At this stage we are not nearly sufficiently well prepared analytically to confront the daunting general question What is income? (It will take us well into the next chapter until we can even begin to express carefully, in a general setting, such a multifaceted concept as "income.") For now, we content ourselves with merely observing what emerges when we attempt to apply a standard well-known income concept here to both of our model economies.

For the sake of argument, suppose we are at time zero in a state of the two-sector putty-clay model where the two capital stocks $K_1(0)$ and $K_2(0)$ are "ideally balanced" in the sense that (49) holds. Then we know that with initial conditions satisfying (45) and (49), the optimal trajectories of the one- and two-sector models are identical (both economies save at the same rate (34)) and both yield exactly the same dynamic welfare.

A well-known concept of income can be paraphrased as saying that income is "the maximum amount that can presently be consumed without compromising future ability to consume at the same level." I think this is a fair phrasing of a widespread notion of income that finds implicit expression throughout a broad range of contexts—from being a free translation of populist public sources such as the report *Our Common Future*, issued by the Bruntland Commission,[1] to being a transliteration of the financial/business concept of "economic earnings,"[2] to being a particular mutual strand of the

---

1. World Commission on Environment and Development (1987), p. 43, which defines "sustainable development" as being "development that meets the needs of the present without compromising the ability of future generations to meet their own needs."

2. See, for example, Bodie, Kane, and Marcus (2002), p. 611, who define "economic earnings" as "the sustainable cash flow that can be paid out to stockholders without impairing the productive capacity of the firm."

conceptual apparatus used by three great economists who did fundamental theoretical work on the concept of income: Fisher, Lindahl, and Hicks.[3]

Irving Fisher (1930) was the first economist to note clearly that "earnings" (what others would call "income"—the headstrong Fisher had already appropriated the term "income" for what others would call "consumption") can fruitfully be conceptualized as a form of interest-like return paid on wealth. Erik Lindahl (1934) argued cogently that the income of a period should be identified with the sum of consumption plus the net increase of wealth over the period. John Hicks (1946) introduced the modern idea, expressed in the definition of the previous paragraph, that income measures maximum present consumption subject to the sustainability-like condition of leaving intact future ability to consume at the same level. In the world of a Robinson Crusoe–like person whose wealth is like a deposit in a bank account paying a constant interest rate, all three measurements (Fisher's "income measured as interest on wealth," Lindahl's "income measured as consumption plus net increment of wealth," Hicks's "income measured as maximum sustainable consumption") coincide. But in almost any other world with even slightly more realistic complications, these three different ways of measuring income may yield different values, and it is not at all clear which one is better—or even for what purposes each might be better. For the sake of specificity, we concentrate here on trying to apply the popular Hicksian concept ("the maximum amount that can presently be consumed without compromising future ability to consume at the same level") to Model B.

A glance at Figure 3 reveals that, for the one-sector aggregate economy (with straight-line production possibilities), the Hicksian definition of income yields

$$aK(0), \tag{57}$$

while for the equivalent two-sector putty-clay version, the same definition of income gives

$$aK_2(0). \tag{58}$$

With conditions (49) and (45) holding, both economies are essentially equivalent in the sense of delivering an identical consumption trajectory,

---

3. I hasten to add that several other concepts of income were also explored by them.

yet the difference in income (as defined above) between the one-sector version (57) and the two-sector version (58) is

$$a(K_1(0) + K_2(0)) - aK_2(0) = aK_1(0). \tag{59}$$

We do not yet have the formal techniques to probe deeper into the situation, but we merely note for later reference that something seems very puzzling about the fact that the above seemingly reasonable standard definition of income yields very different values for what are essentially identical economic situations. From Figure 3, the core problem here seems to be that such a definition of income effectively forces us to compare the hypothetical consumption-producing ability of economies in the region where net investment is zero (that is, where $s = 0$), even when we most emphatically prefer *not* to locate ourselves in such a region (whenever $s^* > 0$).

"The maximum amount that can presently be consumed without compromising future ability to consume at the same level" might be a fine definition of income *if* we happen to want to be consuming at such a maximum sustainable level in the sense that we choose $s^* = 0$. Otherwise, unfortunately, this definition of income depends artificially, and arbitrarily, on the time allowed for an adjustment period and on the elasticity of short-run substitution between the production of consumption and investment, which (at least in this example) is not related to the economy's ability to produce well-being over time. Such a definition, as Samuelson (1961) put it, essentially defines income as "capacity to produce emergency consumption"—and this feature makes it quite idiosyncratically peculiar in any setting other than a situation where consumption and investment are infinitely substitutable. It seems natural enough to want income to be measuring some "sustainable-like" property of present and future consumption possibilities; but this model is hinting very strongly that income should not be defined literally as the highest permanently maintainable level of consumption, and that a proper definition of income (if one exists) may have almost nothing to do with literal sustainability. We will return to the important theme of an appropriate definition of income later, but for now we take leave of this subject—and of the two-sector putty-clay model of nonshiftable capital.

The following situation combines together in one optimal control problem some core elements of the Ramsey and Hotelling models.

MODEL C: RAMSEY-HOTELLING GROWTH

There are three basic types of factors of production, which for brevity may be conceptualized as "labor," "capital," and "oil." The first factor of production represents all fixed factors like labor, land, and so forth, which are held constant in the background. A second factor, aggregate reproducible capital, is denoted $K(t)$ at time t, with corresponding net investment $I(t)$. Finally, $S(t)$ is the aggregate stock of exhaustible resources in the economy at time t, whose corresponding extraction flow rate is denoted $E(t)$. Because labor and other fixed factors are being held constant in the background, the relevant reduced-form technology here can be written as

$$C(t) + I(t) = F(K(t),\ E(t)), \tag{60}$$

where $F(K,\ E)$ is the pertinent aggregate production function.

With $\{C(t)\}$ and $\{E(t)\}$ representing the controls, consider the following two-sector optimal growth problem:

$$\text{maximize} \quad \int_0^\infty C(t)e^{-\rho t}\,dt \tag{61}$$

subject to the capital accumulation differential equations

$$\dot{K}(t) = F(K(t),\ E(t)) - C(t), \tag{62}$$

$$\dot{S}(t) = -E(t), \tag{63}$$

and with the control constraints

$$E(t) \geq 0, \tag{64}$$

$$\underline{C} \leq C(t) \leq \overline{C}, \tag{65}$$

and the state constraint

$$S(t) \geq 0, \tag{66}$$

and having the given initial conditions

$$K(0) = K_0, \tag{67}$$

$$S(0) = S_0. \tag{68}$$

The above optimal growth problem (61)–(68) represents perhaps the simplest meaningful way to combine the Hotelling and Ramsey models. (Versions of this type of combined model appear throughout the literature; see, for example, Dasgupta and Heal (1979).) For ease of exposition in focusing sharply on some central issues, the utility function here is made "as if linear" in consumption (within arbitrary lower and upper bounds)—which (within the bounds) corresponds to a widely noted stylized fact that the own rate of return on consumption has been essentially trendless over time (here specified exogenously by the consumption discount rate ρ). The really important nonlinearity we want to focus upon in this exercise concerns the aggregate production function $F(K, E)$. For the purposes of this problem, the most important thing is that essentially no restrictions are being made about how K and E interact, so that in principle the aggregate production function in (60) could take virtually any form.

How might we describe approximately in words the solution of the two-sector optimal growth problem (61)–(68)? Over time, the exhaustible resource ("oil") is running out. The optimal solution will try over time to substitute the services of capital (and, behind the scenes, of labor) for the services of oil. The outcome will depend on many things—including how large are the oil reserves, how severe is the effect of overall diminishing returns from the background fixed factors like labor, and, perhaps most directly, the degree to which accumulated capital can replace oil. With a low elasticity of substitution between oil and capital (or, for that matter, between capital and labor), there may be severe limits to growth. (In the most extreme case where E is an irreplaceable input in the production process, consumption must ultimately go to zero over time, so that life as we know it would eventually cease.) Conversely, a sufficiently high elasticity of substitution between oil and capital presents much less of a threat to eventual well-being.

We cannot possibly know beforehand the values of the elasticities of substitution among oil and capital and labor in the limit as oil usage approaches zero over time, because this is much too far outside the range of normal experience. And yet this is precisely the kind of detailed information about the future that we would need to know now in order to be able to predict the ultimate impact on consumption of running out of oil. So if we want to gaze ahead into the future to find out what oil scarcity will do to our future consumption we would seem to be in a quandary, because we do not have a crystal ball. But wait a minute—maybe we do have a kind of crystal ball here! After all, we know in a general way that a great deal of information about scarcity is compressed into a competitive price. And we also know from the wealth and income version of the maximum principle that the current Hamiltonian (that is, current income) is a powerful predictor of future gains. Is it possible to use the market value of oil depletion as a leading indicator of how much consumption we will lose by running out of oil? The answer is essentially yes.

Before proceeding formally, we should first appreciate the power of this result. Imagine what kind of a modeling effort would be needed to give an answer to the question: "how much future consumption will be lost by running out of oil?" Among many other things, we would need to assemble a "dream team" of experts who could estimate where the arbitrarily specified aggregate production function $F(K(t), E(t))$ is going over time. These experts would need to know, among many other things, what is the future elasticity of substitution between capital and oil as oil diminishes, what is the overall degree of diminishing returns from the inability to shift away from fixed background factors like labor, and what are the best estimates of oil reserves. Furthermore, the results of any model assembled by the experts would only be as believable as the estimates, projections, and assumptions behind such a model. It is a staggering idea that the current price of oil, as determined by millions of actual buyers and sellers staking their own private fortunes on the outcome, renders, at least in principle, a more accurate judgment of the consumption losses from running out of oil than could be given by the best computer-driven forecasting model constructed by world-class experts.

Let us now use the maximum principle to analyze the problem (61)–(68). The mode of analysis we employ here might be characterized as "semiformal"—being at this stage a mixture of a heuristic extrapolation of formal control theory from the one-dimensional case combined with some intuitive economic arguments. We begin by writing down the Hamiltonian expression

$$H = C + p_k[F(K, E) - C] - p_s E, \tag{69}$$

where p_k represents the efficiency or competitive price of capital, while p_s represents the efficiency or competitive net price of oil. Expression (69) is directly interpretable as NNP.

Because the Hamiltonian (69) is linear in C (or, equivalently, in I), the optimal policy in C (or I) is a most rapid approach to an interior solution where $p_k = 1$. (We are assuming throughout that the consumption bounds (65) do not interfere with being in an interior solution.) But the stationary solution of

$\dot{p}_k = -\partial H / \partial K + \rho p_k$ corresponding to $p_k = 1$, $\dot{p}_k = 0$, from differentiating (69), must satisfy

$$\frac{\partial F}{\partial K} = \rho. \tag{70}$$

Maximizing the Hamiltonian (69) over E yields the first-order condition

$$\frac{\partial F}{\partial E} = p_s, \tag{71}$$

where, by the usual Hotelling-like arguments,

$$\frac{\dot{p}_s}{p_s} = \rho. \tag{72}$$

Without further ado, let us assume that we are in a dynamic competitive equilibrium where (70), (71), and (72) are holding, along with the relevant transversality conditions. The interpretation of (70) is essentially the same as for any interior solution of an optimal-growth problem with productive capital—the marginal product of capital equals the discount rate—while (72), combined with (71), is essentially a version of Hotelling's rule relevant to this two-sector context.

In the general case, (70), (71), and (72) are describing some highly complicated optimal equilibrium trajectory $\{C^*(t), I^*(t), E^*(t)\}$, whose behavior over time is very dependent, among other things, on the assumed form of the aggregate production function $F(K, E)$. Suppose we are located at time t on this optimal or equilibrium trajectory. Then the Hamiltonian expression (69), with $p_k(t) = 1$ along an interior solution, becomes

$$H(t) = C^*(t) + I^*(t) - p_s(t)E^*(t). \tag{73}$$

From the wealth and income version of the maximum principle, we know that $H(t)$ in equation (73) represents the *stationary equivalent consumption* level from time t on. In other words,

$$H(t) = \rho \int_t^\infty C^*(\tau)e^{-\rho(\tau-t)}d\tau. \tag{74}$$

The expression

$$C^*(t) + I^*(t) \tag{75}$$

appearing in (73) represents conventionally measured NNP—that is, consumption plus net investment in human-made capital. What does the expression

$$p_s(t)E^*(t) \tag{76}$$

in (73) stand for? Expression (76) is the total economic depletion or Hotelling rent at time t. In this particular model, however, we can go further and show that the economic depletion term (76) represents exactly the equivalent annual future loss of consumption from running out of oil.

For suppose that we interpret "*not* running out of oil" to mean here that at time t we have been unexpectedly given a sudden miraculous gift of a great many oil spigots distributed throughout the world, which deliver a constant total flow of $E^*(t)$ barrels of oil per year every year into perpetuity starting at time t. In other words, suppose that instead of being a depletable resource, oil was instead a fixed renewable resource able to deliver flow services forever at the current rate. The counterfactual historical thought experiment being proposed here is to imagine what would happen to consumption if everything else were the same in the model economy except that, instead of being constrained in the future by the finite world stock of oil $S(t)$, we were instead constrained in the future by today's constant flow of oil $E^*(t)$, so that, as a fixed factor of production, oil would never become any more scarce than it is now. What, we would like to know, would then happen to future consumption? For sure, consumption must increase with more oil available, but by how much?

The counterfactual thought experiment goes like this. Think of the present time t as being fixed. Future times will be represented by the variable τ, throughout which $E(\tau)$ is the constant value $E^*(t)$. For all $\tau \geq t$, let $\{C^{**}(\tau), I^{**}(\tau)\}$ be a solution of the following counterfactual one-dimensional optimal growth problem:

$$\text{maximize} \quad \int_t^\infty C(\tau)e^{-\rho(\tau-t)}d\tau \tag{77}$$

subject to the capital accumulation differential equation

$$\dot{K}(\tau) = F(K(\tau), E^*(t)) - C(\tau), \tag{78}$$

and with the control constraints

$$\underline{C} \leq C(\tau) \leq \overline{C}, \tag{79}$$

and having the given initial conditions

$$K(t) = K^*(t). \tag{80}$$

Note that the counterfactual "what if" problem (77)–(80) has the exact form of the family firm problem, with the additional feature that the problem happens to start out initially in its stationary solution, because (70) holds. Therefore, the solution of (77)–(80) is to remain forever in the stationary solution, that is,

$$C^{**}(\tau) = C^{**} \equiv F(K^*(t), E^*(t)), \tag{81}$$

and

$$I^{**}(\tau) = I^{**} \equiv 0. \tag{82}$$

for all $\tau \geq t$.
   Since

$$C^*(t) + I^*(t) = F(K^*(t), E^*(t)), \tag{83}$$

comparing (83) and (81) with (73) and (74), we have that

$$p_s(t)E^*(t) = C^{**} - \rho \int_t^\infty C^*(\tau)e^{-\rho(\tau-t)}d\tau. \tag{84}$$

Thus economic depletion of oil represents exactly the difference between C^{**}, which represents what consumption *would be* if we lived in an imaginary "what if" world where oil flows were constant, and the (stationary equivalent) consumption of the world in which we actually do live, where the stock of depletable oil is finite. In the precise sense of this counterfactual thought experiment, from (84), the total Hotelling rent term (76) stands for the "loss of future consumption" from present oil depletion. Although the relationship between E and K may be arbitrarily nonlinear in the aggregate production function $F(K, E)$, nevertheless, the simple linear economic depletion term (76) always—for any aggregate production function—captures exactly the difference in consumption between nondepletable and depletable oil. (Incidentally, for what it is worth, rough calculations based on this theory show that the fact that we here on the planet earth happen to live in a world where oil is exhaustible, rather than perpetually available at today's flow rate, causes an equivalent perpetuity-flow loss of about 1% of annual consumption; see Weitzman 1999 for details.)

In expression (73), H represents what might be called "green NNP" because it subtracts off the economic value of depletion of natural resources $p_s E^*$ from the expression $C^* + I^*$, the latter standing for conventionally measured NNP. Another way of interpreting (73), (74), and (84) taken together is to say that the value of depletion $p_s E^*$ is here a *precise welfare measure* of the degree to which conventionally measured NNP is a misleading indicator of future consumption (because conventionally measured NNP fails to account for the fact that future output will be impaired by depleting current stocks of the nonrenewable resource).

This example presages a number of basic themes to be developed throughout Part II. We can see here that "green NNP" is serving as a welfare-like measure that is compressing a remarkable amount of relevant information about future production possibilities and the future course of economic development into a single number. Furthermore, this single number seems to represent a concept with a "sustainable-consumption-like" flavor, which we might genuinely be interested in knowing and understanding. (After all, we are not really interested in elasticities of substitution or the size of reserve stocks for their own sakes, so much as a means of telling us what the future portends for our consumption possibilities when we are depleting those very stocks of the nonrenewable resources—and this aspect is picked up nicely in reduced form by "green NNP.") In studying this particular "Ramsey-Hotelling" two-sector model, we can sense that there exists an interesting and useful structure tying together concepts such as income, consumption, investment, depletion, wealth, welfare, and so on. And yet this particular problem is of a quite specific form and possesses some very special features. In this particular "Ramsey-Hotelling" model we are seeing the tip of an iceberg, and we would naturally like to know what general structure lies below the surface. We now begin the detailed task of revealing the exact architecture of the relationship between income, consumption, investment, depletion, wealth, welfare, and so forth in a very general model of optimal multisector growth and dynamic competitive equilibrium.

The General Multisector Optimal Growth Problem

Beginning in this chapter and continuing throughout the next, we deal with the multidimensional maximum principle expressed in terms of the so-called multisector optimal growth problem. However, no loss of generality is involved in using this particular terminology or handling this particular case. Merely by substituting the word "gain" for the word "utility," we could equally well be describing a multidimensional optimal control model for any economic unit (not just a national economy) maximizing present discounted gains.

Previously we were using the maximum principle primarily to "solve" specific problems—in the sense of providing either a closed-form solution or a very sharp characterization of an optimal policy. The one-dimensional case lends itself especially well to deriving such explicit characterizations. By using the key solution concept of the "stationary rate of return on capital," a reader who has carefully studied Part I should be able to solve and to analyze routinely any prototype-economic optimal control problem with just one capital stock—which is quite a useful accomplishment.

As a practical matter, optimal control problems are typically more difficult to solve with two or more state variables, and sometimes they are much more difficult to solve *even* for just two state variables. With more than one capital good, the concept of a stationary solution tends to lose its primacy, because, among other reasons, it is much less frequently approached as a limit since *all* of the capital stocks must admit of stationary solutions. (Think of the Ramsey-Hotelling model of an economy producing output from reproducible capital and an exhaustible resource; the economy tries over time to substitute capital for the nonreproducible resource, but a stationary state is not typically attainable because the economy cannot maintain any stationary positive value of the nonrenewable resource.)

With multiple heterogeneous capital goods there is no general analogue of the simple concept of a stationary rate of return on (homogeneous) capital, which was so useful for analyzing models having just one capital good. There is no simple general answer to the thought-experiment question "do I want to stay at this capital stock level indefinitely," which was so easy to formulate and answer with just one capital good. Furthermore, even if a stationary solution exists, and even if access to a stationary solution is unblocked, an optimal trajectory need not approach the stationary state with more than one capital good. It may be that convergence to a stationary state depends upon initial conditions. Some multidimensional problems *never* converge to a stationary state unless the problem happens to start there.

Yet another headache with multiple capital goods is that there is no multidimensional analogue of the extremely useful condition $R'(K) < 0$, which makes the stationary solution of a single homogeneous capital good vary inversely with the discount rate. In the multidimensional heterogeneous case, stationary-solution capital stocks can in general behave perversely as the discount rate ρ is varied parametrically—it can even happen that a higher value of ρ is associated with greater capital intensity. There may be multiple stationary solutions—sometimes the optimal trajectory will converge to one of them, but sometimes it will not converge to any of the multiple stationary solutions.

With one capital good, there were only two differential equations (in quantity and price) to analyze, and it is relatively easy to envision in a simple two-dimensional phase diagram what is happening. With two capital goods there are four differential equations to analyze. And truly anomalous things can happen, including chaotic behavior, in nonlinear differential equation systems of three or more dimensions. Even without chaos, the general analysis of nonlinear differential equation systems is difficult in three dimensions and can be essentially intractable for four or more dimensions.

So the bad news about most optimal control problems involving two or more capital goods is that we cannot explicitly solve them (not generally, anyway). The good news is that the extremely powerful maximum principle continues to characterize completely an optimal solution, even though the solution itself can only rarely be solved in closed form.

Instead of trying to solve multidimensional optimal control problems, we now focus much more sharply on the descriptive side, stressing the wealth and income version of the maximum principle for the general case. In this second part of the book, we use the maximum principle more as a description of an economy in dynamic competitive equilibrium than as a practical technique for solving actual problems. We will see that, although it may be very difficult in practice to give explicit closed-form solutions of multidimensional optimal control problems, the theory remains powerfully applicable and useful. In particular, the theory can be used to give a general interpretation of the meaning of net national income in a dynamic competitive economy where some renewable capital stocks are being built up over time while some other nonrenewable capital stocks are being drawn down.

What we are trying to do in Part II, ultimately, is to create a theory of comprehensive national income accounting. There are a number of big questions in this area that we intend to address. What is national income measuring? Which activities or items should be included in national income, and how should they be included? How might or should national income expressed in monetary units, which is all we can ever really hope to observe, be deflated into "real" national income? What is the exact relationship between national income, expressed in monetary units of account, and Hamiltonian income, expressed in terms of unobservable utility? How can "real" national income be used to make welfare comparisons over time or across space? What does national income mean in a world of uncertainty?

Another shift in emphasis that begins with this chapter concerns the mathematical level of abstraction and sophistication. In Part I, no familiarity with the maximum principle was assumed. Now the mathematics will be much more compressed, and some previous familiarity with the maximum principle will be assumed. We will be dealing in Part II with a multidimensional version of the maximum principle, which we will state but not prove.

The rest of this chapter proceeds as follows. We first state and prove rigorously a generalized wealth and income version of the maximum principle for the multisector optimal growth problem. Next, we state without proof the standard version of the maximum principle. We then explore the connection between the standard version and a simplified form of the wealth and income version.

Almost without exception, the usual textbook versions of the maximum principle are stated as if utility were directly observable and as if all prices were expressed in the numeraire of utility. This may be fine for problems representing profit-maximizing firms, since the objective is already stated in money terms; but at the level of a national economy, actually using such a "utility Hamiltonian" to draw practical conclusions represents a genuine intellectual challenge. The second half of this chapter is devoted to breaking free from the dependence of the maximum principle upon measuring everything in utiles. This is a very important link to where we are wanting to go, because in the actual world of national economies we do not observe utility functions or rates of pure time preference. The most we can possibly hope to observe is a monetary economy in dynamic competitive equilibrium with all prices expressed in terms of the (arbitrary) monetary unit of account. Our primary aim in this chapter is to indicate what a dynamic competitive equilibrium would look like in such a money-based economy.

Chapter 6 will reverse the causality of this chapter. In the current chapter, we are going from a multisector optimal growth problem to a statement of what the corresponding dynamic competitive equilibrium would look like when expressed in terms of the monetary unit of account—via the standard version of the maximum principle. In the next chapter we will go from observations on a monetary economy in dynamic competitive equilibrium to making some inferences about the relation between the economy's current money net national product and the future welfare it is able to deliver—via the wealth and income version of the maximum principle. The next chapter is centered on explaining the welfare significance of net national product; this chapter explains how net national product arises in the first place in a dynamic competitive economy and what conditions it satisfies.

The wealth and income version of the maximum principle is the key relation that will allow us to go from observations about an economy in dynamic competitive equilibrium to inferences about future welfare. However, there are many steps to be taken before such inferences can be made. In essence, we seek a methodology to translate welfare statements about utility income ("the Hamiltonian") into welfare statements expressed in terms of money income ("money NNP"). Prior to posing rigorously questions about the welfare significance of comprehensive national income accounting and attempting to answer them, however, we must state carefully what is the dynamic competitive equilibrium we are talking about. This is the overarching task of the current chapter.

It is important to state clearly at the outset that the results to be obtained in this and the next chapter do not depend on any tricky or unorthodox assumptions. The assumptions are the usual familiar ingredients of the conventional multisector optimal growth model. It is possible, of course, to criticize these assumptions, or this model of economic growth. For better or for worse, however, on no substantive point does this formulation deviate from the standard representative-agent "consensus" version of intertemporal optimization—here with multiple heterogeneous consumption and investment goods.

Let the vector C represent a m-dimensional fully disaggregated consumption bundle. (More specifically, component i of $C(t)$ measures the *instantaneous flow of consumption services* from consuming at the rate of $C_i(t)$ units of commodity i per unit time at time instant t, for $i = 1, 2, \ldots, m$.) The consumption vector C is conceptualized as a complete list containing everything that influences current well-being, including environmental amenities and other externalities. Consumption here would ideally include all components that influence the true "standard of living"—not just the goods we buy in stores and the government services "purchased" with our taxes, but also nonmarket commodities, such as those produced at home, and environmental services, such as those rendered by natural capital like forests and clean air. For the sake of developing the core theory, we assume that national income accounting is "complete" in the sense that comprehensive consumption is presumed to be fully observable, along with its associated m-vector of competitive or efficiency prices. We will also presume to know or be able to observe the relevant short-run market demand function in the domain over which any consumption comparisons are to be made.

For all feasible consumption-flow time series $\{C(t)\}$, it is supposed that it is meaningful to measure overall intertemporal well-being by the familiar expression:

$$\Omega(\{C(t)\}) \equiv \int_0^\infty e^{-\rho t} U(C(t))\, dt, \tag{85}$$

where $U(C)$ is some given concave, nondecreasing, instantaneous utility function with continuous second derivatives defined over all non-negative consumption flows C, while ρ is some given rate of pure time preference.

As practically every economist will attest, for better or for worse formula (85) is the standard workhorse dynamic-consistent objective function used widely in economics as a maximand in intertemporal optimization problems. Also for what it is worth, a linear functional taking the form (85) of an integral of present discounted utilities can be given an axiomatic justification as representing the appropriate dynamic preference ordering whenever independence, stationarity, continuity, and a few other seemingly reasonable conditions are postulated.[4]

Despite widespread acceptance in practice, especially for applied work, the form (85) has not been without its critics in the literature.[5] All of this is pointed out here because, for better or for worse, the analytical thrust of this part of the book will depend critically on the welfare ordering (85). It is by relying on the particular form (85) that the book's central concept of "sustainability equivalence" will be defined, motivated, and finally put to use.

The parameter ρ is interpreted as being the underlying rate of pure time preference. In a probabilistic version of the problem, ρ could also be interpreted as the probability that the world ends in any period, with zero utility obtained thereafter.

A wide variety of different preferences are accommodated by expression (85) as ρ is made to vary from zero to infinity and the curvature of the utility

4. See, for example, Koopmans (1960).
5. See, for example, Heal (1998), chap. 2.

function ranges from zero to minus infinity. Without further ado here, (85) is presumed to measure dynamic welfare.

The notion of "capital" used in this multisector model is intended to be quite a bit more general than the traditional produced means of production like equipment and structures. Most immediately, subsoil mineral resources are unquestionably considered to be forms of capital. Forms of human capital, such as education, should in principle be included, and also the knowledge capital accumulated from R&D-like activities. Generally speaking, every possible type of capital ought to be included—to the extent that we know how to measure and evaluate the associated net investment flows. Under a broad interpretation, renewable resources in particular and environmental assets more generally should be treated as forms of capital. From this perspective, environmental quality would be viewed as a stock of capital that is depreciated by pollution and invested in by abatement.[6] The underlying ideal is to have the list of capital goods be as comprehensive as possible, subject to the practical limitation that meaningful competitive-market-like efficiency prices are available for evaluating the corresponding net investments.

Suppose that altogether there are n capital goods, including stocks of natural resources and other nonorthodox forms. The stock of capital of type i $(1 \leq i \leq n)$ in existence at time t is denoted $K_i(t)$, and its corresponding net investment flow is $I_i(t) = \dot{K}_i(t)$. The n-vector $K = \{K_i\}$ denotes all capital stocks, while $I = \{I_i\}$ stands for the corresponding n-vector of net investments. Note that the net investment flow of a natural capital asset like a timber reserve would be negative if the overall extraction rate exceeds the replacement rate. Generally speaking, net investment in environmental capital should be regarded as negative whenever the underlying asset is being depleted or run down more rapidly than it is being replaced or built up.

In a spirit of focusing sharply for the sake of developing the core theory, we assume that the "attainable possibilities" of the underlying production and distribution system are time autonomous.[7] For theoretical purposes, we are thus imagining an idealized world where the coverage of capital goods is

6. Mäler (1991) contains a good discussion of some of the relevant issues here.

7. For treatments of the time-dependent case, see Nordhaus (1995), Weitzman (1997), or Weitzman and Löfgren (1997), and the further references cited therein. Time dependence introduces a host of messy complications, but a modified (and much less pretty) version of the result presented here can usually be found, contingent on some simplifying assumptions that accommodate an exponential form of time dependency growing at a constant rate.

so comprehensive, and the national accounting system is so complete, that there remain no unaccounted-for residual "atmospheric" growth factors. Thus national income is assumed to be "perfectly complete," because (in addition to including all relevant consumption flows evaluated at market-like competitive prices) all sources of future growth have been attributed as proper investments, which are fully "accounted-for" by being valued at their proper efficiency prices and included in national income.

Unfortunately, we do not now live in a world where national income accounting is complete, even though our theoretical models typically assume this feature. Completeness is perhaps best envisioned as a limiting case, which some real-world accounting systems approach in coverage but few attain. In our actual world we cannot measure accurately all investments, many externalities are not corrected or internalized, it is often difficult to impute market-like prices for nonmarket goods, imperfect competition and other second-best conditions exist, there are various atmospheric sources of positive or negative growth, which we cannot or do not include in net national product, and so on.[8] (The omitted atmospheric contributions are identified primarily as a residual, which is obtained by subtracting off from actual growth the effects of all known, properly attributed, sources of growth.)

Note that, technically speaking, it is always possible to convert any time-dependent system into a time-autonomous system merely by relabeling "time" as the $(n + 1)$st capital good, whose corresponding investment flow is the positive constant $+1$. And this approach would be fine for national income applications, provided we knew the efficiency price of time. Then complete accounting for a time-dependent system would include as the price of the $(n + 1)$st "investment" the value to the welfare-producing system of the passage of calendar time itself. The difficulty with this approach, which was pointed out very early in the green accounting literature, is not theoretical, but rather empirical. We are not sure where to look in a real-world economy for a decent market-based measure of the value of changes dependent on calendar time, such as the value of exogenous technological progress or other elements of the "residual."

All of these misgivings notwithstanding, it is eminently reasonable to begin an inquiry into the welfare significance of national income by first examining the case of perfectly complete accounting. One justification traditionally

8. Some ideas about how to treat imperfectly competitive and second-best market economies are discussed in the book by Aronsson, Johansson, and Löfgren (1997).

given for studying the pure theory of complete accounting in a real world of incomplete accounting is that the pure theory can indicate the route to greater completeness—by suggesting what activities to include, and how best to include them, in comprehensive national income. Another possible justification is that the pure theory of complete accounting is important because it will indicate how to use current income-like data to make welfare comparisons over time or across space. Either way, we want to begin an investigation into the meaning of national income with an examination of the case where national income accounting is perfectly complete.

As a precondition for having a perfectly complete accounting system, it is required that the attainable possibilities of consumption and investment at any time can be described in reduced form as a function only of the capital stocks existing at that time. Therefore, by making this assumption we are allowed to denote the $(m + 2n)$-dimensional attainable possibilities set here as A (rather than $A(t)$), where the consumption-investment pair $(C(t), I(t))$ is attainable at time t from the capital stock $K(t)$ if and only if

$$(C(t), I(t), K(t)) \; \varepsilon \; A. \tag{86}$$

To the extent that we conceptualize labor or land as fixed factors (in contrast with capital, which can be accumulated), they are already included in the definition of A by being held constant in the background. If labor (or labor-augmenting technological progress) is conceptualized as a factor that grows at a constant exponential rate, then there is a well-known trick that converts such a situation into a time-autonomous system merely by expressing all variables in per capita terms. (An explicit example of this kind of procedure was given in the formulation of Problem 4, Ramsey neoclassical optimal growth, of Chapter 2.) If it were considered desirable to treat labor participation as an endogenous choice variable, leisure might be included in the utility function. Thus in this framework, the treatment of labor (or land) can be seen as fairly unrestrictive.

As is usual in economic problems, the set of attainable possibilities A is presumed to be convex. We also assume that the constraint $K \geq 0$ is included in A. It should be appreciated that (86) represents an extremely general form for describing attainable possibilities, although, to be sure, the underlying technology is required to be time independent. In this discussion, A could be envisioned as reflecting technological, trading, political, and/or behavioral constraints, depending on the context. A technological constraint expresses the restrictions imposed by the usual laws of physical production as embodied, say, in standard production functions. An example of a trading constraint is the linear tradeoff schedule that a small nation trading at world prices might face. A political constraint may reflect a government-imposed restriction on what can be produced legally or a mandate to produce minimal amounts of certain "necessities." A behavioral constraint reflects limitations inherent in human nature that may override utility-maximizing combinations of (C, I, K), which are actually producible in a physical or trading sense.

There might be all sorts of underlying causes for constraints on attainable possibilities, including legal, constitutional, institutional, ethical, political, social, psychological, or other restrictions on what can be done. For example, the government may be limited, for any of a number of reasons, in what actions it can undertake to correct certain externalities. The important overarching point here is that all of the theory still holds, provided we interpret (86) as a reduced-form description of the allowable combinations of C and I that society actually confronts with capital stock K. Thus when we speak of optimization, it is always with respect to the allowable combinations described by the set A. (With an extreme interpretation, one could even model a completely "dysfunctional" society where the economy is so extremely nonoptimizing that A effectively prescribes uniquely determined values of C and I as a function of K.)[9] In this spirit it might be more accurate to refer to A as the "attainable possibilities set" rather than as the "production possibilities set." It should be noted, however, that this whole issue is entirely of an interpretational nature, since nothing on the substantive mathematical side is affected. It is just that such a general interpretation allows a somewhat broader coverage "for free," as it were—or, more accurately, at the expense of being required to construct the relevant as-if-competitive dual shadow prices, rather than merely assuming they are observable in the marketplace.

A key methodological assumption here is that competitive-like market prices can be observed (or at least imputed). This is not, of course, always true in practice. The degree to which some market prices are observable, or can be imputed, or are "competitive-like" will differ from economy to economy, depending, among other things, on the amount and degree of market distortion that is present. Even in the most developed and smoothly running capitalist economies, there are uncorrected (or at least not optimally corrected) externalities. The assumption of observable competitive-like market prices is useful

<hr/>

9. Dasgupta (2001) describes such an extreme nonoptimizing economy as "Kakatopia."

and necessary to begin with, but it is sometimes unrealistic. Nevertheless, even for the most dysfunctional underdeveloped economy, the starting point of almost any economic analysis would be the positing of imputed "shadow prices" that obey the same conditions as if they came from a dynamic competitive equilibrium—so there is no escaping the necessity of dealing with the kind of theory that will be developed in this and subsequent chapters.

This completes the background description required to formulate the basic optimal control problem of this chapter.

The *multisector optimal growth problem* is of the form to

$$\text{maximize} \quad \int_0^\infty U(C(t))e^{-\rho t}\, dt \tag{87}$$

subject to the constraints

$$(C(t), I(t), K(t)) \; \varepsilon \; A, \tag{88}$$

and the differential equations

$$\dot{K}(t) = I(t), \tag{89}$$

and obeying the initial conditions

$$K(0) = K_0, \tag{90}$$

where K_0 is the initially given capital stocks.

We are about to state and prove rigorously a generalized wealth and income version of the maximum principle for the above problem. Because at this stage we are not assuming any smoothness or differentiability, other than what is implied implicitly by a convex environment, we must formulate this rigorous wealth and income version in terms of tangent hyperplanes and directional derivatives, which represents a generalization to this convex environment of the concept of differentiability. First we restate the basic assumptions being made in this chapter.

Assumption 1. The set of attainable possibilities A is convex with free disposal.

Assumption 2. The utility function $U(C)$ is concave.

Assumption 3. A solution to the optimal growth problem exists for all $K_0 \geq 0$.

Let us employ the notation $X = K_0$. Then assumption 3 means that the state evaluation function for the multisector optimal growth problem $V(X)$ exists for all $X \geq 0$. ($V(X)$ is just the optimized value (87) of the problem (87)–(90) expressed as a function of the initial conditions, where $K(0) = X$ replaces (90).) It is relatively straightforward to prove, using the same approach that we employed for the one-dimensional case, that $V(X)$ *is a concave function of X* for all $X \geq 0$.

An unappreciated mathematical fact is that concave (or convex) functions are extraordinarily regular. In mathematical jargon, concave functions are what is called "C^2 almost everywhere"—signifying they have continuous second partial derivatives everywhere except possibly on a set of measure zero. It means that if we randomly choose a point $X \geq 0$, the probability that $V(X)$ has continuous second partial derivatives at that point is essentially one. At every interior point $X > 0$, a concave function has directional derivatives in all directions, and the probability that it fails to have a set of full partial derivatives at any randomly chosen point is essentially zero.

Now for any $K \geq 0$ and for any I producible from that K, define the tangent-hyperplane vector-valued function $\Psi(K, I)$ as being any solution of the following two conditions

$$V(X) - V(K) \leq \Psi(K, I)[X - K],\tag{91}$$

for all $X \geq 0$, and

$$\Psi(K, I)I = \lim_{h \to 0^+} \frac{V(K + hI) - V(K)}{h},\tag{92}$$

which solution must exist by concavity of $V(X)$. The function $\Psi(K, I)$ represents the *directional derivative along the tangent hyperplane of $V(K)$ at K in the direction of $K + I$*. If $V(K)$ is fully differentiable, then $\Psi(K, I)$ is just the vector of partial derivatives $\nabla V(K)$.

Under Assumptions 1, 2, and 3, we have the following simple, powerful, completely rigorous, and very general characterization of a solution to the multisector optimal growth problem.

Theorem (Generalized Wealth and Income Version of the Maximum Principle). *For the feasible trajectory $\{C^*(t), I^*(t), K^*(t)\}$ to be optimal under*

Assumptions 1, 2, and 3, it is necessary and sufficient that there exists a concave state evaluation function $V(X)$ and a price trajectory $p(t)$ satisfying for all $t \geq 0$ the condition

$$\rho V(K^*(t)) = U(C^*(t)) + p(t)I^*(t)$$

$$\geq \underset{(C,I)|(C,I,K^*(t)) \, \varepsilon A}{U(C) + \Psi(K^*(t), I)I,} \tag{93}$$

where

$$p(t) \equiv \Psi(K^*(t), I^*(t)). \tag{94}$$

Proof of Necessity. Following the same line of reasoning as the proof in Chapter 3, the wealth function

$$W(t) \equiv V(K^*(t)) \tag{95}$$

is differentiable with respect to time and satisfies the basic wealth equation

$$\dot{W}(t) = \rho W(t) - U(C^*(t)). \tag{96}$$

Combining (92), (94), and (95), it must hold everywhere along an optimal trajectory that

$$p(t)I^*(t) = \dot{W}(t). \tag{97}$$

Combining (95), (96), and (97), at all points along an optimal trajectory

$$\rho V(K^*(t)) = U(C^*(t)) + p(t)I^*(t). \tag{98}$$

Again paralleling the proof of necessity for the one-dimensional case of Chapter 3, for the time interval between time t and time $t + \tau$, consider *any feasible trajectory* $\{C(t), I(t), K(t)\}$ that begins at time t with the initial condition $K(t) = K^*(t)$, and after time $t + \tau$ follows an optimal trajectory starting from the then-initial state $K(t + \tau)$. The difference between the value of such a policy and the optimal policy starting from time t, discounted back to time t, is

$$\varphi(\tau) \equiv \int_t^{t+\tau} U(C(s))e^{-\rho(s-t)}ds$$

$$+ e^{-\rho\tau}V(K(t + \tau)) - V(K^*(t)). \tag{99}$$

By the definition of the function (99), we have that

$$\varphi(\tau) \leq 0 \tag{100}$$

and

$$\varphi(0) = 0. \tag{101}$$

Next, define the function

$$\psi(\tau) \equiv \int_{t}^{t+\tau} U(C(s))e^{-\rho(s-t)}ds + e^{-\rho\tau}\{V(K^*(t))$$

$$+ \Psi(K(t+\tau), I(t+\tau))[K(t+\tau)) - K^*(t)]\} \tag{102}$$

$$- V(K^*(t)).$$

We note that

$$\psi(0) = 0, \tag{103}$$

while, comparing (102) with (99) in the light of (91) (with $X \equiv K^*(t)$ and $K \equiv K(t+\tau)$) implies

$$\psi(\tau) \leq \varphi(\tau). \tag{104}$$

Now note from (99) and (102) that both $\varphi(\tau)$ and $\psi(\tau)$ are differentiable from the right at $\tau = 0$, which, from (100), (101), (103), and (104) must imply that

$$\psi'(0) \leq 0. \tag{105}$$

Differentiating (102) at $\tau = 0$, while remembering the "initial condition at time t" is $K(t) = K^*(t)$, and then applying (105), yields, for all feasible $I(t)$, the condition

$$U(C(t)) + \Psi(K^*(t), I(t))I(t) - \rho V(K^*(t)) \leq 0. \tag{106}$$

Combining (106) with (98), we have just proved the necessity of condition (93). ∎

Proof of Sufficiency. Let $(C(t), I(t), K(t))$ be any feasible trajectory with initial condition $K(0) = K_0$. Then, applying *to this feasible trajectory at any time t* the necessary optimality condition (93), which $V(K(t))$ must satisfy, we have that

$$U(C(t)) + \Psi(K(t), I(t))I(t) - \rho V(K(t)) \leq 0. \tag{107}$$

Now rewrite (107) as

$$U(C(t))e^{-\rho t} \leq [\rho V(K(t)) - \Psi(K(t), I(t))I(t)]e^{-\rho t}, \tag{108}$$

and rewrite the equality of (93) as

$$U(C^*(t))e^{-\rho t} = [\rho V(K^*(t)) - \Psi(K^*(t), I^*(t))I^*(t)]e^{-\rho t}. \tag{109}$$

Making use of the directional derivative property (92), mechanical time differentiation yields

$$[\rho V(K(t)) - \Psi(K(t), I(t))I(t)]e^{-\rho t} = -\frac{d}{dt}[V(K(t))e^{-\rho t}] \tag{110}$$

for *any* trajectory. Combining (108), (109), and (110), we then obtain

$$\int_0^\infty U(C^*(t))e^{-\rho t}\, dt - \int_0^\infty U(C(t))e^{-\rho t}\, dt$$

$$\geq \int_0^\infty \frac{d}{dt}[V(K(t))e^{-\rho t}] - \int_0^\infty \frac{d}{dt}[V(K^*(t))e^{-\rho t}]. \tag{111}$$

Because $V(K(0)) = V(K^*(0))$ and the limiting values of $V(K(t))e^{-\rho t}$ and $V(K^*(t))e^{-\rho t}$ are both zero, the right-hand side of the inequality in (111) is zero. Thus, the left-hand side of (111) is non-negative, which is the sufficiency result to be proved. ∎

Equation (93) shows that the previously treated one-dimensional state-ment of the wealth and income version of the maximum principle (in Chap-ter 3) generalizes powerfully to a situation with an arbitrary number of capital goods. The economic interpretation of (93) is essentially the same as for the one-dimensional case. Current income (direct gain plus the comparable net value of all investments) represents future "power to consume" in the pre-cise sense that the current-value Hamiltonian measures exactly the stationary equivalent of the future gains the system is capable of delivering over an in-finite time horizon. The main difficulty in connecting (93) with the existing optimal growth literature is not its lack of rigor or economic content, but the fact that (93) is of an unorthodox or "not-standard" form. The "prices" of capital $\Psi(K^*(t), I)$ that appear in (93) may depend on the direction in which investment is taking the capital stock, which, when it occurs, corresponds to an unconventional interpretation of equilibrium prices; however, there is nothing really wrong or incorrect about the concept, since $\Psi(K^*(t), I)$ *are* equilibrium prices—evaluated in the direction relevant for such an equilibrium concept. (When the state evaluation function is genuinely differentiable—meaning, for a concave function, that right- and left-hand-side derivatives are equal along a line in any direction—then all of these technical issues vanish.) However, rather than attempting the ambitious task of re-creating optimal growth and dynamic competitive equilibrium theory in the image of equation (93), which could be done, we instead opt here for the path of least resistance.

The Multidimensional Maximum Principle

We describe the appropriate standard version of the maximum principle for the above problem by a multidimensional generalization of the one-dimensional standard version described in Chapter 3. We have already proved in Chapter 3 the standard version of the maximum principle rigorously for one dimension. And we have here in this chapter just proved rigorously a "generalized" wealth and income version of the maximum principle for n dimensions. We will make no attempt here to prove the standard version of the maximum principle in n dimensions, although it could be done, as in the one-dimensional case, by using the generalized wealth and income version of the maximum principle. (Additional regularity assumptions are required to ensure the existence of all relevant derivatives, or else we must define carefully how to state a standard version of the maximum principle in terms of directional gradients of concave functions; overall, a higher level of mathematics is required and the proof is technically demanding.) It is hoped that some of the intuition of the one-dimensional case will carry over to the case of more than one dimension. From this point on, we are more interested in using the maximum principle to give general economic insights than to solve particular problems, and we do not pay so much attention to the exact conditions under which it holds or other such mathematical details.

We introduce the n-dimensional vector p. To maintain uniform notation throughout the remainder of this book, all *prices are row vectors* and all *quantities are column vectors*. The dual variables p will stand here for the *shadow prices of capital*. As in static optimization theory, whenever the state evaluation function is differentiable, p represents the extra value of the objective function that could be obtained upon reoptimization after relaxing the corresponding constraint equation by one unit. (However, p also exists at points where the state evaluation function is *not* differentiable.) The constraint equation corresponding to p here is (89). In this dynamic setting, $p(t)$ is what is sometimes called the (vector-valued) "co-state variable" associated at time t with the state-variable differential equations (89). (This shorthand vector notation just means that component i of $p(t)$ is the co-state variable to differential equation i of the differential equation system (89).)

We write mechanically the Hamiltonian expression:

$$H \equiv U(C) + pI. \tag{112}$$

A function of K and p that will again play a critical role in the maximum principle is the *maximized Hamiltonian* expression

$$\tilde{H}(K, p) \equiv \underset{(C,I)|(C,I,K)\,\varepsilon\,A}{\text{maximum}} \{U(C) + pI\}. \tag{113}$$

Because A is a convex set and the utility function is concave, the function $\tilde{H}(K, p)$ is concave in K for any given p, which means that a directional derivative exists in *every* direction of K. And a concave function must be differentiable "almost everywhere," as the mathematicians put it—meaning everywhere except on a set of measure zero. Without further ado we simply assume that $\tilde{H}(K, p)$ is fully differentiable, or at least there are only a finite number of points along an optimal trajectory where $\partial \tilde{H}/\partial K$ is not defined.

The trajectory $\{C(t), I(t), K(t)\}$ is called *feasible* if it satisfies conditions (88)–(90).

Having seen in Chapter 3 a rigorous proof for one dimension, and having just seen a rigorous proof of the n-dimensional generalized wealth and income version, we accept here on faith that under reasonable regularity conditions the solution of the optimal control problem (87)–(90) can be characterized as follows.

Multidimensional Standard Maximum Principle. *For the feasible trajectory $\{C^*(t), I^*(t), K^*(t)\}$ to be optimal, it is necessary and sufficient that there exists a continuous non-negative price trajectory $\{p(t)\}$ satisfying for all $t \geq 0$ the condition*

$$[\#1]: \qquad U(C^*(t)) + p(t)I^*(t) = \tilde{H}(K^*(t), p(t)), \tag{114}$$

and satisfying for all t ≥ 0 along the trajectory {C*(t), I*(t), K*(t)} (except possibly at points of discontinuity of I*(t)) the differential equations

$$[\#2]: \qquad \dot{p}(t) = -\frac{\partial \tilde{H}}{\partial K} + \rho p(t), \tag{115}$$

and satisfying the transversality condition

$$[\#3]: \qquad \lim_{t \to \infty} p(t) K^*(t) e^{-\rho t} = 0. \tag{116}$$

Let the relevant state evaluation function for the multisector optimal growth problem be $V(K)$, which exists everywhere along an optimal trajectory and must be concave. The *simplified wealth and income* version of the maximum principle here is the statement

$$[\#4]: \qquad \rho V(K^*(t)) = U(C^*(t)) + p(t)I^*(t) \\ = \tilde{H}(K^*(t), p(t)). \tag{117}$$

The "simplified" wealth and income version (117) is simpler than the "generalized" wealth and income version (93) in the sense that the simple price vector $p(t)$ replaces the more complicated subgradient $\Psi(K^*(t), I)$ in (93). Expression (93), although it has a plausible economic interpretation, is too cumbersome to be used without further development of the accompanying theory, whereas (117) is already expressed in a very convenient and familiar form for analyzing economic problems. We now show how we can prove condition [#4] directly from conditions [#1], [#2], and [#3]. Throughout the rest of the book we will make repeated use of the following important result.

Theorem. *The maximum principle conditions [#1], [#2], and [#3] imply the wealth and income condition [#4].*

Proof. Condition [#1] is exactly the second equality of [#4]. It therefore remains only to prove the first equality of [#4].

Differentiating the maximized Hamiltonian $\tilde{H}(K(t), p(t))$ and evaluating it along the optimal trajectory, we have

$$\frac{d\tilde{H}}{dt} = \frac{\partial \tilde{H}}{\partial K} \dot{K}^*(t) + \dot{p}(t) \frac{\partial \tilde{H}}{\partial p}. \tag{118}$$

Along an optimal trajectory, by the definition of $\tilde{H}(K^*(t), p(t))$ and using [#1], we must have the restricted-profit-function property

$$\frac{\partial \tilde{H}}{\partial p} = I^*(t). \tag{119}$$

Combining (119) and [#2] with (118), and canceling like terms, then turns (118) into

$$\frac{d\tilde{H}}{dt} = \rho p(t) I^*(t). \tag{120}$$

Use [#1] to change (120) into the equivalent linear differential equation

$$\frac{d\tilde{H}}{dt} = \rho \left(\tilde{H} - U(C^*(t)) \right), \tag{121}$$

which has the solution

$$\tilde{H}(K^*(t), p(t)) = \rho \int_t^\infty U(C^*(s)) e^{-\rho(s-t)} \, ds \tag{122}$$

$$+ \lim_{\tau \to \infty} [U(C^*(\tau)) + p(\tau)I^*(\tau)] e^{-\rho(\tau-t)}.$$

Now if a solution of the original problem exists, it must be true that

$$\lim_{\tau \to \infty} U(C^*(\tau)) e^{-\rho\tau} = 0. \tag{123}$$

From [#3], we must have

$$\lim_{\tau \to \infty} p(\tau)[K_0 + \int_0^\tau I^*(\tau) d\tau] e^{-\rho\tau} = 0, \tag{124}$$

which cannot hold unless

$$\lim_{\tau \to \infty} p(\tau) I^*(\tau) e^{-\rho\tau} = 0. \tag{125}$$

Making use of (123) and (125) to eliminate the second term of equation (122), it then becomes

$$\tilde{H}(K^*(t), p(t)) = \rho \int_t^\infty U(C^*(s)) \, e^{-\rho(s-t)} \, ds, \tag{126}$$

which signifies that we have the desired result

$$\tilde{H}(K^*(t), p(t)) = \rho V(K^*(t)). \blacksquare \tag{127}$$

Where do we stand now on the multidimensional case? We have proved rigorously a generalized wealth and income version of the maximum principle (with tangent hyperplane subgradients that are interpretable as directional prices). We have also proved rigorously that a simplified wealth and income version of the maximum principle follows from the standard version of the maximum principle. What we have not shown rigorously, but instead are taking on faith, is that with reasonable regularity assumptions, the standard version of the multidimensional maximum principle can be proved.

The Real Economy and the Nominal Economy

Starting with the standard version of the multidimensional maximum principle (114), (115), (116) as a point of departure, we are about to examine the corresponding description of a dynamic competitive multisector equilibrium with a representative agent whose intertemporal welfare function is of the form (85). Our ultimate aim is to infer future welfare from present observations of the current competitive economy. But, the reader may be asking, if that is the aim, why not just invoke the simplified wealth and income version of the maximum principle (117) to infer future welfare from the current Hamiltonian?

There are two major problems yet to be confronted in trying to infer future welfare from the current Hamiltonian. First of all, the Hamiltonian here is of a form which, in effect, aggregates all consumption goods into a utility function that is unobservable to a national income accountant. Second, prices of investment goods are expressed in "utiles"—that is, with utility as numeraire—and the national income accountant does not know how to deflate money prices into utiles. In a sense the problem is that we have a "utility Hamiltonian" or "utility-based income" in the theory, whereas all that we can ever hope to observe in actual practice is national income expressed in money or nominal terms.

The national income accountant is, at best, observing consumption and investment aggregated at their competitive money prices. The utility-valued wealth and income version of the maximum principle will not be useful, except for special cases, unless it can be translated into an operational procedure for making welfare statements in terms of what is observable. We will move toward an observable description of a dynamic competitive multisectoral equilibrium in two steps. The first step is to replace the role of the utility function by the role of aggregate consumption evaluated in utility prices. The second step is to replace a formulation expressed in terms of utility prices into a formulation expressed in terms of money prices.

We envision the representative agent as being simultaneously a utility-maximizing consumer and a profit-maximizing producer. Let q be an m-vector of consumption goods prices (with utility as numeraire). To facilitate thinking more directly about the dynamic-competitive-equilibrium interpretation of the maximum principle, define the *aggregate utility-valued production function* (of K, for given utility-based prices p and q) as

$$f(K \mid p, q) \equiv \underset{(C,I)\mid(C,I,K)\,\varepsilon\,A}{\text{maximum}} \{qC + pI\}. \tag{128}$$

Now define

$$q(t) \equiv \nabla U(C^*(t)), \tag{129}$$

where ∇ denotes a vector of partial derivatives. The optimality condition [#1] requires that the Hamiltonian expression should attain its maximum everywhere along an optimal trajectory. In the representative-agent interpretation, and with the problem having a convex structure, maximizing the Hamiltonian is equivalent to the more economically intuitive combination of two equilibrium conditions. The first condition describes the representative *consumer*'s decentralized behavior in choosing among consumption goods C and net savings when consumption goods prices are normalized so that the marginal utility of income saved is one:

$$[\#1a]: \quad U(C^*(t)) - q(t)C^*(t)$$
$$= \underset{C \geq 0}{\text{maximum}}[U(C) - q(t)C]; \tag{130}$$

the second condition describes the representative *producer*'s decentralized static-equilibrium profit-maximizing behavior:

$$[\#1b]: \quad q(t)C^*(t) + p(t)I^*(t) = f(K^*(t) \mid p(t), q(t)). \tag{131}$$

We leave it as an exercise to prove that, under convexity, $(C^*(t), I^*(t))$ is a solution of conditions [#1a] and [#1b] if and only if it is a solution of condition [#1]. (It is a fairly straightforward application of the separating hyperplane theorem.)

Condition [#2] in this new notation becomes

$$[\#2a]: \qquad \dot{\boldsymbol{p}}(t) = -\left.\frac{\partial f}{\partial \boldsymbol{K}}\right|_{*(t)} + \rho \boldsymbol{p}(t), \qquad (132)$$

where the notation "$|_{*(t)}$" means evaluation along the optimal trajectory at time t.

The transversality condition [#3] remains the same here.

We have taken a first step toward an observable description of a dynamic competitive equilibrium by expressing the maximum principle in terms of what might be called "utility prices" of consumption and investment. To be helpful as a guide for national income accounting, however, both the prices of consumption goods and the prices of investment goods at any time should be expressed in terms of the nominal unit of account at that time as numeraire. What remains before us is to take the second step of converting utility prices into observable money prices.

Toward that end, we write *money* or *nominal* prices at time t in the form

$$\boldsymbol{P}(t) \equiv \frac{\boldsymbol{p}(t)}{\lambda(t)}, \qquad (133)$$

and

$$\boldsymbol{Q}(t) \equiv \frac{\boldsymbol{q}(t)}{\lambda(t)}. \qquad (134)$$

The coefficient $\lambda(t)$ appearing in (133) and (134) can be regarded at this point as being simply an arbitrarily chosen reduced-form "scaling factor" that converts utility prices at time t into nominal prices. In the model, $\{\lambda(t)\}$ may be chosen arbitrarily because it represents an extra degree of freedom that merely parameterizes the marginal utility of money income, which can be given a life of its own, related behind the scenes of the real economy to the money supply and other background, purely monetary, factors that determine the price level. For example, let $M(t)$ be the exogenously determined "stock of money" circulating in the economy at time t. Then, with a crude quantity theory of money and with "monetary policy" envisioned as costless helicopter drops of new cash, we can think of $M(t)$ as "essentially" determining $\lambda(t)$ via the equation

$$\lambda(t) = \frac{Q(t)C^*(t) + P(t)I^*(t)}{M(t)v(t)}, \tag{135}$$

where $v(t)$ represents some given *velocity of money* at time t. (We note in passing that far greater doses of generality, sophistication, and realism are possible for describing the role of money, but they would play no genuine role in the model—worse, they would distract attention from the main points that need to be made here. This is the reason why our analysis uses the simplest imaginable concept of money as being merely a mechanical transmission mechanism that determines the price level.)

The primary interpretation of $\lambda(t)$ comes directly from combining (129) and (134) into the statement

$$\nabla U(C^*(t)) = \lambda(t)Q(t). \tag{136}$$

Equation (136) means that $\lambda(t)$ can be interpreted as *the marginal utility of income at time t*. In a sense, part of what we are attempting to do in this chapter is to make use of this interpretation (136) of $\lambda(t)$, even though we cannot observe $\lambda(t)$ directly.

What matters for the allocation of resources in the *real* economy—through the classical-dichotomy veil of arbitrary $\{\lambda(t)\}$, so to speak—are the real utility-based prices, which are denominated in terms of the contemporaneous value of utility serving as numeraire, and are therefore invariant to $\{\lambda(t)\}$. In other words, changing the exogenous specification of $\{\lambda(t)\}$ within this kind of classical world would merely induce inversely proportional scaling changes in $\{P(t)\}$ and $\{Q(t)\}$ without altering $\{p(t)\}$ or $\{q(t)\}$. (Almost without exception, the literature on optimal growth theory specifies unceremoniously that all prices are to be expressed in "real" utility-valued units. The reason we must deal carefully with the issues raised by arbitrary $\{\lambda(t)\}$ is because our ultimate goal here is to translate observable market values, denominated in the arbitrary nominal units of a monetary economy, into statements about welfare, expressed, ultimately, in utiles.)

It is essential to note that no one (neither consumers, nor producers, nor government central bank authorities, nor anyone else) thinks directly in terms of utility prices. Indeed, if the economy is growing, then utility prices are declining over time (from diminishing marginal utility), and yet no actual monetary authority in real life would countenance the deflationary monetary policy that would generate a declining price level (as conventionally measured). For this reason alone it is important to state the conditions for a dynamic competitive equilibrium in terms of the nominal money prices existing at the time.

Let us now calculate the nominal interest rate that corresponds to the money prices described by equations (133) and (134). We begin with the observation that, in terms of utility, the utility interest rate or rate of return on utility is ρ all along an optimal path. If, in any period, we were to postpone enjoying a unit of utility until the next period, we must be able to receive back ρ *extra* units of utility in that next period without disturbing subsequent utility possibilities—or else the program would not be optimal.

To determine the *nominal interest rate*, we need to calculate the corresponding *money rate of return on consumption*. Suppose we are moving along an optimal trajectory. If in period t we abstain from one dollar's worth of consumption, then we forgo the enjoyment of $\lambda(t)$ units of utility. During the following period $t + dt$, we could then enjoy a splurge of $(1 + \rho\, dt)\lambda(t)$ units of utility (because the rate of return on utility over this period is $\rho\, dt$) without disturbing anything else in the future after that. But this is equivalent to consuming in period $t + dt$ the dollar amount

$$\frac{(1 + \rho\, dt)\lambda(t)}{\lambda(t + dt)} \tag{137}$$

of consumption without otherwise threatening subsequent possibilities. (The marginal utility of income appearing in the denominator of (137) is being used to convert from utility to consumption at time $t + dt$.) Because it represents the money rate of return that a bank would pay on a dollar deposit of "withheld consumption," the short-term nominal interest rate, denoted $r(t)$, must be related to (137) by satisfying the condition

$$1 + r(t)\, dt = \frac{(1 + \rho\, dt)\lambda(t)}{\lambda(t + dt)}. \tag{138}$$

Now rewrite equation (138) as the equivalent expression

$$(1 + r(t)dt)\lambda(t + dt) = (1 + \rho\, dt)\lambda(t), \tag{139}$$

and then let the length of a period in equation (139) become progressively shorter. In the limit as the length of a period dt becomes infinitesimally small, equation (139) becomes

$$r(t) = \rho - \frac{\dot{\lambda}(t)}{\lambda(t)}. \tag{140}$$

Expression (140) is considered to be *the* fundamental equation linking the instantaneous money interest rate along an optimal trajectory to the rate of pure time preference and the behavior of the marginal utility of income over time.

The implicit causality we have been using is that $\{\lambda(t)\}$ is viewed as being arbitrarily chosen, with $\{r(t)\}$ then being determined by (140). But we can reverse this causality. We can envision the schedule of nominal interest rates $\{r(t)\}$ as being arbitrarily chosen by the monetary authorities, while $\{\lambda(t)\}$ is determined by integrating the differential equation (140), which then becomes

$$\lambda(t) = \lambda(0) \, \exp(\int_0^t (\rho - r(\tau))d\tau). \tag{141}$$

Therefore we are entitled to envision any one of the triple $\{M(t)\}$, $\{\lambda(t)\}$, $\{r(t)\}$ as being exogenously chosen, while the other two are then determined by equations (135), (140), or (141). As was already stated, the easiest interpretation is simply to regard the time series of coefficients $\{\lambda(t)\}$ as being an arbitrarily chosen reduced-form "scaling factor" that converts nominal prices at time t into utility prices. However, if we want to, we are entitled to think of the monetary authorities setting money-stock targets $\{M(t)\}$ or even targeting the money rate of interest $\{r(t)\}$ by open market operations. In principle, at the level of abstraction of the underlying multisector model, none of this detail matters for the allocation of real resources.

Define the *aggregate money-valued production function* (of K, for given nominal prices P and Q) as

$$F(K \mid P, Q) = \operatorname*{maximum}_{(C,I)\mid(C,I,K)\,\varepsilon\,A} \{QC + PI\}. \tag{142}$$

We now seek to state conditions [#1a], [#1b], [#2a], and [#3] in nominal terms. From (133), the nominal version of [#1a] is

$$\{\#1\}: \quad U(C^*(t)) - \lambda(t)Q(t)C^*(t)$$
$$= \operatorname*{maximum}_{C\geq 0}[U(C) - \lambda(t)Q(t)C], \tag{143}$$

while from (134) the nominal version of [#1b] is

$$\{\#2\}: \quad Q(t)C^*(t) + P(t)I^*(t) = F(K^*(t) \mid P(t), Q(t)). \tag{144}$$

Using (133) and (140), the nominal version of [#2a] is

$$\{\#3\}: \qquad \dot{P}(t) = -\left.\frac{\partial F}{\partial K}\right|_{*(t)} + r(t)P(t), \qquad (145)$$

where the notation "$|_{*(t)}$" means evaluation along an optimal trajectory at time t.

Finally, the nominal version of the transversality condition [#3] is

$$\{\#4\}: \qquad \lim_{t \to \infty} \alpha(t)P(t)K^*(t) = 0, \qquad (146)$$

where

$$\alpha(t) \equiv \exp(-\int_0^t r(\tau)d\tau) \qquad (147)$$

is the corresponding nominal discount factor for time t, which is equal to the present discounted money value of a dollar at time t.

Why have we have expended so much algebra and space on the minute details of showing the equivalence of conditions [#1], [#2], and [#3] of the maximum principle with conditions {#1}, {#2}, {#3}, and {#4}, which characterize a nominal dynamic competitive equilibrium in the corresponding representative-agent economy? It is because conditions {#1}, {#2}, {#3}, and {#4} are interpretable as a set of competitive market-equilibrium conditions whose units are expressed in familiar economic terms, since the numeraire at any time is the monetary unit of account at that time. This will prove to be useful for making a more realistic description of a dynamic equilibrium, and, more important, because the output of the "aggregate production function" is expressed in the proper units to be able to correspond to a genuinely observable money-valued net national income concept.

It will be fundamentally important for all that follows to comprehend fully that conditions {#1}, {#2}, {#3}, and {#4} can be interpreted as describing a money-valued economy in dynamic competitive equilibrium. In other words, if we tried to write down a description of a competitive equilibrium for the economy being considered here, even without any knowledge of the maximum principle, then conditions {#1}, {#2}, {#3}, and {#4} would be the natural candidates we would turn to. Because this interpretation is so important, we investigate each condition in some detail.

Condition {#1} describes the representative consumer's decentralized behavior in choosing among consumption goods **C** and net savings, where the "price" of net savings, corresponding to the nominal prices of consumption goods, is the marginal utility of income. We will return shortly to condition {#1}, because we will want to see how this static description meshes with the dynamic consumption plans of a consumer maximizing lifetime utility subject to a lifetime budget constraint requiring that total consumption spending should not exceed lifetime wealth.

Condition {#2} describes in reduced form the static production side of a perfectly competitive economy, where each producer is maximizing profits with prices taken as given. Behind this reduced-form condition on final (consumption and net investment) goods might be millions of individual producers, each one of whom is maximizing individual profits. The important point here is that the production sector is in static competitive equilibrium if and only if condition {#2} holds—irrespective of the intermediate microeconomic details of who produces what and who sells to whom. An entire world of unspecified intermediate goods might be being netted-out in the background. So the economy behind the reduced-form description {#2} might be as complicated and intricate as can be imagined—the beauty of the reduced-form approach taken here is that we are describing in one fell swoop an arbitrarily complicated production and distribution economy, which we do not need to specify explicitly because the sine qua non of perfect competition in production is that the economy be located on its production possibilities frontier at a point where all marginal rates of substitution between final goods are equal to their price ratios, that is, where {#2} is satisfied.

Taken together, conditions {#1} and {#2} constitute a reduced-form statement that the economy at all times obeys the static marginal conditions of a competitive market system. Each representative agent—all producers and all consumers—effectively take prices at any time t as given and act in such a way as to equate the marginal rates of transformation or substitution between any two goods with their corresponding price ratios. In other words, at any given instant the economy acts *as if* it were in a perfectly competitive static equilibrium.

Condition {#3} is for dynamics what conditions {#1} and {#2} are for statics. Equation {#3} is the fundamental stock market equilibrium condition for a perfect capital market whose nominal rate of return on capital is $r(t)$ at time t. If {#1},{#2} represents a photograph of a static economy in competitive equilibrium, then {#3} is the complete movie from which the still frame of

{#1},{#2} is taken at any particular time. Condition {#3} portrays a stock market in a dynamic competitive price equilibrium where no arbitrageur can make pure profits by any movement of funds among alternative investment vehicles. This condition can be explained by the following thought experiment.

Consider a world of no uncertainty with a perfectly competitive capital market. Suppose a potential investor at time t decides to forgo one dollar's worth of consumption during the period between time t and time $t + dt$ in favor of buying $1/P_j^*(t)$ units of capital stock j. If the investor plans to carry this investment forward for just one period, the "income dividend" yielded during the period by putting the extra $1/P_j^*(t)$ units of capital stock j to its most profitable use is

$$\frac{\left.\frac{\partial F}{\partial K_j}\right|_{*(t)} dt}{P_j^*(t)}. \tag{148}$$

If the stock is sold at time $t + dt$, the expected capital gain would be

$$\frac{P_j^*(t + dt) - P_j^*(t)}{P_j^*(t)}. \tag{149}$$

The total one-period return on a dollar's worth of capital would then be

$$\frac{\left.\frac{\partial F}{\partial K_j}\right|_{*(t)} dt}{P_j^*(t)} + \frac{P_j^*(t + dt) - P_j^*(t)}{P_j^*(t)}. \tag{150}$$

In a perfect capital market, the nominal rate of return on capital for this dollar investment at time t must equal the prevailing money interest rate $r(t)$. Thus

$$\frac{\left.\frac{\partial F}{\partial K_j}\right|_{*(t)} dt}{P_j^*(t)} + \frac{P_j^*(t + dt) - P_j^*(t)}{P_j^*(t)} = r(t)\, dt. \tag{151}$$

Since equation (151) is just an alternatively written version of equation (145), it means that condition {#3} is describing the dynamic equilibrium of a perfectly competitive stock market. If condition {#3} were *not* met, a disequilibrium situation exists and arbitragers could make positive pure profits by straddling markets, thereby setting in motion, with their buying and selling activities, stock price changes that would end by re-equilibrating {#3}.

Finally, the "transversality condition" {#4} disallows a speculative bubble from continuing forever. If {#4} did *not* hold, then an arbitrager could in principle broker a sequence of overlapping buying and selling swaps that would end up making pure positive profits. The economic story behind the logic of the transversality condition {#4} for the general equilibrium scenario is so close to the economic story behind the logic of the transversality condition [#3] for the multidimensional maximum principle, which in its turn is so close to the economic story behind the logic of the transversality condition [#3] for the one-dimensional maximum principle (explained in detail in Chapter 3), that we leave it as a fruitful exercise for the reader to fill in whatever details remain. (The remaining details essentially consist of rephrasing the one-dimensional economic story so that it holds where the symbol "n"—for the number of capital goods—replaces the symbol "1"—for the case of a single capital good already treated fully in Chapter 3. Doing this is a good exercise, especially for the novice, because it highlights the connections between the maximum principle in one dimension with the maximum principle in n dimensions with the nominal dynamic competitive equilibrium interpretation in n dimensions.)

The kind of dynamic equilibrium represented by conditions {#3} and {#4} is sometimes called an "equilibrium in expectations" or a "perfect foresight equilibrium." No one really believes that today's prices are literally satisfying conditions {#3} and {#4}. These conditions are rather describing the target trajectory around which prices may tend to fluctuate (ideally only slightly), rather than representing a literal story of how prices change over time. The hope is that the actual approximation is close enough to make applications of the theory, such as those of this book, fit reasonably well with the facts.

The nominal dynamic competitive equilibrium description {#1}, {#2}, {#3}, and {#4} and the multisector optimal growth problem (87)–(90) are two sides of the same coin. In the setup here, with convexity, a solution of the optimal growth problem must generate nominal efficiency prices that constitute a dynamic competitive equilibrium, and any nominal dynamic competitive equilibrium must be a solution of the optimal growth problem. Throughout the remainder of the book, we will use both sides of this basic duality repeatedly. We will use the dynamic competitive equilibrium side to evaluate and interpret various prices and quantities. And we will use the optimal growth side to justify using the "as if optimized" objective function (85) in order to provide some crucial welfare measures.

The duality between optimal growth and dynamic competitive equilibrium is crucial for the main purpose of Part II, which is to investigate thoroughly the welfare basis of comprehensive national income accounting. This explains the large effort being made in this chapter to show the equivalence between optimization and equilibrium for a system of goods money prices that correspond to how a national income statistician would actually evaluate national income in the real world.

There is one more important issue to be dealt with now. It concerns consumer behavior. We have described the consumer's *static* optimizing behavior at any time by condition {#1}. Let us now examine the relationship of {#1} with the consumer's *dynamic* optimizing behavior of maximizing present discounted utility subject to a lifetime budget constraint limiting total consumption expenditures to be no more than total lifetime wealth.

What is the representative consumer's lifetime wealth? At time zero (now), the representative agent in this economy owns the current capital stocks $K(0)$, whose present cash value is

$$P(0)K(0). \tag{152}$$

Furthermore, the representative agent is entitled to all future cash-flow returns to labor (and other noncapital factors of production like land and so forth), which are fixed in the background and supplied by the representative agent to the work process. Because the representative agent "represents" all consumers and producers (present and future), the relevant lifetime spans an infinite horizon. By the marginal productivity theory of distribution, the present discounted money value of returns to fixed factors like labor, land, and so forth supplied by the representative agent is

$$\int_0^\infty [Y(t) - \frac{\partial F}{\partial K}\Big|_{*(t)} K^*(t)]\alpha(t)\, dt, \tag{153}$$

where

$$Y(t) \equiv F(K^*(t) \mid P(t), Q(t)) \tag{154}$$

is nominal aggregate output at time t, while $\alpha(t)$ is the nominal discount factor at time t defined by (147).

Therefore the representative agent's total lifetime wealth (at time zero) W_0 is the value of initial stock holdings (152) plus the present discounted value of lifetime earnings (153) of all noncapital fixed factors of production, like labor, land, and so forth, or

$$
W_0 = P(0)K(0) + \int_0^\infty [Y(t) - \frac{\partial F}{\partial K}\bigg|_{*(t)} K^*(t)]\alpha(t)\, dt. \tag{155}
$$

The representative agent's lifetime consumption allocation problem is to

$$
\text{maximize} \quad \int_0^\infty U(C(t))e^{-\rho t}\, dt \tag{156}
$$

subject to the lifetime budget constraint

$$
\int_0^\infty \alpha(t)Q(t)C(t)\, dt = W_0. \tag{157}
$$

Making use of (140) and (147), it is not difficult to show that, aside from corner solutions at zero consumption, the solution of the above constrained optimization problem (156),(157) satisfies at all times t the first-order condition

$$
\nabla U(C^*(t)) = \lambda(t)Q(t), \tag{158}
$$

which signifies that condition {#1} is exactly the solution of the representative agent's lifetime consumption allocation problem. Therefore, since condition {#1} is equivalent to the solution of (156),(157), we have the option of choosing either description of the representative consumer's behavior. If we tend to choose {#1}, it is only because this formulation is simpler.

We now turn our attention to specifying the representative consumer's demand function in this dynamic competitive equilibrium framework. Whenever someone talks about a demand function, the very first question to ask is: for what time horizon is this demand function defined? Here, we are talking about the representative consumer's short-run demand function.

Consistent with traditional economic usage, consumption is measured as a flow of services. At least in theory, this means the "short run" is envisioned as being a period of arbitrarily short duration, with the corresponding prices of consumer durables, like owner-occupied houses (or automobiles or refrigerators), imputed as competitive-market-equivalent rental flow rates.[10] Practically, for most commodities and for most applications, it probably suffices to think of short-run consumption as occurring over a period of, say, a year, or, for the most extreme cases, maybe a month. Theoretically, however, we are eliminating time aggregation altogether by going to the limit in distinguishing among commodities consumed at each instant of time.

The current short-run consumer demand function is the representative consumer-agent's response to the following counterfactual question: At what rate would you choose to consume (throughout a vanishingly short time interval starting now) if the instantaneous rental prices of consumption service flows (during this interval) were Q (but the rest of the consumer-goods price path did not change)? The traditional way of formalizing this question is to represent consumption choices over time by an intertemporal budget constraint of the form

$$\int_0^\delta \alpha(t)QC(t)\,dt + \int_\delta^\infty \alpha(t)Q(t)C(t)\,dt = W_0 \tag{159}$$

for some "vanishingly small" δ. The short-run consumer demand function (at time zero) is the limiting optimized value of $C(= C(0^+))$, expressed parametrically as a function of Q, which maximizes the intertemporal utility function (85) subject to budget constraint (159), as $\delta \to 0^+$.

An equivalent (but much neater) description of the short-run consumer demand function (at any time t) comes straight out of the representative consumer's equilibrium condition {#1}, where the consumer's static problem is of the form to find a value of $C \geq 0$ to

$$\text{maximize} \quad U(C) - \lambda(t)QC, \tag{160}$$

with Q representing the counterfactual parametrically fixed short-run money consumption prices, while $\lambda(t)$ is the (not observable to an outsider) given-as-if-fixed marginal utility of income at time t.

The short-run demand function is simply the optimized value of C in (160) expressed parametrically as a function of Q. The important implication here

10. This very imputation is used to include owner-occupied housing services in national income accounts. See, for example, Boskin et al. (1998) for a discussion of imputed rents aimed at applications.

for consumer demand theory is that in the short run, the consumer's utility function is quasilinear. Intuitively, this quasilinear form (160) is inherent in a continuous-time formulation, because the consumer can fully offset, via changes in savings behavior, any and all possible income effects of a short-run price change—merely by shifting the tiniest bit of saved income across time. It is for this reason that (160)—with $\lambda(t)$ treated as a given constant—describes the same short-run instantaneous demand function of Q as would a rigorous limiting argument when $\delta \to 0^+$ in the intertemporal budget constraint (159).[11]

We write the directly observable *short-run consumer demand function* at time t as $D_t(Q)$. The vector function $D_t(Q)$ is the implicit maximizing solution of the above problem (160) at time t, which therefore satisfies, for all parametrically given hypothetical values of $Q \geq 0$, the standard duality condition

$$\nabla U(D_t(Q)) = \lambda(t)Q \tag{161}$$

(leaving aside trivial corner solutions representing zero consumption).

Reflecting the fact that there are no income effects as Q is varied hypothetically in the short run, $\lambda(t)$ is seen by the representative consumer as if being fixed in (161), that is, $\lambda(t)$ is implicitly contained as a parameter in the demand function $D_t(Q)$.

For completeness, we now identify the corresponding short-run *demand function for capital* at time t, denoted $D_t^k(P)$. Wherever the state evaluation function is differentiable (which, because it is concave, holds almost everywhere), $D_t^k(P)$ is the implicit solution to the condition

$$\nabla V(D_t^k(P)) = \lambda(t)P. \tag{162}$$

Note the aesthetically pleasing symmetry between (162) and (161). Suppose the (arbitrary) marginal utility of income is normalized to unity and let us wave aside the (essentially uninteresting) mathematical issues about "corner solutions" at zero and "correspondences" replacing functions. Then the demand function for consumption is essentially the inverse of the marginal utility function, while the demand function for capital is essentially the inverse of the marginal state evaluation function.

---

11. A proposition very close to this is proved rigorously in Bewley (1977).

6

✳

The Pure Theory of Perfectly Complete
National Income Accounting

This chapter investigates the theoretical welfare significance of net national income or product—what it is and how to use it—in a perfectly complete accounting system. Before jumping into the mathematical details, however, let us first introduce the topic.

Recent times have witnessed a greatly heightened awareness of the interactions between economic, social, and environmental issues. People throughout the world have become much more sensitive to the important possible links between their own human societies and the natural environmental surroundings within which these societies may thrive or fail. Terms like "green accounting" and "sustainability" have found their way into the popular lexicon. There has appeared a widespread interest in the idea of extending the concepts and measurement of national income to include important nonmarket activities in related areas that bear on welfare and productivity—in particular environmental goods and services (including natural resources), but also human capital formation, unpaid home production (possibly including leisure-time activities), the services of consumer-owned durables, near-market research and development, and so on.[1]

Many questions have been raised about augmented national income accounting, ranging from broad concerns, posed at a high level of abstraction, about its welfare foundations, through basic issues touching upon the design of green national income accounts, down to narrow advice on which particular activities to include and how to include them. In response, there has arisen a branch or application of economic analysis that might be called the "pure theory of comprehensive national income accounting." Through the

1. For more background and details, set in a practical context, see National Research Council Panel on Integrated Environmental and Economic Accounts (1999).

core of this theory runs a common strand attempting to connect a currently observable index of comprehensive net national income or product with some appropriate but not currently observable welfare measure of future power to consume, which typically has a "sustainability-like" flavor or undertone about it.

As a historical aside, we note briefly that the recent interest in comprehensive income accounting may be seen as being closer to the revival of a classic economic theme than as something that is brand new. Great classical economists such as Fisher, Lindahl, Hicks, Pigou, Hayek, and many others were very much interested in the concept of income—and in linking this concept to other important concepts in capital theory.[2] Today, we have the advantage of being able to explore this classic theme with the analytical tools of modern dynamic optimization theory.

To be observable in the first place, net national product or income must essentially take the form of a production-based index of the money value of current aggregate output, whereas the concepts that show up naturally in optimal growth theory, such as the Hamiltonian, are essentially utility-based measures. This is not a problem at the level of a firm, because the stock market value of the firm, its dividends, its income, and the interest rate representing the firm's cost of capital are, at least in principle, observable. But this situation represents a significant intellectual challenge at the level of the nation. The broad mandate of this chapter is to make dynamic welfare inferences based only on currently observable market information. (Perhaps more accurately, the market information is "in theory observable or measurable.") In this spirit we seek to answer a pair of basic questions: What *is* net national income or product (what does it *represent*, in terms of both utility-equivalent and consumption-equivalent units)? How are we actually supposed to *use* national income and other currently observable market demand information (at least in principle) to make rigorous welfare comparisons among different economies, or in the same economy over time?

We have just laid out a fairly specific motivation for this chapter in the form of basic questions about national income that we intend to answer. Now let us go to the opposite extreme and provide a rather fuzzy motivation in terms of "sustainability"—or what we will later argue might more properly be called "sustainability equivalence." The purpose of this particular exercise is not to demolish the concept of "sustainability," which has, I believe, a legitimate

---

2. Relevant writings on this theme are collected in Harcourt, Parker, and Whittington (1986).

core essence, but rather to eliminate the fuzziness by formalizing and making operational the basic economic ideas underlying the concept. As we will see by the end of this chapter, there is a fundamental connection between "national income" and "sustainability equivalence."

The word "sustainability" is often used but rarely defined carefully. It can have quite a few meanings, which may vary greatly depending on the user and the context of the usage (see Pezzey 1992). At the broadest level, sustainability refers in some way to the ability to "sustain" in the sense of keeping constant *something* across time. That is, the word sustainability connotes a *constancy-like property* of "something."

The various notions of sustainability then seem to differ primarily in the "something" that is supposed to be sustained—usually in the *degree of specificity* of the "something" to be sustained. We begin the discussion by using a classification scheme based on the specificity of the "something" having the "constancy-like property" as an organizing principle, discussing in turn three major categories that operate at three different levels of abstraction. We start first with the most specific articulation of the constancy-like property, which might be called the micro-specific approach to sustainability. Then we discuss as a second example the Rawlsian maximin utility approach. Finally, there is a discussion of the most abstract conceivable formulation that still retains as the foundation of its analytical structure the core concept of a criterion like constancy or like constancy equivalence over time—which constancy-like abstraction we will thereafter take to be the most useful analytical essence of the concept of sustainability.

Starting with the most specific interpretation, "sustainability" here refers to maintaining at constant levels something quite particular—a wooded area, or wetlands, or oil reserves, or fisheries—so that future generations might enjoy the same usage of these specific forms of natural resource capital as we do now. Although "sustainability" in this most narrow sense might sometimes be a practical shorthand way of expressing certain desirable conservation goals, it seems too arbitrary to serve as a general principle for guiding economic development. As a practical matter, we simply cannot have economic growth, with its attendant goal of raising people out of poverty, while preserving everything that has any conceivable natural or aesthetic value.

Taken to an extreme, the injunction to pursue "sustainable development" in this most narrowly specific sense of leaving intact particular forms of natural capital would paralyze development, since no growth is possible without causing levels of something to decline somewhere. The injunction to pursue sustainable development in this micro-specific sense strikes an economist as being very much like the welfare criterion that "no project should be approved unless every component element of the population is made better off." It is not so much that this criterion is wrong, as that it is almost completely useless in practice because there never has been or will be an actual project that improves every component. Somewhere, someone or something will be hurt. Such a narrow Pareto-like welfare criterion represents an extraordinarily conservative criterion that would have the practical effect of completely freezing the status quo, because no project could ever actually pass this test in practice. Whether intended or not, if narrow micro-specific criteria of sustainable development were widely applied they would result in a de facto moratorium on economic growth.

Sector-specific or use-specific or micro-specific definitions of "sustainability" are highly problematic in several ways. From the beginning, it is left up in the air *what* is the particular set of specific resources to be sustained at all costs, and *who* selects the list. And this matters a great deal. In technical terms, the principle of sustainable development at this level of specificity is not invariant to aggregation and is highly sensitive to *which* sector's gross output is chosen to be sustained. What is sustainable for individual trees may be unsustainable for the forest ecosystem as a whole and vice versa.

The micro-specific formulation means that no amount of substitution, or at least very little substitution, is allowed between the particular specific natural capital resource chosen to be sustained at all costs and any other resources that happen not to be granted this special status. If killer whales are selected to be sustained, but not the porpoises they eat, then in the most extreme example we are not allowed to harvest just one more killer whale even if it allows one thousand more porpoises to live. The core problem remains even without such an extreme formulation: the sustainability of killer whales at high population levels depends on lowering the equilibrium population of porpoises, while the sustainability of porpoises at high population levels depends on lowering the equilibrium population of killer whales. The "sustainability" of one population at higher numbers invariably means the "nonsustainability" of another population at higher numbers. In ecology, as in economics, there are very few win-win situations. Who gets to choose whose sustainability is enhanced and whose sustainability is diminished—and on the basis of what criteria?

As an example of how deeply problematic the concept of micro-specific sustainability can be as a general criterion for guiding economic development, consider the case of the North American tallgrass prairie. What is today the best large farmland area in the world was a mere century and a half ago the largest virgin tallgrass prairie in the world. The tallgrass prairie ecosystem of the American Midwest is a relatively recent phenomenon—less than ten thousand or so years old. If a farmer were forced to abandon Iowa farmland today, it would pass through several successional stages, with its climax vegetation reverting not to prairie, but to some form of mature woodland. Prairie existed in the Midwest in the first place, rather than woodland, because of recurrent periodic fires. These well-documented large-scale burns were set by Native Americans—mostly deliberately, for hunting purposes. Today, what is called "prescribed burning" is an essential part of almost all serious prairie restoration projects.[3]

Imagine what would have been said in the name of sustainability to the Native Americans who created the tallgrass prairie beginning some ten thousand years ago. They would have been told by the Environmental Protection Agency to stop setting fires—to not change what was then sustainable postglacial woodland into what might be called nonsustainable tallgrass prairie, dependent on human fires. This same micro-specific sustainability principle is cited nowadays as an underlying rationale to preserve what still remains of the tallgrass prairie—which itself is human made. A principle that can be used to argue both sides of an issue seems suspect.

Although these anecdotal examples are extreme, they drive home the main point. The micro-specific sustainability principle is highly problematic as an *overall* conceptual guide to economic development.

For the idea of sustainability to make sense as an overall conceptual guide to development, it must refer to generalized well-being at a very high level of abstraction. The broader definition of sustainability, and therefore the more meaningful definition economically, focuses on sustaining well-being or utility itself. In the broadest sense, sustainability (or, perhaps more accurately, the degree of sustainability) stands for some overall measure of the ability of an economy to sustain the utility of consumption into the future. (Remember: in principle the utility of consumption might include the existence of the tallgrass prairie, or some weighted composite of killer whales and porpoises.)

Suppose, as a thought experiment, that we tried to sustain utility by *maximizing the minimum* level of utility over time. This *maximin* objective (which is sometimes also called "Rawlsian" after the philosopher John Rawls who

3. See Krech (1999, chap. 4) for Indian burning and Packard and Mutel (1997) for prairie restoration.

championed it), might be characterized as being at an intermediate level of specificity. Overall, using the maximin objective is less rigid than using micro-specific sustainability criteria (because we are sustaining the utility of all goods, rather than just a selected few). However, we will argue, maximin is still far too rigidly specific a welfare indicator to serve as a useful principle for guiding development.

An immediate problem with using the Rawlsian maximin principle is that it would condemn poor societies to perpetuate poverty forever by not putting any weight on increased future consumption from present savings. Think of a fishery-based economy that has badly run down its fish stocks by past overfishing. Strict application of the Rawlsian criterion would not allow this economy to declare a temporary moratorium on fishing, which would hurt the present generation, in order to build up fish stocks to levels that would permit a higher amount of sustainable harvesting, thereby benefiting all future generations. This is an extremely contradictory consequence of using a welfare criterion that purports to weight the needs of future generations more equitably than ordinary capitalistic-sounding discounting. In other words, the maximin-utility principle of sustainability, which sometimes advertises itself as if marching under the banner of an altruistic-sounding *zero* discount rate, in this case, by perpetuating the misery of poverty forever, has the actual effect of marching under the banner of an extremely self-centered present-oriented *infinite* discount rate.

Here is another problem. In the presence of technological progress, the maximin criterion would require society to choose a constant level of consumption per head when it could easily have exponentially growing consumption per head by investing just a small amount in the new technologies. This kind of problem represents a serious generic defect of all overly specific definitions of "sustainability" that, in effect, lock an economy into rigid adherence to constant consumption as an ideal. Such definitions are misplaced, as they seem intended mainly to prevent the present generation from consuming more than future generations, while this is probably not the problem we actually face. Because of technological progress and capital accumulation, it is quite likely that, for the world as a whole, future generations will enjoy a higher average standard of living than generations alive today. This is certainly what has happened on average in the past. For this more realistic world scenario, rigid application of the literal principle of highest maintainable consumption is a terrible criterion because it will choose between two consumption paths, both of which are growing over time, by favoring the one that has higher consumption now, which translates into a criterion that encourages present consumption at the expense of the growth of future consumption.

The root flaw of the Rawlsian maximin criterion is that it is so rigidly specific that absolutely no substitution is allowed between present and future utility. Although the maximin-utility criterion of sustainability is more general than sector-specific criteria in allowing substitution among sectors "across space" in producing utility, it is still fantastically rigid "over time" in specifying a welfare criterion (essentially, an unchanging utility of consumption level), which must hold for every future date. The sacrifice of one-millionth of a utile is not permitted in any period, even if it would result in an increase of a trillion more utiles for every other period. It is difficult to have any more faith in the development advice given by the extreme maximin zero-elasticity-of-substitution, fixed-coefficients welfare criterion than in the opposite extreme of an optimal growth program generated by maximizing an infinite-elasticity-of-substitution objective function that is strictly linear in consumption across periods. Both extreme cases are unacceptable, because without careful selection of the weighting coefficients, they are capable of generating untrustworthy outcomes that are useful mainly for the pedagogic purposes of illustrating what happens when extreme assumptions are made about the curvature of the utility function. Nobody believes in using an intertemporal welfare function that just adds up unweighted consumption linearly across periods, except, maybe, as an "as if" approximation. But, somewhat surprisingly, the opposite extreme, the Rawlsian maximin interpretation of sustainability, is still sometimes taken seriously.

Does all of this mean that the concept of sustainability is useless? The answer, I believe, is "no," or even more strongly, "not at all." In its appropriate form, the idea of sustainability is so extremely appealing as a highly intuitive conceptual device for thinking seriously about the environmental big-picture side of economic development that it is difficult to imagine how we might do without it. When it is allowed to have practical force by being freed from excessively rigid specifications, the concept of sustainability provides an intuitively appealing way to frame a relatively simple question and give a relatively simple answer to the complex issue of where our development is taking us and what comprehensive national income is measuring. But to make further progress with this concept of "sustainability," we need to abstract even more than the Rawlsian formulation of maximin utility, which is still much too specific.

The concept of sustainability to economic dynamics should be almost like the concept of energy is to dynamics in physics. Just as physicists in the past like

Lagrange, Hamilton, or Maxwell made great progress in physics by generalizing expressions of physical laws to their most abstract possible form, typically centered on the concept of energy, so too should economists generalize the notion of sustainability to its most abstract possible formulation, centered on the ultimate abstraction of the constancy-like or constancy-equivalence-like property, in order to move forward here.

Employing an analogy closer to home, narrow and specific definitions of sustainability are like narrow and specific versions of the Pareto criterion. What economists have found most useful about the Pareto idea as a practical welfare measure is not so much its initial and very specific version, but rather its generalized or abstract form. The Pareto criterion says that one situation is better than another if and only if everyone is (weakly) better off in the one than in the other. The problem with this kind of "win-win" criterion is that it is never fulfilled in actuality, so it has almost no real-world applicability. (Can you think of any change that does not hurt someone, somewhere?) A generalization or abstraction of the Pareto principle, however, has turned out to be so useful to economists that it might truly be called the cornerstone of modern welfare economics. Instead of judging a situation by whether it actually achieves a Pareto improvement, which is too narrow to be useful in practice as a principle for benefit-cost analysis, we judge a situation by whether it could or might attain a Pareto improvement under an ideal redistribution mechanism. (This is sometimes called the Kaldor-Hicks criterion.) I am arguing by analogy that rather than judging a situation by some measure of its actual literal sustainability, we should be judging a situation by some measure of its welfare-equivalent sustainability under an ideal equalizing redistribution of utility across time.

What we need to understand by the word "sustainability" as applied to any particular development program is the sustainable-equivalent gain or utility that the program generates. In other words, the sustainability of a development program is to be identified with the hypothetical level of constant utility over time that would yield the same degree of overall well-being as what the actual development program may yield. We can build a theoretically powerful and practically useful theory centered on the important and intuitive concept of sustainability provided only that we identify correctly this concept in what is truly its most general or abstract form: the word "sustainability" applied to an economy, an economic situation, or an economic program stands for, and is measured by, the corresponding level of "sustainable-equivalent utility."

So long as we adhere carefully to the "sustainability-equivalence" generalized interpretation of sustainability, we will be on solid analytical ground. But when we descend into more specific concepts of sustainability—especially micro-specific criteria, but even Rawlsian maximin-utility formulations—we find ourselves on a slippery slope. We start sliding into analytical trouble almost from the beginning, and we must be prepared to deal with paradoxical situations and disturbing outcomes.

A brief point of notational order having to do with the nomenclature to be followed throughout the rest of the book. This book is about theory. At the level of abstraction of the models we are using, the following concepts are equivalent: net national product, net national income, net domestic product, and net domestic income. For convenience, we will simply refer to all such summary national income concepts as "NNP."

Speaking generally, the proper definition of "income" is one of the most elusive and controversial subjects in all of economics. It is also one of the most important, as witnessed by the enormous interest in national income accounting, or, for that matter, in income accounting more generally. Whatever difficulties there may be in measuring income, such measures are attempted very frequently in practice, and they are attempted at almost every level of aggregation and throughout almost every sector of a modern economy. Put simply, there is no other practically attainable measure that can even come close to giving as coherent and inclusive a picture of a nation's overall economic activity as its comprehensive national income accounts. This having been said, we postpone a more complete discussion of the important concept of "income" until the end of this chapter, when the full analytical apparatus for the general multisector case will have been developed. For the time being, we employ the concept of "NNP as income" intuitively and informally.

With regard to NNP as income, it seems fair to say that contemporary national income accounting is centered on what is frequently identified as the "Hicksian" concept of income, typically paraphrased as something like last chapter's definition: "the maximum amount that can presently be consumed without compromising future ability to consume at the same level." The exact phrase that Hicks (1946) used to define his production-based measure is "the maximum amount which can be spent during a period if there is to be an expectation of maintaining intact the capital value of prospective returns." Hicks went on to add "it equals consumption plus [net] capital accumulation," but this is an inferred property, which holds under certain conditions, rather than a proper definition. Hicks's definition of income makes good sense for a Robinson Crusoe–like person whose single capital good acts like a deposit in a bank account paying a constant interest rate (where the Hicks concept of income coincides with Fisher's "interest on wealth," as well as with Lindahl's "consumption plus net wealth increment"). But, as the preliminary discussion of income following Model B of Chaper 5 illustrates, it is not clear what exactly the Hicksian metaphor is supposed to mean at the level of a nation with multiple consumption goods and an enormous diversity of differently acting forms of capital, which are transformable only via highly complicated nonlinear tradeoffs.

To recast the discussion of Chapter 5 into a more general mold, it is well to remind ourselves that a modern industrial economy contains a vast multitude of extremely heterogeneous forms of consumption and capital goods. What, then, does it mean operationally in a modern economy to speak of "the maximum amount that can presently be consumed without compromising future ability to consume at the same level"? Suppose, for the sake of argument, we were to set aside the extremely formidable problems of aggregation that would have to be faced head on in making operational any realistic definition of income. Even allowing that such broad concepts as "aggregate consumption," "aggregate investment," and the capacity base of "aggregate capital" can be meaningfully defined, in a modern economy the "capacity to produce consumption" is quasi-fixed at any given instant of time because "aggregate capital" is not instantaneously shiftable from the "investment-goods sector" to the "consumption-goods sector." Therefore, "the maximum amount that can presently be consumed without compromising future ability to consume at the same level" depends arbitrarily on—among other things—the speed with which it is assumed that the artificial thought experiment of mobilizing a gigantic economywide "crash conversion program" can transform the generalized capacity to produce investment goods into the generalized capacity to produce consumption goods.

If economy A has much better inherent growth potential and can deliver significantly more consumption than economy B in every future period, but economy B can deliver a higher level of "crash mobilization" consumption for this period only because it happens to have a higher short-run elasticity of substitution between the production of consumption and investment, are we willing to say that net national income is higher in B than in A? And if so, on what grounds? On the grounds that B is capable of mounting a faster "emergency consumption sprint" than A during some arbitrarily defined short-run period during which net investment is artificially made zero? Does this definition in terms of the ability to sprint an "emergency consumption dash" make sense for a situation where in actual fact both economies are behaving more like marathon runners pacing themselves to have significantly positive investment so that their consumption can grow over a long course of time?

In practice, at the level of the nation, the production-based Hicksian concept defines NNP as consumption plus net investment, all evaluated at market prices—on the entirely heuristic grounds of crude analogy that if the production possibilities frontier were a simple linear surface, then Hicksian NNP is a measure of what aggregate price-weighted consumption would be when price-weighted aggregate net investment is set equal to zero (thereby keeping price-weighted aggregate capital stock intact, at least conceptually). In this spirit, recent attempts to "green up" NNP by making it more comprehensive may be seen as an effort to include in the net-production index broader measures of consumption and net investment than are customary in standard national income accounting—but without really asking seriously, "what does green NNP represent?"

The question we ultimately want to address in this chapter concerns the welfare interpretation of national income when there are multiple consumption and investment goods in a monetary economy with a nonlinear production possibilities set of arbitrary complexity. As a first step in this direction, and for the sake of focusing sharply on the core theory, we need to assume that all relevant consumption and investment goods are properly "accounted for" and that the "attainable possibilities" of the production-distribution system are time autonomous. Chapter 5 detailed the meaning and significance of these completeness assumptions, so we can be brief here. (A reader of this chapter who is unsure about what the concept of "perfectly complete accounting" means would do well here to consult the much fuller background discussion of Chapter 5.) First of all, we are assuming that the coverage of consumption goods is comprehensive in the sense that everything affecting utility is part of the consumption vector (including environmental amenities and other externalities) and we know the corresponding efficiency prices. Second, also for the sake of developing the core theory, we are imagining an idealized world where the coverage of capital goods is so comprehensive, and the national accounting system is so complete, that there remain no unaccounted-for residual "atmospheric" growth factors. In this kind of world, all sources of future growth have been attributed as proper investments (including depletion or degradation of natural capital as negative investments), which are fully "accounted for" by being valued at their proper efficiency prices and included in national product.

An ideally comprehensive or fully inclusive accounting system like the one we are postulating might be called "perfectly complete" because we are assuming perfect accounting of all relevant consumption and investment goods at their competitive-market-like efficiency prices. The main point here is that if we cannot develop a sound theory for this fully inclusive time-autonomous case, then the incomplete-accounting case will be nearly hopeless. Conversely, any insights from the case of perfectly complete accounting will be useful as a point of departure for analyzing the case of incomplete accounting.

Unfortunately, as was pointed out in the last chapter, we do not now live in a world where national income accounting is perfectly complete, even though our theoretical models typically assume this feature. Perfect completeness is a limiting case, which some real-world accounting systems approach in coverage but few attain. To summarize the previous discussion of Chapter 5, in our actual world we cannot measure accurately all investments, many externalities are not internalized, it is often difficult to impute market-like prices for non-market goods, there are various "atmospheric" sources of positive or negative growth, which we do not include in net national product, and so forth.

The primary justification usually given for studying the pure theory of complete accounting in a real world of incomplete accounting is that the pure theory can serve as a guiding beacon lighting the way toward greater completeness—by suggesting what activities to include, and how best to include them, to "green up" national income into a more comprehensive aggregate reflecting more accurately what the future portends relative to the present. Also, the pure theory of complete accounting may be important because it will indicate how to use current income-like data to make rigorous dynamic welfare comparisons—at least in principle. Generally speaking, what we hope to show in this chapter is that there exists a theoretically powerful and conceptually useful connection between the comprehensive production-based Hicksian-inspired index of present NNP and a future-looking sustainability-like measure of overall welfare.

The theory of national income accounting, which we will develop in this chapter, is closely related conceptually to the wealth and income version of the maximum principle, as applied to the multisector optimal growth model of Chapter 5. We will ask, and seek to answer, three basic questions in this chapter.

NNP Question no. 1: What is the welfare interpretation of nominal (or money) NNP—in terms of the utilitarian objective function?

NNP Question no. 2: What is the descriptive interpretation of nominal NNP—in terms of real future consumption?

NNP Question no. 3: How can money NNP and currently observable market-demand information be used to make welfare comparisons across space or over time?

NNP Questions 1, 2, and 3 will be answered, respectively, by Theorems 1, 2, and 3—coming later in this chapter. But before turning to the general case, which these theorems address, we begin with a special case. As well as being of considerable interest in its own right, this special case is useful as an intuition-building bridge to the more general case. Suppose, then, that there are multiple heterogeneous capital goods, but just one homogeneous consumption good. (This was for a long time the only situation treated in the literature, and is still the standard predominant case in most books and articles on green accounting.) Suppose further that utility is linear in the single homogeneous consumption good. Then, essentially, utility *is* the single consumption good and the economy acts like it is maximizing present-discounted consumption, where ρ in this context is interpretable as the consumption discount rate (as well as, in this case, the utility discount rate).

As an aside relevant to empirical work, if we are observing an economy (possibly with a curved utility function) moving along an efficient growth trajectory and having a constant own rate of interest on the single consumption good, then the situation is as if utility were linear, while ρ under this interpretation parameterizes the constant rate of return on consumption. This is probably a decent approximation for a great many practical purposes, because it accords with a well-known stylized fact that the real rate of interest has been essentially trendless over time, at least throughout the measurable past.[4] One could argue that the measurable entity corresponding most closely to this concept is the annual after-tax real return on capital (because it approximately defines the relevant intertemporal consumption tradeoff faced by the average citizen in deciding how much to save). As a rough approximation, a trendless round figure of 5% per year might then be used for this real interest rate in the postwar period or even, perhaps, over longer historical periods. So there is

4. Nordhaus (1994), in his section entitled "Empirical Evidence on the Return on Capital," summarizes a large number of studies that are consistent with a trendless interpretation. Indeed, this is one of Kaldor's famous "stylized facts" about the growth of advanced industrial economies. (For a discussion, see Solow 1970, p. 3.) Nordhaus (1995), Jorgenson (1994), or Feldstein (1997) could each be cited to justify a trendless fluctuation around 5% per year.

some rough empirical justification for pretending that the economy acts as if it were maximizing the present discounted value of consumption at a constant consumption discount rate.

It should be clearly understood that we do not want to let the theory rest on the stylized empirical fact that recent history looks as if society has been maximizing present discounted consumption at a constant (or at least trendless) rate of return. Over and above any practical applications, we would like to understand theoretically what happens with a curved utility function of many consumption goods and services. Yet even though we will end up in this chapter with a fully rigorous and fully general treatment covering multiple consumption commodities and a concave utility function, it is still conceptually useful to begin by analyzing the special case where utility is identified with a single measurable consumption good.

In terms of optimal control theory, identifying utility "as if equal" to a single measurable consumption good means that "gain" (here consumption) is directly observable and the prices of the n investment goods can all be measured in terms of consumption as numeraire. The welfare interpretation of NNP is then a straightforward, almost literal, application of the wealth and income version of the maximum principle. (This is to be contrasted with the general case where utility is not directly observable, and, other than the flow quantities themselves, we can only observe the money prices of the m consumption goods and n investment goods.)

What are the answers to the three questions posed above for the special case where utility is a single measurable consumption good? We will answer each question in turn. Questions 1 and 2 are really the same question in this particular case, because there is no distinction between utility-equivalent welfare units and consumption-equivalent descriptive units.

NNP Question no. 1: What is the welfare interpretation of nominal NNP—in terms of the utilitarian objective function? *Answer:* NNP (with consumption as numeraire) equals stationary-equivalent (that is, sustainable-equivalent) utility at the utility discount rate ρ. *NNP Question no. 2:* What is the descriptive interpretation of nominal NNP—in terms of real future consumption? *Answer:* NNP with consumption as numeraire equals stationary-equivalent (that is, annuity-equivalent) consumption at the consumption discount rate ρ.

NNP Question no. 3: How can money NNP and currently observable market-demand information be used to make welfare comparisons across space or over time? *Answer:* One situation gives higher present discounted utility (or consumption) than the other if and only if current real NNP (with the single consumption good as the common real numeraire) is higher in the one situation than in the other.

The above answer to NNP Question no. 3 is so simple that its power can easily be overlooked. Imagine any two dynamic economic units (or economies). The two economic units are arbitrarily different. They may have completely different endowments or completely different production opportunities. For example, one economy may have oil reserves, but cannot use machines to grow. Another economy may be able to use accumulated machines to grow, but does not have oil reserves. And so forth. The only thing in common between the two economic units is that they both are behaving as if they are maximizing present discounted consumption at the same discount rate. (It does not even have to be called "consumption"—we could instead label it the "gain" of the economic unit if we wanted to be more general.) The two economies may grind out completely different growth trajectories.

Suppose we want to compare dynamic welfare between the two economic units. We want to know what is the difference in present discounted consumption (or gain). Suppose further that the only thing we can observe about the two economies is their real NNP with the single consumption good as numeraire. (This is equivalent here to observing money NNP in both economies and being able to convert the money NNP of one economy into the monetary units of the other by using as a price deflator the ratio of their consumption-good prices.) The economist knows nothing else about these two economies except their real NNP. Then the striking result is that the difference in present discounted consumption between the two arbitrarily different economies is exactly the difference in real NNP divided by the consumption discount rate. With complete accounting in this situation all relevant information for making dynamic welfare comparisons is contained in current NNP. In this situation, current real NNP is a sufficient statistic for any dynamic welfare comparisons.

As we will see by the end of the chapter, this spectacular result about the present's being a sufficient statistic for the future generalizes to a situation with an arbitrary number of consumption goods and a curved utility function. The generalization is (naturally) more complicated, but it is in the same spirit as the above result. In the more general situation of a multisector economy with complete accounting, we additionally need some information about the short-run consumer demand function for one of the economies (in the range between the two consumption vectors being compared). However, the same basic principle will hold: with complete accounting, all relevant information for making dynamic welfare stock–like comparisons is contained in currently observable market flow behavior.

We turn now to the far more challenging situation where there is a curved utility function of multiple heterogeneous consumption commodities. If only we knew the utility function, then we could calculate directly "utility-valued NNP," which would be exactly the Hamiltonian of the multisector optimal growth problem treated in the last chapter. With such perfect knowledge of the utility function, the wealth and income version of the maximum principle gives a straightforward interpretation of utility NNP as being the stationary equivalent (that is, sustainable equivalent) of the utility level the economy is actually capable of achieving over time. With knowledge of utility-valued NNP, we have all the information we need for making dynamic welfare comparisons. Alas, the national income statistician does not know the utility function and can only observe current consumption and investment in terms of current money prices (as opposed to "utility prices"). So the issue before us is to construct a unified theory of price deflators and welfare measures that will allow us to infer the relationship between currently observable money NNP and present discounted utility using only currently observable market information. We begin this journey with some observations on what it signifies to have a welfare measure expressed in the form of present discounted utility.

In effect, we have already postulated in Chapter 5 that we are living in a world as if the welfare evaluator

$$\Omega \equiv \int_0^\infty U_t e^{-\rho t}\, dt \tag{1}$$

is being maximized over all feasible alternatives. Here we want to note some properties of (1) that will play an important role in what follows.

Expression (1) is, of course, the standard workhorse version of the objective function used for intertemporal optimization problems. A linear functional taking the form of an integral of discounted utilities can be given an axiomatic justification as the appropriate welfare criterion whenever independence, stationarity, and a few other standard, and arguably reasonable, conditions are postulated.[5] Despite extremely widespread acceptance in practice, especially for all sorts of applied theory, expression (1) has not been without its critics

5. See, for example, Koopmans (1960) and the references cited there.

in the literature.[6] I point all of this out here because, for better or for worse, the basic message of this chapter will depend critically on the welfare ordering induced by the above form of Ω. It is from relying on specification (1) that the central concept of "sustainability equivalence" will be defined, motivated, and, finally, put to use.

Implicit in a utilitarian objective functional of the linearly additive form (1) is the idea that it is conceptually meaningful to think, if we wish to, in terms of a highly abstract thought experiment about the welfare implications of transferring utility from one time period to another. Although we do not typically engage in such thought experiments, there is not really any fundamental distinction with the more familiar thought experiment that we do routinely envision—about hypothetically transferring goods and services from one person to another—in our customary description of the modified Pareto (or Kaldor-Hicks) criterion as a basis for making welfare comparisons.

Now we will push the rationale of this interpretation all the way through to its logical conclusion. Suppose the economy can attain some feasible consumption trajectory $\{C(t)\}$. Define the sustainable equivalent utility of the sequence $\{U(C(t))\}$ to be the hypothetical constant level $\overline{U}$ satisfying

$$\int_0^\infty \overline{U} e^{-\rho t}\, dt = \int_0^\infty U(C(t)) e^{-\rho t}\, dt. \tag{2}$$

We say that $\overline{U}$ is the sustainable equivalent of $\{U(C(t))\}$ in the following exact sense. An outside observer with social welfare function (1) would be indifferent if forced to choose between the hypothetically constant "as if sustainable" utility level

$$U_t \equiv \overline{U}, \tag{3}$$

which (probably) cannot actually be attained by the economy, and the nonconstant path

$$U_t \equiv U(C(t)), \tag{4}$$

which represents the utility sequence that the economy actually achieves for the given feasible program.

6. See, for example, the discussion contained in Heal (1998).

Of course we do not yet know how to calculate sustainable-equivalent utility—most immediately because we do not know directly the utility function or the rate of pure time preference—so the above definition may seem abstract or even obscure. In a way, the purpose of this chapter can be seen as being to make operationally useful the concept of sustainable-equivalent utility. In all that follows here, the guiding precept of the sustainability-equivalence approach is to express each utility-based welfare measure on the left-hand side of an equation in terms of some currently observable market variables on the right-hand side of the equation, with all values normalized relative to existing base-economy money prices as the benchmark.

We have already pointed out that it may not be a bad empirical approximation to view an economy as if it is maximizing the present discounted value of aggregate consumption at a constant discount rate, since that is not a bad historical description of the last century or so. Although it may be a tolerable empirical approximation to use directly the wealth and income version of the maximum principle to give a plausible welfare interpretation of NNP for some purposes, we aspire here to a more general theory. In this spirit, the central task now before us is to elaborate rigorously the connection between comprehensive money-valued NNP evaluated at time zero,

$$Y(0) = Q(0)C^*(0) + P(0)I^*(0) \tag{5}$$

(coming from the money-valued dynamic competitive equilibrium described in Chapter 5), and the associated welfare maximand $\Omega(\{C^*(t)\})$, coming from the solution of the associated optimal growth formulation.

From the wealth and income version of the maximum principle as described in Chapter 5, we have directly that

$$\int_0^\infty [U(C^*(0)) + p(0)I^*(0)]e^{-\rho t}\, dt = \int_0^\infty U(C^*(t))e^{-\rho t}\, dt. \tag{6}$$

Condition (6) means that, within the idealized circumstances of the model, the "utility NNP" expression

$$U(C^*(0)) + p(0)I^*(0) \tag{7}$$

is what might legitimately be called the "sustainable equivalent" of the welfare that is actually attained. With the thought experiment of a hypothetical redistribution of utility across time that delivers the same level of utility in each period, but also yields the same overall social welfare, the "sustainable-equivalent" constant utility that is to be received each year is given by the "utility NNP" expression (7).

Unfortunately, this welfare interpretation is not really useful for optimal-growth applications, or even operational for a problem whose direct gain is not a money-valued observable function. Everything in (7) is ultimately being expressed in terms of the utility "value of consumption at time zero," rather than in terms of the money "value of consumption at time zero." The former is not observed, and perhaps is not even measurable, while the latter represents the consumption part of today's NNP, which is actually being estimated in the real world.

At this point in the argument, let us pause to take a bearing on where are we going. Essentially, we are trying to answer NNP Question no. 1: What is the welfare interpretation of nominal NNP in terms of the utilitarian objective function? We are trying to go in the direction of constructing a general theory of a "sustainability-equivalence principle," which would connect together by a strong natural link a NNP-like index of the form (5) with some measure of sustainable-equivalent utility—in the spirit or style or manner of equation (6). That is to say, in the place where the nonoperational utility-NNP expression (7) appears within the square brackets of the left-hand side of equation (6), we would like to be able to insert instead the money-NNP expression (5). Obviously, there can be no hope of being able to meaningfully transform (6) in this way unless "money NNP" at time zero, (5), and "utility NNP" at time zero, (7), are somehow made commensurate in the transformed version of expression (6) that we are seeking.

Since the prices of the "money consumption" expression $Q(0)C^*(0)$ and the utility function of the "utility consumption" expression $U(C^*(0))$ have each been normalized completely arbitrarily in absolute magnitude, they are a fortiori normalized arbitrarily relative to each other. And since "money consumption" represents a tangible entity in the real world, which people have an intuition for and statisticians are actually trying to measure and to include in national income accounts—while "utility consumption" is not operationally observable or even, perhaps, directly measurable—it makes much more sense to envision normalizing "utility consumption" in terms of "money consumption," rather than the other way around.

Any instantaneous utility function that is a (positive) affine transformation of $U(C)$ gives the same welfare ordering as (1). For this reason, the magnitude of Ω depends utterly on how utility is measured. Therefore, by itself Ω cannot possibly acquire any absolute welfare interpretation. Standing alone, Ω can be a meaningful cardinal concept only if the absolute value of $U(C)$ is pinned down to something familiar by some strongly intuitive scaling convention. Typically, nothing much is made of this observation, because we don't usually attribute significance to the magnitude of Ω per se. Here, however, we now wish to use this observation to cardinalize $U(C)$ with an operationally meaningful normalization as a so-called money-metric utility function constructed from current price and income data.

Because any positive affine transformation of the utility function $U(C)$ induces the same welfare ordering as $U(C)$ itself, the instantaneous utility function

$$U_{a,b}(C) \equiv aU(C) + b \tag{8}$$

gives a welfare ordering that is independent of a or b (so long as a is positive) in the welfare expression:

$$\Omega_{a,b} \equiv \int_0^\infty e^{-\rho t} U_{a,b}(C(t))\, dt. \tag{9}$$

Thus the optimal growth problem (5.60)–(5.63) under consideration has the same solution no matter what values of a and b are selected in (8) and (9) to calibrate $U_{a,b}(C)$ as an instantaneous utility function. Since the parameters a and b represent two degrees of freedom that can be pinned down any way we want, we are entitled to ask the following question. Is there any useful way we would *like* to calibrate, or to normalize, or to scale, or to anchor, or even just to think about the utility of consumption?

I contend that it is "natural" to scale $U_{a,b}(C)$ so that utility at time zero is commensurate with the money-metric value of consumption at time zero, in the sense that

$$U_{a,b}(C^*(0)) = Q(0)C^*(0) \tag{10}$$

and

$$\left.\frac{\partial U_{a,b}}{\partial C}\right|_{*(0)} = Q(0). \tag{11}$$

The "money-metricizing" normalization (10),(11) is accomplished by choosing a in expression (8) as one over the marginal utility of income

$$a \equiv \frac{1}{\lambda(0)}, \tag{12}$$

while b is chosen as

$$b \equiv Q(0)C^*(0) - \frac{U(C^*(0))}{\lambda(0)}. \tag{13}$$

Let the utility function scaled by the money-metricizing normalization (12),(13) be denoted $U^*(C)$. That is to say, the utility function $U^*(C) = U_{a,b}(C)$ is defined uniquely by substituting the value of a in (12) and b in (13) into the formula (8) for $U_{a,b}(C)$, thereby obtaining

$$U^*(C) \equiv Q(0)C^*(0) + \frac{U(C) - U(C^*(0))}{\lambda(0)}. \tag{14}$$

There is no way to "prove" that the natural way to scale or cardinalize $U_{a,b}(C)$ is by calibrating it exactly to the point value of the money-metric utility function at time zero, via the normalization (10),(11). All I can do here is to point out that imposing such a normalization is exactly what we do every time when we interpret in applied work the "area under the demand curve" as some measure of utility or welfare representing "total willingness to pay." (Using the description of the representative consumer's demand function from equation (5.161) as being essentially equal to the marginal utility function, it can readily be confirmed that, when the marginal utility of income at $C^*(0)$ is normalized to unity, the expression $U^*(C) - U^*(C^*(0))$ measures exactly the "area under the current short-run demand function" integrated along any path connecting $C^*(0)$ to C—that is, it is the "total willingness to pay" for the consumption change $C - C^*(0)$.)

The overarching critical point here is that, by money-metricizing it, we have converted the utility function from a somewhat metaphysical concept into an operationally measurable entity. The money-metric utility function here represents exactly the money-normed "area under the demand curve" or the "total willingness to pay," which are such familiar everyday concepts throughout applied economics. Money-metricized utility corresponds here precisely to Pigou's (1932) definition of economic welfare as being "that part of social welfare that can be brought directly or indirectly into relation with the measuring-rod of money."

If we accept the "natural" normalization (10),(11) for the rescaled utility function $U^*(C)$, then the underlying nominal standard, to which everything else is calibrated, becomes the unit of money value at time zero. In this money metric, the expression

$$\int_0^\infty U^*(C(t))e^{-\rho t}\, dt \tag{15}$$

stands for the relevant utilitarian welfare measure of summed-up discounted "total willingness to pay" or "area under the demand curve" utilities—relative to the money value of consumption at time zero.

For completeness and continuity, we restate NNP Question no. 1, which we are trying to answer here: What is the welfare interpretation of nominal NNP—in terms of the utilitarian objective function? The answer comes in the form of the following proposition.

Theorem 1 (Sustainability-Equivalence Principle). *When the instantaneous utility function is "money metricized" at time zero by the normalization (14), then*

$$\int_0^\infty [Q(0)C^*(0) + P(0)I^*(0)]e^{-\rho t}\, dt = \int_0^\infty U^*(C^*(t))e^{-\rho t}\, dt. \tag{16}$$

Proof. Invert definition (14) to yield

$$U(C) = \lambda(0)U^*(C) + U(C^*(0)) - \lambda(0)Q(0)C^*(0). \tag{17}$$

Plug expression (17) into equation (6), which, after canceling identical terms from both sides of the equation and rearranging, then becomes

$$\int_0^\infty [\lambda(0)Q(0)C^*(0) + \lambda(0)P(0)I^*(0)]e^{-\rho t}\, dt$$

$$= \int_0^\infty \lambda(0)U^*(C^*(t))e^{-\rho t}\, dt. \tag{18}$$

After canceling $\lambda(0)$ from both sides of the equation (18), we have the desired conclusion (16). ∎

Translated freely into words, the proof of the proposition says something like the following. Suppose we think abstractly about the "natural" money-metric normalization of the instantaneous utility function at time zero, which transforms (6) into (16). If we think in terms of a "transformation operator" being applied to both sides of equation (6), this operator then makes two transformations. On the left-hand side, it converts the "utility NNP" index (7) within the square brackets of (6) into the more amenable "goods NNP" index (5), which is expressed in terms of the monetary unit of account at time zero. On the right-hand side of (6), this operator calibrates utility (and there-fore the sum of present discounted utilities) to be commensurate with the money value of consumption at time zero (in the consumer-surplus spirit of "area under the demand curve" or "total willingness to pay"). In this way both sides of equation (6) become transformed into the money-valued equivalent expression (16). The simple point is that when all units are expressed relative to initial income, so that the utility of consumption at time zero is "money metricized" to the money value of consumption at time zero, then compre-hensive NNP becomes the "sustainable equivalent" of the money-metricized utility that is actually delivered over time.

Of course, we do not know directly what is the value of sustainable-equivalent money-metricized utility, because we cannot directly evaluate the integral on the right-hand side of equation (16). To begin with, neither the utility function nor the rate of pure time preference is directly observable. Furthermore, we do not know the future part of the consumption trajectory $\{C^*(t)\}$. In such a context, equation (16) would not represent an empirically refutable proposition.

Paradoxically, this very feature of optimal-growth theory—that we do not actually know the optimized value of the objective function—highlights a great strength of the sustainability-equivalence principle. For, if we can con-ceptualize a future unfolding in the generic form of a dynamic competitive equilibrium, then we are entitled also to conceptualize the economy as max-imizing an objective having the *form* of the right-hand side of equation (16), even when we do not actually know $U^*(C)$ or ρ or $\{C^*(t)\}$. And then the principle still holds that a truly comprehensive measure of NNP reflects sustainable-equivalent utility exactly. Put slightly differently, present compre-hensive NNP is probably the closest we can actually come to measuring the sustainable-equivalent utility of the future development path we have em-barked upon. In a sense, the principle is saying that most of what we care about in the future will be picked up and measured by present NNP, if only this current money-valued accounting measure can be made sufficiently comprehensive and accurate.

The ultimate welfare justification for NNP from within the optimal growth/dynamic competitive equilibrium paradigm is the idea that, with perfectly complete accounting, comprehensive or inclusive NNP is an exact proxy for the appropriately weighted measure of sustainable-equivalent utility that is implicit in the whole framework. Because it tells us what NNP is supposed to be measuring in welfare terms, the sustainability-equivalence principle provides a potentially very useful organizing principle for conceptualizing which items should be included in comprehensive NNP, and how they should be included. For example, it should now be clear that the depletion of exhaustible natural resources belongs in comprehensive NNP as a (negative) investment evaluated at Hotelling "net price" equal to selling price minus marginal extraction cost. So calculated, the current depletion value of exhaustible natural resources is quantifying exactly the future loss of sustainable-equivalent money-metricized "total willingness to pay" utility—which will be reduced in the future by their present drawing down.

With the sustainability-equivalence principle, we have answered NNP Question no. 1—what is the *welfare* interpretation of nominal NNP?—in terms of money-metricized units of "willingness to pay" at prices normalized to current values. It would also be very informative to be able to answer NNP Question no. 2—what is the *descriptive* interpretation of nominal NNP?—directly in terms of units of "real aggregate consumption." There is an old idea that NNP represents an economy's *overall capacity to produce consumption*. It would be nice to have a rigorous statement of this idea, which we will call a "capacity-equivalence principle."

In trying to formalize a description of NNP in terms of "overall capacity to produce consumption," we will be trying to find a constant-equivalent consumption stream, which is purely hypothetical in the sense that relative prices representing tradeoffs are assumed incorrectly *not* to change when doing the transformation from the actual to the hypothetical constant path. In fact, we already have such a description close at hand in the form of the traditional "simplistic" interpretation of NNP. If relative prices can be interpreted as specifying rates of transformation for nonmarginal changes, so that the production possibilities frontier is as-if linear in the relevant range, then $Y = QC + PI$ is exactly the maximum constant amount of price-aggregated consumption that could be consumed indefinitely—after converting all investments into consumption and remaining in such a stationary state forever by selecting $I \equiv \dot{K} \equiv 0$. We might legitimately be satisfied to call this simplistic interpretation the "capacity-equivalence principle" and be done with the matter. However, it turns out that it is possible to develop a second version of a "capacity-equivalence principle" with one higher degree of sophistication, so to speak. This slightly more sophisticated version will still suffer from the fact that relative prices representing tradeoffs (including, here, the interest rates) are being assumed incorrectly *not* to change when doing the transformation from the actual to the hypothetical constant path—but it will have the advantage of providing a link between current NNP and future consumption. What we will henceforth be calling *the* "capacity-equivalence principle" is this second-version idea that NNP is the production-smoothed constant-durable-capacity equivalent of an economy's actual consumption trajectory.

Such a "consumption version" of the sustainability-equivalence principle as we are now seeking in the form of *the* capacity-equivalence principle does not have the rigorous welfare connotations (nor perhaps quite the same mathematical tidiness) as the "utility version." Nevertheless, this "consumption version" represents a very useful result as an intuitively appealing description of NNP, because, as we will show, there exists a rigorous sense in which we are allowed to think of current NNP as being a "production-smoothed constant-capacity equivalent" of real aggregate consumption (present and future), where the rate of transformation being used at any time to convert future consumption into present consumption-capacity-equivalent units is exactly the actual real rate of interest prevailing in the economy at that time. Thus, it turns out, we have the symmetric result that current NNP is both a time-weighted average of future utility—with time weights at any time being the time derivative of the utility discount factor—and simultaneously a time-weighted average of future real aggregate consumption—with time weights being the time derivative of the real discount factor (and aggregation weights being real prices) on consumption at that time.

Where are we now in the argument and where are we trying to go? We are seeking to evaluate the "production-smoothed constant-durable-capacity equivalent" of a given consumption stream. Such a description of the economy's overall capacity to produce consumption represents, perhaps, a more intuitive concept than the welfare functional of the original optimal growth problem, just because the underlying components seem more familiar. Among other things, we would like to know the relationship between these two proxies for national wealth. We will show that the seemingly abstract entity of "sustainable-equivalent utility" essentially equals a reasonable measure of "constant-capacity-equivalent aggregate consumption"—as it might actually be measured under a particular set of idealized circumstances. For a perfectly complete national income accounting system, then, the following three concepts will turn out to be essentially identical: (1) comprehensive NNP; (2) sustainable-equivalent utility; and (3) constant-capacity-equivalent consumption.

We begin this part by facing up to the task of providing a reasonable definition of "production-smoothed constant-capacity equivalent" aggregate consumption. Unfortunately, however, in our framework of a dynamic competitive equilibrium with multiple heterogeneous consumption and investment goods (and an arbitrarily complicated, if convex, feasible-possibilities set), it is far from obvious what should be meant by such a concept. There is simply no getting around the fact that any interpretation of any weighted average of present and future consumption—including "capacity-equivalent consumption"—will be intuitive and descriptive only, since such a hypothetical constant consumption level does not generally represent a consumption trajectory that is actually attainable by the economy. To remind ourselves yet again, we are struggling here to find a constant-equivalent consumption stream, which is "purely hypothetical" in the sense that relative prices representing tradeoffs (including interest rates) are assumed incorrectly *not* to change when doing the transformation from the actual to the constant path. A rigorous welfare interpretation of NNP (in terms of money-metricized "total willingness to pay" or "area under the demand curve") has already been provided by the sustainability-equivalence principle; the purpose here is not to try to supersede this welfare interpretation, but to supplement it by giving an intuitively plausible analogue expressed in terms of constant-equivalent capacity to produce real aggregate consumption.

The methodology here is as follows. Our immediate point of departure is the observation (or calculation) at any time of something called the "marginal product of capital"—without yet specifying exactly where such a number comes from. Our goal is to tell a story about how to use the marginal product of capital to convert a given consumption stream into a constant-capacity production-smoothed "equivalent" stationary flow. Then we will specify how to calculate plausibly the marginal product of capital in the dynamic competitive equilibrium of a money-valued economy with multiple heterogeneous consumption and investment goods—and also how to aggregate an m-dimensional consumption vector into a plausible one-dimensional measure of aggregate real consumption. We begin by specifying for the simplest case our definition of the relevant "smoothing" or "annuitizing" operation, and we move slowly toward our ultimate goal of telling a plausible story by a large number of small intuitive steps.

To develop the line of argument most simply, suppose at first that there is just one consumption good, whose production at time t is denoted $c(t)$. Let the exogenously given "marginal product of capital" at time t be denoted $i(t)$, while the corresponding discount factor is

$$\beta(t) = \exp(-\int_0^t i(s)\, ds).\tag{19}$$

In developing the concept of "constant capacity-equivalent consumption" with a time-varying $i(t)$, the very first question to ask here is: "what is to be understood by $i(t)$ representing the marginal product of capital at time t?" A widespread interpretation is that $i(t)$ might stand for the interest rate being paid at time t on a hypothetical bank account held by the representative consumer. If this were the appropriate interpretation, then a reasonable definition of "stationary-equivalent consumption" might be

$$\frac{\displaystyle\int_0^\infty c(t)\beta(t)\, dt}{\displaystyle\int_0^\infty \beta(t)\, dt}.\tag{20}$$

For better or for worse, however, the bank-account parable is here a bad (or at least inappropriate) one-dimensional analogy. The more apt analogue for good story-telling purposes here is *not* the "point-input, point-output" interest paid on the banking of an extra unit of consumption withheld from last period. Expression (20) may be an intuitive measure of the overall capacity of consumers in the economy "to consume." By contrast, in trying to understand NNP we are seeking an intuitive measure of the capacity of the economy *to produce* consumption. The marginal product of capital $i(t)$ in this context is more appropriately represented by the "point-input, continuous-output" investment tradeoff between producing an extra unit of consumption at time t and increasing the durable capacity to produce consumption at a permanently higher level throughout the indefinite future after time t. We are seeking to specify here an appropriate definition of "production-smoothed constant-capacity-equivalent consumption" consistent with the notion that the marginal product of capital at any time should represent the increased "durable capacity to produce consumption" that can be bought at the expense of a unit of current consumption. The key idea here is to understand the concept of a "consumption annuity" in terms of production functions rather than in (the more familiar) terms of bank accounts.

We begin by analyzing the smoothing of a discrete-time production plan. We conceptualize the simplified one-good economy as facing in each period a fixed linear schedule of annuity-like production-smoothing tradeoff possibilities. The economy can smooth its production by trading a unit of nondurable consumption produced in period t for an annuity of durable capital producing $i(t)$ units of consumption into perpetuity starting from period $t + 1$. In other words, for the interpretation here, *consumption-producing durable capacity* of vintage t trades off linearly against nondurable consumption at time t in the ratio $i(t) : 1$.

Suppose the economy just so happened to produce at consumption level $c(1)$ in period 1 and $\bar{c}(2)$ in every period thereafter. The economy could have chosen instead to produce the constant consumption level in each period

$$\tilde{c}(1) = x, \quad \tilde{c}(2) = x, \quad \tilde{c}(3) = x,$$
$$\tilde{c}(4) = x, \quad \tilde{c}(5) = x, \ldots, \tag{21}$$

where, by the rules of the consumption-annuity tradeoff available in period 1,

$$[x - \bar{c}(2)] = -i(1)[x - c(1)]. \tag{22}$$

In this situation it is therefore natural to call the level of x satisfying (22), that is,

$$x = \frac{i(1)c(1)}{1 + i(1)} + \frac{\bar{c}(2)}{1 + i(1)}, \tag{23}$$

the "constant-capacity equivalent" consumption level.

Next, suppose that the economy happened to produce consumption $c(1)$ in period 1, $c(2)$ in period 2, and $\bar{c}(3)$ in every period thereafter. This economy could have chosen instead to produce the consumption profile

$$\tilde{c}(1) = c(1), \quad \tilde{c}(2) = x', \quad \tilde{c}(3) = x',$$
$$\tilde{c}(4) = x', \quad \tilde{c}(5) = x', \ldots, \tag{24}$$

where, by the rules of the consumption-annuity tradeoff available in period 2,

$$[x' - \bar{c}(3)] = -i(2)[x' - c(2)], \tag{25}$$

or

$$x' = \frac{i(2)c(2)}{1 + i(2)} + \frac{\bar{c}(3)}{1 + i(2)}. \tag{26}$$

By our previous reasoning, however, instead of producing the consumption profile (24), the economy could have chosen instead to produce the constant consumption level in each period

$$\tilde{c}(1) = x'', \quad \tilde{c}(2) = x'', \quad \tilde{c}(3) = x'',$$
$$\tilde{c}(4) = x'', \quad \tilde{c}(5) = x'', \dots, \tag{27}$$

where

$$x'' = \frac{i(1)c(1)}{1 + i(1)} + \frac{x'}{1 + i(1)}. \tag{28}$$

Combining (26) with (28), it is natural here to call

$$x'' = \frac{i(1)c(1)}{1 + i(1)} + \frac{i(2)c(2)}{(1 + i(1))(1 + i(2))} + \frac{\bar{c}(3)}{(1 + i(1))(1 + i(2))} \tag{29}$$

the "constant-capacity equivalent" consumption level for this situation.

Continuing inductively in this manner, we find that the general formula for the "constant-capacity equivalent" of the consumption trajectory $\{c(t)\}$ is

$$x = \sum_{t=1}^{\infty} \beta(t)i(t)c(t), \tag{30}$$

whose continuous-time version is

$$x = \int_0^{\infty} \beta(t)i(t)c(t)\, dt, \tag{31}$$

where $\beta(t)$ is defined by (19).

A more concise (but somewhat more abstract) backward-induction derivation of (31) proceeds as follows. Imagine that time is broken up into discrete periods of length ε. Suppose that the constant-capacity production-smoothed equivalent of the consumption stream $\{c(s)\}$ from time $s = t + \varepsilon$ to time

$s = \infty$ is given by $x(t + \varepsilon)$. Then the constant-capacity equivalent of the consumption stream $\{c(s)\}$ from time $s = t$ to time $s = \infty$, denoted $x(t)$, should satisfy the annuity-equivalence production-smoothing tradeoff condition at time t:

$$[x(t) - x(t + \varepsilon)] = -\varepsilon i(t)[x(t) - c(t)]. \tag{32}$$

Taking the limit as $\varepsilon \to 0$ in equation (32), we have the basic differential equation

$$\dot{x}(t) = i(t)[x(t) - c(t)], \tag{33}$$

whose solution (with the terminal condition $\beta(\infty)x(\infty) = 0$) is

$$x(t) = \frac{\displaystyle\int_t^\infty \beta(s)i(s)c(s)\,ds}{\beta(t)}. \tag{34}$$

Note that for the special case where i is independent of time and β is therefore exponential, formulas (31) and (20) yield identical definitions of "constant-equivalent consumption." In the more general case of time-varying interest rates, however, the two different ways of "annuitizing" or "smoothing" consumption represented by (31) and (20) typically yield different (but related) values. In a sense, formula (20) represents more the solution of a consumer's constant-equivalent smoothing exercise, while (31) perhaps represents more the solution of a producer's constant-equivalent smoothing exercise. These two conceptually distinct ways of smoothing consumption yield the same constant-equivalent result for fixed interest rates—but otherwise they may yield different results. Neither smoothing formula has a rigorous welfare underpinning; the most that can be hoped for is some intuitive connection with other economic concepts.

A theory of income for the time-dependent case could be built around equations (31) and (20), but we do not pursue the subject formally here. Essentially, if an economy or individual is characterized in the first instance as maximizing a present-discounted-consumption expression of the form (20)—for any given time-dependent discounting function $\beta(t)$—then current consumption plus the net value of all investments (NNP) is always interpretable as representing "constant-capacity-equivalent consumption" in the sense of (31).

The next natural question for us to ask is, What should we do about multiple heterogeneous consumption goods whose prices are expressed in arbitrary monetary units?

We have outlined in some detail in the previous chapter the form of a dynamic competitive equilibrium expressed in nominal prices (which is all that we could ever hope to observe directly). We now seek a "reasonable" price deflator to turn nominal prices into real prices and a nominal interest rate into a real interest rate. Given a time series of nominal consumption prices $\{Q(t)\}$ starting from time $t = 0$, the *Divisia consumption-goods price index* $\mu(t)$ is defined at time t to be the solution of the differential equation

$$\dot{\mu}(t) = \frac{\dot{Q}(t)C^*(t)}{Q(t)C^*(t)}\mu(t), \tag{35}$$

with the initial condition

$$\mu(0) = 1. \tag{36}$$

Following Sefton and Weale (2001), the vector of real prices at time t is then

$$(Q^*(t), P^*(t)) \equiv \frac{(Q(t), P(t))}{\mu(t)}, \tag{37}$$

while the money inflation rate at time t is $\dot{\mu}(t)/\mu(t)$ and the corresponding real interest rate is therefore

$$r^*(t) \equiv r(t) - \frac{\dot{\mu}(t)}{\mu(t)}. \tag{38}$$

Note that, although it is also applied to deflate investment goods, the price deflator is defined only in terms of consumption goods, which makes investment-goods prices and real NNP be measured and expressed in units of aggregate consumption. This Divisia consumption-goods price index has some very important welfare properties that are not possessed by the conventional procedure for deflating NNP—that is, deflating investment goods by their own separate investment-goods deflator expressed in investment-goods units.[7] Thus we are about to put forward a strong theoretical argument for why measuring aggregate consumption plus aggregate investment in real aggregate

7. For a penetrating empirical exploration of what actual differences this might make, see Oulton (2001). Usher (1994) and Scott (1990) are also critical of the standard practice of deflating investment goods over time by their own separate investment-goods deflator.

consumption units is superior to the standard practice of separately deflating consumption and investment, and then adding the two of them together to obtain "real NNP."

The real discount factor at time t corresponding to (38) is

$$\alpha^*(t) \equiv \exp\left(-\int_0^t r^*(\tau)d\tau\right), \tag{39}$$

which expresses the *present discounted real value of a dollar* at time t.

In the general case of multiple consumption goods, a natural generalization of the one-good formula (31) would use in (31) the corresponding "real" analogues

$$c(t) \equiv Q^*(t)C^*(t), \qquad i(t) \equiv r^*(t), \qquad \beta(t) \equiv \alpha^*(t). \tag{40}$$

Plugging the values (40) into the formula (31), the reduced form of our definition of constant-capacity-equivalent aggregate consumption (at time zero) becomes:

$$X = \int_0^\infty \alpha^*(t)r^*(t)Q^*(t)C^*(t)\,dt. \tag{41}$$

We have come to the point now where we are ready to answer NNP Question no. 2: What is the descriptive interpretation of nominal NNP—in terms of real future consumption? Let

$$Y = Q(0)C^*(0) + P(0)I^*(0) \tag{42}$$

symbolize current money NNP (at time zero). The following result (first proved by Sefton and Weale (2001)) shows that NNP may be interpreted as a production-smoothed constant-durable-capacity equivalent of an economy's overall power to produce present and future consumption.

Theorem 2 (Capacity-Equivalence Principle).

$$X = Y. \tag{43}$$

Proof. Real NNP at time t with deflated prices (37) is

$$Y^*(t) \equiv Q^*(t)C^*(t) + P^*(t)I^*(t). \tag{44}$$

From condition {#2} of the maximum principle (in nominal terms) applied to the above situation, we have

$$Y^*(t) = F(K^*(t) \mid P^*(t), Q^*(t)). \tag{45}$$

Taking the time derivative of (45), we obtain

$$\dot{Y}^*(t) = \left.\frac{\partial F}{\partial K}\right|_{*(t)} I^*(t) + \dot{P}^*(t) \left.\frac{\partial F}{\partial P}\right|_{*(t)} + \dot{Q}^*(t) \left.\frac{\partial F}{\partial Q}\right|_{*(t)}. \tag{46}$$

We also know from condition {#3} of the maximum principle (in nominal terms) applied to the above situation that

$$\dot{P}^*(t) = - \left.\frac{\partial F}{\partial K}\right|_{*(t)} + r^*(t)P^*(t). \tag{47}$$

Now substitute from equations (47) into (46), and use the conditions, which must hold all along an optimal trajectory, that

$$\left.\frac{\partial F}{\partial P}\right|_{*(t)} = I^*(t), \quad \left.\frac{\partial F}{\partial Q}\right|_{*(t)} = C^*(t), \quad \dot{Q}^*C^*(t) = 0 \tag{48}$$

to cancel terms and obtain the basic differential equation

$$\dot{Y}^*(t) = r^*(t)[Y^*(t) - Q^*(t)C^*(t)]. \tag{49}$$

By employing an argument very similar to what was used in last chapter's proof of why the wealth and income condition [#4] follows from the maximum principle, it is a straightforward but tedious exercise here to show that

$$\lim_{t \to \infty} \alpha^*(t)Y^*(t) = 0, \tag{50}$$

so that the solution of (49) evaluated at $t = 0$ is

$$Y^*(0) \equiv \int_0^\infty \alpha^*(t)r^*(t)Q^*(t)C^*(t) \, dt, \tag{51}$$

which is the desired conclusion. ■

A more symmetric way of viewing the relationship between the sustainability-equivalence principle and the capacity-equivalence principle is in terms of weighted time averages of utility and consumption. The sustainability-equivalence principle may be expressed in the form

$$Y = \int_0^\infty w_u(t)U^*(C^*(t))\, dt, \tag{52}$$

where the "utility time weight" is

$$w_u(t) = -\frac{d}{dt}e^{-\rho t} = \rho e^{-\rho t}, \tag{53}$$

while the capacity-equivalence principle, it can be shown, may be expressed in the form

$$Y = \int_0^\infty w_c(t)Q^*(t)C^*(t)\, dt, \tag{54}$$

where the "consumption time weight" is

$$w_c(t) = -\frac{d}{dt}\alpha^*(t) = r^*(t)\alpha^*(t), \tag{55}$$

and it is readily confirmed that both sets of time weights are non-negative and sum to one.

Having answered the question What is NNP? by the sustainability-equivalence principle (in terms of welfare-rigorous money-metricized utility) and the capacity-equivalence principle (in terms of a precise descriptive story told about the economy's overall capacity to produce consumption), we turn now to the third, and perhaps most important, question about national income accounting: At least in principle, how are we actually supposed to *use* national income statistics and other currently observable market flow information to make rigorous welfare comparisons among different economies, or the same economy over time? Taken seriously, such inferences would appear to require the computation of inherently dynamic, wealth-like, present-discounted-utility magnitudes.[8] Is there a way to circumvent these daunting calculations, or at least to relate such wealth-like welfare-stock magnitudes to some simpler, and more readily observable, static income-like flow surrogates located within the national income statistician's "production boundary"?

8. This point was first made forcefully by Samuelson (1961).

Posed this way, the question addresses the dynamic version of a fundamental issue of welfare economics. When we have two inherently dynamic situations whose welfare we wish to compare, then in theory we should be directly evaluating the two conceptually correct wealth-like present-discounted-utility magnitudes. But such welfare-stock measures seem very remote from anything that is actually observed, or that is even observable in principle. Meanwhile, within the "production boundary" of observable statistics we have some flow information about current prices and quantities—including price-quantity pairs observed along the current consumer-demand curves. (For nonmarket services, like environmental externalities, it is assumed that an "as if" demand function is available in the form of (the inverse of) a known willingness-to-pay function.) The fundamental question is, What relationship connects the currently observable incomes (and consumer demands) with the not directly observable difference in dynamic welfare between the two situations we wish to compare?

In a basic sense, the answer to this third NNP question must of necessity move us beyond the pure theory of perfectly complete national income accounting—if "national income accounting" is interpreted narrowly to be only about a price-weighted linear index of aggregate net output flows.

One of the most important and useful results in all of static welfare analysis is the idea that the not directly observable difference in utility between any two stationary income-price situations can be operationally measured by the famous formula "income difference plus change in consumer surplus." What we are now about to show is that this same static flow methodology also covers dynamic welfare comparisons, where "income difference" here refers to differences in real comprehensive NNP. The fact that NNP behaves exactly like income in a natural dynamic generalization of the famous static formula for measuring welfare differences should boost our confidence in interpreting NNP as a rigorously based index of "national income." As an income concept, NNP "walks the walk and talks the talk" in the rigorous sense that it looks just like income and acts just like income in its traditional role of measuring welfare changes.

Our approach here treats fully disaggregated consumption as a natural formulation, and will also show how to reconcile static money-valued production-based national income flows with dynamic utility-based welfare. It turns out that when static consumer-welfare theory is placed in its proper dynamic setting, the analysis actually becomes simpler—and considerably more revealing. By embedding short-run consumer behavior within the unified theory of an optimal growth framework, the theory to be developed will cast new light on some old but important controversies in consumer-surplus theory and index-number theory—as well as shedding some new light on the old question What is income?

It should be understood that although the formulation of this chapter has been framed thus far in terms of the theory of national income accounting, by showing how to use current market information to make dynamic welfare comparisons we will effectively be providing a proper dynamic generalization of the standard static formula for the welfare evaluation of economic changes. As a contribution to the theory of consumer surplus and cost-benefit analysis, the theory about to be developed may therefore also have potential applications in several areas of economics other than the theory of comprehensive national income accounting.

Suppose we are interested in comparing the dynamic welfare achievable by two different economies across space or two different economic situations over time. The formulation here is intended to be quite general, in principle covering actual real-world welfare comparisons across space and over time, as well as "with project" and "without project" hypothetical benefit-cost evaluations. (Benefit-cost evaluations are done prospectively "with project" and "without project" by comparing the welfare attainable from a hypothetical "after the project is included" attainable-possibilities set with the welfare delivered by the existing "sans project" status quo attainable-possibilities set.) Let the economy "type" or "role" in what follows be indexed by the superscript indicator variable j. The index value $j = 1$ indicates the given *base* economy. The index value $j = 2$ indicates some particular *comparison* economy. Both economies share the same preferences, but they may have arbitrarily different endowments and/or arbitrarily different attainable possibilities sets. The goal is to compare the welfare criterion (1) across the two economies relying only on currently observable market information.

Both economies or economic situations $j = 1$ and $j = 2$ are postulated to exhibit dynamic behavior as if they are solutions, respectively, to a pair of optimal growth problems of the form:

$$\text{maximize} \quad \int_0^\infty U(C^j(t))e^{-\rho t}\, dt \tag{56}$$

subject to the constraints

$$(C^j(t), I^j(t), K^j(t)) \ \varepsilon \ A^j, \tag{57}$$

and the differential equations

$$\dot{K}^j(t) = I^j(t), \tag{58}$$

and obeying the initial conditions

$$K^j(0) = K_0^j, \tag{59}$$

*where K_0^j is the initially given capital stocks—all of the above holding for $j = 1$
and $j = 2$.*

Concerning the above formulation (56)–(59), note that the "attainable-
possibilities sets" (or "technologies") A^j in (57) and the "endowments" K_0^j in
(59) are allowed to differ arbitrarily between the base economy ($j = 1$) and the
comparison economy ($j = 2$), while "preferences" are identical, as indicated
by the shared objective (56). Unless preferences are postulated to be comparable in some way across the two situations, it is impossible to make rigorous general welfare comparisons. The standard static framework, remember,
yields a bona fide welfare-change indicator only by assuming that, in essence,
the same consumer faces two different price-income situations.

The goal here is to infer the difference in the value of the optimized objective function (56) between the two economies from currently observable
market information alone—without actually having to solve the pair of optimal growth problems (56)–(59). This might appear to be a formidable (or
even impossible) task, since no additional structure is being imposed on the
technologies or endowments of the two economies.

In what follows, it is assumed that the pair of problems (56)–(59) corresponding to $j = 1$ and $j = 2$ are meaningfully posed, so that solutions exist.
Let $\{C^{*j}(t), I^{*j}(t), K^{*j}(t)\}$ represent the optimal trajectory for economy j.
As is well known from the optimality-equilibrium duality theory of the last
chapter, the solutions of (56)–(59) for both economies will generate corresponding dynamic competitive prices, denoted here by the m-vector time
series $\{Q^j(t)\}$ for consumption-goods (money) prices, and by the n-vector
time series $\{P^j(t)\}$ for investment-goods (money) prices in economy j. Then
(money) national income or product for economy j at time t is

$$Y^j(t) \equiv Q^j(t)C^{*j}(t) + P^j(t)I^{*j}(t). \tag{60}$$

Let $\lambda^j(t)$ represent the nonobservable (to an outsider) marginal utility of
money income along an optimal trajectory in economy $j(= 1, 2)$ at time t.

The investment-goods price n-vector, expressed in current-value utility terms for economy $j (= 1, 2)$ at time t is then

$$\lambda^j(t)\mathbf{P}^j(t), \tag{61}$$

while the corresponding consumption-goods price m-vector, also expressed in current-value utility terms for economy $j (= 1, 2)$ at time t is

$$\lambda^j(t)\mathbf{Q}^j(t). \tag{62}$$

In the model, $\{\lambda^j(t)\}$ may be chosen arbitrarily because it represents an extra degree of freedom that merely parameterizes the marginal utility of money income, which can be given a life of its own, related behind the scenes of the real economy to the money supply and other background, purely monetary, factors that determine the price level. What matters for the allocation of resources in the real economy—through the classical-dichotomy veil of arbitrary $\{\lambda^j(t)\}$, so to speak—are the real prices (61) and (62), which are denominated in terms of the contemporaneous value of utility serving as numeraire, and are therefore invariant to $\{\lambda^j(t)\}$. In other words, changing the exogenous specification of $\{\lambda^j(t)\}$ would merely induce inversely proportional changes in $\{\mathbf{P}^j(t)\}$ and $\{\mathbf{Q}^j(t)\}$ without altering (61) or (62). (Typically a paper on optimal growth theory specifies, without ceremony, all prices to be expressed in "real" utility-valued units. The reason we must deal carefully with the thorny issues raised by arbitrary $\{\lambda^j(t)\}$ here is because our goal is to translate observable market values, denominated in the arbitrary monetary units of the two different economies, into a statement about their real welfare difference, expressed, ultimately, in utiles.)

As we have already shown, the duality conditions corresponding to (56)–(59) can be given an interpretation as if describing a decentralized perfectly competitive economy in dynamic equilibrium with a single representative agent having the preference ordering (1). We will emphasize this decentralized market interpretation throughout, concentrating especially on how the observable short-run market demand function of the representative consumer-agent can be used to reveal critical aspects of the agent's underlying preferences.

The first type of optimality condition requires that a Hamiltonian expression should actually attain its maximum everywhere along an optimal trajectory. In the representative-agent dynamic-competitive equilibrium interpretation, maximizing the Hamiltonian is equivalent to the combination of a condition describing the representative consumer's decentralized behavior in choosing among consumption goods C and aggregate net savings or investment Z:

$$\{\#1\}: \quad U(C^{*j}(t)) - \lambda^j(t)P^j(t)I^{*j}(t)$$

$$= \underset{Q^j(t)C+Z=Y^j(t)}{\text{maximum}} \{U(C) + \lambda^j(t)Z\}, \tag{63}$$

along with a condition describing the representative producer's decentralized static-equilibrium behavior:

$$\{\#2\}: \quad Q^j(t)C^{*j}(t) + P^j(t)I^{*j}(t)$$

$$= \underset{(C,I)|(C,I,K^{*j}(t)) \, \varepsilon \, A^j}{\text{maximum}} \{Q^j(t)C + P^j(t)I\}. \tag{64}$$

A second set of optimality conditions can be translated as describing a perfect capital/stock market in dynamic competitive equilibrium:

$$\{\#3\}: \quad \dot{P}^j(t) = - \left. \frac{\partial F^j}{\partial K} \right|_{*j(t)} + r^j(t)P^j(t), \tag{65}$$

where the notation "$|_{*j(t)}$" means evaluation along the optimal trajectory of economy j at time t, $r^j(t)$ is the nominal interest rate in economy j at time t, and

$$F^j(K|P, Q) = \underset{(C,I)|(C,I,K) \, \varepsilon \, A^j}{\text{maximum}} \{QC + PI\} \tag{66}$$

is the aggregate production function in economy j (of K, for given nominal prices P and Q).

The final optimality condition here is the transversality requirement

$$\{\#4\}: \quad \lim_{t \to \infty} \alpha^j(t)P^j(t)K^{*j}(t) = 0, \tag{67}$$

where

$$\alpha^j(t) \equiv \exp(- \int_0^t r^j(\tau)d\tau) \tag{68}$$

is the nominal discount factor at time t corresponding to the nominal discount rates $\{r^j(t)\}$.

If conditions (66) or (67) did *not* hold, then pure positive profits could be made by intertemporal arbitrage operations, which would induce a change in (66),(67)—meaning these equations could *not* have been describing a dynamic competitive equilibrium in the first place.

Because of the underlying convexity of problem (56)–(59), the duality conditions (63)–(67) are both necessary and sufficient for an optimal solution. Thus whenever we postulate or observe here a dynamic competitive equilibrium of the form (63)–(67), it is the same as if we are postulating or observing the solution to an optimal growth problem (56)–(59).

From now on in the exposition, we deal with flow observations of market behavior made only at the present time $t = 0$. More precisely, we take on faith that the dynamic optimality-equilibrium conditions describing the coupled systems (56)–(59), (63)–(67) will hold over all future time, but, aside from this general knowledge, everything we are permitted to know or infer at the present time $t = 0$ must be based solely on what is, at least in principle, the current directly observable market behavior of the representative consumer. (To the extent that the consumption vector C includes nonmarket services, like environmental externalities, an imputation of current market-like behavior must be made, based on an imputed current demand function for nonmarket services.) In keeping with this restriction on knowable information, the symbol $X^{*j}(0)$—for all pertinent variables X—is henceforth simply referenced by the symbol X^j.

Consistent with long-standing economic usage, all consumption enumerations, including the current consumption vector C^j, are conceptualized as flows of services. If we recall a basic message of Chapter 5, this means the "short run" is envisioned as being a period of arbitrarily short duration, with the corresponding prices of consumer durables imputed as competitive-market-equivalent rental flow rates. Although for most commodities and for most applications it probably suffices to think in terms of short-run consumption as occurring over a period of, say, a year, we are theoretically eliminating time aggregation altogether by going to the limit in distinguishing among commodities consumed at each instant of time.

The current short-run consumer demand function in economy j is the representative consumer-agent's response to the following counterfactual question: At what rate would you choose to consume (throughout a vanishingly short time interval starting now) if the instantaneous rental prices of consumption service flows (during this interval) were Q (but the rest of the rental price path did not change)? As was noted in the previous chapter, the traditional way of formalizing this question is to represent consumption choices over time by an intertemporal wealth-budget constraint of the form

$$
\int_0^\delta \alpha^j(t) QC(t)\, dt + \int_\delta^\infty \alpha^j(t) Q^j(t) C(t)\, dt
$$
$$
= \int_0^\infty \alpha^j(t) Q^j(t) C^*(t)\, dt
$$

(69)

for some "vanishingly small" δ. The short-run consumer demand function in economy j is the limiting optimized value of $C(= C(0))$, expressed parametrically as a function of $Q(= Q(0))$, which maximizes the intertemporal utility function (1) subject to the wealth-budget constraint (69), as $\delta \to 0^+$.

As we have already shown in Chapter 5, a concise description of the short-run consumer demand function comes straight out of the maximum principle of optimal control theory. The act of "maximizing the Hamiltonian" translates behaviorally into having the representative consumer-agent in situation $j(= 1, 2)$ solve a decentralized problem of the reduced form:

$$
\text{maximize} \quad U(C) + \lambda^j Z,
$$

(70)

subject to the budget constraint

$$
QC + Z = Y^j,
$$

(71)

where Q stands for the counterfactual parametrically fixed short-run money consumption prices, Y^j represents the given as-if-fixed national income, $\lambda^j = \lambda^j(0)$ is the (not observable to an outsider) given as-if-fixed marginal utility of income, and Z symbolizes aggregate net savings or investment, to be chosen along with $C \geq 0$ by the representative consumer in j.

The short-run demand function is simply the optimized value of C in (70),(71) expressed parametrically as a function of Q. The important implication here for consumer demand theory is that the Hamiltonian is a quasilinear utility function. Intuitively, this quasilinear Hamiltonian objective form (70) is inherent in a continuous-time formulation because the consumer can offset by changes in savings all possible income effects of a short-run price change— merely by shifting the tiniest bit of investment income across time. It is for this reason that (70),(71) with $\lambda^j(0)$ constant describes the *same* short-run instantaneous demand function of Q as would a rigorous limiting argument when $\delta \to 0^+$ in the intertemporal wealth-budget constraint (69).

We write the directly observable short-run consumer-demand function in economy $j (= 1, 2)$ as $D^j(Q)$. Informally, leaving aside corner solutions or "kinks" in the concave utility function, this demand function is essentially the implicit solution of the equation $U'(D^j(Q)) = \lambda^j Q$, which is the relevant first-order condition—*given* the marginal utility of income. Since the marginal utility of income at any given instant is forward looking, it does not depend explicitly on the prices at that instant. Hence, short-run demand $D^j(Q)$ is essentially the implicit solution of $U'(D^j(Q)) = \lambda^j Q$, where the prices Q may vary in defining the demand function, but not the marginal utility of income λ^j.

Slightly more formally (by allowing here for zero-consumption corner solutions), the vector demand function $D^j(Q)$ is the implicit non-negative solution of the above problem (16), (17), which therefore satisfies, for all parametrically given hypothetical values of $Q \geq 0$, the standard duality conditions

$$U'(D^j(Q)) \leq \lambda^j Q, \tag{72}$$

and

$$[\lambda^j Q - U'(D^j(Q))]D^j(Q) = 0. \tag{73}$$

Reflecting the fact that there are no income effects as Q is varied hypothetically in the short run, $\lambda^j = \lambda^j(0)$ is seen by the representative consumer of economy j as if being fixed in (70)–(73), that is, λ^j is implicitly contained as a parameter in the demand function $D^j(Q)$. Concerning the ratio of marginal utilities, λ^2/λ^1 is not directly observable to an outsider, but rather must be inferred indirectly from observing the ratio of inverse demand functions. The relevant inverse-demand ratio takes the form here of an "ideal price deflator," to which subject we now turn.

The ultimate goal of this last part of the current chapter is to be able to make rigorous welfare comparisons between dynamic economic situations, solely on the basis of currently observable market behavior. Because observable prices are always denominated in arbitrary monetary units, the very first item on this agenda is to deflate current money-price levels to a common standard. The natural common standard to use here is the price level of the base economy. Thus the immediate task before us is to express the "price level" of the comparison economy relative to the "price level" of the base economy. We proceed to derive a price index unified with our theory of a dynamic competitive equilibrium as follows.

Over all consumption flows $C \geq 0$, define the directly observable short-run inverse-demand function in economy $j (= 1, 2)$, denoted $Q^j(C)$, to be (any) solution of the equation:

$$D^j(Q^j(C)) = C. \tag{74}$$

The corresponding short-run consumer-expenditure function in economy $j (= 1, 2)$ is

$$E^j(C) \equiv Q^j(C)C. \tag{75}$$

The expenditure formula (75) describes the expense to consumers in economy j of purchasing the fixed market basket of consumption goods C. In familiar terms, expression (75) is just exactly the short-run "revenue function" from basic economics, which a hypothetical monopolist would face in economy j.

The concept, now introduced here, of an *ideal "market-basket price index"* is intended to be an abstraction or idealization of a consumer price index (CPI) or a purchasing power parity (PPP) deflator, which uses, instead of the actual existing prices $Q^j (= Q^j(C^j))$, the imputed market-clearing prices $Q^j(C)$ that would be observed in economy $j (= 1, 2)$ if the market basket being consumed in j were the quasi-fixed benchmark basket C.

Definition. *An ideal "market-basket price index" for deflating the current prices of comparison economy 2 into the current prices of base economy 1, evaluated at the fixed-benchmark market basket of consumption goods C, is defined as the expenditure ratio*

$$\theta(C) \equiv \frac{E^1(C)}{E^2(C)}. \tag{76}$$

Expression (76) may be seen, perhaps, as an abstraction representing that ideal measure toward which the makers of a CPI or PPP-type price index are implicitly striving when they are trying to select judiciously a representative market basket straddling the two economies. The intent of the index makers is to choose a benchmark basket representing, at least conceptually, consumption goods and services *"of the same quantity and quality"* in both market-like situations across which the comparison-pricing imputation exercises are being performed.[9]

The index $\theta(C)$ is a local measure of the price level in economy 1 relative to the price level in economy 2—in the vicinity of the fixed market basket C. That there may be some kind of an imputation issue involved in calculating (76) should perhaps come as no more of a surprise here than the idea that the appropriate "price" of owner-occupied housing needs to be imputed as what "would be" the observed rental price in the economy at some given level of housing consumption-flow services. The appropriate prices to use in (75) and (76) are the counterfactual, other-things-being-equal imputed prices that would be observed in the marketplace of each economy ($j = 1$ and $j = 2$), if the consumption-flow basket being purchased were the benchmark C.

In practice, this is not usually a difficult imputation to make for economies that are structurally very similar, like the United States and Canada, or like the United States from one year to the next, because the index number comparison implicit in (76) then typically reduces to attributing the existing observed market prices Q^j to the given well-specified representative market basket of consumer goods C. Even so, in any actual real-world comparison-pricing exercise, surprisingly many imputations are required to deal with so-called comparison-resistant items "of the same quantity and quality" as the particular consumption market basket chosen to be representative in the comparisons. And there is absolutely no way of escaping the central necessity to make some genuine price imputations in constructing a market-basket price index when the two comparison economies differ substantially in structure— so that, for example, one economy may have commodities in its marketplace that are not purchased at all in the marketplace of the other economy. The concept defined below may help to shed some analytic light on this important set of issues.

Definition.   *An ideal market-basket price index is called "benchmark invariant" if $\theta(C)$ defined by (76) is independent of the market basket of consumption goods C chosen as benchmark, so that we are permitted to write as an identity*

$$\theta(C) \equiv \theta \tag{77}$$

holding for all possible $C \geq 0$.

9. Summers and Heston (1991, p. 329), emphasis added. This paper contains a good practical overview, employing standard terminology, and also contains some further references.

The following result is of prime theoretical importance for getting to where we are trying to go in this dynamic-welfare-comparison argument. It also may have some implications for index-number theory more generally.

Lemma. *Under the assumptions of the model, the ideal market-basket price index (76) is benchmark invariant, meaning (77) holds here as an identity.*

Proof. From (72),(73) and the definition (74), it follows that the equation

$$U'(C) = \lambda^j Q^j(C) \tag{78}$$

holds for $j = 1$, $j = 2$, all $C \geq 0$.

An immediate consequence of comparing (78) with the definitions (75), (76) is that

$$\theta(C) = \theta \equiv \frac{\lambda^2}{\lambda^1} \tag{79}$$

for all $C \geq 0$. ■

Equation (79) represents a stronger-than-required form of the conclusion to be proved in the statement of the lemma, because θ here is not just a constant, but actually equals λ^2/λ^1. If in two different dynamic settings we know a given consumer's short-run demand function, then we can invert this demand function to obtain the ratio of marginal utilities. Thus we have shown how to infer ratios of marginal utilities of income from observations of short-run market demand behavior embedded in a lifetime consumption model.

Since the lemma (77) permits it, we will henceforth *replace the symbol $\theta(C)$ by the symbol θ*. Because the expenditure ratio (76) resulting from the exercise of pricing-out "the same quantity and quality" of consumption flows in both economies always turns out to be the identical constant (independent of the market basket C chosen as benchmark), the expenditure index θ in (77) may be conceptualized as being a truly global deflator for converting "*the* price level" of comparison economy 2 into "*the* price level" of base economy 1.

An old-fashioned intuitive way of relating price levels across two situations is to compare the cost or expenditure required to attain "the same quantity and quality" as some quasi-fixed representative market basket of consumption. The treatment here, based on (76), is in the spirit of this formerly favored approach. A utility-theoretic approach, currently more favored, is fashioned in a somewhat different spirit, being also based on a ratio of expenditures, but with the main conceptual difference being that a quasi-fixed representative utility level u takes the place in (76) of a quasi-fixed representative market basket C. Here we legitimize the old-fashioned concept of a market-basket-type price deflator, insofar as we will show rigorously that an index-number theory based upon (76) is intrinsically unified in a desirable way with the underlying optimal growth/dynamic competitive equilibrium framework.

We come now to what is perhaps the most startling result of this chapter. With complete accounting, all relevant information for making dynamic welfare stock-like comparisons is contained in market flow behavior that is currently observable within the domain of the relevant current comparison. Equation (80) shows that the theoretically correct but nonobservable dynamic welfare index on the left-hand side of the equality sign is exactly the familiar, even famous, currently observable static welfare formula on the right-hand side.

Theorem 3 (Dynamic Welfare-Comparison Principle). *Under the assumptions of the model,*

$$\frac{\rho}{\lambda^1}[\int_0^\infty U(C^{*2}(t))e^{-\rho t}dt - \int_0^\infty U(C^{*1}(t))e^{-\rho t}\, dt]$$

$$= \theta Y^2 - Y^1 + \int_{\theta Q^2}^{Q^1} D^1(Q)dQ. \tag{80}$$

Proof. We start with the wealth and income version of the maximum principle for the optimal multisector growth problem:

$$\rho \int_0^\infty U(C^{*j}(t))e^{-\rho t}\, dt = U(C^j) + \lambda^j Q^j I^j. \tag{81}$$

Taking the difference of (81) between comparison and base economies gives

$$\rho[\int_0^\infty U(C^{*2}(t))e^{-\rho t}dt - \int_0^\infty U(C^{*1}(t))e^{-\rho t}dt]$$

$$= U(C^2) + \lambda^2 Q^2 I^2 - U(C^1) - \lambda^1 Q^1 I^1. \tag{82}$$

Now just using basic mathematical considerations arising from smooth differentiability of the function $U(C)$, we have

$$\int_{C^1}^{C^2} \nabla U(C)dC = U(C^2) - U(C^1),\qquad(83)$$

where the left-hand-side integral of (83) is path-independent because the second mixed partial derivatives of $U(C)$ are equal by the assumption of continuous second derivatives.[10]

Now (78) implies directly that

$$\int_{C^1}^{C^2} \nabla U(C)dC = \lambda^1 \int_{C^1}^{C^2} Q^1(C)\,dC.\qquad(84)$$

Because $\{Q^1(\bullet)\}$ and $\{D^1(\bullet)\}$ from (72), (73), and (74) are inverse functions to each other, integration by parts along any continuous connecting path yields the equation

$$\int_{C^1}^{C^2} Q^1(C)dC = Q^1(C^2)C^2 - Q^1(C^1)C^1 - \int_{Q^1(C^1)}^{Q^1(C^2)} D^1(Q)\,dQ.\qquad(85)$$

Picking $C = C^2$ in (75) for $j = 1$ and for $j = 2$, and then comparing the resulting expression with (76) implies

$$Q^1(C^2) = \theta Q^2(C^2).\qquad(86)$$

Now, by the definition (74),

$$Q^j(C^j) = Q^j.\qquad(87)$$

10. Actually, because the function $U(C)$ is concave, the assumption of differentiability is not even required here, since the singular points where the second derivatives fail to exist or are not continuous have measure zero in the relevant domain. However, the slight gain in generality from recasting the argument without any differentiability assumptions is not worth the messy and excessively mathematical notation that would thereby be required. But it could be done.

Making use of (86) and (87), expression (85) can be transformed into the equivalent form

$$\int_{C^1}^{C^2} Q^1(C)dC = \theta Q^2 C^2 - Q^1 C^1 - \int_{Q^1}^{\theta Q^2} D^1(Q)\, dQ. \tag{88}$$

Next, substitute (88) into (84) into (83) to yield the equation

$$U(C^2) - U(C^1) = \lambda^1 [\theta Q^2 C^2 - Q^1 C^1 - \int_{Q^1}^{\theta Q^2} D^1(Q)\, dQ]. \tag{89}$$

Finally, substitute (89) into the right-hand side of equation (82) and use (81) to obtain the equation

$$\rho[\int_0^\infty U(C^{*2}(t))e^{-\rho t}dt - \int_0^\infty U(C^{*1}(t))e^{-\rho t}dt]$$

$$= \lambda^1 [\theta Q^2 C^2 + \theta P^2 I^2 - Q^1 C^1 - P^1 I^1 - \int_{Q^1}^{\theta Q^2} D^1(Q)\, dQ]. \tag{90}$$

Using (60) to abbreviate (90) and rearranging terms, we have, at last, equation (80), which is the result to be proved. ∎

Expression (80) can be conceptualized as "compressing" or "reducing" the wealth-like dynamic welfare ordering within the square brackets of the left-hand side of the equation into the isomorphic income-like static welfare ordering on the right-hand side. A way to think about the theoretical equivalence of these two welfare orderings is to envision economic situations $j = 1$ and $j = 2$ as varying over all possible technologies and initial endowments. Then situation $j = 2$ will be "better" than situation $j = 1$ by welfare criterion (1) if and only if the right-hand side of equation (80) is positive. It follows that, for the purpose of making comparisons, the dynamic welfare ordering induced by $\Omega(\{C(t)\})$ in (1) is equivalent to the static welfare ordering induced by the expression

$$\theta Y^2 - Y^1 + \int_{\theta Q^2}^{Q^1} D^1(Q)\, dQ. \tag{91}$$

The basic result (80) can thus be interpreted as proving that expressions (1) and (91) are here just different representations of the same underlying dynamic welfare ordering. The currently observable flow-based static expression (91) might even be called a *sufficient statistic* for comparisons based upon the standard but not currently observable stock-based dynamic welfare criterion $\Omega(\{C(t)\})$—because expression (91) exhausts *all* of the relevant welfare-comparison information contained in (1). In principle, the information content of the currently observed flow component of a dynamic market process is sufficient to reveal the most important single summary statistic of its future welfare. In a sense, this startlingly strong result is the ultimate version of the economist's dictum that current competitive market prices (along with current market demands) summarize "all relevant information" for drawing inferences or making decisions. Equation (80) is telling us that if we can envision or imagine the evaluation of a proposed project in terms of the familiar static formula (91), then we are entitled to envision or imagine that we have effectively calculated the overall amount by which present discounted utility will change as the project affects the economy over time.

The unobservable "normalization constant"

$$\frac{\rho}{\lambda^1}, \tag{92}$$

which appears on the left-hand side of (80), involves a compounding of two "conversion coefficients." The pure-time-preference coefficient ρ converts the utility wealth-stock expression within the square brackets of (80) into an annuitized income flow of stationary-equivalent or sustainable-equivalent utility. The coefficient $1/\lambda^1$ represents an arbitrary and inessential scaling constant for converting from units of utility into units of current income in the base economy.

Without any loss of generality, by taking a positive affine transformation of $U(C)$ we are free here to impose the base-economy money-metric normalization:

$$\lambda^1 \equiv 1. \tag{93}$$

When scaled in dollar-utile units defined by (93), equation (80) may then be expressed more neatly in the equivalent form:

$$\int_0^\infty [U(C^{*2}(t)) - U(C^{*1}(t))]e^{-\rho t}\, dt$$

$$(94)$$

$$= \int_0^\infty [\theta Y^2 - Y^1 + \int_{\theta Q^2}^{Q^1} D^1(Q)\, dQ]e^{-\rho t}\, dt.$$

Note the very simple symmetry of the isomorphism parable being told by (94). The difference in sustainable-equivalent utility between the comparison economy 2 and the base economy 1 (money metricized at base-economy prices) is exactly the answer to the following standard question of classical static welfare analysis: How much extra money must the representative base-economy consumer facing prices Q^1 with income Y^1 be paid to be equally as well off as when facing prices θQ^2 with income θY^2? The answer here to this standard question in economic statics is given by the famous expression (91), where the "substitution term"

$$\int_{\theta Q^2}^{Q^1} D^1(Q)\, dQ$$

$$(95)$$

stands for the appropriate change in classical, old-fashioned, Marshall-Dupuit consumer surplus. It is because the Hamiltonian itself is in the form of a quasi-linear utility function that the answer to the narrow question posed above is such a simple direct function of observable short-run market demands, entirely free of messy and extraneous income-effect corrections.

It would appear to follow from the general theory justifying (94) that there is no need to apologize for using the old-fashioned consumer surplus expression (95) routinely in welfare comparisons, whenever consumption is conceptualized as being a short-run flow of services embedded within a larger dynamic competitive equilibrium—and this, it could further be argued, is the half-hidden backdrop implicit in most economic settings. The distinction between "compensated" and "market" demand functions appears in this light to be the extraneous residue from a fuzzy specification of the short run, since the magnitude of any income effect depends directly, and somewhat artificially, upon the length of the time period over which the act of consumption is supposed to occur or be measured. Equation (94) seems to be telling us that when the full economic dynamics of a welfare comparison are properly specified, and the demand function is genuinely short run, then the rigorously correct term accounting for substitution effects is precisely the Marshall-Dupuit consumer surplus expression (95). For this reason, the standard optimal growth/dynamic competitive equilibrium framework may be viewed as opening a door on rehabilitating old-fashioned intuitive consumer surplus as a useful apparatus of some quite general respectability.

To see more clearly the exact sense here in which static welfare comparisons can be viewed as a special case of dynamic welfare comparisons, define the (static) indirect utility function:

$$\Phi(Q, \mu; y) \equiv \text{maximum}\{U(C) + x\} \tag{96}$$

subject to

$$QC + \mu x = y. \tag{97}$$

As is well known, with a quasilinear utility function the utility difference between any two static economic situations differing in income and prices can be measured by the famous static welfare formula of type (91)—consisting of the change in real income plus consumer surplus.[11] An exact translation to the notation of this chapter would take the form

$$\Phi(Q^2, 1/\lambda^2; Y^2) - \Phi(Q^1, 1; Y^1) = \theta Y^2 - Y^1 + \int_{\theta Q^2}^{Q^1} D^1(Q)dQ. \tag{98}$$

It is a welfare relation of the generic form (98) that is typically cited behind the scenes to justify applying a formula of type (91)—thereby easing the way for this kind of formula to have become, historically, a veritable workhorse of static partial-equilibrium welfare analysis.[12] Although the details are omitted here, it is readily demonstrated that the static equation (98) is just a special stationary case of the more general dynamic equation (94).

The reader should be able to see, or at least intuit, that using the ideal market-basket price deflator θ defined by (75),(76) in (98) is exactly equivalent here to making the quasilinear good x in (96),(97) serve as the measuring stick for welfare comparisons. In textbook quasilinear settings, this

11. See, for example, Varian (1992, sec. 10.4, "Quasilinear utility and money metric utility").
12. For a survey of applications, see Hines (1999).

particular normalization is imposed routinely by economists (typically without comment) because it enormously facilitates the conceptualization of the analysis. Whenever we use the "area to the left of the demand curve" as a partial-equilibrium measure of a welfare change, then we are implicitly selecting $\theta = 1$, which may be rationalized from (94) on the grounds that hypothetical expenditures for any fixed market basket must be the same, in the same economy, before and after the change whose value is being read off the demand curve. Any other price deflator than θ—based, say, on choosing one of the nonquasilinear consumption goods C_i as numeraire—will generally wreck the simplicity of formula (91) by introducing messy income effects. In the pure theory of dynamic competitive equilibrium, then, income effects essentially appear as an extraneous artifact of using either the "wrong" price deflator, the "wrong" time period, or both.

Because (98) is a special static case of (94), and because (98) has proved itself to be of great practical importance in many fields of applied economic analysis, it might be hoped that its dynamic generalization (94) may also find useful applications. Result (94) shows that expressions (1) and (91) are two operationally equivalent representation forms for the same underlying dynamic preference ordering. An economist is therefore free to choose whichever representation is more convenient to work with. For most economic applications, the income-like form (91) is probably simpler, more intuitive, and more useful than the equivalent wealth-like form (1), which is unlikely to be directly observable anyway.

To summarize this part of the chapter, a relatively straightforward shorthand application of static consumer-welfare theory—which involves only comparing presently observable prices and quantities along the relevant parts of the short-run consumer-demand function—gives the "correct answers" to some seemingly complicated general questions, the longhand versions of which must intrinsically involve comparing wealth-like "true indicators" of dynamic welfare. Put slightly differently, every time we perform a familiar consumer-surplus-like economic analysis of the welfare difference between two static situations, we are implicitly answering a dynamic question posed in terms of an underlying dynamic welfare comparison. The final part of this chapter has therefore derived a kind of "dynamic welfare-comparison principle," which lets us compare dynamic welfare between situations rigorously, yet relies only on currently observable prices and quantities evaluated along the current short-run consumer-demand function within the current consumption-comparison domain. The underlying isomorphism assures us that it is permissible to translate dynamic welfare-stock comparisons into a simple as-if-static flow story told in terms of conventional, old-fashioned consumer welfare theory. The simple-minded parable gives the correct answers to complicated questions that intrinsically involve comparing wealth-like dynamic welfare measures across any two economic situations differing arbitrarily in technologies or endowments.

Postscript: What Is Income?

We note that at this point we have answered all three of the fundamental NNP questions that we posed at the beginning. Of course we have answered these questions only from within the context of a particular multisector optimal growth model with perfectly complete accounting, which, while representing a standard formulation, is nevertheless highly idealized and far from being the most general possible description of a dynamic economy.

The end of this chapter might also be a fitting place to sum up what has been accomplished in terms of understanding, within this model, the basic properties of "national income." The title of this chapter is, after all, "the pure theory of perfectly complete national income accounting." One might fairly conclude that it is high time to stop stalling and to start addressing more centrally the fundamental question: What is income?

Of all the difficult concepts that we have been wrestling with in this chapter—including "utility," "welfare," "sustainable-equivalent utility," "capital," "wealth," "aggregate consumption," "real aggregate consumption," "the real rate of return," "constant-capacity-equivalent consumption," "aggregate output," "real aggregate output," and so forth—the trickiest by far is "income." (We have also noted previously that there is no practical substitute for income, a concept ubiquitously measured by practically every economic entity at almost every level of aggregation and in almost every sector and subsector throughout a modern economy.) As we have seen, in the ultra-simple Hicks-Lindahl-Fisher idealized economy of a Robinson Crusoe–like agent whose wealth is a deposit in a bank account paying dividend flows at a constant rate of interest, all reasonable definitions of income amount to the same thing. However, "income" is an extremely elusive concept in even slightly more complicated economies, because all of the simple-sounding formulas (Fisher's "interest on wealth," Lindahl's "consumption plus net wealth increment," Hicks's "maximum sustainable consumption") start to break apart from each other and may become either contradictory, or ambiguous, or misleading, or even meaningless.

As we have stated already, more than any other single income-like flow concept, the guiding principle behind modern national income accounting is identified with the Hicksian definition of income, which, in his words, is: "the maximum amount which can be spent during a period if there is to be an expectation of maintaining intact the capital value of prospective returns."[13] Hicks moved very quickly from this definition of income to the interpretation that "it equals consumption plus [net] capital accumulation." We have noted also that it is essentially meaningless to attempt to apply literally such a sustainability-specific definition to a modern industrial economy with its vast multitude of extremely different consumption and investment goods, whose proportions are de facto quasi-fixed in the short run.

Hicks was well aware that all concepts of income are at best a "rough approximation" with "far too much equivocation in their meaning"—as opposed to constituting a "strict logical category." He characterized examples of his own approach as "an approximation to the central meaning of the income concept," to be contrasted with "an analysis which aims at logical precision." All of this notwithstanding, Hicks was firm in his own mind about his "central meaning" when he wrote "the calculation of income consists in finding some sort of *standard* stream of values whose present capitalized value equals the present value of the stream of receipts which is actually in prospect. It is a standard stream in that it maintains some sort of constancy, as against the actual expected stream of receipts, which may fluctuate in any manner whatsoever . . . . We ask, not how much a person actually does receive in the current week, but how much he would be receiving if he were getting a standard stream of the same present value as his actual expected receipts. That amount is his income."[14]

Understood sympathetically in this way, there is something intuitively (or perhaps even spiritually) appealing about Hicks's core idea that the "central meaning" of national income is to be found in the metaphor of a hypothetical standard stream, which is some kind of a "constant equivalent" to what the economy is actually capable of generating over the long run. In a perceptive

13. Unless otherwise noted, quotations here are from Hicks (1946), chap. 14.
14. Hicks (1946), p. 184, emphasis in original.

essay entitled "The Concept of Income in Economic Theory," Nicholas Kaldor
has characterized Hicks's approach to defining income:

> The novelty of this [Hicks] approach to the income concept is that it eschews
> any connection between the notion of income and the notion of capital.
> Fisher, Lindahl, and the other writers on the subject invariably looked upon
> income as the yield derived from some *given source*: in the case of Fisher, it
> is the *net* yield of capital goods after elimination of all 'double counting'; for
> the others, it is *net* yield after deducting (or adding as the case may be) what-
> ever is necessary to maintain the 'source' or the 'corpus' constant. In Hicks's
> approach the source or corpus from which the income is derived disappears
> altogether as a separate entity—capital appears only as the capitalized value
> of a certain future prospect and income as the 'standard stream equivalent' of
> that prospect. Capital and income are thus two different ways of expressing
> the same thing, not two different things.[15]

Suppose we follow Kaldor in interpreting Hicks's "central meaning of the
income concept" as being the standard-stream equivalent of "the capitalized
value of a certain future prospect" and push this idea through to its logical
conclusion. Is *this* a good candidate for "income"—in the sense of capturing
its central meaning? The most useful first step toward a general answer is
to translate the lofty phrase "central meaning" into a more down-to-earth
rendition, which simply asserts that "income is what income does." The more
abstract question then becomes transformed into the slightly more specific
version: What is it that income is supposed to do?

One of the things "income is supposed to do" is to serve as a kind of
stationary-equivalent proxy summarizing in a single number the complicated pattern of present and future gain flows that a general multisector nonlinear dynamic economy is capable of achieving over time. The
"sustainability-equivalence principle" and the "capacity-equivalence principle" express rigorously two ways in which NNP possesses this income-like
property in the general case. If we succumb to the almost-irrepressible urge
to have one simple summary indicator of the stream of national welfare delivered over all future time, then the sustainability-equivalence principle indicates that inclusive NNP is a welfare-rigorous money-metricized measure of a
nation's overall power to produce utility, while the capacity-equivalence prin-

15. Kaldor (1955), chap. 5, sec. 4 (income as "standard stream"), italics in original.

ciple indicates that inclusive NNP can be interpreted as a story or description of a nation's overall power to produce consumption.

Another thing that income is supposed to do is to serve as a component indicator of welfare differences in the famous formula "welfare difference equals income change plus change in consumer surplus." The "dynamic welfare comparison principle" shows rigorously that real NNP plays exactly this income-like role. If real consumption prices remain the same between two situations, as might be expected for the evaluation of "small" projects, then changes in real NNP accurately measure dynamic welfare differences. When real consumption prices change, then a supplementary term reflecting the difference in consumer surplus is required. With differing real consumption prices, it is clearly asking too much to require that NNP alone should indicate accurately dynamic welfare differences, since even in the simplest static framework the change of income between two situations must be supplemented by the change of consumer surplus in order to reflect accurately the difference in money-metric utility between the two situations when consumption prices differ.

In summary, I believe it is fair to say that it has been shown in this chapter that, at least in principle, the inclusive net aggregate production index number $NNP(\equiv QC + PI)$ has all of the essential income-like generic properties that one could realistically aspire for it to have in a general setting. The seemingly inexorably intertwined notions of "income" and "sustainability" are two of the most elusive concepts in economics—and for essentially similar reasons. This chapter has tried to show the theoretical cohesion and practical usefulness of a neo-Hicksian approach, which would say that income is the standard stream equivalent of what is actually attainable over time, or, as we might put it in the terminology of this book, *present income is the sustainable equivalent of future prospects.*

Bibliographic Note

The literature on the subject matter of this chapter has grown enormously over the last few decades. For a good comprehensive overview, see Aronsson, Johansson, and Löfgren (1997). The February and May 2000 special issue of *Environment and Development Economics* was devoted to the theme "Advances in Green Accounting," and the review articles contained therein give some indication of the current state of knowledge. (I especially recommend the summary article by the guest editor, Jeff Vincent, and the article by Geir Asheim entitled "Green National Accounting: Why and How?") Pezzey (1992) contains an oft-cited discussion of the many meanings of "sustainability."

The organization and emphasis in this chapter very much reflects my own views on the subject of green accounting and sustainability. The idea that the Hamiltonian of a multisector optimal growth problem has an interpretation as ideally accounted NNP was first stated and proved in my 1970 Cowles Foundation Discussion Paper, a special case of which was broken out and published later in Weitzman (1976). Theorem 2 (the "Capacity-Equivalence Principle") is a modification and economic interpretation of a result first stated by Sefton and Weale (2001). Theorem 1 (the "Sustainability-Equivalence Principle") was first stated in Weitzman (2000). The treatment in this chapter of Theorem 3 (the "Dynamic Welfare-Comparison Principle") closely follows Weitzman (2001).

There are many other views on the subject of green accounting and sustainability, too many to list or categorize here. However, it is appropriate to mention explicitly the original and influential work of John Hartwick, beginning with Hartwick (1977), which has spawned a tradition of "sustainability" with an emphasis and interpretation quite different from my own. The most careful and rigorous presentation of "Hartwick's Rule," which also contains an excellent discussion of its domain of applicability and its limitations, is Asheim and Buchholz (2000).

7

❋

The Stochastic Wealth and Income Version
of the Maximum Principle

Introduction

We now extend the basic framework to deal with uncertainty in the accumulation of capital.

At each stage of this book, we have systematically layered increasingly greater mathematical complexity onto the underlying model. We began with the one-capital-good prototype-economic calculus of variations problem, which by now should look fairly simple and seem pretty tame as a special one-variable case where the Hamiltonian has an interior maximum characterized by the appropriate first-order condition. Then we generalized to the one-dimensional optimal control version of the prototype-economic problem by additionally requiring net investment to lie in a control region, which might depend upon the value of the state variable. Although we were able to provide a rigorous proof of the maximum principle for this one-capital-good case, it was considerably more complicated than the corresponding proof for the calculus of variations formulation (where we could ignore the constraints on the control variable). Next came the multidimensional optimal growth problem. Although we gave a rigorous statement and proof for a generalized wealth and income version of the maximum principle, the statement itself involved a subgradient directional derivative of the value function, and we made only gestures toward stating formally or proving rigorously the standard version or the simplified wealth and income version (where partial derivatives replace directional derivatives) of the maximum principle with heterogeneous capital in multiple dimensions.

The introduction of uncertainty ratchets up the required level of analysis yet another several notches on the scale of mathematical complexity. To treat the subject of this chapter rigorously and at the level of generality of the multidimensional economic growth problem of Chapter 5 could easily double the size of this book and would be out of all proportion to its intended purpose (even presuming that it could be done). As a result of the inherent mathematical complexity of the subject, in this chapter we make almost no attempt at being rigorous or general. Instead, to focus as sharply as possible on the core content of the wealth and income version of the maximum principle under uncertainty, we assume the simplest imaginable stochastic generalization of the basic one-dimensional prototype-economic calculus of variations control problem of Chapter 1, along with whatever assumptions it takes to make all of the relevant functions well behaved for the purpose at hand. Then we content ourselves with stating the relevant results in an intuitively reasonable fashion and providing an "economist's proof" consisting of mathematically plausible, but ultimately heuristic, arguments. Economic applications of stochastic diffusion processes constitute what is by now an important area of economics. There exist several books treating this topic at varying levels of mathematical sophistication, which the interested reader is encouraged to consult.[1]

Because it is easy to get lost in the mathematical details of stochastic diffusion processes, whose rigorous foundation is quite intriguingly sophisticated, we should keep our well-defined goals sharply in view. These limited goals represent a logical continuation of the major theme of Part II. We are seeking to connect income with wealth (or welfare)—under uncertainty. The major issue here boils down to giving a convincing wealth-and-income economic interpretation of the (so-called) Hamilton-Jacobi-Bellman equation for the simplest stochastic generalization of the prototype-economic problem of Chapter 1. This chapter, then, assumes some prior knowledge of probability theory and stochastic processes; it is more directed at using such a framework to shed light on the stochastic relationship between income and wealth (or welfare) than at rigorously explaining the probabilistic framework itself.

As we shall see, the stochastic connection between income and wealth depends critically on subtle issues of timing, measurement, and information. For example, it will become crucial to specify carefully what is being measured as income, when is it being measured, and how is it being measured. In the deterministic case the appropriate timing and measurement of income flows were so apparent that no special discussion was warranted. With stochastic diffusion processes, all of this can change dramatically, since seemingly slight

---

1. Part II ("Mathematical Background") of Dixit and Pindyck (1994) is particularly recommended as a first introduction to the subject.

differences of specification about when in the production period the price term of a chain-linked Divisia production index is evaluated (beginning, middle, or end) can give quite different relations between wealth and income. In a stochastic-diffusion economy, it matters how index numbers of income or production are constructed.

The workhorse model of this chapter treats the one-dimensional firm (or investment opportunity) under uncertainty. In this case direct gain is measurable in money terms as a dividend or payout, the firm's stock market value is observable, and income will refer to *expected* true earnings (dividends plus expected net investment evaluated at opportunity cost). Within this context, the main objective of the chapter is to state and prove a stochastic wealth and income version of the maximum principle. (The main result will be that forward-looking comprehensively accounted expected-immediate-future true earnings must exactly equal the firm's opportunity cost of capital times the observed stock market value of all its outstanding shares.)

Just as Chapters 2–6 may be seen as representing various deterministic generalizations of the simplest prototype-economic calculus of variations control problem of Chapter 1, so is it possible to generalize the stochastic results of this chapter analogously into stochastic versions of Chapters 2–6. However, we make no serious effort to develop formally such generalizations. (To do so, like developing a mathematically rigorous version of the present chapter, would require a book of its own.) Instead, we content ourselves here with the hope that, from a good intuitive understanding of the most basic stochastic control model, which we will endeavor to convey, the reader will develop a sense of what should be the broad outlines of the analogous "stochasticized" versions of Chapters 2–6.

The Deterministic Case in Terms of Policy Functions

We begin by reviewing the simplest case of the deterministic one-capital firm with "perfectly complete" income accounting. We will recast the solution to this problem in a somewhat nontraditional form to ease the transition to, and emphasize the connection with, the stochastic version, which will be the primary focus of our attention here. Although the main stochastic result generalizes to multicapital cases with various constraints on the control variables and many other complications, we purposely choose here the simplest imaginable one-dimensional unconstrained version in order to focus as sharply as possible on the core relationship between wealth and income under uncertainty. It is all the more essential to deal with the simplest imaginable case here because, even so, there will be some tricky conceptual (and mathematical) issues involved in the timing and measurement of "expected true earnings," a concept that, though generalizable, is best examined initially in a pure form that is as free as possible of any conceivable distracting complications.

Although all kinds of generalizations are possible (including consumer portfolio choice formulations), for the sake of having a particularly sharp image with a crisp statement and a vivid storyline we interpret the one-dimensional prototype problem as modeling the dynamic behavior of a firm whose shares are publicly traded. A good specific example to keep in mind might be the optimal extraction of a fixed pool of oil by a publicly held Hotelling monopolist, Problem 5 as stated in Chapter 2 and solved in Chapter 4. Another particularly good example to carry along for viewing in the mind's eye could be a firm described by the q-theory of investment (Problem 2, covered in Chapters 2 and 4), whose shares are competitively traded. Of course the theory of the stochastic maximum principle covers a much more general situation than just these two applications, but it can help the conceptualization and intuition greatly to keep in mind, as we develop the concepts of this chapter, a specific example or two. In particular, it will aid clear thinking throughout what follows to think of investment and capital in *real or physical* terms—that is, barrels of oil, numbers of trucks, and so forth. This will automatically reinforce the core idea that, even in the multisector case, we are assuming that every investment has an internal shadow accounting price for the firm, which can vary with changes in the current level of investments or as the background stocks of capital are altered over time.

Let us start with the details describing the one-dimensional firm's environment. As usual by now, the control variable is taken to be net investment I. Essentially, any other control variable (or variables) could be transformed into this reduced-form instrument by a change of variables. For simplicity we are assuming that the choice of I is unconstrained so that, at least in principle, I is allowed to take on any value. The direct gain is represented by the variable G. Since we are interpreting the control problem as being a model of a publicly owned dynamic firm, the relevant direct gain here is best conceptualized as being a dividend that the firm pays out to its shareholders. G can be expressed as a function of I (for a given level of K) by the equation $G = G(K, I)$. The implied "production possibilities frontier" between G and I, for a given fixed value $K = K(0)$, is depicted as the curve in Figure 4.

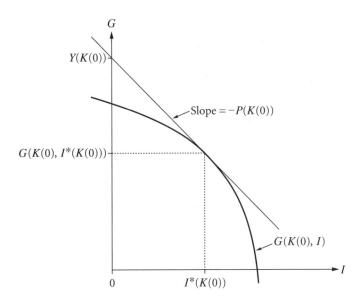

Figure 4 The firm's true income or earnings.

It is important to recognize that here—in this time-autonomous formulation—the firm's "production possibilities frontier" $G = G(K, I)$ does not depend on time explicitly. The time autonomy of the firm's "technology" for trading off dividends against (net) investments for a given level of capital means that all sources of future dividend and investment possibilities are correctly "accounted for" by changes in capital stocks. It might therefore be said that we have "complete accounting" here—in the sense that there are no residual forces of growth having their origin in unaccounted-for time-dependent atmospheric changes.

The firm's risk-class-adjusted "opportunity cost of capital" or its "competitive rate of return" is given as the parameter ρ. The firm seeks to maximize, over an infinite horizon, the present discounted value of dividends paid out to its shareholders.

We have already expressed the firm's dynamic optimal control problem in a traditional form in Chapters 1 and 2. (In the language of Chapter 2, this problem is a special calculus of variations case where the control set essentially allows any value of I to be assumed—implying that the firm will not wish to choose "crazy" values of I, even if it can, because of the implicit deleterious effects on G.) We are attempting to rephrase the wealth and income version of the maximum principle in this deterministic model so that the transition to its natural stochastic generalization is made easier and more understandable.

If we try to place it in the finance literature, the wealth and income version of the maximum principle is itself a substantive generalization of the extremely simple Gordon model for calculating the stock market value of a firm with a constant rate of dividend growth. The Gordon formula says that the competitive stock market value of a firm paying dividends (of current value D_0), which will grow exponentially at rate g, is $V = D_0/(\rho - g)$, where ρ represents the firm's opportunity cost of capital. This Gordon model can be seen as a very special limiting case of the deterministic wealth and income version of the maximum principle. (In this case, it is as if $G(K, I) = \rho K - I$, $K(0) = D_0/(\rho - g)$, and, in this limiting degenerate case of an optimal control problem where the instrument $I(t)$ is constrained to be equal to $gK(t)$, the efficiency price of investment $p(t)$ is always one.) When we present the stochastic wealth and income version of the maximum principle, which we are now leading up to, we will have generalized yet further the scope of a methodology whose simplest conceivable originating example is the Gordon model.

By this stage, we should be used to conceptualizing the optimal policy and expressing the optimality conditions as a function of (the) time. What we want to do throughout this chapter is to conceptualize the optimal policy and express the optimality conditions as a function of (the) state. Let us therefore think of a "policy function" $I(K)$ as expressing the control I as a function of the state variable K. Then an "optimal policy function" $I^*(K)$ expresses the optimal control setting as a function of the capital stock K. What exactly do we mean by this notation?

Any policy function $I(K)$ generates a corresponding time trajectory $K(t)$, which satisfies the differential equation

$$dK(t) = I(K(t))\, dt, \tag{1}$$

along with the initial condition

$$K(0) = K_0. \tag{2}$$

(For reasons that will soon become apparent, we are using the seemingly arcane notation of (1) here to describe the ordinary differential equation $\dot{K} = I$.) In particular, the optimal policy function $I^*(K)$ generates a corresponding time trajectory $K^*(t)$, which also satisfies the relevant versions of (1) and (2), that is,

$$dK^*(t) = I^*(K(t)) \, dt \tag{3}$$

and

$$K^*(0) = K_0. \tag{4}$$

Waving aside mathematical technicalities and difficulties (as will be our custom throughout this chapter), our definition of the optimal policy function $I^*(K)$ is that it satisfies (3),(4) and for any other policy function $I(K)$ satisfying (1),(2), it must hold that

$$\int_0^\infty G(K^*(t), \ I^*(K^*(t)))e^{-\rho t} \, dt \geq \int_0^\infty G(K(t), \ I(K(t)))e^{-\rho t} \, dt. \tag{5}$$

Since the calculus of variations form of the problem is a special case of optimal control theory where there are no constraints on the control variable (here net investment), the Hamiltonian formulation works as a special case where the maximized Hamiltonian (with respect to net income) is obtained at an interior solution. (An additional assumption that the control I is constrained to be in a control interval, so that $m(K) \leq I \leq M(K)$, could readily be handled by the model, but we are trying to convey here the basic message as simply and as directly as possible.)

With (5) representing an optimal net investment policy, we can define the corresponding accounting price of investment as a function of the capital stock here as

$$P(K) \equiv -G_2(K, I^*(K)). \tag{6}$$

Next define for all K_0 the state evaluation function

$$V(K_0) \equiv \int_0^\infty G(K^*(t), \ I^*(K^*(t)))e^{-\rho t} \, dt, \tag{7}$$

where the corresponding trajectories $\{K^*(t)\}$ satisfy conditions (1)–(5) above. In words, $V(K_0)$ is the state evaluation function because it represents the value of an optimal policy expressed parametrically as a function of the initial condition $K(0) = K_0$.

Of course we know from previous considerations (see, for example, Chapter 3) that it is also true (wherever $V(K)$ is differentiable) that

$$P(K) = V'(K). \tag{8}$$

For reasons that will become apparent presently, we choose here to emphasize the less customary current-rate-of-transformation accounting-price interpretation of equation (6), by making it into a definition of $P(K)$, while equation (8) then appears here in the form of a derived result or theorem. (The more customary order, of course, is exactly the opposite—namely, to define $P(K)$ first by (8), and then to derive equation (6) as a theorem.) With the primary interpretation being (6), $P(K)$ can then be viewed more conspicuously as a theoretically observable shadow or accounting price representing the current marginal rate of transformation between investments and dividends, when the capital stock is at level K.

In order to motivate the definition of the firm's true income or earnings, it is convenient to invent and apply, in a thought experiment, the fiction of an "ideal accountant." Suppose the firm is currently at the level of capital stock K. This means the firm is located on its production possibilities frontier at the point where $I = I^*(K)$ and where $G = G(K, I^*(K))$, and that the firm is acting as if it is using $P(K)$ as an internal shadow price to represent the appropriate current marginal rate of transformation of I into G. It is assumed that the ideal accountant knows all of this information. Thus the ideal accountant observes the current dividend flow $G(K, I^*(K))$, the current investment flow $I^*(K)$, and also knows the firm's corresponding current internal efficiency price of investment in terms of dividends, $P(K)$.

In this situation, a not unreasonable definition of the firm's true income or true earnings (as a function of its capital stock) is

$$Y(K) \equiv G(K, \ I^*(K)) + P(K)I^*(K). \tag{9}$$

Formula (9) represents a not unreasonable definition of income because it is a direct analogue of the intuitive idea that income is measured as consumption plus the value of net investment, where the accounting price of investment is taken as its opportunity cost in terms of marginal consumption foregone. The geometric relationship between G, I, P, and Y, for the initial value $K = K(0)$, is depicted in Figure 4.

The wealth and income version of the maximum principle applied to this situation is the theorem that, under the stated assumptions of the model,

$$\rho V(K) = Y(K),\tag{10}$$

which holds for all K.

Let us now review very carefully the intended operational meaning of theorem (10) as a description of a dynamic optimizing firm whose shares are publicly traded. The variable ρ measures the firm's opportunity cost of capital or its competitive rate of return, and is assumed to be known. (The simplest example to have in mind here is an environment of risk neutrality, where ρ represents the available risk-free return—although more general interpretations are possible via so-called risk-neutral evaluation.) The state evaluation function $V(K)$ is observable as the competitive market value of all shares in this firm, when the capital stock is K. Essentially, $V(K)$ must equal this competitive share value because it equals the (maximized) present discounted value of all future dividends that will be paid out by the firm, which a "share" entitles the owner to have.

The left-hand side of equation (10), $\rho V(K)$, represents the flow of return payments that the holders of shares of this firm could expect to obtain on alternative comparable investments made elsewhere in the economy. The right-hand side is genuine income, $Y(K)$, as defined by formula (9).

Equation (10) is a genuine theorem relating two independently measured concepts. There is nothing in the least degree tautological or circular about (10). True earnings are measured by the ideal accountant, who need know absolutely nothing about the stock market value of the firm or its competitive rate of return. (It is completely irrelevant to the ideal accountant even whether the firm is privately held or issues shares that are publicly traded.) The cost of capital times the stock market value of shares is noted by a stock market observer, who may know absolutely nothing about the true currently accounted earnings of the firm—except insofar as it manifests itself through the share price. The theorem embodied in (10) says that, in the above model, these two independently measured entities must theoretically be equal.

If earnings could be comprehensively and accurately measured, with all investments evaluated at true opportunity costs, then the ratio of true earnings to share valuation should equal exactly the firm's competitive rate of return on capital. All of the information about the future that is embodied in competitive asset pricing is in principle also captured by current perfectly comprehensively accounted income. Thus we have here a theory of ideal income accounting explaining quite sharply why someone attempting to understand asset pricing might be very interested, at least in principle, in examining true economic earnings. The essential idea here is that ideally measured income and wealth are, at least in principle, two independently observable sides of the same coin. Although financial economists who specialize in theories of asset pricing occasionally make passing or indirect reference to earnings or income, the centrality of the kind of tight conceptual connection revealed by (10)—which is at least useful as a theoretical organizing principle for thinking about what earnings or income is ideally supposed to be measuring or representing—seems not to have been grasped in the finance literature.

Of course, equation (10) is only a theoretical result about the relationship between ideal comprehensively accounted income and wealth. The real world of accounting may actually be very different from the theoretical idealizations of this model. The overarching point here, however, is that there *is* a theoretically tight connection between idealized measures of income and wealth. A tight theoretical relation like this can serve as a valuable starting point for focusing our thinking about some important possible financial (or even welfare) connections between stock values and flow values.

Stochastic Wealth and Income

Thus far, the precise connection between ideally accounted comprehensive income and perfectly competitive share evaluation has been developed for what is essentially a deterministic dynamic firm. But since asset pricing is widely believed to be associated with uncertainty in a genuinely essential way, it will be interesting to see what happens to the relation (10) when the underlying dynamic model of the firm is augmented by uncertainty.

We now follow a long modeling tradition by introducing uncertainty as a stochastic diffusion process appended to the accumulation equation (1). (The analytical power that stochastic diffusion processes can bring to bear on many dynamic optimization problems is one of the reasons that many modelers like them in the first place.) This particular form of uncertainty is far from innocuous and in a sense will drive the strong results that come out of the model. Modeling uncertainty as a continuous-time stochastic diffusion process in the accumulation of capital stocks certainly has ample precedence in the economics and finance literature, and, one might argue, such a formulation at least approximates some realistic situations. As we will show, this formulation in terms of a stochastic diffusion process will turn out to be a good starting point for thinking about the introduction of uncertainty into the basic model—because with this formulation we will still be able to obtain a striking connection, in the spirit of (10), between ideally measured stochastic income and stochastic wealth.

By defining the deterministic problem in the unusually roundabout form that we just did—in terms of policy functions—we have greatly eased our transition to an analysis of the proper stochastic generalization. We now introduce genuine uncertainty by replacing (1) with its stochastic generalization

$$dK(t) = I(K(t))\,dt + \sigma(K(t))dZ(t), \tag{11}$$

and (3) by its corresponding stochastic generalization

$$dK^*(t) = I^*(K^*(t))\,dt + \sigma(K^*(t))dZ(t). \tag{12}$$

In the above problem, dZ represents the stochastic differential of a simple Wiener process, while the function $\sigma(K)$ represents the standard deviation per unit time of "unintended" or "unexpected" capital accumulation at stock level K. The control variable is the unconstrained net investment level I. In (11), the level of I is chosen at time t by the policy function $I(K(t))$, conditional on observing the state variable $K(t)$. Similar comments apply to (12) for $I^*(K^*(t))$.

Were this a book whose main theme was about applications of stochastic optimal control theory to economics or finance, then much more effort would be spent explaining the stochastic diffusion equation (11) (or (12)). Even so, it is worth noting that almost all such books for economists on the subject (which I know of) do not define rigorously the exact meaning of the underlying stochastic diffusion equations or the exact meaning of an optimum. Nor is the treatment of the dual optimality conditions in such books fully rigorous. The inherent mathematical complexity of a rigorous treatment is such that it is far more "economical" for most economists to rely heavily on intuitively plausible explanations and heuristic proofs. Here, we shortchange even this approach to the subject by relying on other texts, which are more centered directly on the economics or finance applications of stochastic diffusion processes, to provide a more detailed heuristic background explanation of stochastic diffusion processes themselves.

The ultimate purpose of this chapter is to develop a stochastic wealth and income version of the maximum principle for the simplest possible one-sector dynamic stochastic model, which generalizes what was done previously in the deterministic part of this book. We concentrate our detailed heuristics on those mathematical aspects that are particularly relevant for defining the concept of stochastic income and relating it to stochastic wealth.

Stochastic diffusion processes, used here in the basic model, are mathematically quite tricky. Such processes are continuous almost everywhere, but they fluctuate so violently, per unit time in the limit, that they are differentiable almost nowhere. The *variances* of such processes are of order dt in time, so that the standard deviations are of order $\sqrt{dt}$—which means we must be very careful in taking differentials of stochastic functions, because we must consider the impact of the second-order terms of a Taylor series expansion in standard deviations to ensure that we have retained all relevant first-order terms.

Our one modest attempt here at an "explanation" of the meaning of (11) (or (12)) is to provide an *as if* heuristic story, which will be useful later in interpreting the concept of stochastic income. In fact, this explanation is so contradictory from a strictly rigorous mathematical viewpoint that it cannot even be carried out meaningfully. Nevertheless, the *as if* story is exceedingly useful as a first introduction, because it conveys, albeit in misleadingly simple terms, the "spirit" of what remains after the real mathematicians, like Wiener, Kolmogoroff, Itô, and Stratonovich, have performed their magic with rigorous definitions and proofs.

Suppose we want to conceptualize the diffusion process (11) as the limit of a finite-difference version (with infinitesimally small step sizes), which is analogous to the very useful usual way of thinking about an ordinary differential equation as being the limit of what happens to a finite-difference story—in the limit as the step size goes to zero. (Everyone begins by intuiting the stochastic diffusion story along these lines, even the great mathematicians who provided a precisely rigorous description in order to "patch up" the parts where the *as if* story goes wrong.) Let the step size be h, which is to be interpreted as some very small positive number. Then the *as if* story that equation (11) is trying to tell us goes something like this. Given $K(t)$ at time t, the situation is *as if* there is a fair-coin-flipping probability of one-half that the coin comes up "heads," in which case the realized value of K at time $t + h$ is

$$K^1(t + h) = K(t) + I(K(t))h + \sigma(K(t))\sqrt{h} + O(h^{3/2}), \qquad (13)$$

while the situation is *as if* there is a fair-coin-flipping probability of one-half that the coin ends up "tails," in which case the realized value of K at time $t + h$ is

$$K^2(t + h) = K(t) + I(K(t))h - \sigma(K(t))\sqrt{h} + O(h^{3/2}), \qquad (14)$$

where the expression $O(h^{3/2})$ stands for all terms of order 3/2 or higher in h.

Note the informational timing in the above description, which turns out to be a crucial aspect of the *as if* story. First, at time t the value $K(t)$ of the state variable is observed. Almost simultaneously, at almost that same time instant of t but just *immediately after* the value $K(t)$ of the state variable is observed, the value of the control variable $I(K(t))$ is chosen. The observation of $K(t)$ and the subsequent choosing of $I(K(t))$ *both occur before* the fair coin is flipped. This "observing and then choosing" at time instant t is subsequently followed by a period of length h, during which the fair coin is flipped and the outcome is observed at time $t + h$. From (13) and (14), the actual realized value $K(t + h)$ of the state variable at time $t + h$ may then be conceptualized, for small enough h, *as if* it has taken on the value $K(t) + I(K(t))h$ plus or minus the standard deviation $\sigma(K(t))\sqrt{h}$.

The other appropriate change that must be noted in going over to a stochastic diffusion generalization of a prototype-economic control problem is that the deterministic criterion defining the optimal investment function (5) must be changed to its appropriate expected-value version. Omitting mathematically significant details, our definition of the optimal policy function $I^*(K)$ is that it satisfies the stochastic diffusion process (12),(4) and for any other policy function $I(K)$ satisfying the stochastic diffusion process (11),(2), it must hold that

$$E[\int_0^\infty G(K^*(t), I^*(K^*(t)))e^{-\rho t}\, dt]$$

$$\geq E[\int_0^\infty G(K(t), I(K(t)))e^{-\rho t}\, dt]. \qquad (15)$$

The notation $E[\bullet]$ refers to the expectation of the random variable contained within the square brackets. In the case of (15), what is inside the square brackets is a relatively simple example of a so-called *stochastic integral*. For any given realized stochastic trajectory of $\{K(t)\}$ (or of $\{K^*(t)\}$), the integrals within the square brackets of (15) can be understood in the usual (Riemann-Stieltjes) sense. Thus we are allowed to conceptualize each sample path of realized $\{K(t)\}$ (or $\{K^*(t)\}$) as yielding a corresponding realized value of the stochastic integrals appearing inside the square brackets of (15). Because what is inside the square brackets is, by this procedure, a well-defined random variable, there is no problem with interpreting its expected value in the usual way.

It will be useful to note for later reference that the stochastic version of the "prototype-economic control problem" (15) embodies the stochastic analogue of the idea that all sources of future growth are correctly accounted for via changes in capital stocks. With the stochastic version, however, future capital and capital changes are unknown at the present time. As usual in such problems, it is mathematically trivial here to extend the model to include atmospheric time-dependent stochastic diffusion shocks—provided we are allowed to account for them properly by knowing their correct efficiency prices. (For this mathematically trivial extension of the theory, we merely treat the variable that is being shocked over time "as if" it were just another capital-stock-like state variable—and then apply the existing time-free theory.)

We now want to make use of a particular application of a famous result from the theory of stochastic diffusion processes, which application we will here call "Itô's Expectation Formula." This result is a specific case of what is known in the stochastic-diffusion literature more generally as "Itô's Lemma." We do not really need the more general form here, and there is no sense cluttering up the presentation of this chapter with it. Any book dedicated to stochastic diffusion processes, including books on applications to economics and finance, will contain a full discussion of Itô's Lemma.

What we are calling here "Itô's Expectation Formula" can be seen as a generalization of a right-direction version of Taylor's Theorem. Consider any function $F(K)$ that has everywhere a continuous second derivative. The result we need for this chapter, in the notation of this chapter, is the following.

Lemma ("Itô's Expectation Formula").   *For $h > 0$,*

$$E[F(K(h))] = F(K(0)) + \{F'(K(0))I(K(0))$$
$$+ \frac{1}{2}F''(K(0))\sigma^2(K(0))\}h \qquad (16)$$
$$+ O(h^{3/2}),$$

where the expression $O(h^{3/2})$ stands for all terms of order 3/2 or higher in h.

From staring at (16), it should become fairly evident the sense in which (the right-handed version of) Taylor's Theorem about a first-order deterministic approximation can be seen as a particular instance of Itô's Expectation Formula applied to the special case $\sigma^2(K(0)) = 0$.

Itô's Expectation Formula looks very simple, but this is a deception. Behind the scenes, Itô had to define precisely what he meant by a stochastic integral, whose integrator is the outcome of a stochastic diffusion process (here $\{K(t)\}$) having unbounded variation within any time interval $[0, h]$. The issues involved in a rigorous definition of an Itô stochastic integral, which lie just below the surface of (16), are mathematically quite sophisticated. We limit our discussion to an attempt to convey the basic idea verbally of why the timing implicit in an Itô stochastic integral is compatible in an essential way with stochastic optimal control theory. We also try to indicate preliminarily why we may want to express projected stochastic income as the expectation of a differently defined "Stratonovich stochastic integral," even though Itô's is the concept compatible with the information-timing sequence implicit in the kind of stochastic-diffusion optimal control problem that forms the backbone of this chapter. (Whenever we employ such terms as "Itô stochastic integral" or "Stratonovich stochastic integral" throughout this chapter, it is essentially for background, motivational, or heuristic purposes not really requiring a rigorous mathematical definition.)

In the deterministic dynamic model of a firm's optimal policy, there was no need to make a distinction between infinite horizon optimal plans completely specified now, without revision, and infinite horizon optimal plans when revision is later allowed—because in the absence of uncertainty no revision is required. But here, in the presence of uncertainty, we specify that an optimal program allows instantaneous updating based on new information and that the "optimality" is with respect to maximizing the present discounted *expected* value of gains given the current state and with future updating allowed. Essentially, we are working with a concept of information and timing that is compatible only with an "Itô stochastic integral"—meaning, heuristically, that in the limiting process defining the integral, all relevant functions are evaluated at the *left endpoint* of time subintervals of form $[t, t + dt]$. This kind of stochastic integration concept is completely appropriate for measuring functions in the context of a dynamic decision process of "nonanticipating control"—meaning the firm decides $I(t)$ at time instant t based on observed $K(t)$, but only *after* this decision is made is the value of $dZ(t)$ revealed and allowed to exert its influence throughout the vanishingly small time interval $(t, t + dt]$.

Although the treatment of stochastic diffusion processes presented here has been heuristically rudimentary, it is only fair to warn the reader that some truly deep mathematical issues underlie a genuinely rigorous mathematical formalization. Speaking generally and for the most part, there usually is not a complete need for an economist to plumb down to the full depths of mathematical rigor to understand the essential take-home economic messages that emerge from such stochastic control models in economics or finance. However, it turns out that for the particular application in which we are interested, the treatment of stochastic income will force us to rethink at least one basic issue that goes to the core of what a stochastic diffusion process means as a representation of economic dynamics. This basic issue has to do with some delicate matters of timing and information, involving ex post and ex ante measurement of index numbers, that seem not to have been encountered or noticed so far in other economic applications of stochastic processes, but which come to the fore in trying to define the concept of stochastic income operationally in terms of the thought experiment by which it is supposed to be accounted.

The stochastic control problem represented by (15) is describing a situation where, in the discrete version whose limit it is, the action taken at time t, at the beginning of a (vanishingly small) period of length dt, could depend on the knowledge of the current state $K(t)$, but not on any knowledge of the random future state $K(t + dt)$. If time is truly continuous, the two times t and $t + dt$ cohere in the limit as dt vanishes. To rule out any kind of seeing-ahead or clairvoyance property, the mathematical limiting process must be carefully modeled so as not to allow current choices to depend on information available even the tiniest instant ahead.

The limiting process that rules out clairvoyance, by in effect forcing strategies to be continuous from the left while the uncertainties are continuous from the right, gives rise in a natural way to the construction of an Itô stochastic integral. In fact, this is a major reason why the particular Itô way of constructing a stochastic limiting process is the only concept of stochastic integration ever encountered by most economists. We would not need to spend so much time belaboring the point except that when it comes time to give a proper definition of how to measure "expected stochastic income," it will *not* be based on the interpretation of an Itô stochastic integral of the value of capital accumulated within a (vanishingly small) period of time.

As we will presently argue in more detail, for measuring stochastic income a different kind of stochastic integral than Itô's is required, which is based on the "trapezoid rule" of averaging the price values at both endpoints of each tiny time interval, rather than evaluating it, as Itô does, only at the left endpoint of the limiting interval used to define the stochastic integral. Thus, it turns out, one famous kind of stochastic integral, called an Itô integral, is appropriate (behind our heuristics) for formulating and evaluating the firm's stochastic optimal control problem, while another, also very well known, competing kind of stochastic integral, called a Stratonovich integral, is more appropriate (behind our heuristics) for measuring stochastic income.

We can readily provide an intuitive explanation for why (16) holds, which is at the same level of heuristic description as our treatment of (13) and (14). If we make use of the interpretation in the story that outcomes (13) and (14) are *as if* determined as a result ("heads" or "tails") of the random flipping of a fair coin, by expanding $F(K(h))$ as a *second-order* Taylor series expansion evaluated at time $t = 0$, we can tell a new *as if* story about *it*. The new *as if* story told "in the spirit of Itô" is that for the given $K(0)$ at time $t = 0$, the situation is *as if* there is a fair-coin-flipping probability of one-half (case 1: the coin comes up "heads") that the realized value at time $t = h$ of the stochastic function $F(K(h))$ is

$$F^1(K(h)) = F(K(0)) + F'(K(0))I(K(0))[K^1(h) - K(0)]$$
$$+ \frac{1}{2}F''(K(0))[K^1(h) - K(0)]^2 + O^3, \tag{17}$$

while the situation is *as if* there is a fair-coin-flipping probability of one-half (case 2: the coin comes up "tails") that the realized value at time $t = h$ of the stochastic function $F(K(h))$ is

$$F^2(K(h)) = F(K(0)) + F'(K(0))I(K(0))[K^2(h) - K(0)]$$
$$+ \frac{1}{2}F''(K(0))[K^2(h) - K(0)]^2 + O^3, \tag{18}$$

where the notation "O^3" stands for all terms of third or higher order in $[K(h) - K(0)]$.

Combining (17) and (18) into an expected value expression, we then have

$$E[F(K(h))] = F(K(0)) + \frac{1}{2}F^1(K(h)) + \frac{1}{2}F^2(K(h)) + O^3. \tag{19}$$

Now substitute from (13) (for $t = 0$) into (17), and from (14) (for $t = 0$) into (18). Then combine the resulting expressions for (17) and (18) in terms of h into the formula (19), cancel all redundant terms, and collect all terms of order 3/2 or higher in h. The resulting equation is (16), the lemma we want.

We will now reinforce our intuition about the exact timing that is involved in describing the expectation of an Itô stochastic integral by generating heuristically a very important condition that must be met by the optimal policy function $I^*(K)$. This famous condition is known as the *Hamilton-Jacobi-Bellman equation*, hereafter abbreviated as HJB. Some version of HJB shows up in a very high fraction of stochastic control problems, ranging from physics to finance.

We begin our development of HJB by constructing the state evaluation function here, in this stochastic setting, as an obvious generalization of the deterministic case. Define for all K_0 the state evaluation function

$$V(K_0) \equiv E[\int_0^\infty G(K^*(t), I^*(K^*(t)))e^{-\rho t} \, dt], \tag{20}$$

where the corresponding trajectories $\{K^*(t)\}$ satisfy conditions (2), (4), (11), (12), and (15). In words, $V(K_0)$ is the state evaluation function because it represents the *expected value* of an optimal policy expressed parametrically as a function of the initial condition $K(0) = K_0$.

We now proceed heuristically from (20) to HJB. From the basic dynamic programming principle of optimality, we have for any positive h that (20) can also be expressed recursively as

$$V(K(0)) = E[\int_0^h G(K^*(t), I^*(K^*(t)))e^{-\rho t} \, dt] \\ + e^{-\rho h} E[V(K^*(h))]. \tag{21}$$

Combining (15), (20), and (21), we have that for any policy function $I(K)$ satisfying (11) and (2), it must hold for all positive h that

$$V(K(0)) \geq E[\int_0^h G(K(t), I(K(t)))e^{-\rho t} \, dt] \\ + e^{-\rho h} E[V(K(h))]. \tag{22}$$

In (21),(22) and what follows, the stochastic variables within the square brackets are being understood "in the spirit of Itô." This means, loosely speaking, that for any time instant t the state $K(t)$ is observed and then the policy $I(K(t))$ is chosen at the left end of time instant t *just before* the random variable $dZ(t)$ becomes known at the right end. "In the spirit of Itô" signifies that the timing of a stochastic diffusion process is to be understood in the order that "dZ moves just ahead" of the state and control variables. The timing/information sequence we are postulating for an Itô process may here be written symbolically as:

$$K(t) \mapsto I(K(t)) \mapsto dZ(t) \mapsto K(t+dt)$$
$$[= K(t) + I(K(t))dt + \sigma(K(t))dZ(t)] \tag{23}$$
$$\mapsto I(K(t+dt)) \mapsto dZ(t+dt) \mapsto \ldots$$

The main point about being "in the spirit of Itô" here is this. The timing/information convention described by the sequence (23) must be followed whenever expressing any Taylor series expansions of random variables "in the spirit of Itô."

From the fundamental theorem of the calculus and Taylor's Theorem, the following result is just a particular application here of a condition that must hold for any well-defined stochastic integral:

$$E[\int_0^h G(K(t), I(K(t)))e^{-\rho t}\, dt]$$
$$= G(K(0), I(K(0)))h + O(h^2). \tag{24}$$

We now apply Itô's Expectation Formula (16) to the state evaluation function $V(K)$. Setting $F(K) = V(K)$ in (16), we obtain

$$E[V(K(h))] = V(K(0))$$
$$+ \{V'(K(0))I(0) + \frac{1}{2}V''(K(0))\sigma^2(K(0))\}h \tag{25}$$
$$+ O(h^{3/2}).$$

It should be evident that the second-order Taylor series expansion (25) is being carried out and evaluated "in the spirit of Itô."

We know that

$$e^{-\rho h} = 1 - \rho h + O(h^2). \tag{26}$$

Combine (26) with (25) and collect all terms of order higher than 3/2 to obtain the expression

$$e^{-\rho h} E[V(K(h))] = (1 - \rho h)(V(K(0)) + \{V'(K(0))I(K(0))$$
$$+ \frac{1}{2}V''(K(0))\sigma^2(V(K(0)))\}h) \quad (27)$$
$$+ O(h^{3/2}).$$

Next, plug (27) and (24) into (22). Then expand out the resulting expression and consolidate all terms of order 3/2 or higher. We thereby obtain

$$V \geq V - \rho V h + G h + V'I h + \frac{1}{2}V''\sigma^2 h + O(h^{3/2}), \quad (28)$$

where all functions are evaluated "in the spirit of Itô" at time $t = 0$ when the capital stock is $K(0)$.

Now cancel V from both sides of the inequality (28), divide by positive h, and go to the limit as $h \to 0^+$. Then rewrite the resulting expression out fully as

$$\rho V(K(0)) \geq G(K(0), I(K(0))) + V'(K(0))I(K(0))$$
$$+ \frac{1}{2}V''(K(0))\sigma^2(K(0)). \quad (29)$$

The above procedure carried out "in the spirit of Itô" converted the inequality (22) into the equivalent inequality (29). If we apply exactly the analogous procedure to the equality (21), we obtain the equivalent equality

$$\rho V(K(0)) = G(K(0), I^*(K(0))) + V'(K(0))I^*(K(0))$$
$$+ \frac{1}{2}V''(K(0))\sigma^2(K(0)). \quad (30)$$

Combining (30) with (29), we then obtain the famous Hamilton-Jacobi-Bellman equation for this situation:

$$\rho V(K(0)) = \max_{I}[G(K(0), I) + V'(K(0))I]$$
$$+ \frac{1}{2}V''(K(0))\sigma^2(K(0)). \quad (31)$$

The question we now want to ask is, What is the proper economic interpretation of HJB as a relation between income and wealth? The answer is not immediately obvious. From (30) (or (31)), the term

$$G(K(0), I^*(K(0))) + V'(K(0))I^*(K(0)) \tag{32}$$

certainly looks like true current income at properly accounted prices, but what does the term

$$\frac{1}{2}V''(K(0))\sigma^2(K(0)) \tag{33}$$

stand for? The conventional answer is very mechanical. In some technical sense, term (33) represents the expected loss of value from the concavity of the value function—because Jensen's Inequality plays a significant role when the underlying stochastic process is fluctuating so violently per unit time in the limit as a Wiener process does when the time interval is made infinitesimally small.

In this "explanation," the Jensen's Inequality term (33) is being "explained" by the *as if* risk aversion of a shadow central planner who "owns" the state evaluation function $V(K)$. For such a story, $V''/2$ stands for the "price of risk," while σ^2 represents the "quantity of risk." But if the uncertainty in the model is firm-specific in the first place, why cannot such "risk" be diversified away by shareholders in the usual way—merely by holding just a small amount of this firm's stock in a portfolio? Why should any kind of "risk adjustment" be necessary here? In this Jensen's Inequality way of looking at the world there is a fundamental inconsistency with the basic principles of finance. Surely we can tell a better story for an economic interpretation than this!

The second derivative of the state evaluation function is an endogenously derived construct, rather than an exogenously given primitive. Where do we look in a stochastic economy to find $V''(K(0))$ (or, for that matter, $\sigma^2(K(0))$)? The Jensen's Inequality story may be technically correct as a pure mathematical description, in some narrow sense, but what does it mean operationally in terms of measurement? Which index number might we have our ideal accountant calculate in order to account for the Jensen's Inequality term (33)? What is the economic interpretation of the HJB condition (31) in terms of some well-defined thought experiment linking stochastic income with stochastic wealth?

We are now ready to begin to confront formally the issue of stating rigorously the stochastic analogue of the deterministic "wealth and income" equation (10) and explaining its relation to HJB. For convenience in seeing some useful analogies, we employ the same notation and use a conceptually similar apparatus to what was developed to explain the deterministic case, only henceforth it is intended that *all notation refers to the stochastic solution.*

Because the control variable I is being treated as if it could in principle take any value, the solution of the HJB equation (28) must satisfy the marginalist-interior first-order condition

$$V'(K) = -G_2(K, I^*(K)). \tag{34}$$

Following the methodology of the deterministic case, let us first define here the primary relationship to be the accounting price of investment in state K—that is,

$$P(K) \equiv -G_2(K, I^*(K)). \tag{35}$$

Then, as with the deterministic case, we are conceptualizing the derived secondary relationship

$$P(K) = V'(K) \tag{36}$$

as being in the form of a theorem obtained by combining the definition (35) with the inference (34). (If the standard deviation depends upon I as well as K, so that we must write $\sigma(K, I)$, it is then not possible to define so simply (as by using (35)) the accounting price of investment goods. Nevertheless, the theory goes through if accounting prices are then defined by (36), with the only other modification being that I is then chosen to maximize *expected* immediate-future income, rather than actually realized current income.)

As before in the deterministic case, the variable ρ here measures this stochastic firm's risk-neutral-evaluated opportunity cost of capital or its competitive rate of return, and is assumed to be observable (or at least it can be calculated from applicable financial-market considerations and data). The state evaluation function $V(K)$ is again observable in the stochastic case here as the competitive stock market value of all shares in the firm, when the capital stock is K.

Essentially, $V(K)$ must be the competitive share value by the usual arguments—because it equals the (maximized) expected present discounted value of all (here stochastic) future dividends that will be paid out by the firm, and which a "share" entitles the owner to have. The expression $\rho V(K)$ represents the flow of returns that the holders of shares of this firm could expect to obtain on competitively equivalent alternative investments made elsewhere in the economy. Thus what is going to appear on the left-hand side of the stochastic generalization of equation (10) has essentially the same interpretation as in the previous deterministic case—it is interpretable as the firm's cost of capital times the stock market value of its shares.

The more challenging issue here is to define rigorously what is the appropriate proxy for expected true earnings on the right-hand side of the appropriate stochastic generalization of equation (10). We are groping here to find, for this simple stochastic model, a rigorous definition of the concept of "projected earnings." We again employ the useful fiction of the "ideal accountant." Only now, in this stochastic setting, the ideal accountant is endowed with even more powerful abilities and is being asked to take on an even more daunting thought-experimental task.

Ideally measured earnings in the near future are themselves a random variable. Stated heuristically, the ideal accountant will be asked to evaluate true future earnings along all realizable stochastic trajectories throughout a given near-future period—and then to estimate their expected value per unit time (in the limit as the length of the future period goes to zero). Intuitively, therefore, we are searching for a reasonable definition of the expected value of forward-looking future stochastic income over what might be called loosely the "immediate future." The ideal accountant is effectively asking himself: On the basis of current information, what do I *expect* that I will have measured as the true income of this firm over the immediate future? The ideal accountant is nonanticipating, in the strict mathematical sense that he is using only current information to estimate or project expected true income over the immediate future, which is a legitimate construction to make on the basis of nonanticipating current information.

Let us first begin by fixing the length of the near-future interval at h, which is some arbitrarily given positive number that will eventually be made to go to zero in the limit. What we define rigorously as "expected future income" over the time interval $(0, h]$ is intended to be a stochastic generalization of the right-hand side of formula (9). Up to this point in the argument we could essentially finesse the issue, but now we must seriously face up to this question of what exactly we mean by a stochastic generalization of true income (or earnings). We now pose this issue very sharply in terms of which price index of investment goods to use.

For any chosen value of the parameter λ, where $0 \leq \lambda \leq 1$, define the *weighted-average accounting price* of capital accumulated throughout the interval $[0, h]$ to be the random variable

$$P_\lambda(K^*(h)) \equiv (1 - \lambda)P(K(0)) + \lambda P(K^*(h)). \tag{37}$$

What we are now going to ask the ideal accountant to measure as forward-looking immediate-future expected income (per unit time, now, at time $t = 0$) is an expected-value generalization of the deterministic case, taking here the form

$$
\begin{aligned}
EY(\lambda) \equiv\ & G(K(0), I^*(K(0))) \\
& + \lim_{h \to 0^+} \frac{1}{h} E[P_\lambda(K^*(h))(K^*(h) - K(0))],
\end{aligned}
\tag{38}
$$

where the relevant underlying stochastic process is

$$dK^*(t) = I^*(K^*(t))\, dt + \sigma(K^*(t))dZ(t), \tag{39}$$

and $K(0)$ is given as an initial condition.

The critical question before us then becomes very specific: What value of λ should we instruct the ideal accountant to use? The choice will very much matter for the evaluation of the second term on the right-hand side of (38). Everything is now a stochastic random variable in this setup. The efficiency price of investment (in terms of dividends) and the capital being accumulated are both changing stochastically throughout the time interval $[0, h]$. There is an efficiency price of investment at the beginning of the interval, $P(K(0))$, and there is a (different) efficiency price of investment at the end of the interval, $P(K(h))$. If $\lambda = 0$, it corresponds to using the initial price to evaluate the capital that has been accumulated throughout the interval $[0, h]$. If $\lambda = 1$, it corresponds to using the final price to evaluate the capital that has been accumulated throughout the interval $[0, h]$. If $\lambda = 1/2$, it corresponds to using the average price throughout the interval to evaluate the capital that has been accumulated throughout the interval $[0, h]$. In a deterministic setup (that is, $\sigma^2(K(0)) = 0$), it makes no difference what value of λ is chosen in definition (38). In a stochastic-diffusion setting, however, this choice can make a significant difference.

The case $\lambda = 0$ corresponds to making the random variable within the square brackets of (38) be effectively an Itô stochastic integral of $P(K(t))dK(t)$ between $t = 0$ and $t = h$—meaning the price function $P(K)$ is to be understood as being evaluated at the *left endpoint* of the tiny subintervals that, in the limit, define this Itô stochastic integral. The case $\lambda = 1/2$ corresponds to making the random variable within the square brackets of (38) be effectively a Stratonovich stochastic integral of $P(K(t))dK(t)$ between $t = 0$ and $t = h$—meaning the price function $P(K)$ is to be understood as being based upon the "trapezoid rule" of averaging the price function values at both endpoints of the tiny subintervals that, in the limit, define this Stratonovich stochastic integral. In any event, we come back again to the very specifically posed critical question here: Which value of λ should we instruct the ideal accountant to use to evaluate the capital that is being accumulated stochastically within the interval?

I think that most economists would agree on the answer to this question. We should use some measure of the average efficiency price that occurs within the interval—that is, we should take the average of the price that occurs at the beginning of the interval and the price that occurs at the end of the interval. This is essentially a natural extension of the idea that it is best to measure a finite-difference approximation of a Divisia index of the value of capital accumulation by using the average investment price, which corresponds to the midpoint of an interval, for evaluating the amount of capital that has been accumulated during the interval.

It turns out that—with the unboundedly violent fluctuations that occur in realized capital stock changes per tiny subinterval as the tininess of the subinterval approaches zero, which degree of violence is inherent in the nature of a Wiener process—it matters at which point of the tiny subinterval we evaluate the stochastically changing price (when we define rigorously, as a limiting process, the stochastic integral implicitly contained within the square brackets of (38)). If we want to base the efficiency price on the "trapezoid rule" of having the ideal accountant average the price values at both endpoints of the tiny subintervals, which intuitively seems more plausible than picking either of the extremes of the price at the beginning left endpoint or the price at the ending right endpoint, and which is consistent with best-practice real-world construction of Divisia indexes, then the concept of integration we should be using to evaluate (38) is the Stratonovich stochastic integral corresponding to the case $\lambda = 1/2$. Once we buy into the notion—whether intuitively or on the basis of a formal result from index number theory—that it is better for comparisons to use some average of Laspeyres and Paasche price indices, rather than using either price index alone, then by logic we should also buy into the notion of using $\lambda = 1/2$ for measuring expected income.

The Stratonovich stochastic integral of $P(K(t))dK(t)$ corresponding to $\lambda = 1/2$ is symmetric backward and forward, which is an essential property for a Divisia-like index of real capital accumulation to possess in the setting of a stochastic diffusion process. If, in a thought experiment, we *de*-cumulated capital symmetrically by retracing our steps backward along the same realization of the stochastic trajectory along which we *ac*-cumulated it, when we arrived back at the initial state we would then want our index of the total value of real net accumulated capital to register *zero*. This is precisely the forward-backward symmetry that characterizes the Stratonovich stochastic integral, because the Stratonovich path integral is always zero around any closed loop. However, in the above thought experiment, the path-dependent Itô stochastic integral of $P(K(t))dK(t)$, corresponding to $\lambda = 0$, would yield some *nonzero* forward-backward round-trip value of net total capital accumulated, when there actually has been zero net total capital accumulated. As we will later show formally, the expected value of the difference-from-zero biased-measurement error of such an Itô ($\lambda = 0$) "round-trip evaluation" of net capital accumulated, per unit time, into the immediate future and back, exactly accounts for the Jensen's Inequality term (33).

Thus, it turns out, our stochastic integral of choice for formulating and evaluating the stochastic optimal control problem is unquestionably the Itô integral, which is most appropriate for this particular application—but our stochastic integral of choice for measuring expected true income in (38) is the Stratonovich stochastic integral corresponding to $\lambda = 1/2$, which represents the undeniably appropriate concept for that particular application. Such a distinction matters only for the evaluation of the "accumulated-capital" part of expected income—because both the amount of capital accumulated and the accounting price of capital accumulated are jointly changing stochastically, which with a continuous diffusion process must be accounted for instantaneously, even within the tiniest measurement interval.

Therefore, to make a long story short, our mathematically rigorous definition of the firm's *ideally measured immediate-future expected stochastic income* is

$$EY(1/2) \equiv G(K(0), I^*(K(0)))$$

$$+ \lim_{h \to 0^+} \frac{1}{h} E\left[\frac{P(K(0)) + P(K(h))}{2}(K(h) - K(0))\right], \tag{40}$$

which, it is readily confirmed, corresponds to the special $\lambda = 1/2$ "Stratonovich case" of (38).

Because the outcome will hinge on subtle questions of timing in what might be called "stochastic-diffusion index number theory," it has been absolutely crucial here to specify carefully what is being measured as the properly accounted net value of capital accumulated over a near-future period, when is it being measured, and how it is being measured. To make more vivid the image of a forward-looking trapezoidal accountant working on the left-hand side of the stochastic wealth and income version of the maximum principle, let us call our ideal accountant "Mr. Strat." From an economist's standpoint, Mr. Strat is the world's greatest accountant. Mr. Strat is the leading authority on the theory and practice of projecting forward a firm's expected true economic earnings. Expression (40) is the expected immediate-future value of the firm's true income, representing exactly what Mr. Strat *expects* he will be measuring as complete income over the immediate future. In this sense, Mr. Strat's expected immediate-future income measurement (40) can be interpreted as the mathematical formalization, which is appropriate to this stochastic setting, of the idea of a firm's "projected true earnings."

The stochastic generalization of the deterministic wealth and income statement (10) is the following theorem, which is the main result of this chapter.

Theorem (Stochastic Wealth and Income Version of the Maximum Principle).

$$\rho V(K(0)) = EY(1/2). \tag{41}$$

In asserting that *expected income is the return on expected wealth*, it is directly apparent that (41) represents a stochastic generalization of (10). We will "prove" the stochastic wealth and income version of the maximum principle here in two steps. First, applying Itô's Expectation Formula to (38) and (37) will give us a useful general result holding for any λ. Second, we will then obtain (41) by just plugging into this general result the specific parameter value $\lambda = 1/2$.

Proof. Define the function

$$F(K) \equiv [(1 - \lambda)P(K(0)) + \lambda P(K)][K - K(0)], \tag{42}$$

and note that

$$F(K(0)) = 0. \tag{43}$$

Taking first and second derivatives of $F(K)$ from (42), and then evaluating at $K = K(0)$, we obtain

$$F'(K(0)) = P(K(0)), \qquad (44)$$

and

$$F''(K(0)) = 2\lambda P'(K(0)). \qquad (45)$$

Plugging (43), (44), and (45) into the right-hand side of (16), we then obtain from Itô's Expectation Formula the result that

$$E[F(K^*(h))] = \{P(K(0))I^*(K(0)) + \lambda P'(K(0))\sigma^2(K(0))\}h \\ + O(h^{3/2}). \qquad (46)$$

Now divide both sides of (46) by positive h and go to the limit $h \to 0^+$, thereby obtaining

$$\lim_{h \to 0^+} \frac{1}{h} E[F(K^*(h))] = P(K(0))I^*(K(0)) \\ + \lambda P'(K(0))\sigma^2(K(0)). \qquad (47)$$

Applying definitions (37) and (42) to (47) then yields

$$\lim_{h \to 0^+} \frac{1}{h} E[P_\lambda(K^*(h))(K^*(h) - K(0))] \\ = P(K(0))I^*(K(0)) + \lambda P'(K(0))\sigma^2(K(0)). \qquad (48)$$

Applying equation (48) to the definition (38) turns the latter expression into

$$EY(\lambda) \equiv G(K(0), I^*(K(0))) + P(K(0))I^*(K(0)) \\ + \lambda P'(K(0))\sigma^2(K(0)). \qquad (49)$$

Since (36) must hold as an identity for all K, by differentiating it we obtain

$$P'(K) = V''(K), \qquad (50)$$

which must also hold for all K. Now use (36) and (50) to compare (49) with the HJB condition (30). We have then just shown that for all λ satisfying $0 \le \lambda \le 1$, the relation must hold that

$$\rho V(K(0)) = EY(\lambda) + (\frac{1}{2} - \lambda)V''(K(0))\sigma^2(K(0)). \qquad (51)$$

The stochastic wealth and income version of the maximum principle (41) follows immediately from plugging $\lambda = 1/2$ into equation (51). ∎

Now all of the pieces should fit. If the accounting is done correctly (which includes using the proper price index number corresponding to $\lambda = 1/2$) expected income is the return on expected wealth. The key economic interpretation of HJB is provided directly by the "stochastic wealth and income version of the maximum principle," which is equation (41) (along with the definition (40)).

Using (51), we can analyze formally the important concept of the measurement error or index-number bias introduced by various values of λ. To do so, let us examine what is measured as the accounting value of the capital accumulated (as investment) along any round-trip forward-backward trajectory. At time $t = 0$, the stochastic trajectory $\{K^*(t)\}$ begins at $K = K(0)$. Throughout the time interval $[0, h]$, the trajectory $\{K^*(t)\}$ grinds out a particular stochastic path realization. At time $t = h$, the stochastic trajectory arrives at $K = K^*(h)$.

Throughout the time interval $[h, 2h]$, let us imagine a hypothetical trajectory, which is exactly the same as the realized trajectory of time interval $[0, h]$, except that time is running backward. For any time t with $0 \leq t \leq h$, the hypothetical trajectory $\{\tilde{K}(h + t)\}$, which we are analyzing as a thought experiment throughout the time interval $[h, 2h]$, is related to the stochastic trajectory $\{K^*(t)\}$, which was actually realized throughout time interval $[0, h]$, by the equation

$$\tilde{K}(h + t) = K^*(h - t). \tag{52}$$

What would be measured by an ideally instructed accountant, given any value of λ, as the value (per unit time) of capital accumulated along such a forward-backward-symmetric path in the full time interval $[0, 2h]$? From (52) and the definition (37), it would be

$$\frac{P_\lambda(K^*(h))[K^*(h) - K(0)] + P_{1-\lambda}(K^*(h))[K(0) - K^*(h)]}{2h}. \tag{53}$$

Now it should be quite intuitive that a truly ideal stochastic index of the value of capital accumulated throughout the time interval $[0, 2h]$ should register that (53) is exactly zero. When zero net capital has actually been accumulated, the properly accounted value of total net accumulated capital should also be zero. It is readily seen that the value of (53) is zero for $\lambda = 1/2$ and is nonzero for any other value of λ.

The degree of expected measurement error in the sense of immediate-future expected index-number bias is then captured by the limiting expected value of expression (53), which "should" be zero but instead is

$$
B(\lambda) \equiv \lim_{h \to 0} \frac{1}{2h} [P_\lambda(K^*(h))[K^*(h) - K(0)] \\
+ P_{1-\lambda}(K^*(h))[K(0) - K^*(h)]]. \tag{54}
$$

Using arguments very similar to what was used to derive (52), it can readily be shown that the definition (54) reduces to

$$
B(\lambda) = (\frac{1}{2} - \lambda)V''(K(0))\sigma^2(K(0)). \tag{55}
$$

From formula (55), it follows immediately that the Jensen's Inequality term (33) can be interpreted as representing precisely the expected index-number bias or measurement error (per unit time) from using the "incorrect" Itô-like beginning-of-period price corresponding to $\lambda = 0$ instead of the "correct" Stratonovich-like midperiod average price corresponding to $\lambda = 1/2$. When capital accumulation is "correctly accounted" ($\lambda = 1/2$), there is no measurement bias and correctly accounted expected income is exactly the return on correctly accounted expected wealth.

Discussion and Conclusion

Note that the stochastic wealth and income version of the maximum principle (41) can readily be interpreted as giving a finance interpretation to the Hamilton-Jacobi-Bellman equation (31). The result (41) means that, for this dynamic stochastic model of the firm, HJB is trying to tell us that the information content of stock market evaluation (times the competitive rate of return) is captured completely by forward-looking expected earnings in the immediate future, provided that these earnings have been ideally accounted.

Notice that it is not current true earnings that line up exactly with the current stock market evaluation. That was true for the deterministic case, but it no longer holds in a genuinely stochastic environment where $\sigma^2(K(0)) > 0$. Rather, in this model it is forward-looking expected true earnings in the immediate future that must equal the current stock market evaluation. The stock market, so to speak, now knows current true earnings and is already looking ahead to projected true earnings in the immediate future. For this model, the entire informational content of competitive stock market asset evaluation (times ρ) is exactly mirrored in expected true earnings for the immediate future. Therefore, to the extent that the stock market value of a firm is correlated with its expected future true earnings for a stochastic diffusion model like this, in principle all of the correlation is explained by the immediate future, and none by periods further ahead than that.

The assumption of ideal comprehensive accounting is very strong here, but it is also able to purchase a very strong focal-point result as a polar case. Perhaps a more balanced way of conceptualizing the possible significance of (the multicapital version of) this basic result for the theory of asset pricing is in its inverse form as a kind of representation theorem.

Asset pricing theory essentially consists of different versions of representing today's asset prices as the expected value of "something" tomorrow. The economic interpretation of the Hamilton-Jacobi-Bellman equation, which is given by the stochastic wealth and income version of the maximum principle (41), gives us a new "something" to look at and ponder. From (a multicapital version of) (41), the current stock market evaluation of a firm's shares must have a representation as the immediate-future expectation of income—or at least of an income-like linearly weighted expression, whose quantities are changes in state variables affecting the firm's ability to pay future dividends, and whose weights for evaluating these changes in capital are shadow accounting prices representing current rates of transformation into dividends. Under ideally complete accounting, this expected-income-like term is exactly the expected immediate-future true earnings of the firm. Otherwise, and in reality of course, this expected-income-like term will be captured by projected immediate-future earnings only to the degree that the firm's accounting system is relatively complete and accurate in being able to assess changes in all those continuously changing capital-like state variables that are relevant for the firm's ultimate dividend-paying ability.

Even in a world of imperfect accounting, such a new representation theorem may be useful for asset pricing theory. Knowing the precise theoretical link between asset value and earned income may lead to new ways of conceptualization and measurement. Also, such a result may serve the theory of income accounting as a kind of guide toward better practice by providing a rigorous conceptual foundation and by suggesting what activities to include as investments and how best to price them.

For an interpretation of the main result of this model in terms of national income accounting, we need to modify the setting appropriately. The relevant prices of capital or investment goods in the setting of a national economy would be observable, in the spirit of Chapter 5, as the result of competitive market processes operating both in a static and in a dynamic sense. The static interpretation is the usual one: it is as if every agent is currently optimizing (the agent's static net utility or static net profits) for the given current prices. The dynamic interpretation in the stochastic economy would involve a dynamic competitive rational-expectations equilibrium in price uncertainty—meaning, essentially, a self-reinforcing equilibrium in expectations where no agents, even when carrying out their optimal actions, can expect to make positive pure profits over time. (While the details are omitted here, what translates into the "zero expected pure profits" condition of a rational-expectations decentralized dynamic competitive equilibrium is precisely the wealth and income version of the maximum principle, (41), which is based implicitly on the case $\lambda = 1/2$.)

Even for a hypothetical situation of perfectly comprehensive accounting, in a stochastic setting the national income statistician is recording as current NNP some just-observed or just-measured index of the value of current economic activity, rather than the expected value of immediate-future income. Therefore, in the rational-expectations competitive dynamic equilibrium of a stochastically evolving economy, current comprehensive NNP is an accurate barometer of expected wealth (or welfare) only to the extent that current income is an accurate barometer of expected immediate-future income. A nation's expected future welfare is not completely reflected by last year's realized NNP, but, rather, it is mirrored completely accurately in next year's expected NNP. The theory is telling us to smooth out the unanticipated shocks of the immediate past, which have distorted last year's recorded NNP, by projecting ahead to next year's expected NNP. This makes the welfare interpretation of present comprehensive NNP somewhat more complicated than the deterministic case, but at least we understand, in the spirit of the stochastic diffusion model of this chapter, what exactly are the theoretical relationships between all of the relevant concepts.

The brevity of this chapter is illusory, because the treatment of stochastic diffusion processes here has been so extremely compressed. Had we really tried rigorously to explain optimal control theory for stochastic diffusion processes, this would have been the longest chapter of the book. Though cursory, the treatment of this chapter should be sufficient to illustrate how the basic principles may be extended into the domain of uncertainty, at least for some classes of stochastic processes. And these basic principles have been the same throughout the book.

The main theme of this book is thus that the wealth and income-accounting side of a dynamic economy is an essential complement to the optimization and equilibrium side—and, with the abstraction of perfectly complete accounting, data based on near-past (or projections made on near-future) competitive market processes are in principle sufficient to reveal useful and important information about future welfare.

Bibliographic Note

Of the books whose aim is to explain the optimal control of stochastic diffusion processes to economists, the best overall introduction is contained in Dixit and Pindyck (1994). A slightly more rigorous approach is taken in Merton (1992). Yet another step up in rigor is the treatment in Malliaris and Brock (1982).

Fully rigorous, yet simplified and introductory, treatments of stochastic integrals and stochastic diffusion-differential equations, along with nice discussions of applications, are contained in Gard (1987) and von Weizsäcker and Winkler (1990). These two books also include a good discussion of the modeling issues involved in the "Itô versus Stratonovich" debate. In this connection, the original book by Stratonovich (1968) may profitably be consulted.

A fully rigorous treatment of stochastic-diffusion optimal control theory is developed in the books of Fleming and Rishel (1975) and Krylov (1980).

The literature on the theory of complete accounting under uncertainty is sparse. A pioneering article laying out the basic issues is Aronsson and Löfgren (1995), which is also presented as Chapter 8 in Aronsson, Johansson, and Löfgren (1997).

References

Aronsson, Thomas, Per-Olov Johansson, and Karl-Gustaf Löfgren. 1997. *Welfare Measurement, Sustainability, and Green National Accounting*. Cheltenham: Edward Elgar.

Aronsson, Thomas, and Karl-Gustaf Löfgren. 1995. National product related welfare measures in the presence of technological change, externalities, and uncertainty. *Environmental and Resource Economics* 5: 321–332.

Arrow, Kenneth J., and Anthony C. Fisher. 1974. Environmental preservation, uncertainty, and irreversibility. *Quarterly Journal of Economics* 88: 312–319.

Arrow, Kenneth J., and Mordecai Kurz. 1970. *Public Investment, the Rate of Return, and Optimal Fiscal Policy*. Baltimore: Johns Hopkins University Press.

Asheim, Geir B. 1994. Net national product as an indicator of sustainability. *Scandinavian Journal of Economics* 96 (2): 257–265.

——— 1997. Adjusting green NNP to measure sustainability. *Scandinavian Journal of Economics* 99 (3): 355–370.

——— 2000. Green national accounting: Why and how? *Environment and Development Economics* 5 (1, 2): 25–49.

Asheim, Geir B., and Wolfgang Buchholz. 2000. The Hartwick rule: Myths and facts. March 16. Photocopy.

Asheim, Geir B., and Martin L. Weitzman. 2001. Does NNP growth indicate welfare improvement? *Economics Letters* 73: 233–239.

Bewley, Truman. 1977. The permanent income hypothesis: A theoretical formulation. *Journal of Economic Theory* 16: 252–292.

Bodie, Z., A. Kane, and A. J. Marcus. 2002. *Investments*. 5th ed. New York: McGraw-Hill, Irwin.

Boskin, Michael, et al. 1998. Consumer prices, the consumer price index, and the cost of living. *Journal of Economic Perspectives* 12: 3–36.

Brearley, R. A., and S. C. Myers. 2000. *Principles of Corporate Finance*. 6th ed. New York: McGraw-Hill.

Brekke, Kjell A. 1994. Net national product as a welfare indicator. *Scandinavian Journal of Economics* 96: 257–265.

————— 1996. *Economic Growth and the Environment: On the Measurement of Income and Welfare*. Cheltenham: Edward Elgar.

Brock, William A. 1977. A polluted golden age. In Vernon L. Smith, ed., *Economics of Natural and Environmental Resources*. New York: Gordon and Breach.

Cass, David. 1965. Optimum growth in an aggregative model of capital accumulation. *Review of Economic Studies* 32: 233–240.

Clark, Colin W. 1990. *Mathematical Bioeconomics: The Optimal Management of Renewable Resources*. 2nd ed. New York: Wiley.

Conrad, Jon M. 1999. *Resource Economics*. Cambridge: Cambridge University Press.

Conrad, Jon M., and Colin W. Clark. 1987. *Natural Resource Economics: Notes and Problems*. Cambridge: Cambridge University Press.

Dasgupta, Partha. 1993. Optimal development and the idea of net national product. In I. Goldin and L. A. Winters, eds., *Approaches to Sustainable Economic Development*, pp. 111–143. Paris: Cambridge University Press for the OECD.

————— 2001. *Human Well-Being and the Natural Environment*. Oxford: Oxford University Press.

Dasgupta, Partha, and Geoffrey M. Heal. 1979. *Economic Theory and Exhaustible Resources*. Cambridge: Cambridge University Press.

Dasgupta, Partha, Bengt Kriström, and Karl-Göran Mäler. 1995. Current issues in resource accounting in P. O. Johansson, B. Kriström, and K. G. Mäler, eds., *Current Issues in Environmental Economics*. Manchester: Manchester University Press.

Dasgupta, Partha, and Karl-Göran Mäler. 2000. Net national product, wealth, and social well-being. *Environment and Development Economics* 5: 69–93.

Dixit, Avinash K., Peter Hammond, and Michael Hoel. 1980. On Hartwick's rule for regular maximin paths of capital accumulation. *Review of Economic Studies* 47: 551–606.

Dixit, Avinash K., and Robert S. Pindyck. 1994. *Investment under Uncertainty*. Princeton: Princeton University Press.

Dorfman, Robert. 1969. An economic interpretation of optimal control theory. *American Economic Review* 59: 817–831.

Environment and Development Economics. 2000. Special Issue: *Advances in Green Accounting* (volume 5, parts 1 and 2).

Feldstein, Martin. 1997. The costs and benefits of going from low inflation to price stability. In C. D. Romer and D. H. Romer, eds., *Reducing Inflation: Motivation and Strategy*. Chicago: University of Chicago Press.

Fisher, Irving. 1906. *The Nature of Capital and Income*. New York: Macmillan.

————— 1930. *The Theory of Interest*. New York: Macmillan.

Fleming, W. H., and R. W. Rishel. 1975. *Deterministic and Stochastic Optimal Control*. New York: Springer-Verlag.

Gard, Thomas C. 1987. *Introduction to Stochastic Differential Equations*. New York: Marcel Dekker.

Goldstine, H. H. 1980. *A History of the Calculus of Variations from the 17th through the 19th Century*. New York: Springer-Verlag.

Hamilton, Kirk. 1994. Green adjustments to GDP. *Resources Policy* 20 (3): 155–168.

Hamilton, K., Atkinson, G., and Pearce, D. 1998. "Genuine Savings as an Indicator of Sustainability." CSERGE Discussion Paper. London.

Hanemann, W. M. 1989. Information and the concept of option value. *Journal of Environmental Economics and Management* 14: 23–37.

Hartwick, John M. 1977. Intergenerational equity and the investing of rents from exhaustible resources. *American Economic Review* 65 (5): 972–974.

———— 1990. Natural resources, national accounting, and economic depreciation. *Journal of Public Economics* 43 (3): 291–304.

———— 1994. National wealth and net national product. *Scandinavian Journal of Economics* 96 (2): 253–256.

———— 1996. Constant consumption as interest on capital. *Scandinavian Journal of Economics* 98 (3): 439–443.

———— 2000. *National Accounting and Capital*. Cheltenham: Edward Elgar.

Hartwick, John M., and Nancy D. Olewiler. *The Economics of Natural Resource Use*. 2nd ed. 1998. Reading, Mass.: Addison-Wesley.

Heal, Geoffrey M. 1998. *Valuing the Future: Economic Theory and Sustainability*. New York: Columbia University Press.

Heal, Geoffrey, and Bengt Kriström. 2001. National income and the environment. Working paper to appear in K. G. Mäler and J. Vincent, eds., *Handbook of Environmental Economics*. Amsterdam: Elsevier.

Hicks, John R. 1946. *Value and Capital*. 2nd ed. Oxford: Oxford University Press.

Hines, James R. 1999. Three sides of Harberger triangles. *Journal of Economic Perspectives* 13: 167–188.

Hotelling, Harold. 1931. The economics of exhaustible resources. *Journal of Political Economy* 39: 137–175.

Hulten, C. R. 1992. Accounting for the wealth of nations: The net vs. gross output controversy and its ramifications. *Scandinavian Journal of Economics* 94: supplement, 9–24.

Intriligator, Michael D. 1971. *Mathematical Optimization and Economic Theory*. Englewood Cliffs, N.J.: Prentice Hall.

Johansson, Per-Olov, and Karl-Gustaf Löfgren. 1985. *The Economics of Forestry and Natural Resources*. London: Basil Blackwell.

Jorgenson, Dale W. 1994. Investment and economic growth. The Simon Kuznets Lectures, Yale University, 11–13 November.

Kaldor, Nicholas. 1955. *An Expenditure Tax*. London: Allen and Unwin.

Kamien, Morton I., and Nancy L. Schwartz. 1991. *Dynamic Optimization*. 2nd ed. New York: North Holland.

Keeler, E., A. M. Spence, and R. Zeckhauser. 1972. The optimal control of pollution. *Journal of Economic Theory* 4: 19–34.

Kendrick, John W. 1995. *The New System of National Accounts*. Boston: Kluwer Academic Publishers.

Koopmans, Tjalling C. 1957. The price system and the allocation of resources. Chapter 1 in *Three Essays on the State of Economic Science*. New York: McGraw-Hill.

——— 1960. Stationary ordinal utility and impatience. *Econometrica* 28 (2): 287–309.

Krech, Shepard III. 1999. *The Ecological Indian*. New York: Norton.

Krylov, N. V. 1980. *Controlled Diffusion Processes*. New York: Springer Verlag.

Lindahl, Erik. 1934. The concept of income. In G. Bagge, ed., *Economic Essays in Honor of Gustaf Cassel*. London: George Allen & Unwin.

Löfgren, Karl-Gustaf. 1999. Ohlin versus Heckscher and Wicksell on forestry: One win (points) and one draw. Department of Economics, Umeå University, December. Photocopy.

Loury, Glenn. 1979. The optimal exploitation of an unknown reserve. *Review of Economic Studies* (October): 621–636.

Lutz, Ernst, ed. 1993. *Toward Improved Accounting for the Environment*. Washington, D.C.: World Bank.

Mäler, Karl-Göran. 1991. National accounts and environmental resources. *Environmental and Resource Economics* 1 (1): 283–305.

Malliaris, A. G., and W. A. Brock. 1982. *Stochastic Methods in Economics and Finance*. Amsterdam: North-Holland.

Merton, Robert C. 1992. *Continuous-Time Finance*. Oxford: Basil Blackwell.

National Research Council Panel on Integrated Environmental and Economic Accounting. 1999. *Nature's Numbers: Expanding the National Economic Accounts to Include the Environment*. Washington, D.C.: National Academy Press.

Nordhaus, William D. 1994. *Managing the Global Commons: The Economics of Climate Change*. Cambridge: MIT Press.

——— 1995. How should we measure sustainable income? Cowles Foundation Discussion Paper no. 1101, Yale University, October.

——— 1999. The future of environmental and augmented national accounts: An overview. *Survey of Current Business* (November): 45–49.

———— 2000. New directions in national income accounting. *American Economic Review* 90 (2): 259–263.

Oulton, Nick. 2001. Productivity and welfare: Or, GDP versus Weitzman's NDP. Structural Economic Analysis Division, Bank of England. Photocopy.

Packard, Stephan, and Cornelia F. Mutel, eds. 1997. *The Tallgrass Restoration Handbook.* Washington, D.C.: Island Press.

Parker, R. H., G. C. Harcourt, and G. Whittington. 1986. *Readings in the Concept and Measurement of Income.* 2nd ed. Oxford: Phillip Allan.

Pemberton, Malcolm, and David Ulph. 2001. Measuring income and measuring sustainability. *Scandinavian Journal of Economics* 103 (1): 25–40.

Pezzey, J. 1992. Sustainable development concepts: An economic analysis. World Bank Environment Paper no. 2. Washington, D.C.: World Bank.

Pezzey, J., and C. Withagen. 1998. The rise, fall, and sustainability of capital-resource economies. *Scandinavian Journal of Economics* 100: 513–527.

Pigou, Arthur C. 1932. *Economics of Welfare.* New York: Wiley & Sons.

Pontryagin, L. S., B. Boltyanskii, R. Gamkrelidze, and E. Mischenko. 1962. *Mathematical Theory of Optimal Processes.* New York: Wiley-Interscience.

Ramsey, Frank P. 1928. A mathematical theory of saving. *Economic Journal* 38: 543–549.

Romer, David. 1996. *Advanced Macroeconomics.* New York: McGraw-Hill.

Samuelson, Paul A. 1961. The evaluation of 'social income': Capital formation and wealth. In F. A. Lutz and D. C. Hague, eds., *The Theory of Capital.* New York: St. Martin's Press.

———— 1976. Economics of forestry in an evolving society. *Economic Inquiry* 14: 466–492.

Scott, M. 1990. Extended accounts for national income and product: A comment. *Journal of Economic Literature* 28 (September): 172–179.

Sefton, James A., and Martin R. Weale. 1996. The net national product and exhaustible resources: The effects of foreign trade. *Journal of Public Economics* 61 (1): 21–48.

———— 2001. Real national income. NIESR, London. Photocopy.

Seierstad, Atle, and Knut Sydsaeter. 1987. *Optimal Control Theory with Economic Applications.* New York: North Holland.

Solow, Robert M. 1970. *Growth Theory: An Exposition.* New York: Oxford University Press.

———— 1974. The economics of resources and the resources of economics. *American Economic Review* 64: 1–21.

———— 1986. On the intertemporal allocation of natural resources. *Scandinavian Journal of Economics* 88 (1): 141–149.

———— 1992. An almost practical step toward sustainability. Fortieth Anniversary Lecture, Resources for the Future, Washington, D.C.

Spence, A. Michael, and David A. Starrett. 1975. Most rapid approach paths in accumulation problems. *International Economic Review* 16: 388–403.

Stokey, Nancy L. 1998. Are there limits to growth? *International Economic Review* 39 (1): 1–31.

Stratonovich, R. L. 1968. *Conditional Markov Processes and Their Application to the Theory of Optimal Control.* New York: Elsevier.

Studenski, Paul. 1958. *The Income of Nations.* New York: New York University Press.

Summers, Robert, and Alan Heston. 1991. The Penn world table (mark 5): An expanded set of international comparisons, 1950–1988. *Quarterly Journal of Economics* 106: 327–368.

Usher, Dan. 1994. Income and the Hamiltonian. *Review of Income and Wealth* 40 (2): 123–141.

Varian, Hal R. 1992. *Microeconomic Analysis.* 3rd ed. New York: Norton.

Vellinga, Nicolas, and Cees Withagen. 1996. On the concept of green national income. Oxford Economic Papers (96): 499–514.

Vincent, J. R. 2000. Green accounting: From theory to practice. *Environment and Development Economics* 5 (1, 2): 1–12.

Vincent, J. R., T. Panayotou, and J. M. Hartwick. 1997. Resource depletion and sustainability in small open economies. *Journal of Environmental Economics and Management* 33: 274–286.

Von Weizsäcker, Heinrich, and Gerhard Winkler. 1990. *Stochastic Integrals: An Introduction.* Braunschweig, Germany: Vieweg.

Weitzman, Martin L. 1970. Aggregation and disaggregation in the pure theory of capital and growth: A new parable. Cowles Foundation Discussion Paper no. 292, Yale University, April.

——— 1971. Shiftable versus non-shiftable capital: A synthesis. *Econometrica* 39 (3): 511–529.

——— 1973. Duality theory for infinite horizon convex models. *Management Science* 19: 783–789.

——— 1976. On the welfare significance of national product in a dynamic economy. *Quarterly Journal of Economics* 90: 156–162.

——— 1997. Sustainability and technical progress. *Scandinavian Journal of Economics* 99: 1–14.

——— 1999. Pricing the limits to growth from minerals depletion. *Quarterly Journal of Economics.* 14: 691–706.

——— 2000. The linearised Hamiltonian as comprehensive NDP. *Environment and Development Economics* 5 (1, 2): 55–68.

——— 2001. A contribution to the theory of welfare accounting. *Scandinavian Journal of Economics* 103 (1): 1–24.

Weitzman, Martin L., and Karl-Gustaf Löfgren. 1997. On the welfare significance of green accounting as taught by parable. *Journal of Environmental Economics and Management* 32: 139–153.

World Commission on Environment and Development. 1987. *Our Common Future* ("The Brundtland Report"). New York: Oxford University Press.

Yong, J., and X. Y. Zhou. 1999. *Stochastic Controls: Hamiltonian Systems and HJB Equations.* New York: Springer-Verlag.

Index